RED SCREAMS

TERROR IN THE NEW MILLENNIUM

Hemlock Books

England

Visit our website:
www.hemlockbooks.co.uk

First published in 2012 by
Hemlock Books Limited,
The Bristol Office,
2nd Floor,
5 High Street,
Westbury-on-Trym,
Bristol
BS9 3BY

©Christopher T Koetting, 2012. Christopher T Koetting has asserted his right to be identified as the Author of this work, in accordance with the Copyright, Designs and Patents Act, 1988.

A CIP catalogue record for this book is available from the British Library.

ISBN 978-0-9557774-6-2

Editor Jim O'Brien. Design by Hemlock Books Limited/James King.

Printed and bound by CPI Group (UK) Ltd, Croydon, CR0 4YY.

Christopher T Koetting

ACKNOWLEDGEMENTS

A book like this would not be possible without the efforts of countless persons in various publications and websites over the years, and I am grateful for their efforts, which I have noted wherever possible in the text. I am also indebted as always to my family for their loving support and my friend and publisher Denis Meikle, who continues to make these endeavours possible.

CONTENTS

For Bart, Marshall and Nora, who read over our shoulders.

INTRODUCTION

Why isn't Hollywood doing anything original? Because there is plenty they can remake. I think they feel if you start with a title that is recognisable then you're already ahead of the game. The problem falls to the writers, actors and directors. They can't just make a movie because it pre-existed.

We are kind of stuck...They aren't really coming to us with originals. All we are getting offered are remakes. So we can boycott them, which is never going to happen, [because] there's always someone standing in the shadows waiting to jump in and start their career. So the only way we can do it is to be passionate, come up with a twist and not phone it in.

–Todd Farmer, co-writer, My Bloody Valentine 3D

Farmer's question is in essence misleading: there is nothing new about remakes. In fact, remakes have been as much a part of Hollywood as overhyped films and overindulged stars. Think of some of Tinseltown's classics—*An Affair to Remember, Ben Hur, Cleopatra, The Magnificent Seven, The Man Who Knew Too Much, Quo Vadis, A Star is Born, The Ten Commandments*—and what do they all have in common? You guessed it: they were all remakes.

The horror film in particular seems to thrive on remakes. The two most famous Universal horror films were themselves remakes: *Frankenstein* (1931) had previously been made in 1910 (and again as *Life Without Soul* in 1915) and *Dracula* (also 1931) had been unofficially adapted as *Nosferatu* in 1922. Universal's successor in the horror field, England's Hammer Films, began their rise to prominence in the 1950s by remaking Universal's horrors: *The Curse of Frankenstein* (1957), *Dracula* (1958) and *The Mummy* (1959). Most of the Edgar Allan Poe films Roger Corman directed for American International Pictures in the 1960s were remakes: the *House of Usher* (1960) had already fallen in 1928 and 1949, *Pit and the Pendulum* (1961) swung all the way back to 1913, *The Raven* (1963) had taken cinematic flight in 1912 and 1935, and *The Masque of the Red Death* (1964) had been adapted by Fritz Lang as *Die Pest in Florenz/The Plague in Florence* in 1921.

The 1970s saw attempts to revive the Dracula and Frankenstein stories with more 'faithful' adaptations (two versions of *Count Dracula* in 1970 and 1978 and *Frankenstein: The True Story* in 1973) or as excuses for blaxploitation (*Blacula, Blackenstein*), sexploitation (*Blood for Dracula, Flesh for Frankenstein*) or comedy (*Love at First Bite, Young Frankenstein*). Once the horror genre hit stratospheric heights with *The Exorcist* (1973) and *Jaws* (1975), those two films saw themselves copied for the rest of the decade by such knockoffs as *Abby, The Antichrist, The Devil Within Her* and *The Omen* in the case of the former and *Barracuda, Orca, Piranha* and *Tintorera* for the latter.

The 1980s began with another rash of imitations of popular horror films: *Dawn of the Dead* was followed by *Cannibal Apocalypse, City of the Living Dead, City of the Walking Dead, Zombie Creeping Flesh* and *Zombie Flesh Eaters*; *Halloween* was followed by *The Boogeyman, Don't Answer the Phone, Graduation Day, He Knows You're Alone* and *New Year's Evil*; *Friday the 13th* was followed by *Body Count, The Burning, Campsite Massacre, I, Madman* and *Sleepaway Camp*. The rest of the decade was pretty much a plethora of sequels, Stephen King adaptations and generic hybrids like *Ghostbusters, Gremlins* (both 1984), *The Witches of Eastwick* (1987) and *Beetlejuice* (1988).

Much the same could be said for the 1990s, although two more attempts were made to 'faithfully' translate Bram Stoker and Mary Shelley to the screen. Francis Ford Coppola's *Dracula* (1992) and Kenneth Branagh's *Frankenstein* (1994) were both big-budget, star-laden bores that failed to add anything new. By the time *The Mummy* was remade in 1999, it was influenced more by Indiana Jones than Boris Karloff.

Gus Van Sant's shot-for-shot remake of Hitchcock's *Psycho* (1998) was certainly one of the more ill-advised concepts of the decade; better luck was had the next year in remakes of both *The Haunting* and *The House on Haunted Hill*. Beginning in 2002, American filmmakers began remaking Asian horror films with *The Ring*, followed by *The Grudge* (2004), *Dark Water* (2005) and *The Eye* (2008).

Then, with the dawn of a new millennium, the floodgates were opened. An entire crop of filmmakers who had come of age in the 1970s and 1980s decided to set their sights on reimagining/reinterpreting/remaking/revising/revisiting/rehashing/rebooting/ what-have-you the horror movies that influenced them as young filmgoers. They were primarily directors who had come up through the commercials/music video route—Samuel Bayer, Andrew Douglas, Marcus Nispel, Zack Snyder, Rupert Wainwright, Rob Zombie—and were used to slick, fast-paced productions. Also, they were not shy about going after the genre's standard-bearers—from *Dawn of the Dead* to *Halloween*; from *Friday the 13th* to *The Hills Have Eyes*; from *The Last House on the Left* to *The Texas Chainsaw Massacre*.

The directors of the original films took varying degrees of interest in these remakes, seemingly in direct proportion to the success of the earlier efforts. John Carpenter co-produced the remake of his *The Fog* but had no involvement in the remake of the film that put him on the map, *Halloween*. Wes Craven co-produced the remakes to his *The Hills Have Eyes* films and *Last House on the Left*, but did not take part in the remake of his most successful pre-*Scream* film, *A Nightmare on Elm Street*. George Romero has had no involvement in the remakes of his *Living Dead* films, but he served as an executive producer on the remake of his nearly-forgotten *The Crazies*. Other directors—Bob Clark, Sean Cunningham, Tobe Hooper—have had nominal involvement with the remakes of their work, often serving as *de facto* producers simply because of rights agreements. So lucrative did the horror remake business become in the first decade of the 21st century that an entire production company—Platinum Dunes—was set up by blockbuster director Michael Bay (*The Rock, Pearl Harbour*) for the express purpose of giving '70s and '80s terror a new lease of life. Between 2003 and 2010, Platinum Dunes produced remakes of *The Amityville Horror, Friday the 13th, The Hitcher, A Nightmare on Elm Stree*t and *The Texas Chainsaw Massacre.*

What follows in these pages is a chronicle of the biggest horror remakes of the new millennium—and the films that inspired them. By giving a side-by-side comparison of each film's production history, script-to-screen transition, cutting room changes, critical and audience reception and legacy, hopefully the reader can judge for themselves whether all this looking backward is truly a re-imagining or simply evidence of a lack of oiginality and imagination.

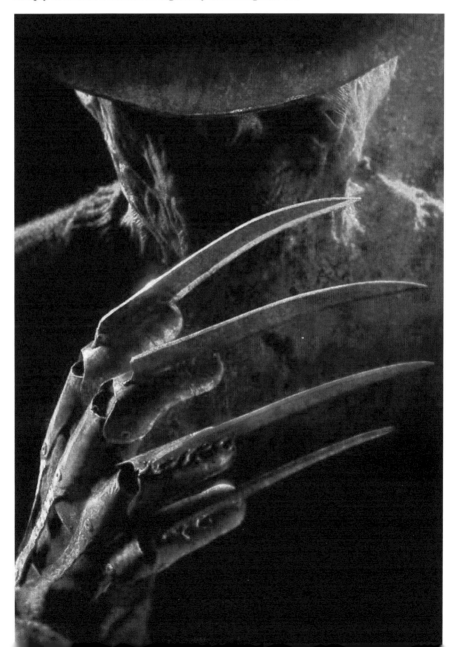

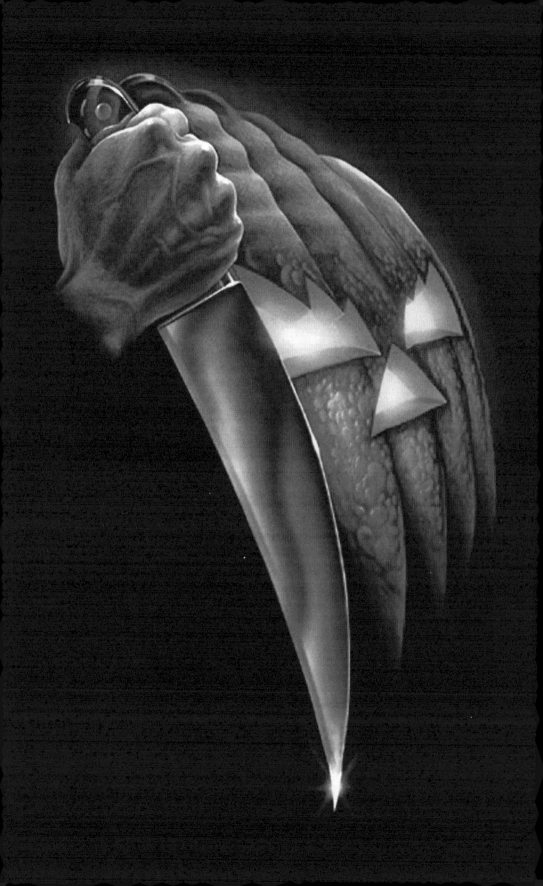

THE CARPENTER COMPLEX

HALLOWEEN

(1978)

Halloween **was a haunted house story and an attempt to do a horror film which incorporates all of the devices that you would expect from a horror film. No need for an extensive plot—just pure evil on the loose on Halloween night. We gave the evil form, and a reason to do what it does—and just let it go from there.**

–John Carpenter, co-writer, director and music composer

I was told that this was a horror film, that it did have a go-ahead, that the budget was \$300,000. And it was a director that was very hot in Europe, but nobody knew him here. That was my information.

–Jamie Lee Curtis, 'Laurie Strode'

At the tender age of five, the future slammed young John Howard Carpenter right between the eyes. The year was 1953, and his mother had taken him to see the 3D science fiction movie *It Came from Outer Space*. 'I sat in the front row,' Carpenter told *Time Out*, 'and this meteor came out of the screen and blew up right in my face. I got up and ran down the aisle, completely and utterly terrified. But by the time I reached the lobby, I knew that this was the greatest thing that had ever happened to me.'

That same year the Carpenters relocated from Carthage, New York to Bowling Green, Kentucky when Carpenter's father Howard got a job teaching music history and theory at Western Kentucky University. Living in a log cabin on the grounds of the Kentucky Museum, John indulged his newfound love of movies by frequenting the cinema and putting his father's 8mm camera to good use making his own monster movies. While in his teens, he also edited, illustrated and self-published a magazine called *Fantastic Films Illustrated*, which ran for three issues.

It was obvious that Carpenter's interests would take him westward, and after two years at Western Kentucky, Carpenter left for the University of Southern California's cinema program in 1968. In 1970, he co-wrote, edited and scored the short film *The Resurrection of Bronco Billy*, which won the Oscar for Best Short Subject. Along with fellow student Dan O'Bannon, he also began making a science fiction spoof called *Dark Star* as his Senior Thesis film. Over the course of the next four years, thanks to the intervention of a Canadian distributor, the budget went from $6,000 to $60,000, and *Dark Star* went from a 16mm, 45-minute short to a 35mm, 83-minute feature. But while its premiere at the 1974 Los Angeles International Film Exposition was met with enthusiasm, its general release the next year fell completely flat.

For the next two years Carpenter earned a living by writing scripts: a western called *Blood River* was bought by John Wayne's company but not produced[1], and a thriller called *Eyes* was bought by Jon Peters and Barbra Streisand as a possible vehicle for the star (it was eventually made as *Eyes of Laura Mars* with Faye Dunaway in 1977). In 1976, Carpenter was offered $150,000 by producer Joseph Kaufman to make any kind of film he wanted. He wrote an urban western called *The Anderson Alamo*, which relocated *Rio Bravo* (1959) and *The Alamo* (1960)—two of Carpenter's favourite films—to a rundown Los Angeles police station under siege from an interracial gang. Retitled *Assault on Precinct 13*, the movie was acquired by a start-up distributor named Turtle Releasing and released that November to near-total indifference.

Turtle had been formed by 42 year-old Irwin Yablans, the brother of former Paramount president Frank Yablans. Irwin had spent nearly 20 years in sales at both Warners and Paramount before producing his first two films, *Badge 373* (1973) and *The Education of Sonny Carson* (1974). After brief stints at Jerry Gross's Cinemation and Tom Laughlin's Billy Jack Enterprises, he decided to go into business for himself, first as Turtle then as The Irwin Yablans Company, where he worked both ends of the spectrum, releasing low-budget Charles Band exploitation flicks (*End of the World*, *Laserblast*) and at the same time serving as a producer's representative for major films like *Hooper* (1978) and *Apocalypse Now* (1979).

While *Precinct 13* had fallen off the radar in America, it met with acclaim at both the 1977 Edinburgh and London Film Festivals, where Carpenter was hailed as a rising young talent. Flying home from London that November, Yablans searched for a way to capitalise on Carpenter's newfound status, as he told *New York* magazine: 'I suddenly thought, "We should do something with a baby-sitter.

---

1 Carpenter's script was eventually made in 1991 as a CBS TV movie with Wilford Brimley and Rick Shroeder in roles originally intended for John Wayne and Ron Howard.

Put some nubile girls together and terrorise them." There's a common denominator there...everybody's been a baby-sitter, or everybody's had one. So I called John and he was somewhat enthusiastic but wasn't jumping up and down. [Then] I had a revelation. Let it all happen in one night. We could save production costs. Let it be Halloween night. I called Carpenter and he unequivocally went crazy. Carpenter said he'd do the movie under three conditions: "I want complete autonomy; I want no interference; I want to write the music." I said fine, and I told him I only had one question: "Can you do it for $300,000?"'

In January 1978, Yablans formed a new company, Compass International Pictures, with 48 year-old, Syrian-born producer/director Moustapha Akkad. Yablans had handled the distribution for Akkad's $17 million epic, *Mohammad: Messenger of God*, which achieved notoriety in March 1977 when Black Muslim extremists protested the film by seizing buildings adjacent to a theatre in Washington DC that was showing the movie. They took 149 hostages and killed a police officer and a broadcast journalist in a 39-hour-long standoff. This effectively put an end to *Mohammad*'s commercial prospects and it ended up being one of the biggest money-losers of the decade. Undaunted, Akkad announced plans for more big-budget, Arab-themed movies— *Omar Mukhtar, The Princess of Alhambra, Saladin and the Crusades*—but being a fellow USC graduate gave him an instant rapport with Carpenter, and he agreed to put up the budget for *Halloween*.[2] Akkad and Yablans would serve as executive producers on the picture, while producing chores would be handled by the woman who was sharing Carpenter's address: his girlfriend, 27 year-old Debra Hill.

Hill was born in Haddonfield, New Jersey and got her degree in sociology from Temple University in 1972. After some documentary filmmaking in New York (her father had worked for Republic and M-G-M in the 1940s and she had inherited a love of movies), she went to San Francisco to do publicity for Evel Knievel and later found work as a script supervisor on the TV series, *The Streets of San Francisco*. Encouraged by co-star Michael Douglas, she made her way into independent features in 1976, doing script supervision for films like *Goodbye Norma Jean* and *Satan's Cheerleaders*. During that time she also served as script supervisor and assistant editor on *Precinct 13,* where she met and fell in love with John Carpenter.

In 1977, Carpenter had sold two scripts to Warners: a female reworking of *Deliverance* called *Prey* and a suspense thriller called *High Rise*. The former, despite having Bob Clark (*Black Christmas*) attached as director for producers Arthur Gardner and Jules Levy, was never made, but *High Rise* entered production in February 1978 as a $1 million TV movie for NBC that Carpenter was allowed to direct. While her boyfriend was at Burbank Studios during the day, Hill worked on the script for *Halloween*: 'I had been a baby-sitter, so I knew a lot about that,' she told an audience at the American Cinematheque. 'I would start with a blank page, write the baby-sitting stuff, and put scenes where [psychiatrist] Sam Loomis would talk, and John would fill all that in.'

---

2 *Omar Mukhtar* was produced in March 1979 in Libya on a $25 million budget, which ended up swelling to $35 million, much of which came from notorious Libyan dictator Col Muammar Gadaffi. Released by United Film Distribution as *Lion of the Desert* in April 1981, it only made $1.5 million in rentals and would be the last film Akkad would ever direct.

Haddonfield, Illinois: Halloween, 1963. Six-year-old Michael Myers brutally stabs his sister to death after she has sex with her boyfriend. Fifteen years later, he escapes from Smith's Grove Sanitarium on the night before Halloween and is pursued by his psychiatrist, Dr Sam Loomis. Myers arrives back in Haddonfield the next day and begins stalking three teenage girls—Annie, Laurie and Lynda. While Loomis enlists the aid of Haddonfield's Sheriff Brackett (Annie's father) in stopping the killer—whom the good doctor insists is the personification of evil—Myers murders Annie, Lynda and her boyfriend Bob. Laurie, babysitting two young kids at a house across the street from the killings, goes over to investigate and finds her dead friends. Myers is waiting for her, and a stalk-and-slash ensues that finally ends with Loomis arriving on the scene and shooting Myers multiple times before the killer falls out an upstairs window. After telling an injured and frightened Laurie that Myers was indeed 'the boogeyman', Loomis discovers to his horror that Michael has somehow escaped yet again.

'We wanted to write a classic kind of horror film about terrorised girls,' Hill told *Cinefantastique*. 'Halloween had never really been used before in the movies and it just lent itself to good things, good symbols.' And good humour—the movie's locale is named after Hill's hometown of Haddonfield, Sam Loomis is named after John Gavin's character in Hitchcock's *Psycho*, Sheriff Brackett is named after author/screenwriter Leigh Brackett (who wrote *Rio Bravo*) and Michael Myers himself is named after the head of England's Miracle Films, which had released *Precinct 13* in the UK in March 1978.

The script for *Halloween* was written in just ten days; on top of that, only three weeks were allowed for preproduction. 'I made a very judicious work schedule,' said Hill, 'with actors coming in when they were needed, rather than signing on for four or five weeks...The entire film was storyboarded, very well prepared...Most of the money went for camera equipment and the lab. I called in a lot of favours.'

Twenty days of principal photography in Pasadena and West Hollywood began on April 25, with the lead role of Laurie Strode going to 19-year-old Jamie Lee Curtis, the daughter of Janet Leigh and Tony Curtis (the couple had divorced when Jamie was four). One of the last contract players at Universal Studios, Curtis had worked her way up from walk-ons in TV shows like *Columbo* and *Quincy* to a regular series role in *Operation Petticoat,* a sitcom based on the 1959 film that co-starred her father. *Halloween* would be her first feature film, and while Curtis was not Carpenter's first choice—he had wanted Anne Lockhart, daughter of *Lassie* and *Lost in Space*'s June Lockhart—she was hardly offended, being of the same opinion as her director. 'I wouldn't have cast myself as Laurie,' she told *Fangoria*. 'I wear tight jeans, have a low voice and big tits. Of course, when I went in for that audition, I wore an old-fashioned dress and no makeup.'

An extra $25,000 had been allocated to the budget for the purpose of securing a 'name' actor for the part of Dr Loomis. Carpenter and Hill had initially approached

British horror star Christopher Lee, who had recently relocated to Hollywood, but he found the part unappealing, as he told author Denis Meikle: 'I said to them, "There's nothing I can do with this; I can't make a contribution. [Loomis] just shows up and says, 'This man's mad and he's dangerous.' I can't do anything with that."'

Next on the list was British character actor Donald Pleasence, who met with Carpenter at Hollywood's famed restaurant The Hamburger Hamlet and promptly told the young filmmaker, 'The only reason I'm here is because my daughter liked one of your movies [*Precinct 13*]. I don't understand this script at all; would you please explain it to me?' Unlike his fellow countryman Lee, Pleasence decided that getting $5,000 a day for just five days' work was worth whatever misgivings he might have about the screenplay and signed on the dotted line.

> **MARION**
> What did he say?

> **LOOMIS**
> He asked me if I could help him find his purple lawnmower.

> **MARION**
> I don't think this is any time to be funny...

> **LOOMIS**
> He said something else. 'It's all right now. He's gone. The evil's gone.'

--Unfilmed exchange, from the original script

Because of the brief period of preproduction as well as the quick shooting schedule, Carpenter and Hill stuck pretty close to the script as written, though there are still some significant differences between the page and the screen, including:

- The opening titles were to have played over Michael's mask instead of a pumpkin. ('It is a large, full-head latex rubber mask, not a monster or ghoul, but the pale, neutral features of a man weirdly distorted by the rubber...')
- After killing his sister, Michael was to have fled his house and gone to the neighbours' to find his parents—as if he wants them to know what he has done—with 'a calm, quiet smile on his face.' In the film, he simply wanders outside just as his parents pull up.
- On his way to Haddonfield, Loomis was to have called his wife back home. This was changed to him calling the Haddonfield authorities because Pleasence did not want Loomis to have a past or a family.
- The scene with a young bully running into Myers outside the schoolyard was to have caused a butcher knife to slip out of the Shape's pocket, with his foot slamming down to hide it. In the film, the youngster simply runs away after encountering Myers.

16

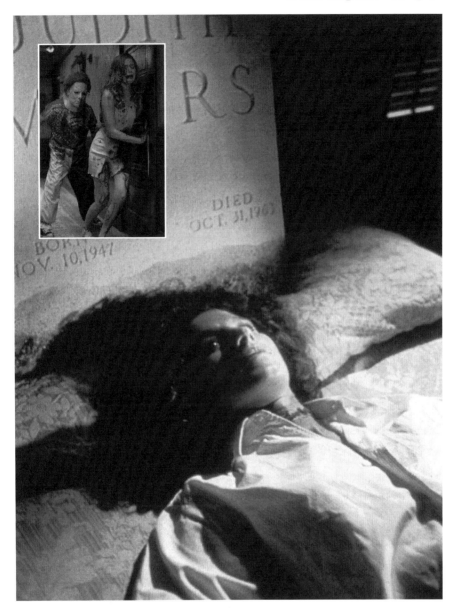

- Michael was to have been permanently unmasked after struggling with Laurie in the Doyle house: 'The Shape, Michael, stares at her with his one eye. He has a dank, white face with blond hair. There is something completely unhuman about his features, the open mouth, the dark staring eye.' In the film, Laurie pulls off his mask, but he puts it back on before we can get a good look at him.
- After being shot by Loomis, Michael was to have crashed backwards through a second story window, then land on top of the camera outside. In the film, he merely falls off a balcony to the ground below.

17

'My idea was to do an old haunted house movie,' Carpenter told *Rolling Stone*. 'When we used to go to state fairs, they always had an attraction called the Haunted House. It would be completely dark and as you stepped on certain boards, things would jump out and scare you. Sort of like the spook ride at an amusement park. That's what I wanted to do: a spook ride on film, taking the audience through twists and turns and having things jump out at them.'

In the case of twisting and turning, Carpenter was speaking literally. *Halloween* was one of the first films to make use of the Panaglide, Panavision's answer to the Steadicam. A harness enabled the camera operator to walk with the camera attached in front, which dampened out the jolts and vibrations that usually accompanied hand-held shots. This greatly increased mobility and eliminated the need for dolly tracks to stabilise moving shots. 'People were still figuring out what to do with it,' *Halloween* cinematographer Dean Cundey told the American Cinematheque, 'they were thinking of it in old terms, and John thought of it in a new kind of way, and we did a shot that was, for the time, quite amazing.'

Cundey was referring to *Halloween*'s celebrated opening Panaglide shot, which was Carpenter's self-confessed homage to the long-take tracking shot that opens Orson Welles' *Touch of Evil* (1958). Here the camera is Michael's point of view as he approaches his house, peers through the window at his sister and her boyfriend making out, walks around back, enters through the kitchen, takes out a butcher knife, waits downstairs for the boyfriend to leave, climbs the stairs to his sister's room, stabs her repeatedly, then goes back downstairs and out the front door just as his parents' car pulls up to the curb. While this all appears to be done in a single take, it is actually two separate shots, with the cut hidden by the donning of a mask.

Beginning with this sequence, the film seems to single out sexually promiscuous young women (and their boyfriends) for a death sentence—while the virginal heroine is spared—a motif that came to be the hallmark of the so-called 'slasher' genre that *Halloween* is often credited with birthing. Carpenter and Hill went to great lengths to deny that this was their intention, saying that Laurie survives simply because she is the only one not so distracted by sex that she is able to surmise that a madman is on the loose and act accordingly. Carpenter even went so far as to suggest to *Cinefantastique* that the confrontation between Laurie and Michael was the consummation of a macabre courtship: 'Ironically, the one girl in the film who does not fool around...is the one who stabs [Myers] over and over with this long knife! She's as repressed as he is, getting rid of this sexual energy. And no one sees this.' Perhaps the reason why audiences did not grasp this concept was because Laurie only stabs Michael once with a knife (after using a knitting needle and a hanger)—a fact that calls into question the potency of Carpenter's after-the-fact argument.

As far as the director was concerned, however, the sexuality of the film was never what mattered anyway: '*Halloween* is not about a crazy guy killing people. That's the story, but not what it's about. The movie is about evil, and...evil never dies. The script was done to a rigid structure, without a lot of agonising. I was aware some people might [object to the ending], but it seemed like the right thing to do at the time... [Michael's] identity is irrelevant. Wait 'til next Halloween: he'll be back to getcha!'

As the son of a music professor, Carpenter had had a lifelong exposure to the art form, as well as a love of rock 'n' roll that led him to play in a band in Bowling Green with classmate Tommy Lee Wallace, who followed Carpenter to USC and, together with Nick Castle, formed a trio called The Coupe De Villes (they are heard playing on the radio in Annie's car before Blue Oyster Cult's 'Don't Fear the Reaper').[3] Carpenter had used a synthesiser to score his two previous films and *Halloween* would be no different, though it was due less to artistry than practicality, as he confessed to *Time Out*: 'I was the cheapest and best person I could get for the money. I would have loved to hire someone else. I used the synthesiser because I can't write or arrange music, but I can hear, and so I would over-dub myself time and again until it was right.'

Getting the score right would literally make all the difference to the film as a whole. 'I screened the final cut, minus sound effects and music, for a young executive from 20th Century Fox,' Carpenter wrote in *Fangoria*. 'She wasn't scared at all.' Determined to save the movie with the soundtrack, Carpenter would make *Halloween* as much an aural experience as a visual one: 'About six months later I ran into the same young executive...Now she too loved the movie and all I had done was add music.'

Desiring to get a broader audience reaction, Yablans arranged for a preview of *Halloween* to 1,000 people in Westwood, California that September. 'We were warned not to do it because there were a lot of kids from UCLA, a lot of sophisticated, wise-ass kids,' Yablans told the American Cinematheque. 'And we knew we were taking a risk, but I believed in this movie implicitly. So, the movie started, and it was quiet for a while, then the laughs started, and they kept coming. And I thought,

3 Both Castle and Wallace were also veterans of the USC cinema studies programme and had worked on Carpenter's other films. On *Halloween*, Wallace was co-editor and production designer while Castle played Michael Myers (masked).

"My God, what did we do? What's wrong with this picture?" I couldn't understand it. Finally, the last time that Jamie Lee Curtis dropped [the knife], somebody yelled out, "You dumb bitch, you deserve to die!" Then I knew we had a hit.'

Halloween premiered in Kansas City on October 25, where Robert Trussell of the *Kansas City Star* greeted it enthusiastically: 'A film has now been made that straddles the line between the utterly believable and the fantastic, and in so doing has earned itself a place in the ranks of other great and near-great horror films. The film is *Halloween*...if it doesn't scare you badly enough to make you want to move very quickly out of the theatre before the final scene, then you have emotions of iron and are a better man than I. In fact it would be fair to say that somewhere toward the middle of the final reel, the film virtually stops being entertainment and becomes an exercise in masochism for the audience...*Halloween* is a tight, professionally made film that demands to be seen by movie-goers who love to be scared. There may not be another scare movie of its calibre for quite a while.'

Horror film fans took Trussell at his word and *Halloween* earned nearly $50,000 in its first week at six Kansas City theatres and two drive-ins; as a result, it was deemed by *Variety* the 'surprise entry of the early fall season.'

Two days after its Kansas City premiere, *Halloween* fanned out to Los Angeles and New York, where it posted opening weeks of $120,000 and $500,000, respectively. Word of mouth spread like wildfire as the film's release broadened, and in just six weeks it had grossed over $5 million. By May 1979, it had earned over $30 million; it would go on to gross nearly $47 million in the US and an additional

20

$20 million overseas, which made it the most successful independently-produced film to that time.[4]

While the audience reaction was unanimous, the critical one was not. Several prominent critics dismissed the film, including *The Washington Post*'s Gary Arnold ('This plodding exercise in sham apprehension would [not] look impressive even if one felt starved for morbid stimulation...*Halloween* is far more proficient at torpor than terror'), *The New Yorker*'s Pauline Kael ('Maybe when a horror film is stripped of everything but dumb scariness—when it isn't ashamed to revive the stalest device of the genre (the escaped lunatic)—it satisfies part of the audience in a more basic, childish way than sophisticated horror pictures do') and the *Los Angeles Times*' Kevin Thomas ('With its tree-shaded small-town American setting, *Halloween* does function metaphorically for the insecure times in which we live. But since it offers nothing more, *Halloween* becomes yet another in the seemingly endless series of films that simply exacerbate our increasing paranoia—and what is the good of this?')

However, many more critics lavished praise on Carpenter's frightfest, including *Newsweek*'s David Ansen ('*Halloween* is a superb exercise in the art of suspense... the most frightening flick in years'), the *Village Voice*'s Tom Allen ('*Halloween* is a movie of almost unrelieved chills and of violence, conjuring up that unique mix of subliminal threat and contrapuntal physicality employed by Hitchcock'), the *New York Times*'s Vincent Canby ('Carpenter is clearly a director who has studied at the feet of the master...Like Hitchcock, Mr Carpenter doesn't waste time on purposeless characterisation and explanation...The point of the movie is to cause us as much distress as possible in the safety of our theatre seats as we watch—happy voyeurs all—the mysterious fellow go about his work'), the *Chicago Sun-Times*'s Roger Ebert ('*Halloween* is an absolutely merciless thriller, a movie so violent and scary that, yes, I would compare it to *Psycho*') and the *Chicago Tribune*'s Gene Siskel ('It is a beautifully made thriller—more shocking than bloody—that will have you screaming with regularity').

In January 1979, Carpenter won the Critics Award at France's Avoriaz Fantastic Film Festival, which was augmented two months later by *Halloween*'s Grand Prix and Jamie Lee Curtis's Best Acting Award at the Paris Festival of Science Fiction and Fantasy Films. That August, Carpenter also won the New Generation Award from the Los Angeles Film Critics Association.

It had begun with the strange pictures in his head at night, pictures of people he had never seen...People in strange costumes, animal skins, armour, leather, drinking and dancing wildly around a fire. One couple in particular. They looked like Judy and Danny, madly in love with each other, dancing in a circle around the huge bonfire, while he, Michael, stood in the crowd hating them, burning up with jealousy.

–From Curtis Richards's novelisation of Halloween

---

4 Carpenter and Hill did not take salaries on the film, opting instead for 10% of the profits, which made them both millionaires.

In October 1979, on the occasion of *Halloween*'s first national re-release, Bantam published a novelisation of the film by Curtis Richards which, while derived primarily from Carpenter and Hill's script, includes a prologue set in medieval Ireland, where a deformed 15 year-old Celt named Enda falls madly in love with the beautiful princess Deirdre. After his advances are spurned and Deirdre is engaged to the handsome Cullain, Enda is driven mad with jealousy and kills the couple during a Samhain celebration. Torn apart by the tribe, Enda's head and heart are carried to the summit of the Hill of Fiends, where a shaman places a curse on his soul, damning it to everlasting wandering and torment. To exact its revenge, Enda's soul has possessed men throughout the ages—including Michael Myers' great-grandfather—and caused them to brutally murder young lovers. Now Enda's spirit has apparently taken hold of Michael and drives him to murder his sister.

Richards' narrative not only explicitly links Michael's madness with the ancient precursor to Halloween but also details his early years at Smith's Grove, where he holds the entire children's ward in a grip of fear through his seemingly supernatural ability to gain revenge against those who wrong him. Once escaped, Michael singles out Laurie Strode for attack because she reminds him of his dead sister; Laurie's friends are murdered because their promiscuousness enrages the spirit that controls Michael.

After *Halloween*'s second re-release in October 1980, NBC-TV paid $4 million for the broadcast rights, only to discover subsequently that the film, when cut for television, was too short for a two-hour time slot. To make up the difference, Carpenter and Hill wrote and shot new material in just three days in April 1981, including two scenes with Loomis at Smith's Grove six months after Michael's incarceration, Loomis discovering the aftermath of Michael's breakout and Lynda coming over to Laurie's house to borrow a silk blouse. 'The additional footage should have been in there in the first place,' Hill told *Fangoria*, 'it integrated very well. It also helps [the film] make more sense.'[5]

Under normal circumstances, it would have been prohibitively expensive and tedious to reunite the cast and crew of a three-year-old movie just for some filler material, but, as luck would have it, the old gang was already back together—for *Halloween II*.

(2007)

If you're just going in to do the same exact movie with different actors...why bother? If you're trying to make it look the same and feel the same, why bother? What I wanted to do was make it a totally different experience, so within the first five minutes of this movie you're going to go, 'There's no sense sitting here comparing.' It's so different, there's nothing to compare.

—Rob Zombie, writer, co-producer and director

---

5 *Halloween* premiered on NBC on October 30, 1981, where it ranked #42 in the week's ratings.

We improvise a lot, because Rob likes a slightly off-kilter and spontaneous kind of thing...You'll be surprised, but he reminds me of Stanley [Kubrick]. Not in looks, you'll be glad to know. It's because he has an absolute belief in what his vision is, but he doesn't come with any preconceived ideas of how to do it.

–Malcolm McDowell, 'Dr Sam Loomis'

On November 9, 2005, 75-year-old Moustapha Akkad and his 34-year-old daughter were both in the lobby of the Grand Hyatt in Amman, Jordan, when it was struck by an Al-Qaeda suicide bomber. Akkad's daughter died instantly, while he died of his injuries two days later. Akkad was in the country scouting locations for his long-cherished project *Saladin and the Crusades*, which he was finally scheduled to shoot with Sean Connery on a budget of $80 million.

Most of that money had come on the back of Michael Myers. After the Myers-less, name-only sequel *Halloween III: Season of the Witch* (1982) failed to draw a crowd, it appeared that the series was dead. Then, in 1986, Cannon Films—which was at that time returning Leatherface to the screen with Tobe Hooper's *Texas Chainsaw Massacre 2*—approached John Carpenter and Debra Hill with the idea of resurrecting Michael Myers for a *Halloween 4*. The duo worked up a script with horror writer Dennis Etchison (who had written the novelisations for *The Fog* and *Halloween II* and *III*), but were soon stopped in their tracks by Akkad, who claimed ownership of the *Halloween* trademark. Akkad won the ensuing legal battle and in April 1988, his Trancas International Films began production on *Halloween 4: The Return of Michael Myers,* which also featured a returning Donald Pleasence and played to strong box office returns that October. Over the next 15 years, Akkad would produce four more *Halloween* films, including *Halloween 5: The Revenge of Michael Myers* (1989), *Halloween 6: The Curse of Michael Myers* (1995), *Halloween: H20* (1998) and *Halloween: Resurrection* (2002). With his son Malek, he also oversaw the merchandising of the Michael Myers character and the licensing of the first, fourth and fifth films in the series (everything from *Halloween 6* on was owned by Miramax, which became the series' benefactor through its Dimension Films subsidiary). While *H20*—featuring a returning Jamie Lee Curtis in what was easily the series' best sequel—had been a hit, its delayed follow-up, *Resurrection*, had not and a 'reboot' of the franchise was sought. Akkad would not live to see that come to fruition, but his son had just the person in mind for the job: Robert Bartleh Cummings—better known by his stage name, Rob Zombie.

Born in January 1965, Zombie founded the heavy metal group White Zombie, which took its name from the 1932 Bela Lugosi film. Besides being a musician, Zombie was also a huge horror movie fan and budding filmmaker, who had directed several of White Zombie's videos himself (in 1995 he became the first self-directed artist to win an MTV Music Video Award). After going solo in 1998, Zombie began a five-year quest to make his own horror film, which went through three studios (Universal, M-G-M and Lionsgate) before finally being released in 2003 as *House of*

1000 Corpses. Produced for just $7 million, the extremely violent film was panned by critics but found enough of an audience to justify a more stylised and successful sequel, *The Devil's Rejects*, in 2005.

In June 2006, it was announced that Zombie would be writing, producing and directing a remake of the original *Halloween* with Malek Akkad and Zombie's long-time manager Andy Gould, who had also produced his previous two films. Miramax impresarios Bob and Harvey Weinstein would serve as executive producers, as they had done on the previous three *Halloween* features; in fact, it was actually Bob Weinstein who had approached Zombie with the idea in the first place.

'My first reaction was I didn't see the point of any of this,' Zombie told MTV. 'Then I went away and thought about it for a couple of months and started thinking that that was maybe a weird attitude to have.' With John Carpenter's remake of *The Thing* (1982) and David Cronenberg's version of *The Fly* (1986) serving as templates, Zombie 'started thinking of ways this could be...done right.'

He was adamant, however, that this was not going to be just another sequel, telling the website The Gauntlet: 'I am not making *Halloween 9*. That series is done, complete, over. But what I am doing is starting totally from scratch. This is the new *Halloween*. Call it a remake, an update, a reimagining or whatever, but one thing that's for sure is this is a whole new start...a new beginning with no connection to the other series. That is exactly why the project appeals to me. I can take it and run with it.' Before he did, however, he felt obliged to get the blessing of the man who had started the race: 'I talked to John Carpenter...and he said, "Go for it, Rob. Make it your own." And that's exactly what I intend to do.'

'It will take a totally different approach to make [*Halloween*] scary again,' Zombie told *The Hollywood Reporter*. 'The look and the feel is going to be completely different. *Halloween* started off as a very terrifying concept, a terrifying movie. But over the years, Michael Myers has become a friendly Halloween mask. But I think the story and the situation is [still] scary.'

Haddonfield, Illinois: Halloween 1978. 10-year-old Michael Myers lives in the ultimate white trash home: his mother is a stripper, her live-in boyfriend Ronnie is an abusive cripple, his teenage sister Judith is a sexpot and his baby sister Boo never stops crying. Michael takes out his frustration by torturing animals—which he records— and masturbating to a scrapbook he has made from hardcore porn magazines and pictures of dead pets. After school, he lures a young classmate into the woods and brutally murders her, all the while recording the incident. That night, Michael goes to an elementary school Halloween party; after coming home, he grabs his tape recorder and a butcher knife and slits a drunken Ronnie's throat. He beats Judith's boyfriend to death with a baseball bat, then goes upstairs and stabs his sister to death. Taking the baby in his bloody hands, he goes outside and waits for his mother to come home. Arrested and convicted of triple murder, Myers is sentenced to life in Smith's Grove Sanitarium, where he spends the next 17 years being

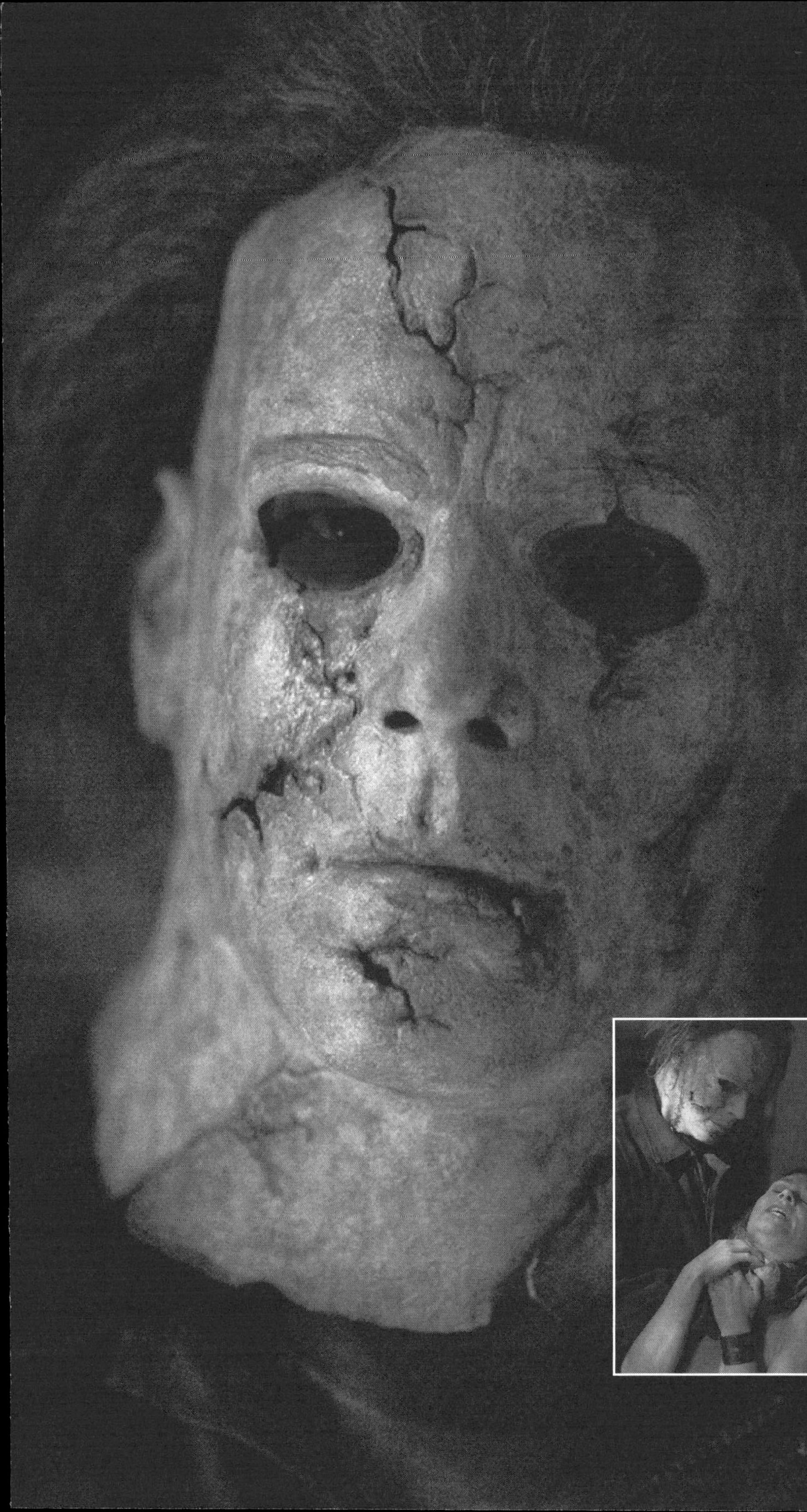

Halloween (2007)

unsuccessfully treated by Dr Sam Loomis, who eventually retires after writing two bestselling books about the case. On the night before Smith's Grove is to be closed, two orderlies bring an inmate into Michael's cell and rape her, giving Michael a chance to escape— leaving four bodies and a ward of freed inmates in his wake. Michael makes his way to his mother's trailer, where she kills herself before her son can learn the whereabouts of his baby sister. Loomis returns to the scene and tracks Myers to Haddonfield, where the madman has singled out three teenagers—Laurie, Lynda and Annie—for attack. Myers systematically kills Laurie's parents and her friends before finally kidnapping her and taking her to the long-abandoned Myers house—it is revealed that Laurie is actually Boo, put up for adoption years earlier by her distraught mother. Laurie wants no part of Michael's family reunion, however, and fights back until Loomis and the police arrive and kill her brother in a barrage of gunfire.

'For me, the idea of firing up this movie with this character, Michael Myers, was exciting,' Zombie told Ain't It Cool News, 'but then I was like, "It needs more," because if you just do what we've already seen, it does become like all the remakes that we all complain about: "Why did you bother? We already saw that movie." To me, those were some of the most interesting missing elements. In the original, Dr Loomis would always sort of refer to the old days of what happened with Michael and we never saw any of it. We never really got any insight into it...I did a lot of research, as in, "What if Michael Myers was a real person? What would he be?" You know, he would be basically a...textbook psychopath, and there really is no 'why' for a psychopath. That's what I found fascinating. They don't have a situation that turns them into that. They're basically born that way.'

With this rationale in mind, it seems rather odd that Zombie went to such great lengths to show Michael growing up in an environment that is every social worker's nightmare. Not only does this completely de-mystify Myers, thus making him less frightening, but renders the film itself schizophrenic, as it begins like a social realist tract then switches gears midway through and becomes a run-of-the-mill, teenage slasher movie. In fact, when asked to explain this apparent contradiction, Zombie seemed to be at odds with his own film: 'The young Michael stuff is not why he is like that... it's not like, "Oh, he had a bad childhood, so he became bad," because that's not the case...It was just seeing him, the mystery of him unravel and yet he still remains a mystery. I mean as much as we see of him through his life, it doesn't [give] any reason why he became what he became.' Then what was the point of showing it at all? And how does Zombie justify Michael's inexplicable metamorphosis from a cherubic psychotic to a hulking reject from World Wrestling Entertainment?[6]

It was not just the character of Michael Myers that Zombie chose to expand upon, however, but also Dr Loomis: 'In the original, [he] doesn't really have a character arc in the sense that we come to him after everything has happened. You know, he's like,

---

6 Literally, in this case, as the man playing the adult Myers—6'9" Tyler Mane—was formerly a professional wrestler.

"He's Michael and we want to keep him locked away... blah blah blah," but this Dr Loomis goes through a change when we meet him early on with young Michael where he feels that there's still somebody there he can reach and there's something he can do and then we watch him go through his failure [and] becoming the other guy, so it's a very different character.'

In order to fill the large shoes of Donald Pleasence, who, after a total of five *Halloween* films had come to be associated in the public's mind with the Loomis role, Zombie turned to another celebrated British actor, Malcolm McDowell, who was just as reluctant to take on the project as his predecessor had been. 'When I first saw [Rob Zombie] sitting there, I thought, "Holy God, I'm having lunch with Charles Manson!" McDowell told the *Baltimore Sun*. 'And he turns out to be the sweetest guy I ever met.'

With a $15 million budget, production on *Halloween* began on February 2, 2007, and lasted for 38 days. During the course of filming, a number of changes were made to the script, including:

- Michael does not tape his killings or have a scrapbook of dirty pictures.
- The confrontation with bullies Wesley and Shane that happens at a cafeteria screening of *Forbidden Planet* was changed to the school bathroom.
- The attack on the girl classmate in the woods was changed to Wesley being killed by Michael.
- Michael's return to the house and the killing of Ronnie was to have been shot POV—with his identity revealed in a mirror. It is all shot objectively in the film.
- As McDowell and Daeg Faerch (who played the young Michael) enjoyed improvising, all of the scripted sessions between Loomis and Michael were discarded, eliminating the youngster watching home movies of himself and talking about how he enjoyed killing his sister.
- Loomis's retirement and his home life with wife Ellen were eliminated (along with a nightmare where Michael kills Ellen).
- An entire subplot involving Loomis, Sheriff Brackett and a file clerk trying to find Boo's adoption papers was dropped.
- Michael was supposed to repeatedly say 'Boo' to Laurie in the Myers basement but Zombie chose instead to keep him silent.

One of the biggest changes was the death of Deborah Myers. In the film, the distraught mother shoots herself while watching home movies of Michael. In the script, however, her death was to have played out rather differently:

Deborah sits watching the TV—in her hands is a LOADED GUN. A SHAPE appears in the window of the door—the doorknob turns. The

door is locked and chained—Boom! The door is kicked in—snapping the chain.

It is Michael.

> ### DEBORAH
> I knew you'd come back for me.

Michael enters, now dressed in Big Joe's clothes and still wearing his paper mask—he walks slowly towards Deborah. In his hands is the same B+W PICTURE of himself as a child holding his BABY SISTER.

> ### DEBORAH (CONT'D)
> I had no choice...I didn't want to give away my babies...but...but...

Michael moves in closer. Michael holds the picture towards Deborah.

> ### MICHAEL
> ### (HOARSE AND RAW)
> Boo.

> ### DEBORAH
> She's dead Michael...you can't find her...she's gone.

> ### MICHAEL
> Boo.

Deborah raises the gun and places it in her mouth. Michael stands towering over Deborah—tears stream down her face.

> ### MICHAEL (CONT'D)
> Boo.

> ### DEBORAH
> You'll never find her.

BOOM! She pulls the trigger. Blood spatters up onto Michael. The screen goes black.

Several scenes that were shot in fact ended up on the cutting room floor, including some interaction between Deborah and Loomis, the adult Michael's parole hearing, Loomis signing his book for eager college kids, Michael letting out other patients and attacking the night watchmen during his escape, Loomis unsuccessfully trying to get Boo's adoption papers and Myers killing the cemetery caretaker while stealing Judith's headstone.

Because Zombie is horror cinema's answer to Quentin Tarantino—namely, a pop-culture junkie whose films are crammed with references to exploitation and cult movies—his casts are liberally padded with weather-beaten faces from those same films. As such, *Halloween* features cameos from Adrienne Barbeau, Sybil Danning, Ken Foree, Clint Howard, Udo Kier, Richard Lynch and Dee Wallace. Zombie also cast his wife, Sheri Moon Zombie, as Michael's mother Deborah, along with Danielle Harris, who had played young Jamie Lloyd in *Halloween 4* and *5*, as Laurie's friend Annie. While the score was mostly recycled John Carpenter—courtesy of Zombie and Tyler Bates—the director also indulged his love of classic rock by including tunes from BTO, Alice Cooper, Peter Frampton, KISS, Nazareth and Rush, along with two doses of Blue Oyster Cult's 'Don't Fear the Reaper' (also heard in the original) and a new rendition of 'Mr Sandman', used previously in

Halloween II and *H20*. For someone who was insistent that his *Halloween* was a film apart, Zombie was still clearly trying to keep all his bases covered, as he told MTV: 'You have to completely reinvent the wheel, but keep the people that love the original wheel thrilled. It's a tricky balancing act.'

While Zombie's self-indulgent, 4½ hour documentary *Michael Lives: The Making of Halloween* paints the picture of a good time had by all, the truth was rather different, as the director would later admit to the website Bloody Disgusting: '*Halloween* was a very troubled shoot from Day One. Sometimes you get a shoot like *Devil's Rejects* where every second goes perfectly, every day is wonderful. And then you get one like *Halloween*...It was one of those ones where, if something could go wrong, it was gonna go wrong.'

Because of this, it was necessary to schedule five days of reshoots beginning on June 25, which would end up comprising a half hour of new footage:

- Michael's escape from the asylum was originally shot to the script. It was replaced by a transfer of Myers in the custody of three security guards, all played by alumni from *The Devil's Rejects*—Leslie Easterbrook, Bill Moseley and Tom Towles—who are summarily dispatched by the madman.
- The scene in which Loomis meets Sheriff Brackett (Brad Dourif) at the graveyard and discovers Judith's missing headstone was replaced by two new scenes—first with Loomis being led to the gravesite by the caretaker (played by Sid Haig, another Zombie regular) to find the headstone replaced by a crucified coyote, and second with Loomis meeting Brackett at a hamburger joint.
- The death of Bob (Nick Mennell), Lynda's boyfriend, was originally written with him being attacked by Myers in a ghost sheet outside the boy's van and impaled to a tree. It was instead shot with Bob being pulled into the van and stabbed by Myers. This was in turn changed to a demise that was more like the original film, with him being impaled on a wall with a butcher's knife.

The biggest change was the ending, again originally shot to the script, then replaced with a more extended climax that has Michael chasing Laurie (Scout Taylor-Compton) through the dilapidated Myers house until they both fall off the outside balcony. Laurie then uses Loomis's gun to shoot Myers before screaming herself into madness. 'We were kind of rushed because, filming in Pasadena, it's like 11:00 and—boom!—they shut you down...the cops would step in front of the cameras,' Zombie told MTV. 'We were shut down and I thought, "Well, maybe we have it." Then I started editing, and it didn't feel like I had the end of the movie. Luckily, I had the luxury of going back. Now, by the end of the movie, on those final frames you're going to think, "Wow, that *is* Michael's sister." The other way, it was more like she was a victim being rescued. Now, she becomes her own person.'

The release version of *Halloween* is 11 minutes shorter than Zombie's unrated 'director's cut', which includes more of young Michael and Loomis's sessions, the original rape scene in the asylum, the administrative meeting after Myers escapes, Myers following Laurie home from school and some more interplay between Laurie and her babysitting charges. Contrary to popular belief, the extended version is no more violent or graphic than the R-rated release. 'I don't think that people are more scared if things are bloody or more violent,' Zombie told Scripps News Service. 'I don't really think that scares people necessarily. I think movies are about the style and the execution, and that's how you get to people. It's just the way you tell them the story; it just has to be different...Basically, people get scared when they get really sucked into a movie and they feel like they're there and they feel like they're living in the situations with the characters. That's what scares people. Not blood and gore.'

The film was originally set for an October theatrical release, which was changed to August 31, to avoid competing with *Saw IV*. *Halloween* had a record-breaking debut, earning $30.5 million over the four-day Labor Day weekend. This meant that the movie paid for itself right out of the gate; however, *Halloween*'s opening ended up accounting for over half of its *entire* gross, since its final tally in the US was $58 million. An additional $22 million was raked in overseas.

Critics were polarised on the film, with the positive side represented by the *New York Post* ('The *Batman Begins* of slasher movies, and one of the more frightening stabathons of recent years'), *Premiere* magazine ('*Halloween* is a real, classic-style horror movie, not an exercise in gross special effects...for those who've missed Carpenter's classic, this will scare the candy corn out of you'), the *San Francisco Chronicle* ('Zombie puts his own spin on *Halloween*, while at the same time paying tribute to Carpenter's film, and he's mostly successful at both') and the *Village Voice* ('Horrific as it is, *Halloween* isn't so much a horror film as a biopic, and a superb one at that...Zombie's portrait is every bit as reverent, scrupulous, and deeply felt as any Oscar-grubbing horror show. Note the strange circumspection, the discipline of tone, the utter lack of snark, the absolute denial of gore-for-gore's sake...Can you feel the love?').

In the other corner were the *Chicago Tribune* ('It's a more polished, high-fidelity version of a story that's played out on screen many times since 1978, but once Zombie runs out of subtext, he's right back to the same old slasher text: "Blood. Guts. The end"'), *Entertainment Weekly* ('Zombie's identification with the killers in his films is the creepiest thing about them, but that's a mixed blessing: This Myers is more problem child than boogeyman. Zombie's embroidery of the 1978 *Halloween* never quite revives its fear factor'), the *New York Times* ('The film's obligation to serve up the expected body count prevents Mr Zombie from laying the groundwork for the explosion of tragic feeling that the movie's finale deserves. The new *Halloween* has sympathy for the Devil, but not enough') and *Variety* ('This bloodier, higher-body-count version leaves nothing to the imagination: Michael Myers is always right there in plain sight, committing mayhem sans suspenseful build-up or mystique').

On the occasion of *Halloween*'s release, Zombie insisted to Ain't It Cool News, 'I definitely would not do sequels...I wanted to make a movie with a beginning, a middle, and an end, so it's a movie-going experience. It's not a franchise-going experience, because I think that's part of what ruins these movies...I don't give a shit about a part 2 or 3, 4, 5. I want to make one great movie and then whatever happens, happens.' But with a worldwide gross of over $80 million, there was definitely going to be yet another outing for Michael Myers—and Zombie would be forced to eat his words when he signed on for the tentatively-titled *H2*.

THE FOG

(1979)

When I was in England...I took a drive out to see Stonehenge. There was a tremendous mood to the countryside. I looked across, and there was this fog sitting there. It was very visual, eerie, white, and ghostly. I thought, 'What if some dark shape just walked out of that thing and started coming toward me?' I'd have gone right through the roof of the car! Imagine a small town, with this fog bank drifting quietly across the road. Suddenly it surrounds your house, and you hear a knocking at the door. The things you could do with that!

–John Carpenter, music composer, co-writer and director

Working with the fog was an ordeal. It was made out of kerosene and water and we all stank for weeks.

–Adrienne Barbeau, 'Stevie Wayne'

After the runaway success of *Halloween*, John Carpenter seemed to be living a charmed life. On New Year's Day, 1979, he married actress Adrienne Barbeau (best known for playing Bea Arthur's divorced daughter on the TV series *Maude*), whom he had met during the filming of *High Rise* (aired in November 1978 as *Someone's Watching Me*), at a courthouse in Carpenter's hometown of Bowling Green, Kentucky. Then, on February 11, his second made-for-TV movie, the three-hour biopic *Elvis*, scored an unprecedented audience of 64 million viewers, despite being up against broadcasts of *Gone With the Wind* and *One Flew Over the Cuckoo's Nest*. That same month, it was announced that Carpenter's next project would be *The Prometheus Crisis*, based on the bestseller by Thomas Scortia and Frank Robinson (authors of *The Glass Inferno*, one of the books that formed the basis for Irwin Allen's blockbuster *The Towering Inferno*) about a nuclear plant meltdown. Set to roll in June on a $7 million budget, the film was beaten to the punch by the March release of *The China Syndrome* and was never made.

Carpenter had no time for regrets, however. He and his ex-girlfriend-turned-partner Debra Hill had now entered into a two-picture deal with Avco Embassy Pictures, the first film of which was to be a ghost story called *The Fog*. 'I came up with an idea before I connected it to a ghost genre,' Carpenter told *Rolling Stone*, 'an idea of fog. It's a frame in which to do certain cinematic things with ghosts. You don't really see ghosts as much as you think you see them. The fog moves around, it glows, it comes under doorways, through windowpanes, through your clothes...I think, in its own way, *The Fog* will allow me the same kinds of opportunities that *Halloween* did.'

On April 21, 1880, the clipper ship Elizabeth Dane carries its crew towards Antonio Bay, California, where they have purchased land to set up a colony. A bonfire on the beach lures the ship in through an unusually dense fog, where it crashes against the rocks. The ship sinks and the crew is drowned.[7] One hundred years later, Antonio Bay is celebrating its centennial. At midnight on April 21, fisherman Nick Castle picks up hitchhiker Elizabeth Solley when suddenly all the windows in his truck explode. At the same time, alcoholic priest Father Malone is startled when a stone slab crashes to the floor of his rectory, revealing an open hole in the wall which contains his grandfather's diary. Meanwhile, the fishing trawler Seagrass, fifteen miles offshore, is engulfed by a glowing fog bank that destroys the boat's generator. After encountering a ghost ship, the three men on the Seagrass meet their deaths from unseen assailants. Nick and Elizabeth, in bed at Nick's beach house, are interrupted by a loud knocking at the door that ends when the radio announces one o'clock; a series of footprints leading from the ocean to Nick's front door are the only evidence of trespass. The next morning, beachcombing seven-year-old Andy Wayne sees a gold coin on the rocks which suddenly turns into an old piece of driftwood when a wave hits it. He brings it home to his mother, Steve Wayne—the owner of the local lighthouse and radio station, where she serves as its night time deejay—who cleans it off to find letters underneath the dirt and slime: Dane. That afternoon, city councilwoman Kathy Williams and her secretary Sandy Fadel go to visit Father Malone to check on his participation in the evening's festivities. They find him totally distressed from having read the diary, where he has learned the truth about Antonio Bay's past: his grandfather, also the town priest, was one of twelve men who conspired to murder Captain Blake and the leprous crew of the Dane and steal their gold in order to build the church and grow the town. Arriving at the lighthouse for work, Steve has brought along the driftwood, which suddenly starts glowing with the inscription '12 Must Die' before violently bursting into flames. That night, a huge, glowing fog bank rolls in to assault Antonio Bay, killing the weatherman, cutting the phone lines, destroying the power station and encircling Steve's home, where Andy is alone with his babysitter. Steve frantically broadcasts for help and Nick and Elizabeth arrive in time to save Andy but not his elderly companion. As the fog spreads, Steve advises everyone to get out of town. Nick, Elizabeth and Andy make it to the church, followed immediately by Kathy and Sandy. Meanwhile, the fog surrounds the lighthouse and an intruding spectre forces Steve outside to the railing. At the church, the five survivors and Father Malone seek shelter in the priest's study, while

---

7 Carpenter was partly inspired by the actual wreck of the *Fama*, a schooner that got lost in the fog and ran aground at Daniels Hill, Goleta, California, in February 1846.

The Fog (1979)

the ghostly crew of the Dane assault the parish. As it turns out, not all of the stolen money was spent—Malone's grandfather secreted it away after the church was built. Ripping open the wall, the survivors find a huge wooden chest full of gold coins. As the ghosts break into the study, Malone confronts Blake in the sanctuary and spills the chest's contents at the feet of the captain, asking him to take Malone as a final sacrifice. Blake lifts up Malone by the neck to strangle him, catching the priest's robe on the burning candles, which sets the two of them on fire. After a sudden explosion, the ghosts, the gold and the fog are all gone—only Malone's charred body remains. The curse has finally been lifted.

As evidenced by the above, *The Fog* was totally unlike *Halloween*. Instead of being simple and straightforward, *The Fog* was plot-heavy and actually had a triple-focus narrative (Nick and Elizabeth; Steve in the lighthouse; Kathy, Sandy and Father Malone) where only two strands eventually intersect at the church (although Nick does talk to Steve on the phone). This was due largely to contrivances off-screen that resulted in the casting of the director's new wife, his starlet and her famous mother all in the same movie. 'For me it was very difficult because John and I had been a…couple prior to [his marriage to Barbeau],' Hill told a BBC documentary crew. 'So, while they were on their honeymoon, I was writing…[what] I think is the best character Adrienne's ever played.'

Just as Steve (later changed to Stevie) Wayne was written for Barbeau, so the character of Elizabeth Solley was written specifically for Jamie Lee Curtis, who,

much to Carpenter's surprise, had found herself out of work after *Halloween*. As the actress told the *Los Angeles Times*: 'I was always asked when I went out for jobs, "Have you got any film on yourself?" Before, I would always say, "No. I've only done TV," and I'd show them *Petticoat* or something and not get the job. Finally, I had a 91-minute film that I pretty much had the lead in and I couldn't get a job for seven months. John and Debra realised this and wrote me a big role in *The Fog*.' She further elaborated to *Rolling Stone*: 'Elizabeth's really neat...the first time you see me, I'm hitchhiking. The second time you see me, I'm in bed. With the guy. And it's nice. She's not a whore. She's got a reason.'

Carpenter had a reason, too—his casting of Curtis was not merely altruism but also an avenue to securing his third leading lady, Curtis's mother Janet Leigh, who had achieved immortality by taking a fatal shower in Hitchcock's *Psycho* (1960). The novelty of casting past and present scream queens was not lost on Leigh, but she nevertheless was grateful not only for the chance to work with her daughter but also to play a role suited to her: 'Most scripts I'm offered want to cast me younger than I am or older than I am,' the 52-year-old actress told the Associated Press. 'What I really want to do is play my own age.' As for the film itself, Leigh commented, '[*The Fog*] has no pretence except to be a ghost story, and it should be accepted for what it is.'

There *was* some pretence, however. Academy Award winner John Houseman (*The Paper Chase*) had been signed to cameo as an old fisherman who tells a group of children the story of the *Elizabeth Dane* in the pre-title sequence. And, once again, Carpenter approached Christopher Lee to play Father Malone. However, not having learned his lesson from turning down *Halloween*, the actor once again let opportunity pass him by. 'I told them I didn't think that [Malone] was the person the community would turn to,' Lee told Denis Meikle. 'He needed to be a strong

man.' Lee's loss was *The Fog*'s gain, however, as the role went to Tony and Emmy award-winner Hal Holbrook (*Mark Twain Tonight*).

With the cast set, Carpenter and Hill took a weekend and drove up the coast of California to scout locations, finally stopping at the lighthouse in Inverness, north of San Francisco (just a few miles north was Bodega Bay, where *The Birds* was shot). Nearby Point Reyes Station would double for Antonio Bay, while interiors were filmed at the Raleigh Studios in Hollywood.

The Fog was a $1 million co-production between Avco Embassy and the newly -formed film division of Bantam Books, Entertainment Discoveries, which had also produced the TV movie *The House on Garibaldi Street* (1979). On the strength of *Halloween*, Avco Embassy was able to rack up $7.5 million in pre-sales for *The Fog*, including a deal with ABC-TV for $1.2 million. 'The day we went into production,' Hill told her hometown newspaper the *Burlington County Times*, 'we had our negative cost back due to the sale to ABC.'

FATHER MALONE
I have been haunted for years by nightmares. Not dreams exactly. More like memories...of that night a hundred years ago, almost as if I inherited my grandfather's memory. His black corruption is in my blood...

KATHY
I admit that this puts a little different light on things, but you're taking this too far. We inherit nothing but a name from our ancestors. Now I don't want this up in lights on a marquee but I don't assume

the blame. They wanted a town. Your grandfather wanted a church...

FATHER MALONE

They were lepers!

SANDY

That is a little worse than if they were bankers.

—Unfilmed exchange, from the original script

Production began on April 2, 1979 and saw many changes from the script, not least of which was dialogue between Nick and Elizabeth, which was completely different (ie, the 'Are you weird?' hitch-hiking exchange was apparently improvised), as well as her character given some depth as an artist. Other alterations included:

- Bennett Tramer, the church custodian, was written to be a 14-year-old kid. In the film he is played by director Carpenter in an uncredited cameo.[8]
- After answering the door at Nick's beach house, he and Elizabeth were meant to see a series of footprints on an otherwise smooth beach that lead from the water's edge to the front porch. This was changed to having Nick simply stare out into the receding fog.
- Before the driftwood blows up at Stevie's station, Carpenter added the effect of Blake's voice on her tape recorder.
- The number of conspirators was changed from twelve to six.
- The treasure chest full of gold coins was changed to a golden cross.
- Malone's death was changed from burning to decapitation by Blake.

'It's not as frightening as *Halloween*, it's not supposed to be,' Carpenter told *The Washington Post*. 'This is a fantasy from the word go, I can't emphasise that enough. It's ghosts, you see ghosts rise up from the deep depths of the water. It's one illusion from beginning to end, with no basis in reality, nothing for the audience to hook onto.' Unfortunately, there was not much for the director or his crew to hook onto either when it came to the title character, which was every bit as unwieldy in reality as it was in fantasy. 'We shot thousands and thousands—*hundreds* of thousands of feet to get that fog right,' an exasperated Carpenter told *Fangoria*. 'It was the most film I've ever shot on one feature; take after take with the widest shots imaginable.'

Despite the logistical problems, Carpenter was adamant that *The Fog* be a very different experience than *Halloween*. 'There's less violence,' he told *Cinefantastique*, 'it's less overt, more in the mood. I'm relying on parallel cutting rather than a lot of camera movement. And we don't need cattle-prod shocks here. Mood and story will carry it.' But Bob Rehme, president of Avco Embassy, was not so sure. 'We'll get the film-buff audience,' he told *New York* magazine. 'But I'm concerned that there are

---

8 Bennett Tramer is one of many Carpenter characters based on real-life friends who pop up repeatedly in his movies. Tramer is also the name of the boy Annie fixes Laurie up with in *Halloween* and who is mistaken for Michael Myers and accidentally killed in *Halloween II*.

an awful lot of horror movies out now. That's why we're going with the hard sell.'

That summer, a rough cut of *The Fog* was screened for Rehme and the Avco sales team, with Carpenter, Hill and Barbeau in attendance. It did not go well, as Barbeau would relate in her 2006 autobiography, *There Are Worse Things I Could Do*: 'Halfway through....John asked me to step outside to talk. He felt he had failed; the movie wasn't scary. And the pain of making it was killing him. He asked if it would be all right with me if he quit directing. Of course it would, I said. Whatever he wanted to do was fine with me.'

Once he got over his initial despair, Carpenter decided to take a second pass at making the film more frightening, both through re-editing and reshooting. 'John was going to pay for [the reshoots] himself,' Barbeau wrote. 'Avco Embassy couldn't believe he was so conscientious, telling him most directors just turn in their cut and walk away. They volunteered to absorb the cost.'[9] With that, Carpenter wrote and directed five new scenes, including:

- A title sequence with poltergeist activity wreaking havoc in Antonio Bay.
- More explicit deaths for Baxter (James Canning), Wallace (George 'Buck' Flower) and Williams (John Goff), the sailors on the *Seagrass*.
- While waiting for the Coast Guard on board the *Seagrass*, Nick (Tom Atkins) tells Elizabeth a sailor's yarn about his father finding an abandoned ship and a disappearing gold coin. Then Baxter's corpse falls on Elizabeth (originally she found his dead body snagged in tackle equipment).
- In the morgue, Baxter's reanimated corpse attacks Elizabeth.
- After retreating outside, Stevie climbs to the top of the lighthouse and fights off the ghosts.

'I came to a point on *The Fog* where I said, "They have seen *Alien, Halloween, Phantasm,* and a lot of other movies," Carpenter told *Fangoria*. "If my film is going to be viable in the marketplace, it's got to compete with those." Originally I was trying to compete only with Val Lewton movies—very understated horror with a brooding atmospheric feel to it. But if you released *Isle of the Dead* [1945] today, I don't think it could compete because it doesn't have those visceral shocks.'

Avco Embassy spent $3 million promoting *The Fog* (including skywriting and fog-machines in theatre lobbies) before its release on February 8, 1980, the most the company had spent since *The Graduate* in 1967-68. While the film was certainly profitable, grossing $21 million, it was a far cry from *Halloween*'s returns, and several of the critics who had favourably reviewed that film found themselves disappointed by Carpenter's follow up. '*The Fog* is constructed of random diversions,' said Vincent Canby. 'There are too many story lines, which necessitate so much cross-cutting that no one sequence can ever build to a decent climax. The movie looks quite pretty but prettiness of this sort is beside the point in such a film.' 'The problem is with the fog,' observed Roger Ebert. 'It must have seemed like an inspired idea to make a horror movie in which clouds of fog would be the menace,

---

9 Carpenter and Hill had a 25% stake in *The Fog*'s profits, so it was in their best interest to ensure the film's viability at the box office.

but the idea just doesn't work out...The movie's made with style and energy, but it needs a better villain. And it also needs a slightly more plausible plot.' What most people want to know about *The Fog* is whether it's as scary as *Halloween*,' wrote Gene Siskel. 'The answer is simple: No way. To be fair to Carpenter, it's not the same kind of film. But to be fair to the audience, *The Fog* is not very good for what it's trying to be.'

Not everyone saw it that way. Tom Allen once again took the lead in championing John Carpenter as a talent on the rise: 'There is a Carpenter touch. It is entertaining, intelligent, frequently derivative, and quintessentially American in its creative comfortableness with genre forms. *The Fog* is merely a holding action compared to Carpenter's transcendence of old forms in *Assault on Precinct 13* and *Halloween*. But the movie does confirm that few have mastered cinema craft so quickly and so totally, and now we wait to see whether there is an original voice to keep pace with the technique.' Kevin Thomas found *The Fog* 'an elegant and scary thriller of the supernatural that's far more impressive and satisfying than Carpenter's grisly and pointless (but profitable) *Halloween*,' while *Variety* enthused: 'Alfred Hitchcock he isn't, but John Carpenter demonstrates he has a finger right on the pulse of today's film going public with *The Fog*. This well-made suspenser looks to be a good bet to equal or surpass the returns of Carpenter's sleeper hit *Halloween*.'

Initially, Carpenter was to follow *The Fog* with the equally ethereal *Without a Trace*, a 'top secret' project about The Philadelphia Experiment.[10] When he 'couldn't come up with a third act,' as he told *Variety*, the film was scrapped and replaced with something he had written years earlier for 20th Century Fox: *Escape from New York*. *Escape* would reunite Carpenter with *Elvis*'s Kurt Russell as criminal antihero Snake Plissken, who in 1997 is sent into New York City—now the sole maximum-security penitentiary for the United States—to rescue the President. Produced in August 1980 on a $6 million budget, the film was released the following summer to strong reviews and $25 million at the box office.

From there, Carpenter made his bid for the big time by directing a remake of his favourite horror film, Howard Hawks' *The Thing* (1951), for Universal. The $15 million production, which the studio had originally intended for Tobe Hooper in the mid-70s, involved such intricate and ground-breaking effects work that it took over a year to complete. Released in June 1982, *The Thing* had the bad fortune to follow in the wake of Steven Spielberg's saccharine and manipulative—but phenomenally successful—*ET* (also from Universal), and was savaged by critics and ignored by audiences. Its failure put the kibosh on Carpenter directing a $17 million version of Stephen King's *Firestarter* for Universal, though he would simply segue into directing a $10 million production of King's *Christine* for Columbia instead.

Over the years, *The Thing* has gained a huge following and come to be recognised

---

10 Supposedly a true story, though now widely disbelieved, The Philadelphia Experiment is meant to have occurred aboard the USS Eldridge in the Philadelphia Naval Shipyard in 1943. An experiment in unified field theory is said to have rendered the ship invisible for a time, resulting in disembodiment and illness for the crew. After he became president of New World Pictures in early 1984, Bob Rehme reactivated the project with Carpenter as executive producer and Stewart Raffill (*Across the Great Divide*) as director. *The Philadelphia Experiment* was released that August to negative reviews and poor box office.

as one of the best horror films of the 1980s. Its mind-blowing effects and palpable sense of paranoia eventually found enough of an audience that in 2002 Universal licensed a video game version of the film, while putting a second remake into production in 2010 under Dutch commercial director Matthijs van Heijningen Jr. Its release in October 2011 showed that lightning could indeed fail to strike twice, as it too was a box-office failure.

(2005)

You finished watching *The Fog* and you're left with all these questions. And you know there's the whole ending where Adrienne Barbeau is talking about whatever it was, it came, it went, it disappeared. We have no idea what happened. In this movie we try and answer some of those questions...And there's a whole other storyline that is to do

with [Elizabeth] and sort of a strange connection with the past that
you wouldn't expect.

–Rupert Wainwright, director

I am a producer, but I [just] come in and say hello to everybody. Then
I go home...and watch basketball games on TV.

–John Carpenter, co-producer

After collaborating on five films, John Carpenter and Debra Hill went their separate
ways in 1983. Carpenter would direct such films as *Starman* (1984), *Big Trouble in
Little China* (1986), *Prince of Darkness* (1987), *They Live* (1988), *Memoirs of an
Invisible Man* (1991), *In the Mouth of Madness* and *Village of the Damned* (both
1995). Hill produced *The Dead Zone* (1983), *Adventures in Babysitting* (1987), *Big
Top Pee Wee* (1988), *The Fisher King* (1991) and Showtime's *Rebel Highway* series
of AIP remakes in 1994. In 1996, the two reunited with Kurt Russell to make the
sequel *Escape from LA*, which proved to be a huge disappointment, both critically
and commercially.

Carpenter tried to bounce back in 1998 with the critically-acclaimed *Vampires*,
but it lost $10 million at the box office. An even bigger flop followed in 2001 with
Ghosts of Mars, which lost over $20 million and ended his feature-directing career
for the rest of the decade. After *Escape from LA*, Hill only produced one film, the
flop comedy *Crazy in Alabama* (1999), before being diagnosed with terminal cancer
in February 2004.

Receiving the news actually spurred Hill into action, and she put two films on
the fast track—one about the 9/11 attacks called *World Trade Centre* and the other a
remake of her personal favourite of her collaborations with Carpenter. '*The Fog* was
something that...was near and dear to her heart,' Carpenter told Bloody Disgusting. 'She
always wanted to remake that film. So it was from her perseverance that it got made.'

That October, it was announced that Carpenter and Hill had done a deal with
Revolution Studios to produce a new version of *The Fog* in association with veteran
producer David Foster, who had co-produced Carpenter's *The Thing*. '[The] cultural
mindset these days...says if anything's over 15 years old, it's old-fashioned and old-
school,' Carpenter told the website Dark Horizons. '[But] audiences have maybe
heard of it, so the thing to do is to take it out and prop it up and put a fresh coat of
paint on it and see how it goes.'

Cooper Layne, co-writer and co-producer of the sci-fi flop *The Core* (2003) for
Foster's company, was engaged to write the screenplay. In December, while Layne
was still working on the script, Rupert Wainwright (*Stigmata*) was signed to direct.
Wainwright would tell the audience at the 2005 Comic Con in San Diego: 'I didn't
even interview with [Carpenter] to get the job because he didn't want to be in the
position of interviewing directors, as a director himself...I mean, he was supervising
the script...but he really wanted to let us to do our version of the movie and not...
come out [with his] stamp all over it.'

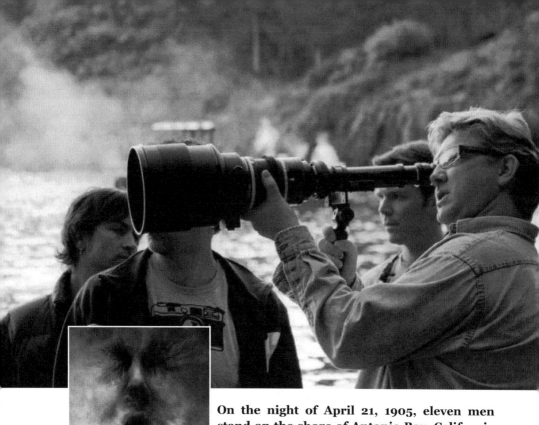

On the night of April 21, 1905, eleven men stand on the shore of Antonio Bay, California and watch as Father Patrick Malone and two oarsmen row out through a fog bank to meet the clipper ship Elizabeth Dane. On board is Captain Blake, his wife and a large contingent of fellow lepers, who have come to set up a colony. Malone and the oarsmen board the ship and are met by Blake and a chest full of gold. But Malone demands all the gold the ship is carrying; when Blake refuses, the men douse the Dane in kerosene. After the oarsmen fetch the gold below decks, Malone locks them in with the lepers and sets fire to the ship, barely escaping with the gold on one of the Dane's lifeboats. One hundred years later, Antonio Bay is celebrating its centennial. Local fisherman Nick Castle picks up his girlfriend Elizabeth Williams, who is returning home from college, and takes her to a beach party, which is crashed when Nick's first mate Brett Spooner drives their boat the Seagrass right up onto the beach, pouring out beer and two party girls. Nick has to take Elizabeth home, so their friend Sean Reed volunteers to get the Seagrass back to the marina. Once at sea, the Seagrass runs out of gas just as it is enveloped by a huge fog bank and encounters a ghost ship. Suddenly, both girls and Sean are killed by unseen forces, while the fog enters into Spooner. After an argument with her mother, local Chamber of Commerce president Kathy Williams,

Elizabeth goes home with Nick. Their lovemaking is interrupted by a pounding at the door, but a series of footprints leading from the ocean to Nick's front door are the only evidence of trespass. The next morning, beachcombing youngster Andy Wayne finds an old, golden hairbrush. He brings it home to his mother, Stevie Wayne, the owner of the local lighthouse and radio station, where she serves as its night-time deejay. Meanwhile, Nick learns that the Seagrass never made it to the marina, and he and Elizabeth set out to find the boat. When they do, they also find three dead bodies and Spooner—half-dead and hiding in the freezer. Arriving at the lighthouse for work, Stevie has brought along the hairbrush, which suddenly turns red hot and ignites her son's drawings on the wall. The fire leaves an opening in the wall, from which Stevie recovers the journal of Patrick Malone. She takes the journal to Father Bobby Malone, but he merely turns her away, wanting no part of his great-grandfather's legacy. At the hospital with Spooner, Elizabeth is attacked by Sean's reanimated corpse. During the commotion, Spooner, accused of murder by Sheriff Tom Malone, escapes out the window. Stevie arrives at the hospital and gives the journal to Malone; Elizabeth and Nick steal it, go to a local bar and examine the contents. That night, a huge, glowing fog bank rolls in to assault Antonio Bay, killing the weatherman, cutting the phone lines, creating a flood, destroying the power station and invading Stevie's home, where Andy is alone with his babysitter, Mrs Kobritz. With no power, Stevie leaves the lighthouse for home, but her car is swallowed up by fog. Mrs Kobritz is attacked by a malignant

spirit that leaves her a rotting, decomposed mess; Andy hides in his room. Stevie is trapped in her car as the fog propels it towards a cliff; she manages to escape just before the car tumbles over into the ocean. Making her way back to the lighthouse, Stevie fires up the generator and frantically broadcasts for someone to help her son. Nick and Elizabeth arrive just in time to save Andy from the attacking ghosts. The fog creates chaos in town, assaulting and killing the townspeople, who flee in a panic; with the road out of town ruined by the flood, Stevie advises everyone to head for the safety of the church. Spooner is already there. Nick, Elizabeth and Andy join him, followed immediately by Kathy and Tom Malone. The survivors and Father Malone seek shelter in the cellar, but Kathy is ripped through a window by the fog. Meanwhile, the fog surrounds the lighthouse and a parade of ghosts stream by the windows, seeking entry. At the church, the fog explodes from inside Spooner, who is ripped apart, then attacks Tom Malone, literally dragging him outside and through the woods. In the lighthouse, a spectre ushers Stevie outside at knifepoint. The fog dragging Tom Malone lets him go, then turns into Blake and his crew; the ground they are standing on is the land the lepers purchased and it engulfs Malone. Blake and his wife embrace and then they, with all the ghosts, dissolve. The fog, and the threat, is gone. In the church, Father Malone places the journal into a hole in the wall and bricks it up, hopefully for good.

Layne's first draft had dutifully followed the plotline of the original *Fog* fairly closely, even duplicating several key scenes, including the opening title sequence of supernatural mischief:

INT. MERRY MARKET—ANTONIO BAY—NIGHT

A BAG BOY picks up his broom, cranks the volume on his radio, as the song Stevie just cued plays in the b.g. He goes to straighten a display of canned goods, when something makes him stop...

He looks around the store, eying the creepy old curios dangling from the ceiling, hanging on walls, etc. –

Shaking it off, he starts to sweep, when the lights inside the soda cases begin to flicker and buzz.

BOTTLES start CLINKING together on the shelves. The whole place starts to RATTLE AND HUM now, as stuff falls and breaks in the aisles.

BAG BOY
Shit! It's the big one!

He drops his broom and races for the exit, when he sees:

THE AUTOMATIC DOORS slamming open and shut all on their own, fast, and erratic—lethal even—and when he turns, he sees something that freezes him in his tracks:

MICROWAVE POPCORN starts to POP. Still in the packages. Right on the shelf.

EXT. ANTONIO BAY SAVINGS AND LOAN—NIGHT

The screen on the ATM begins BUZZING with a weird, sepia-tone FLUX. It looks like there's an IMAGE trying to form somewhere in

there, but then we hear the KA-CHUNK of the cash dispenser, as TWENTIES begin spitting from the machine.

An OLD LADY passes by, her eyeglasses on a decorative chain around her neck. At first she just keeps walking, but when she realises no one is watching, she goes back, scooping the bills into her purse.

EXT. SERVICE STATION—NIGHT

Closed. Dark. The AIR HOSE DING-DINGs. But there's nobody there.

One of the gas NOZZLES falls off the pump, begins discharging GASOLINE, which slowly spreads across the parking lot...

EXT. PET WORLD—NIGHT

Through the window, we see DOGS GOING NUTS in their cages, barking at the moon, spinning, chasing their tails...

EXT. REAL ESTATE OFFICE—NIGHT

There's a cherry SIGN out front, with a digital TIME/TEMP display. The thing is going haywire—34 o'clock, 299 degrees, etc. And for the briefest moment, we could swear it spells out a word: DANE.

Layne had, however, allowed himself certain liberties with the property and managed to concoct some fairly hair-raising sequences, including the one where Stevie finds Patrick Malone's journal:

STEVIE'S POV—INSIDE THE WALL

SHE SEES SOMETHING wedged between the studs, but the light doesn't quite hit it. Whatever it is, it appears to be wrapped, or wound in something...

POV—INSIDE THE HOLE—A MINUTE LATER

STEVIE'S ARM REACHES IN...fingers feeling around blindly, straining for the thing, but she can't quite reach it, when

SOMETHING LASHES AROUND HER WRIST!!

ON STEVIE'S TERRIFIED FACE

As she tries to pull her arm from the hole! THE LIGHTS and ELECTRONICS in the room begin to flicker and buzz, and whatever has her, PULLS HER INTO THE WALL, with force enough to send the rest of the bricks cascading down around her...

SHE FALLS, SHRIEKING in horror at what's now attached to her hand!

CLOSE ON HER HAND—AN OLD BOOK IS TETHERED TO IT BY A LIVING SNARL OF LONG, BLACK HAIR, LACED WITH SAND AND SLIME AND UNDULATING SEAWEED!!!

She goes for a pair of SCISSORS on the desk, HACKING AT THE SLIMY MASS. YELLOW OOZE spurts from the SEAWEED TENDRILS, as whatever it is FINALLY LETS GO and the book falls to the floor.

She checks her wrist where the thing had hold of her—red, puffy, rising welts...

She looks down at the book, only now it's just a dusty old, leather-bound book. No sign of anything strange.

She tilts her head to make out the gold-embossed words on the book's cover...

JOURNAL OF PATRICK MALONE

This and many other scenes were drastically changed in the rewrite that Wainwright oversaw, as he sought to move his version of *The Fog* further away from the one that had gone before:

- The location was changed from Antonio Bay in California to Antonio Island in Oregon.
- The timeframe was changed from 100 years to 134, with the trigger event being the dedication of a statue of Antonio Island's founding fathers—the men who robbed Blake and set fire to the *Dane*—instead of the town's centennial.
- Stevie discovering Patrick Malone's journal behind the lighthouse wall was changed to Elizabeth finding it in a wall in Nick's boathouse.
- Originally, Stevie narrowly escapes the fog pushing her car off a cliff then returns to the lighthouse to warn the community. This was changed to her being trapped underwater in her car and seeing a ghost before escaping and making her way to town where she is reunited with her son.
- Instead of sheltering in the church, the survivors congregate at the town hall.
- The scene with the fog exploding out of Spooner was dropped.
- The scenes of Stevie being attacked at the lighthouse were dropped.
- Instead of surviving the ordeal, Father Malone is killed by flying glass shards.
- Instead of being swallowed up by the lepers' land, Tom Malone is set ablaze by Blake.

The biggest changes involved the character of Elizabeth, who now returns to Antonio Island after being plagued by nightmares while living in New York, instead of simply coming home from college. Her nightmares are in fact flashbacks of what happened on the *Dane*; a series of added scenes see her haunted by scales that turn out to be a Nineteenth century hallmark from manufacturers on Canada's Prince William Island, which was deserted after an outbreak of leprosy. She slowly comes to realise that she is in fact the reincarnation of Blake's wife, and only she can end the fog's reign of terror.

All this was part and parcel of Wainwright's take on the material, as he remarked in the featurette *Whiteout Conditions*: 'I decided...that it wasn't enough just to have a horror story where ghosts come back for a gold cross. It's fun, but why do ghosts want a gold cross? What are they gonna do with it? So I always felt there had to be something more that they were after. One of the main things that I wanted to do was explore the idea of Elizabeth going on this totally unique journey...[with Blake] reaching out to find the love of his life. So, in a sense, adding romance to it and adding this sort of blurring between the two worlds. It seems to me much more likely that ghosts will come back for a person they're in love with rather than a piece of gold.'

On March 7, 2005, Debra Hill died at age 54. Exactly one week later, *The Fog* began shooting in Vancouver on an $18 million budget. Carpenter picked up where his late partner had left off, as co-star Maggie Grace (from the TV series *Lost*) would tell the Comic Con audience: 'I think we all felt that there was a really beautiful ambiance, just with Mr Carpenter's involvement. He was very much a presence on the set, especially in the beginning, which was really lovely...to have his support.

He gave us, obviously, a wonderful template that's been kind of an indie film/ horror filmmakers' ideal forever…It was lovely to meet him and talk with him about everything surrounding the first one. But I think he was extremely gracious as far as allowing Mr Wainwright to do it.'

'This version of *The Fog* is updated,' co-star Tom Welling (from the TV series *Smallville*) told Dark Horizons. 'It's more modern. The other one was great for what it was, but…we have taken the ages of the [first film's] characters and divided them by two. This is younger, it's quicker, and it's a little bit edgier.'

EXT. A COMMUNITY PARK—NEAR THE COAST—NIGHT

TWO LITTLE BOYS play on a swing set in the kiddie-park. We hear it CREAKING as they go back and forth. Back and forth.

BEHIND THEM, UNNOTICED, THE FOG SWEEPS OUT FROM A CLUMP OF TREES, UNSEEN, COMING CLOSER AND CLOSER.

SILENTLY, it overtakes them from behind, temporarily obscuring them from view…

…but when it has passed, ONLY ONE LITTLE BOY IS LEFT SWINGING. He looks over to the swing beside him which just a moment ago was occupied by his friend…

CLOSE ON THE EMPTY SWING—dangling at the end of its chains.

–From Layne's original draft; unused

'The fog is a central character to the piece,' Layne remarked in *Whiteout Conditions*. 'In the original they weren't able to manipulate the fog the way we can do it now. Nobody wanted characters made out of fog but we did want the fog to actually have a life of its own…We started with the fog really able to do a lot of things that regular fog wouldn't be able to do and then we had to scale that back…so that eventually what it does is believable.'

'We tried to get all the fog effects practically,' Wainwright said in the featurette, *Feeling the Effects of the Fog*, 'so we have like angry fog and sneaky fog and all these different [characteristics] because the fog is a personality.' In this, he was aided by special effects coordinator Bob Comer, but Wainwright came to rely just as much on digital effects supervisor Chris Watts and his team of computer artists. 'There are a variety of other things that we can do now with CG fog,' Wainwright told Dark Horizons. 'There is a whole bunch of other things we can use to make it scary, ominous and weird.'

'What we've really tried to do is add stuff to the original, rather than switch it out,' Wainwright would tell the Comic Con audience. 'We're not trying to throw away what's good about the original…We want to scare people. This is a scary movie with a scary premise, a scary idea...the fog does all sorts of very bizarre, weird things to people and you have no idea how or why...for a PG-13 movie it's as gory as it can get.'

Columbia decided not to screen *The Fog* in advance for critics (a practice more and more common for genre pictures), and the studio was wise not to do so, given the overwhelmingly-negative reaction the film received. 'Carpenter has co-produced a remake...that actually manages to be even more inertly inept than his 1980 original,' said *Entertainment Weekly*. The *New York Daily News* deadpanned, 'The fog...does something genuinely eerie: It causes everyone in the cast to deliver dreadful performances and display inappropriate reactions when their friends are drowned, burned, stabbed or thrown into glass display cases.' *Time Out* commented, 'Carpenter's silly 1980 weather thriller...certainly doesn't suggest remake material; it's merely the way-station between *Halloween* and *Escape from New York*. Apparently, that wasn't enough to prevent this misguided attempt...Never will you wish more fervently for an Adrienne Barbeau cameo, just for old time's sake. Your prayers will be in vain.' *Variety* observed, 'At once slicker and blander than John Carpenter's 1980 shocker of the same title, this low-voltage remake drifts rather aimlessly through scenes of mayhem sufficiently subdued to ensure a PG-13 rating,' while the *Village Voice* rendered a similar judgment: 'Making concessions at every turn to the youth-horror market, the film slashes the ages of its protagonists by some 15 years, and its IQ follows suit.'[11]

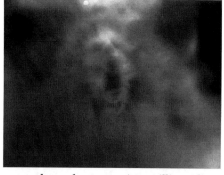

The Fog opened on October 14, with an $11.7 million haul, which was good enough to rank first for the weekend, on its way to an eventual gross of $29 million in America, with an additional $16 million accrued overseas. Debra Hill's other posthumous production, *World Trade Centre*—which was based on the true story of Will Jimeno and John McLoughlin, two New York cops who were trapped under the wreckage of the WTC while rescue teams fought to save them—became a $65 million Oliver Stone film and was shot in late 2005. Released by Paramount in the summer of 2006, it garnered good reviews and $163 million in worldwide box-office.

The year 2009 saw production on the first John Carpenter feature in nearly a decade with *The Ward*, the story of an institutionalised young woman (Amber Heard) who is terrorised by a ghost.[12] Produced for $10 million, the film premiered at the Toronto International Film Festival in September 2010 and played several

---

11 The PG-13 rating had been determined before shooting began. In fact, there is only a three-minute difference between the theatrical version and the unrated DVD, mostly involving shortened scenes of people burning to death (on the *Dane*, Dan the weatherman, Tom Malone).

12 Although this is Carpenter's first feature film in several years, he did direct two well-received episodes of Showtime's *Masters of Horror* cable series: 'Cigarette Burns' (2005) and 'Pro-Life' (2006).

other festivals in the first part of 2011, as well as being released overseas, but distributor Warner Brothers decided to forego a US theatrical release and sent it straight to DVD that August.

HALLOWEEN II
(1981)

The villain in *Halloween*...has never really been done in any of [the rip-offs] that followed. They never quite caught the essence of how frightening he was, for various reasons. They try to work on who he was, which doesn't matter, and they try to work on inventive ways of killing people, which is not that important either; it's really the style with which you do it.

–John Carpenter, co-music composer, co-writer and co-producer

Quite frankly, *Halloween II* stinks. It's a terrible movie. I should never have done it. The only reason I did it was out of loyalty to John and Debra. But it was definitely a mistake.

–Jamie Lee Curtis, 'Laurie Strode'

Irwin Yablans had spent two fruitless years trying to duplicate the success of *Halloween* with films like *Tourist Trap* (1979) and *Fade to Black* (1980); he had even tried to capitalise on *Saturday Night Fever* with a disco comedy (*Nocturna*) and a disco roller-skating musical (*Roller Boogie*), neither one of which saw much in the way of returns. Little wonder that he was eager to get the ball rolling on *Halloween II*, and he began presales on the film at the 1980 Cannes Film Festival, where the rights were bought by Filmways Pictures. In December, Yablans and Moustapha Akkad ended their partnership, though Akkad would continue to have an interest in any *Halloween* sequels.

Shortly thereafter, facing financial difficulties in the wake of their buy-out of American International Pictures, Filmways was forced to divest itself of some of the properties it had in development, including *Halloween II* and Ridley Scott's *Blade Runner*. The former was picked up by Dino De Laurentiis, while the latter went to The Ladd Company.

It was first announced that *Halloween II* would have Laurie Strode going off to college and being stalked there by Michael Myers ('Imagine the possibilities, a whole dorm filled with nice, juicy co-eds!' Yablans told the *Los Angeles Times*). That was then changed to Laurie living in another town and residing in a high-rise apartment complex when Myers—still pursued by Dr Loomis—finds her on Halloween night.

HALLOWEEN II

ALL NEW

From The People Who Brought You "HALLOWEEN"..
More Of The Night *He* Came Home.

MOUSTAPHA AKKAD PRESENTS A DINO DE LAURENTIIS CORP. FILM
JAMIE LEE CURTIS
DONALD PLEASENCE
'HALLOWEEN II' · A JOHN CARPENTER / DEBRA HILL PRODUCTION · JOHN CARPENTER AND DEBRA HILL · RICK ROSENTHAL
PRODUCED BY DEBRA HILL AND JOHN CARPENTER · IRWIN YABLANS · JOSEPH WOLF · BARRY BERNARDI · DEAN CUNDEY
A UNIVERSAL RELEASE PANAVISION® **R** RESTRICTED

This too was rejected, which led Debra Hill to question whether an entirely new approach was needed. 'We wondered whether the characters of Laurie Strode and Sam Loomis had run their course, really,' she told *Cinefantastique*. 'At one point, John and I thought of starting the picture with Laurie dead and then, like *Psycho*, introduce a new set of characters. One of our motivations for trying that approach was Jamie Lee Curtis. She's matured and developed so much in the last three years that we wondered whether the audience would still believe her as a high schooler. Finally, though, we reasoned that any girl who'd been through *that* much in one night, would have to look a little more mature! Also, we think that the audience wants the struggle between these two representatives of good and evil to continue.'

For her part, Curtis had become the cinema's reigning 'scream queen' after appearing in five consecutive horror films and was eager to move her career in another direction.[13] 'I didn't want to make another horror movie,' she admitted to *Fangoria*. 'But then I realised that I have a terrible loyalty to John and Debra—who am I to say no to them when they gave me a career? And also to the audience; most of all to the audience. Since it takes up directly from where the first one ends, the audience has the right to see the same person in the same role.'

As far as John Carpenter was concerned, he had gone from a relatively unknown talent to being in high demand—he was trying to do post-production on *Escape from New York,* write *Halloween II* and prepare *The Thing* all at the same time. Something was bound to suffer, and that something was the script for *Halloween II*. As the man himself would later tell *Time Out New York*, 'I said, "Well I don't wanna direct it, but I'll sit down and write something." Big mistake! Middle of the night, chugging beer, trying to come up with some ideas. What is there? There's nothing left to say.'

Haddonfield, Illinois: Halloween, 1978. After being shot six times by Dr Sam Loomis and falling off a second-floor balcony, homicidal maniac Michael Myers manages to escape. Loomis and Sheriff Brackett continue to pursue the madman, while his would-be victim Laurie Strode is taken to Haddonfield Medical Clinic and treated for her injuries. Myers kills a television news producer and takes her car to Haddonfield Medical to continue his pursuit of Laurie, who, while under sedation, is having dreams of visiting Michael in Smith's Grove Sanitarium when she was eight years old. Methodically, Myers kills the hospital security guard, an EMT, four nurses and the attending physician before going after Laurie. In the meantime, Loomis learns that Laurie is in fact Michael's younger sister, who was born two years after he was committed for murdering his older sister. Four years later, her parents died and Laurie was adopted by the Strodes, who had the records sealed. Now that he knows the method behind Michael's madness, Loomis rushes to the hospital to find Laurie the

---

13 It was rumoured that Curtis was being sought by producer Michelle Corbin-Hillman for a remake of *Psycho* in which she would play her mother's role but would be murdered in a hot tub instead of a shower. Nothing came of this, however, and it was chalked up to wishful thinking.

only one left alive. Under attack by Myers, Loomis and Laurie lure the killer into an operating room which is rapidly filling with gas. Laurie shoots out both of Michael's eyes; now blinded, her brother cannot prevent Laurie's escape before Loomis blows up the entire ward with his lighter. Consumed by fire, Michael Myers is finally destroyed.

Carpenter was not exaggerating the extent of his writer's block—the *Halloween II* script was a mess. Within just two weeks of delivering a final draft, the piece went through two major rewrites, which altered a full third of the screenplay. The script is in fact so dumbed-down that a good deal of it is underlined and exclaimed, just in case whoever was unlucky enough to direct it failed to grasp all the false scares: 'Suddenly a cat springs out of the trash SCREECHING!' 'Suddenly the shape under the blankets grabs Karen and pulls her down onto the bed!'

The big 'twist' that Carpenter and Hill had come up with was to make Michael Myers and Laurie Strode brother and sister, the horror movie equivalent of making Darth Vader and Luke Skywalker father and son. Not only did this destroy much of the mystery behind The Shape, but it was poorly handled to boot: Laurie claims ignorance to an EMT when he tells her the identity of her attacker, then has a dream/flashback where she goes as a young girl and visits Michael in the asylum! It is also stretching credibility to breaking point to believe that Loomis, for whom Myers was 'an obsession', would not have known about Laurie's existence, especially since she apparently came to visit his patient!

All of this makes a mockery of Carpenter's overly-ambitious comments to *Fangoria* at the time: 'I thought about Coppola's reasons for doing *Godfather II*—sequels are so bad so often, why not try to make a good one? Also there were certain things that happened in the first one that I wanted to 'clear up'; that was very attractive to me—and also kind of a freeing thing. On the business aspect, it was a good move. Then there was the challenge of it—what could we do with a sequel to *Halloween*? Could it be exciting and scary? And then the final thing; after thinking about it a long time, I thought that there really might be another story in it, and I thought it really might be a lot of fun. So I thought, let's try it. But my biggest problem was that I did not want to direct it—I had made that film once, and I really didn't want to do it again.'

Carpenter's first choice to replace him in the director's chair was old friend Tommy Lee Wallace, who was grateful for the offer but not wild about the opportunity, as he told *Starburst* magazine: 'All I would have gotten out of the film—and what a lot of people thought was worth it—was the chance to direct, but I knew it would be hack work, pure and simple.' Wallace was content instead to become a screenwriter, penning the scripts for *Amityville II: The Possession* (1982) as well as two proposed Carpenter films, the western *El Diablo* and the martial arts film *The Ninja*.[14]

---

14 *El Diablo* was to have been produced for EMI and starred Kurt Russell; *The Ninja* was to have been a Zanuck-Brown production for Fox—both projects fell through. *El Diablo* was eventually produced for HBO in 1990 with Anthony Edwards (*ER*) in the Russell role. Carpenter and Hill were not involved, though Carpenter and Wallace's script (co-written with Bill Phillips) was used.

There was then some thought given to making *Halloween II* be Debra Hill's directorial debut, but she had the same misgivings as Wallace, which she explained to *Fangoria*: 'I really didn't want to start with a sequel [to] a John Carpenter film. I'd like to start with an original.' At the time, she had her sights set on directing an adaptation of the popular board game *Clue*, so she too was crossed off the list.[15]

In the meantime, Carpenter's agent David Gersh had seen a half-hour suspense film called *The Toyer* from 31-year-old Rick Rosenthal, a Harvard graduate and American Film Institute alumnus. Based on the play by Gardner McKay, *The Toyer* concerns a psychopath who plays a game of seduction and terror with his female victims. When finished, he severs their brain stems, leaving them helpless, non-functioning living toys. Gersh was favourably disposed towards Rosenthal and recommended him to Carpenter as a possible director for *Halloween II*. 'On a low budget and with very little to work with, [Rick] did an incredibly intense job,' Carpenter told *Fangoria*. 'I was impressed.'

Rosenthal won the toss and was handed a budget of $2.5 million (nearly eight times that of the original *Halloween*), but when production on *Halloween II* began on April 6, 1981, he found himself working with a crew that was used to Carpenter's way of doing things. 'I often felt like I was a rookie quarterback replacing Ken Stabler,' Rosenthal told *Cinefantastique*. 'The first time in the huddle I say, "Red right 42 break!" and nobody breaks. The men look at me and say, "Kenny Stabler never called that play."'

'Conceptually, it's not at all my film,' Rosenthal confessed to the *Los Angeles Times*. 'But in execution it's my vision. You won't see it as a typical horror film. Oh,

---

15 Hill finally produced *Clue* in 1985 for Paramount Pictures with Jonathan Lynn as writer/director. John Landis had once been attached to write and direct, but ended up serving as an executive producer.

there's a woman in danger and all that, but the *visibility* of it...What I tried to do was make a picture that had a little of the visual style of the German expressionists, that hard edge of Von Sternberg...A lot of contrasts, shafts of light and oblique angles.'

'I wanted to do this tableau shot,' Rosenthal continued. 'It goes beyond reality and becomes surreal. Pictorially, the actual shot is a very exciting shot, like a still photograph or a painting. There's a lot of blood, but the blood is part of the composition: the amount of blood, its colour, is very carefully composed. It's done not to get a gross-out reaction but to get an image. That's an image reaction to the action that jolts the audience. It's the topper, pictorially, and it had to do with visuals, not blood and guts.'

Once production wrapped on *Halloween II*, Carpenter and Hill were concerned that there was not *enough* blood and guts to appease the slasher crowd. Accordingly, Carpenter stepped in and directed two new scenes himself: a teenage girl is knifed by Myers in her house and the hospital security guard gets a hammer to the skull when he stumbles upon the killer. An additional close-up was added to Ana Alicia's murder when Myers plunges a hypodermic needle into her temple. Finally, Carpenter shot a linking segment that shows Myers roaming through downtown Haddonfield when he hears a radio broadcast announcing where Laurie was taken and makes his way to the hospital.

'Part of the problem was the pressure of a Halloween release,' Rosenthal explained to *Cinefantastique*. 'There was no time to do a correct director's cut. The film wasn't assembled until two weeks before my cut was due and you just can't cut a film in two weeks. It was tough for John to be a director and not be directing and it was tough to be a director and have another director producing. And Debra, who had worked as producer only with John, found it tough to work with a new first-time director.'

As such, Hill tried to deflect criticism of the film's violence onto Rosenthal. 'Debra is fond of saying I had a little different 'vision' of the film. She implies I was the one who said we needed this type of close-up or this type of killing. [But] if anything, they found my cut of the film too slow.'

Finally she straightens up and lets the jack down. She carries the jack and the jack handle around to the trunk and tosses them on the floor. She doesn't notice that the beer can is missing.

She goes back to get the flat tyre and half-rolls, half-carries it back to the trunk. Her hands and her dress are already filthy. She leans

the flat against the back bumper to catch her breath before lifting it again.

SUDDENLY, THE SHAPE RISES UP FROM UNDER THE BLANKET IN THE TRUNK AND LEAPS ON HER!

There's a blur of silver across her throat and she tumbles to the ground.

HIGH ANGLE
The Shape rushes around to the driver's side and climbs in. The car starts with a ROAR and takes off down the road.

CLOSE ON THE PRODUCER
Lying by the side of the road. Her THROAT SLIT! Behind her, the flat tire spins around and around until finally it comes to as the lights of the car disappear in the distance.

−Unfilmed scene, from the original script

A killing that did not make it off the page, however, involved Debra the TV news producer (played in the film by Catherine Bergstrom) being accosted by a truck driver on a country road when she suffers a breakdown caused by flat tyre. After he leaves, Michael Myers bursts from Debra's trunk and murders her, then takes off with her car (this is how he gets to the hospital, instead of just walking there, as he does in the film). While the scene was dropped, Dennis Etchison nevertheless saw fit to include it in his novelisation of *Halloween II* (written under the pseudonym 'Jack Martin').

Other scenes were in fact shot but left on the cutting-room floor, including much of Lance Guest's role as EMT Jimmy, Tawny Moyer's role as Nurse Jill and Dennis Holahan's role as Morgan Strode, Laurie's adoptive father, which was cut altogether. He was supposed to have appeared in a flashback of the Strodes arguing about taking Laurie to see her brother, which then segues into Pamela Strode (Pamela McMyler) admitting to Laurie that she is not in fact her mother. Only the latter was used. Also, young Laurie's (Nichole Drucker) visit with young Michael (Adam Gunn) was originally longer, with him turning from his cell window and staring at her while she pleads with him not to hurt her.

Released on Halloween weekend by Universal Pictures, the picture pulled in a huge initial haul of $7.6 million, in defiance of almost universally-negative reviews.

'Eyes are pierced by hypodermic needles; a face is dunked in scalding water; throats are slashed,' catalogued *The Boston Globe*. 'Anyway, you get the disgusting picture. Now you don't have to pay to see it.' 'John Carpenter and Debra Hill have hit upon one sure-fire weapon that even the unstoppable Shape cannot survive,' observed *Cinefantastique*, 'a flaccid, implausibility-ridden screenplay.' 'It is not a horror film but a geek show,' wrote Roger Ebert. 'It is technically a sequel, but it doesn't even attempt to do justice to the original. Instead, it tries to outdo all the other violent *Halloween* rip-offs of the last several years.' 'There's a point at which no amount of mastery of form can redeem reprehensible content,' judged Kevin Thomas. 'That point arrived early on in *Halloween* and arrives even earlier in its even gorier sequel.' 'This uninspired version amounts to lukewarm sloppy seconds in comparison to the original film,' said *Variety*. *The Washington Post*'s Tom Shales dismissed the film as 'A splashily bloody, tediously idiotic, doggedly inevitable sequel.' Given that *Halloween II* fully deserved its critical drubbing, one wonders whatever could have possessed Janet Maslin to write, '*Halloween II* is good enough to deserve a sequel of its own. By the standards of most recent horror films, this—like its predecessor—is a class act.'

Bad press and word of mouth quickly caught up with *Halloween II*, and its eventual gross of $25 million was well below its predecessor's tally, though an additional $16 million was found at overseas wickets. With The Shape now dead, Carpenter and Hill set their sights on making *Halloween* into an annual series of unrelated films that centred on the holiday itself rather than a masked maniac. British screenwriter Nigel Kneale, creator of the BBC *Quatermass* serials in the 1950s, happened to be in Hollywood working on Universal's proposed remake of *The Creature from the Black Lagoon* (1954), and was engaged by Carpenter and Hill to write a script for *Halloween III*.[16]

'As I come from the Isle of Man and I remembered that Halloween was a big event,' Kneale told *Starburst*, 'the start of the Celtic year and so forth, I worked out a story about the shops filling up with plastic masks and Halloween toys as it's really a big industry in America. I said we could do a story about a joke factory so that the background would be basically comic. Into this you inject something creepy, magical, frightening. The theme was to be microchip witchcraft. In the old days in order for a witch to put a curse on you she had to make personal contact. With the advent of the microchip, a spell could be transferred through the Halloween gifts. The trademark stamp would carry the device and would spread whatever evil influences it was designed to spread via a trigger mechanism incorporated in a TV programme.' Carpenter and Hill were delighted with Kneale's concept, and six weeks later the writer delivered a script called *Season of the Witch*.

But Kneale's script did not pass muster with executive producer De Laurentiis. 'I was told that evidently a lot of my dialogue didn't translate well into Italian. He was having difficulty understanding it. He finally decided that it should follow a pattern

---

16 The remake was to have been directed by John Landis in 3-D, with original director Jack Arnold producing, but Universal opted to go with *Jaws 3-D* (1983) instead. *Creature* was scheduled for a new remake in 2011 to be directed by Carl Rinsch from a script by Gary Ross (*Big*, *Seabiscuit*), but this has also since gone the way of all flesh.

set by *Halloween II.*' That pattern being clichéd characters, banal situations and graphically-violent death scenes, seemingly. Tommy Lee Wallace, who had inherited the mantle of director when Joe Dante (*The Howling*) exited the production, was tasked with rewriting the script, and it was he who came up with the idea of having warlock-cum-mask maker Conal Cochran somehow manage to steal one of the five-ton monoliths from Stonehenge, cart it off to California and grind it up for the microchips. 'There was nothing in my baby that I could recognise,' Kneale said. 'It was reduced to cardboard sets and a cast of six. So I took my name off it.'

Produced in April 1982 on a $2.5 million budget, *Halloween III: Season of the Witch* tried to make up for what it lost in the Kneale-Wallace translation by including references to *Invasion of the Body Snatchers* (1956)—people are replaced by lookalike androids and Cochran's factory is located in *Body Snatchers*' fictional town of Santa Mira. The result was released that October to poor reviews and a box office of just $14 million. It was enough to kill the annual *Halloween* concept and put the series on ice for six years.

(2009)

Even though I said I wouldn't do *H2*...I was happy to come back, kind of like with *Devil's Rejects*, you want to come back and see how you can take it to another level...This time, I really feel like enough is enough. If somebody else wants to do *H3*, I'd be happy to see what they're going to do with it.

—Rob Zombie, writer, co-producer and director

In the first one I am very earnest. Now he's turned into a total jerk. He's the only one who made money from this desperate, poor family. Of course, that's the American way. Let's write a book about it.

—Malcolm McDowell, 'Dr Sam Loomis'

With the worldwide success of Rob Zombie's *Halloween*, the Weinsteins and Malek Akkad wanted to strike while the iron was hot with regards to a sequel. Zombie had taken himself out of the running, however, and Dimension turned instead to French directors Alexandre Bustillo and Julien Maury, whose intense thriller *À l'intérieur* (*Inside*, 2007) the company had released on DVD. 'We were looking into how we could do a normal sequel,' Akkad told the website Shock Till You Drop. 'We had [Bustillo and Maury] do a draft and we weren't happy at all...it wasn't them so much as we just wanted Rob back...These guys were French so there was something lost in the translation somehow.'

'I was so burnt out after making *Halloween*,' Rob Zombie confessed to Dark Horizons. '[It] was a very difficult shoot. It was not particularly enjoyable. And the thought of doing anything *Halloween* again just seemed like, no way...Weinstein Company didn't even ask me about it, because I was so clear that I didn't want to be part of it...And then I ran into one of the executives...and I asked him, "How's filming on *Halloween II* going?"...And he said, "Oh, man. We haven't even started

Halloween II (2009)

yet. We don't even have a script. We don't even have an idea what to do." So at that point, I had gone on tour, finished a record, been around...And I didn't have my next movie...[so] the idea of coming back to it seemed really interesting to me at that time. Because I had missed all the actors, and...I liked what we had started, and I really, at that point, wanted to continue it.'

In December 2008 it was announced that Zombie would indeed be writing and directing a sequel, initially referred to as *H2*, but he would only have two months for preproduction. 'I was under contract to [the Weinsteins] and I owed them another picture,' Zombie explained to MSN Movies, 'so I was working for them regardless... We talked about this, and I knew the time frame was short for this movie, but I thought that maybe it would work to my advantage. If a movie sits around for too long, that can be bad...because you feel like you just lose the energy. Plus you don't want the company to have too long to think about it, so they can start to go, "We have some ideas..." That's always my biggest fear.'

'I went back and looked at [my] *Halloween*,' Zombie told Dark Horizons, 'and I thought...this film looks a little too clean. It looks a little too safe. It looks a little bit claustrophobic. Everything's confined in this suburban neighbourhood...I really wanted to open up the scope of the movie...I went for a different approach, just from the film stock to the lighting...it's [a] much darker, grainer, grittier, dirtier film. And it seemed appropriate this time, because in the first *Halloween*, you have these characters like Laurie Strode. And they're very, like, happy-go-lucky all-American girl characters. They're not dark and damaged. But now, all the characters have survived this horrible night of murder. So, all the characters are scarred inside and out. So it

made it much easier to concoct this sort of darker, nastier vision of *Halloween*.'

After her confrontation with Michael Myers, Laurie Strode is taken to the hospital while Michael's apparently dead body is put in a coroner's van. On the way to the morgue, the van collides with a cow in the road, killing the driver. Michael is awakened, kills the attendant, and stalks off towards the ghostly image of his mother Deborah. Two years later, Laurie is living with Sheriff Brackett and his daughter Annie while working at a hippy coffee house and attending weekly therapy sessions, which are not helping her chronic nightmares or uncontrollable rages. Meanwhile, Michael has become a hermit, wandering in the fields outside Haddonfield where he interacts with the ghosts of his mother and his younger self. Having survived his encounter with Michael two years earlier, Dr Loomis has gone on the lecture circuit to shamelessly self-promote himself and his new book about Michael, The Devil Walks Among Us. As Halloween approaches, Deborah Myers tells her son that it is time for a family reunion in the afterlife—he must find and kill his sister Angel. Reading Loomis's book, Laurie discovers that she is in fact Angel Myers. Getting drunk, she attends a rave party with her co-workers Mya and Harley, the latter of whom is murdered by Michael. Laurie and Mya go back to the Brackett house to find that Annie has been attacked by Michael; she dies in Laurie's arms. Michael is still

in the house and kills Mya—Laurie manages to escape but is pursued by her brother, who eventually captures her and takes her to a shack where the ghosts of Deborah and young Michael are waiting. The shack is soon surrounded by Sheriff Brackett and the state police; Loomis learns of the standoff while being interviewed at a radio station and races to the scene to intervene. Against Brackett's orders, Loomis enters the shack to try and reason with Michael, who ends up killing his former doctor before being felled in a hail of gunfire. Driven completely mad by the ordeal, Laurie exits the shack, picks up Michael's hunting knife and heads towards Loomis' body before being shot down herself.

With a budget of $15 million, shooting on *H2* began on February 12, 2009, in Covington, Georgia, thanks to the state's generous tax breaks. 'Since [the first film] was a remake I felt some responsibility to retain elements of the original,' Zombie remarked to Bloody Disgusting. 'But with this one I don't feel any responsibility except to go crazy with it...It's really layered and there's a lot to it, but I wanted to pick it up and when you follow all the characters you really [see] how fucked up [they] are from what would have happened. It's not like anyone survived it without being completely a mess...It starts really dark and gets darker. There's really no nice moments in the whole movie. Dr Loomis is kind of living this pseudo-nice life and it all goes bad. So he has a few nice moments, but everyone else is having a bad time trying to deal with it.'

A 13-minute nightmare sequence where Laurie (a returning Scout Taylor-Compton) awakens at the hospital to find that everyone has been slaughtered by Michael (a returning Tyler Mane) would seem to be Zombie's tip of the hat to the original *Halloween II*, but the director was adamant that he had no such intention. 'It never crossed my mind,' he alleged to MSN Movies. 'In fact, I was always downplaying the hospital sequence because I didn't want people to get the wrong idea about the movie. It just seemed like a logical extension of what had happened in the previous one: "Well, if this girl's fucked up and they found her wandering around in the middle of the street, they would take her to the hospital."'

Zombie continued his quest to differentiate *H2* from the rest of the *Halloween* *oeuvre* by making it the first film in the series to have a completely original score (courtesy of a returning Tyler Bates) and not use John Carpenter's signature '*Halloween* Theme' until the end credits. 'This film has just so much become its own thing that [to use Carpenter's theme] was actually very distracting,' Zombie told Ain't It Cool News. 'You get caught up in the vibe of what the film actually is, and when you hear that score, it's just kind of like, "Oh, yeah. Here we are again." It's weird. It just didn't work. It's hard to make people see something differently and then throw that music in there. No matter what you're watching, it makes it feel like you've seen it before. On the first film, it was fine...But in this one it just never made sense." Zombie did, however, continue to indulge his love of classic rock tunes, this time featuring songs from 10cc, Foghat, Lynyrd Skynyrd, The Moody Blues, Ozark Mountain Daredevils and Rod Stewart.

With *H2*, a new villain has seemingly entered the fray—Dr Sam Loomis himself. No longer is he the Van Helsing of the piece; the good doctor is now a money-grubbing, publicity-seeking media whore who is completely ambivalent about profiting from other people's misery and totally irresponsible when it comes to sharing privileged information. 'I kind of thought of it like, if Michael Myers was famous, he'd be like Charles Manson,' reasoned Zombie. 'Thus making Dr Loomis [into] Vincent Bugliosi. Loomis would be a superstar; he'd be a little guy who started as a child psychiatrist [and then] turned into Dr Phil. Meanwhile, people who were affected by all of these events, who are trying to pick up the pieces of their crappy lives...and this guy's out there milking it for all it's worth.'

Once filming was underway, the cash-strapped Weinsteins significantly cut the budget, then demanded that the shooting schedule be shortened by approximately two weeks, with production ending on April 9. As if that was not enough adversity, two actors had to be replaced. Daeg Faerch, who had played young Michael Myers in Zombie's *Halloween*, was supposed to reprise the role, but Zombie felt that he had matured too much in the interim and was not convincing as a 10-year-old (he was replaced by Chase Vanek). Then Zombie stock player Bill Moseley (who was cast as Phantom Jam host Uncle Seymour Coffins) informed the director after just one day of filming that he had gotten a better offer and would be leaving immediately. As a result, Zombie was forced to recruit Jeffrey Daniel Phillips, who was already cast in the film (as Howard Boggs, who has his head smashed by Michael at the Rabbit in Red strip club), for double duty to shoot the rest of Moseley's scenes.

'There were a lot of problems with this movie,' Zombie understated to MSN Movies. 'There were a lot of [financial] problems with the [Weinstein] company, a lot of problems with internal personnel, a lot of problems with everything. If my creative team wasn't so strong and wasn't so loyal, we would have been screwed. I mean, the whole thing is really a testament to how much the crew and the actors and everyone really bonded, because every day there was another huge problem that should have shut the production down.'

Because of the tight schedule, as well as Zombie's desire to play fast and loose with the script (most of the surreal scenes that found their way into the film, including the white horse as well as the *Alice in Wonderland*-style feast, were made up on the spot), additional filming was required that July in New Milford, Connecticut. A new scene was added where country hicks Floyd (Mark Boone Junior), Sherman (Duane Whitaker) and Jazlean (Betsy Rue) come upon Michael wandering in their field. Floyd and Sherman then beat him up until he turns the tables and kills all three bumpkins. At the same time, Zombie reshot the attack on Big Lou (Daniel Roebuck) and Misty Dawn (Sylvia Jefferies) at the Rabbit in Red. The scene originally had Michael—without his mask—smashing Lou into a mirror and chasing a naked Misty outside, breaking her neck and dragging her back inside the club. This was replaced by Michael—with his mask—beating Lou to death and then smashing Misty repeatedly against a mirror.

In a case of *déjà vu*, Zombie also decided to change the ending, which, as with his *Halloween*, had originally been shot as scripted: Michael pushes Loomis through the shack wall, rips off his mask, says 'Die!' and thrusts his hunting

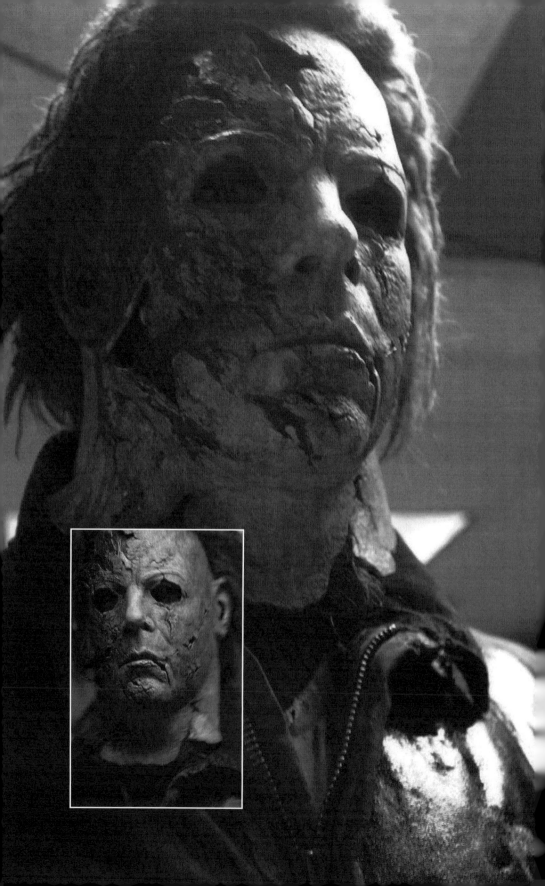

knife into the doctor. He is then killed in a hail of gunfire. Laurie stumbles out of the shack, picks up Michael's knife and approaches Loomis's body before she too is shot down. The scene then dissolves to a tracking shot down a long, whitewashed corridor, at the end of which is Laurie in a hospital gown, sitting on a bed. Looking up, she smiles as Deborah Myers (Sheri Moon Zombie again) and the white horse approach, all while a cover of Nazareth's 'Love Hurts' is heard.

The new ending has a much more violent death for Loomis, as Michael stabs him to death inside the shack before sniper bullets send the madman reeling backwards and he is impaled on farm implements. Laurie tells her brother she loves him, then repeatedly stabs him. She exits the shack with Michael's mask on, falls on her knees, removes the mask and looks at it. The scene then cuts to the same surreal sequence as before, but the score is instead John Carpenter's 'Laurie's Theme'. Apparently she is now actually institutionalised instead of seeing the vision as she dies.

While things were added and changed, a number of scripted scenes that were in fact part of the initial shoot ended up on the cutting-room floor, to include:

- Laurie's therapist Dr. Collier (played by erstwhile Lois Lane, Margot Kidder) telling the girl a Cherokee legend about two wolves in each person that battle for control—fear and hope—and the one that wins 'is the one you feed.'
- *WKRP in Cincinatti*'s Howard Hesseman originally had much more screen time as Uncle Meat, the hippy coffee shop proprietor, first by talking to Mya (Brea Grant) about Tex Ritter and then to the girls about the virtues of records (after which Laurie goes outside and sees herself hanging from a tree in the nearby park).
- At the press conference for his book, Loomis is asked to comment on the phenomenon of 'WWMD (What Would Michael Do)' t-shirts.

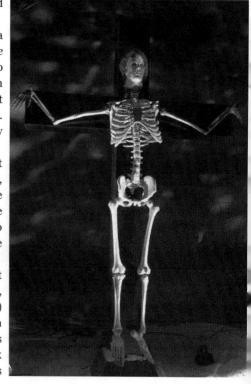

- Eileen Dietz, who doubled for Linda Blair during the vomiting scenes in *The Exorcist*, in a cameo as a housewife who sees Michael going through her trash and calls the police, telling them that she thinks Bigfoot is outside her house. The police then talk about how many Myers sightings have been reported.
- A delivery driver arrives at the Rabbit in Red and finds the bodies of Howard, Big Lou and Misty and calls 911 before being killed himself by Michael. The call is actually answered by Laurie, who is then also killed by Michael before waking from a nightmare.
- Sheriff Brackett (Brad Dourif) first has Annie's (Danielle Harris) nerdish, fanboy friend Darren (Sean Marquette) come over to watch her on Halloween night. He makes her nachos and tries to persuade her to go to a comic book convention with him. After she kicks

him out, Brackett sends Deputy Neale (Greg Travis) to keep vigil outside. Only the latter was used.

• After coming home from the Phantom Jam, Laurie expresses remorse to Mya about the way she has treated Annie before the two of them go upstairs and find Annie's body. An alternate take of Laurie and Mya having tea was used instead.

Whereas Carpenter's *Halloween II* was simply lazy filmmaking, Zombie's sequel is patently offensive. The film is sadistic, brutally violent and full of nasty, hateful people who can seemingly do nothing but curse and yell at each other (Taylor-Compton in particular seems to be trying to break Al Pacino's *Scarface* record for saying 'fuck' the most times in a single movie). Zombie gave his justification for this to Ain't It Cool News: 'I thought all of the characters would be damaged and they would respond in different ways. Everybody knows people in their lives, or themselves, who've had horrible events happen to them, and they change you in certain ways: some people become really introverted, and some people will just go, "Fuck it! I don't care anymore! I'm going out partying every night, and I don't give a shit if I live." That's what I felt Laurie Strode would become. She'd become really outgoing, whereas the Annie Brackett character...would become more agoraphobic and introverted.'

The Weinsteins were understandably concerned that Zombie had turned the *Halloween* series' notional heroine into a foul-mouthed, neurotic bitch and ordered that changes be made. As a result, both scenes of Laurie arguing with Annie were removed, as was the scene where Laurie confesses her murderous thoughts to Dr Collier. This was replaced with an alternate take where she talks about missing her parents. Likewise, a scene where Laurie storms into Collier's office and demands prescriptions before launching into an obscenity-laced tirade was also dropped. In an effort to further soften Laurie's character, two scenes were added: one in which she talks to her stuffed animal and another in which she holds a cat at a petting zoo.

'I think of the movie as a dark psychodrama,' Zombie told the website LifeWhile. 'It's not just about seeing graphic images. First you have to get the audience caught up in the journeys of the characters and get inside their heads. Then, when the violent events happen, that's what disturbs the audience. People have seen so much violence in movies. You have to add much more to it than that.' One of Zombie's means to do that was the Loomis press conference scene. In it, the psychiatrist discusses how the Oedipus complex relates to Myers, Loomis's part in it as Michael's surrogate father and, in answer to a reporter's question, how society has created monsters like The Shape. Again at the behest of the Weinsteins, this was cut out, with the result that the press conference was simply Loomis denying his guilt and insisting that Michael Myers is 'D-E-A-D!'

Dimension Films released the now fully-titled *Halloween II* on August 28. Unlike its predecessor, *Halloween II* did not have the benefit of a four-day weekend and fell far short of *Halloween*'s record-breaking opening, instead placing third for the weekend with $16 million, on its way to an eventual gross of $33 million. The film's international gross was just $6 million, also well below its predecessor's overseas take.

Not surprisingly, *Halloween II* was met with mostly negative reviews, from publications like *The Boston Globe* ('The print ads claim this is the franchise's 'final chapter', but despite Zombie's efforts—or because of them—only the most hardcore fans will have a hard time saying goodbye'), *Entertainment Weekly* ('There isn't really a story in *Halloween II*...And the movie doesn't boast much in the way of characters either'), the *Los Angeles Times* ('Zombie isn't out to engage fans of the genre with a slaughterhouse bonbon like *Halloween II*. Michael Myers may inexplicably get the jump on his victims but Zombie's a looky-loo tradesman whose gory shtick you can see coming a mile away') and the *New York Times* ('If only [Zombie] had more on his mind than his love of 1970s Italian horror films, his meticulous colour schemes and his body count. *Halloween II* is full of in-jokes and references, but nearly devoid of wit').

'I ended the movie in a way I think is an ending,' Zombie told Dark Horizons. 'But unfortunately, you know, with these types of movies, no matter how you end it, somebody thinks you left it wide open for a sequel. So I'm sure there'll be more coming down the road, but not with me.'

With Rob Zombie now seemingly out of the *Halloween* picture for good, the Weinsteins turned instead to Todd Farmer and Patrick Lussier, the writer and director respectively of the hit remake *My Bloody Valentine 3D*. The duo delivered a script for *Halloween 3D* less than a month after the premiere of *Halloween II* and shooting was originally scheduled to begin that November, with Taylor-Compton, Dourif and Mane reprising their roles. However, things ground to a halt shortly after the script's completion because The Weinstein Company ran out of money. Farmer and Lussier instead turned their attention to Millennium Films' *Drive Angry 3D* (2011) with Nicolas Cage. In June 2011, *Halloween 3D* was announced for release in October 2012, but this has progressed no further at time of writing.

THE CRAVEN CONNECTION

LAST HOUSE ON THE LEFT

(1972)

Hallmark said to us, 'Guys, you should make a knock-down, drag-out horror movie,' and they gave us $50,000 to do it. Sean sat down and said, 'Look, I think we can do this in three weeks for $40,000 and pocket the [extra]ten. Can you come up with anything?'

—Wes Craven, writer, director and editor

Wes Craven and I collaborated on it with the idea to make the scariest film possible on a budget that was...well, just laughable.

—Sean Cunningham, producer

O n October 19, 1971, Steve Minasian, general manager for Esquire Theatres of America—one of the biggest theatre chains in the northeastern United States—boarded a 747 jumbo jet at Boston's Logan International Airport for a trip to London, Munich and Paris. According to *Boxoffice* magazine, his plan was 'to call on film producers and consult with foreign film studio heads...he has tentative plans for screening about 40 feature films that are to be available for independent distribution in the US.'

Esquire had just formed a new distributorship, Hallmark Releasing Corporation, and was looking for exploitation films to service its drive-ins. Accordingly, Minasian brought back seven films, two of which were German (*Der verlogene Akt/Sex Scandal, Hexen bis aufs Blut gequält/Witches Tortured Till They Bleed*), three Italian (*La bestia uccide a sangue freddo/The Beast Kills in Cold Blood, Detenuto in attesa di giudizio/In Prison Awaiting Trial, Reazione a catena/Bay of Blood*) and the last two Spanish (*La noche del terror ciego/Night of the Blind Terror, La semana del asesino/Week of the Killer*).

Hallmark's first foray into distribution had come that August when it released a

It rests on 13 acres of earth over the very center of hell..!

MARI, SEVENTEEN, IS DYING.

EVEN FOR HER THE WORST IS YET TO COME!

SHE LIVED IN THE

LAST HOUSE ON THE LEFT

TO AVOID FAINTING
KEEP REPEATING,
IT'S ONLY A MOVIE
..ONLY A MOVIE
..ONLY A MOVIE
..ONLY A MOVIE
..ONLY A MOVIE
..ONLY A MOVIE
..ONLY A MOVIE

SEAN S. CUNNINGHAM FILMS LTD. Presents "THE LAST HOUSE ON THE LEFT" Starring: DAVID HESS • LUCY GRANTHAM • SANDRA CASSEL • MARC SHEFFLER • and introducing ADA WASHINGTON • Produced by SEAN S. CUNNINGHAM Written and Directed by WES CRAVEN • COLOR BY MOVIELAB **R** RESTRICTED
Under 17 requires accompanying Parent or Adult Guardian

softcore porn film called *Together*, a $70,000 opus the company had bought for a mere $15,000 from its writer/producer/director, 29-year-old Sean Sexton Cunningham, a former Broadway stage manager. The movie would achieve notoriety as the first nude performance from 'Ivory Snow' girl Marilyn Briggs, who would change her name to Marilyn Chambers and become a porn superstar in the Mitchell Brothers' hardcore blockbuster *Behind the Green Door* (1972). Described by Cunningham as 'a 90-minute Winston commercial for sex,' *Together* was picked up for national distribution by American International and ended up grossing nearly $7 million at the box office, largely due to Briggs/Chambers' appearance and Hallmark's clever 'testimonial' ad campaign ('See What Your Children Can Show You About Love!').

With such a winner under its belt, Hallmark decided to bankroll Cunningham's next picture. They approached him with the notion of making an all-out horror film, offering a budget of $50,000 to do so. To write and direct such an attraction, Cunningham turned to the man who had helped him piece his last film together, 32-year-old Wesley Earl Craven.

At first glance, Craven hardly seemed the ideal choice. 'I came out of a very religious background,' he told the *Chicago Tribune*. 'As fundamentalist Baptists, we were sequestered from the rest of the world. You couldn't dance or drink or go to the movies. The first time I paid to see a movie I was a senior in college...My whole youth was based on suppression of emotion.' Craven attended the Wheaton Christian liberal arts college outside Chicago, majoring in literature and psychology. After earning his Bachelor's Degree in 1963, he went to Johns Hopkins University in Baltimore where he earned his Master's in writing and philosophy the next year. On marrying, Craven found a job teaching English at Westminster College, a Presbyterian school in Pennsylvania. After a year there, the Cravens moved to Potsdam, New York, where he served as a humanities professor at Clarkson College.

Deciding not to go for his doctorate, Craven left Clarkson and spent the summer of 1968 in New York City, where he worked at the documentary house Leacock-Pennebaker (*Don't Look Back, Monterey Pop*). He returned to Potsdam, taught high school for a year, and then moved his family (the Cravens now had two children) to New York City in 1969 to work for Roland Condon Film Management. That same year, he and his wife divorced and the children stayed with their mother while their father became a full-fledged hippy, living in a commune in New York's Lower East Side. When he was fired from Roland Condon for ruining a premiere by cutting a film in the wrong order, Craven drove a cab during the day and worked on editing jobs at night to keep his hand in the film business. 'I must say there were times of utter despair,' Craven told the *Chicago Sun Times*, 'when I thought that I should just blow my brains out. But I finally made the contact that got me into a place where I could get my foot in the door.' It was during this time that his path crossed that of Cunningham and the two worked feverishly to whip *Together* into releasable shape.

With no other offers on the table, Craven accepted Cunningham's invitation to write the most extreme horror thriller he could come up with. Given his academic background, Craven would find inspiration in Ingmar Bergman's film *Jungfrukällan*, better known as *The Virgin Spring* and Oscar-winner for Best Foreign Film of 1960. Set in 14th century Sweden, it tells the tale of wealthy land-owning parents whose young daughter is brutally raped and murdered by goat herders. In a bizarre twist of fate, the murderers end up seeking shelter from the dead girl's parents, who, after discovering the truth about their lodgers, exact a bloody vengeance. The girl's father (played by Max Von Sydow) subsequently vows to build a church on the site of his daughter's death, causing a spring to magically burst forth from the ground in her honour.

'The core story I knew when I was teaching college and had researched Bergman's use of it,' Craven told the *New York Times*. 'It was...hundreds of years old, and had come out in medieval tales in Sweden, that area of the world...it's so simple and so pure and so powerful, and not only is it about delicious irony, it turns out to be about people who are straight and proper and descend into their own sort of darkness. I just found that very interesting in the time of Vietnam. The humanities professor in me saw a parallel.'

'I wanted to say something about violence and American movies that told us how easy it is to kill someone,' Craven continued to *Cinefantastique*. 'You shoot someone, stab them, and they roll over and die. Don't forget, I made that picture during the Vietnam era when people were watching villages being burned on TV while they ate their evening meals.'

Mari Collinwood and Phylis Stone, two teenage girls in rural Connecticut, are on their way to a rock concert in New York. Once in the city, the two friends decide to buy some marijuana and approach junkie Junior Stillo, who invites the girls back to his apartment. What the two do not realise, however, is that Junior is the son of escaped murderer Krug Stillo, and that he has been sent by his father to bring back young ladies for an orgy Krug intends to have with his bisexual mistress Sadie and fellow convict Fred 'Weasel' Padowski. After spending the night tormenting the young girls, the gang stuffs them in the trunk of their car and drive off towards Canada. In an incredible coincidence, their car breaks down right in front of Mari's house in Connecticut. Oblivious to this fact, the gang take the girls into the woods across the street, where they force them to strip and have lesbian sex with each other and Sadie. After Krug leaves, Phylis runs off in an attempt to lure Sadie and Weasel away from Mari. Mari desperately tries to convince Junior to come with her to her house, even giving him her peace sign necklace and promising him a fix from her doctor father's pharmacy. Meanwhile, Phylis runs into a returning Krug who, together with Sadie and Weasel, proceeds to repeatedly stab, mutilate and eviscerate the young girl. Krug and Weasel then have necrophiliac sex with Phylis' corpse. Afterwards, the gang catch up with Mari and Junior, dropping one of Phylis' severed arms on the ground to intimidate her friend. Krug assaults Mari, carving his name on her chest with a switchblade and raping her. In the aftermath, Mari stumbles to a nearby lake where she is shot by Krug. The gang subsequently clean up at lakeside, change

clothes, and meet Mari's mother Estelle on the road as she is walking the family dog. She offers them hospitality until they can get their car fixed; relaxing in Mari's room, the gang realise from pictures of the girl exactly where it is they have found shelter. That night, Junior is suffering withdrawal symptoms in the bathroom; Estelle offers her aid and notices that the boy is wearing Mari's necklace. She then goes through the gang's luggage and finds their bloody clothes—an overheard conversation tells her the rest. She and her husband John rush to the lake to find Mari on the shore; before the girl dies, she identifies her assailants. Returning to the house with Mari's body, John rigs a number of traps while Estelle seduces Weasel and lures him outdoors, where she orally castrates him. John and Krug get into a fistfight in the living room over Mari's corpse before John retrieves a chainsaw from the basement and decapitates the gang's leader. Sadie flees from the house in a panic, only to be assaulted by Estelle, who beats her with Phylis' amputated arm and then drowns her in the lake.

Hallmark was so impressed with Craven's script that they increased the budget to $90,000, and on October 2, 1971, production began in Westport, Connecticut on what was initially called *Night of Vengeance*. The shoot lasted 22 days and ended, appropriately enough, on Halloween. Due to the practical realities of filmmaking—as well as some sense of propriety—some of the more salacious elements of Craven's script were discarded while other elements, largely improvised on the spot, took their place:

- The script opens with Mari masturbating in the shower. This was changed to have actress Sandra Peabody simply take a shower.
- In the script, both Mari and Phylis share their sexual fantasies—one placid, the other violent—about the rock group Bloodlust. These were to have been visualised but ended up not being shot.
- Phylis was meant to have suffered an especially violent death, with her eyes and tongue gouged out, her breasts severed and her vagina mutilated. None of this was shot. Likewise, the scene of Krug and Weasel's necrophilia with Phylis was nixed.
- A scene with Krug's (David Hess) gang briefly showing remorse after Mari's shooting was added on location.
- A scene where Weasel (Fred Lincoln) has a nightmare about getting his teeth chiselled out by John (Richard Towers) and Estelle (Eleanor Shaw) was added on location.
- Sadie's (Jeramie Rain) death was changed to having her throat slashed by Estelle and drowning in the Collinwood pool.
- After the deaths of Krug and Sadie, the original ending was to have played out this way:

JUNIOR
(Looking towards the fallen form of his father) Is he...dead?

SHERIFF

If he ain't I sure take my hat off to him—he ain't got a head no more. Who're you, anyway?

JUNIOR SLIDES DOWN THE WALL AND SITS ON THE STAIRS, HIS HEAD BACK AGAINST THE WALL.

JUNIOR

I'm his son...(pause) Is she...is the girl...the blond one...is she?

JOHN

She's dead.

JUNIOR

She called me Willow—she gave me a new name. And...(He pulls the Peace Symbol from his shirt and looks at it weakly) She said her father was a Doctor, and could help me...

HE LOOKS AT DR COLLINWOOD. DR COLLINWOOD IS SPATTERED WITH BLOOD.

JUNIOR

You a doctor, mister? You look like a butcher...

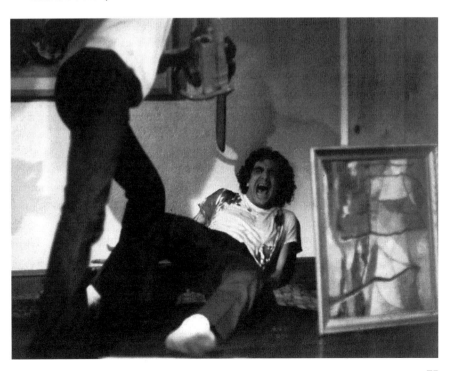

FADE TO BLACK

FADE UP ON THE MOONLIT LAKE, PHYLIS'S HAND AND ARM IN THE FOREGROUND. THE MOONLIGHT LAYS ACROSS THE SEVERED LIMB, THE LAKE RIPPLING SILVER IN THE BACKGROUND. AND WE CAN SEE THAT WITH THE BATTERING OF SADIE, THE HAND HAS LOST ITS FIST. INSTEAD, TWO FINGERS HAVE SPRUNG UPWARDS, MIRACULOUSLY FORMING THE 'V' FOR VICTORY SIGN.

Instead of having Junior (Marc Sheffler) survive to the end of the film, Craven and the actors improvised a scene where Krug bullies his son into committing suicide. Likewise, the echo of *The Virgin Spring*'s miraculous finale with Phylis' hand forming into a 'V' for victory sign was discarded in favour of a conventional fade-out after the parents have exacted their revenge and the arriving police are dumbfounded by the carnage they discover.

'We had looked around at what was being done,' Cunningham told *Fangoria*. 'There were the Clint Eastwood movies, with about 300 people being killed, but that wasn't scary; that was just "bang-bang, you're dead." Then there were those AIP films with Vincent Price—those were mostly escapist costume dramas. So we made this film about a kidnapping and a couple of murders. The budget was very narrow, and we were just figuring out how to *make* a feature film, so our film technique *had* to be primitive. But that primitive style really helped, in a way, because the film took on a newsreel, *verite* look...as if it were a documentary of these ghastly events.'

While Craven and Cunningham went to work on cutting *Night of Vengeance*, Hallmark set the stage for them in January 1972 by releasing *Witches Tortured Till They Bleed,* a more prurient version of Michael Reeves's *Witchfinder General* (1968), featuring Herbert Lom in the Vincent Price role. Changing the title to *Mark of the Devil*, Hallmark made the film a *cause celebre* by declaring it 'Positively the Most Horrifying Film Ever Made!', self-rating it 'V for Violence' and handing out free airsickness bags to patrons. Despite being threatened with a lawsuit by the MPAA over the bogus 'V' rating, Hallmark pressed on with its ballsy campaign, and a film that only cost $40,000 ended up grossing over $3 million.

Hallmark repeated its vomit bag/V rating trick again that May with the release of Mario Bava's body-count prototype *Bay of Blood,* now subtly retitled *Carnage* and advertised as 'The first film that dares to show 'hardcore' violence!'[1] In July, Hallmark released *Night of the Blind Terror* as *The Blind Dead* and, despite a tame PG rating, audiences were still given vomit bags and advised that the company's latest offering 'Makes *Mark of the Devil* look like a fairy tale!'

That same month, Hallmark premiered *Night of Vengeance* under the title *Krug & Company* in two Massachusetts drive-ins, where it failed to click. A token release under the moniker *Sex Crime of the Century* in upstate New York yielded similar results. Casting around for some way to hook an audience, Cunningham took

---

1 The title was changed yet again to the better-known *Twitch of the Death Nerve* that September and the V rating was surrendered in favour of the standard R rating.

advice from one Lee Willis, a Broadway publicist known to the producer from his theatre days, who suggested the title *Last House on the Left*. Craven, however, was less than receptive, as he remarked to Crave Online: 'I was outraged. I went, "What? There's no last house on the left!" And [Sean] said, "Well, [Willis] told me…last, it's like death, it's like the end of it, then house, everybody knows house, it brings back all these memories of being in your house, the place of years and then left, everything in the world is left…sinister and heraldry."' According to Cunningham, it was also Willis who suggested the tag line, 'To Avoid Fainting, Keep Repeating: It's Only a Movie…Only a Movie…Only a Movie…'

On Wednesday, August 23, the newly-titled *Last House on the Left* premiered at two cinemas—the Central and the Paris—in the Hartford, Connecticut area. That Saturday night, after the sequence showing Phylis's disembowelment, some 200 angry theatregoers stormed out of the Paris, gathered outside and demanded that the movie be shut down immediately. 'Sick people made this,' one man told *The Hartford Courant*. 'Stag movies are mild compared to this.' 'It was a very depressing movie,' a thirty-eight-year-old insurance salesman later told *The Boston Globe*. 'It's horror, all right, but there's no suspense and it's too bloody. I'd rather have gone to a Chinese restaurant.' The infuriated patrons signed petitions and gave statements to the police, who were summoned to the scene.

The next day, in the presence of local police and Wethersfield Chief Prosecutor Francis McVane, the Paris theatre management removed three offending passages from their print of *Last House*: Mari and Phylis's forced lesbianism, Sadie's oral sex with Mari and Phylis' disembowelment. In response to similar complaints in his township, West Hartford Police Chief William Rush made the Central theatre neuter its *Last House* print as well. This censoring would be repeated many times in the ensuing months and came to account for the so-called 'lost footage' of *Last House* that has plagued archivists and completists for the past forty years.

For Craven, the extreme reactions that the film provoked told him that he had succeeded in subverting the audience's expectations. 'People came into the theatre to be amused and entertained by violence,' he told the *Journal of Popular Film and Television*, 'the right amount of blood and killing. They certainly expected the director to have the taste to cut away at the right moment. They certainly would not want you to be joking at the same time you were killing people or show sympathy for the murderers. So *Last House* upset everybody.'

One of the most vocal in his objections to *Last House* was Gene Siskel, who wrote in the *Chicago Tribune*:

Three horror films opened recently in the Loop [Asylum, Last House and Private Parts], and if they don't convince you the Earth is flat and we're all very close to the edge, nothing will. The Last House on the Left…is the repulsive story of escaped convicts on the lam who mutilate the bodies of two teenage girls and then attempt to do the same things to one girl's parents. I counted six slashings, one punch in the stomach, three rapes, one act of forced self-degradation, and then I stopped counting. I felt a professional obligation to stick around to see if there was any socially redeeming value in the remainder of the movie and found none. My objection to The Last House on the Left is not an objection to graphic representations of violence per se, but to the fact that this movie celebrates violent acts, particularly adult male abuse of young women. Given the similarity of recent crimes in the Chicago area to the events in this movie I am surprised that any theatre owner would want to make a living by playing it. Theatre owners who do not control themselves invite others to do so.

Last House on the Left would top Siskel's list of the so-called 'Sickest Films of 1972' (which also included *Bluebeard, El Topo, Farewell Uncle Tom, Mark of the Devil, Portnoy's Complaint* and *The Sporting Club*) and many other critics joined in the chorus of disapproval, including *The Christian Science Monitor*'s David Sterritt ('One of the most memorably loathsome pieces of garbage in movie history'), *Cinefantastique*'s David Bartholomew ('This is a coarse, thoroughly repulsive little movie, whose self-indulged ineptitude is alleviated only by sporadic bursts of off-handedly authentic dialogue...Ultimately, the film is that rare, debasing kind which makes one sad, and a bit ashamed, that the motion picture was ever invented'), *Cue*'s William Wolf ('The most obnoxious film around'), the *New York Times*'s Howard Thompson ('The party who wrote this sickening tripe and also directed the inept actors is Wes Craven. It's at the Penthouse Theatre, for anyone interested in paying to see repulsive people and human agony') and the *Pittsburgh Press*'s Edward Blank ('It looks and sounds like someone's ill-conceived and horrendously produced home movie').

Vincent Canby chose to review not just *Last House on the Left*, but Hallmark's overall product thus: 'They are such vivid spectacles of pointless, mindless cruelty that I could almost suspect them of political subversion, though to what end, I'm still undecided. Do they further corrupt the common folk, thereby hastening the end of the old order? Do they preach social anarchy? Or, perhaps, do they numb the mind in such a way as to create a citizenry so apathetic it becomes powerless in its disinterest?'

There were, however, two notable exceptions to the general critical onslaught. One was Roger Ebert, who evaluated *Last House* as 'a tough, bitter little sleeper of a movie that's about four times as good as you'd expect...This movie covers the same philosophical territory as...*Straw Dogs*, and is more hard-nosed about it: Sure, a man's home is his castle, but who wants to be left with nothing but a castle and a lifetime memory of horror?' The other was *Film Comment*'s Robin Wood, who opined that 'No film is more expressive than *Last House* of a national social sickness, and no film is richer in Oedipal references—an extension, in its widest implications, of the minutiae of human relations under patriarchal capitalist culture.'

'We never thought that anyone in our circle of friends and family would ever see it,' Craven told the *New York Times*. 'And I think in some ways that was what freed me to do something so outrageous...if anyone in my family had seen it, they would have been appalled.' Indeed, in Craven's circle of friends, the movie was seen as a major *faux pas*: 'When they went out and saw my film, most of them didn't speak to me anymore.'

Last House had clearly disturbed the waters, and the opportunists at Hallmark decided to make the film's notoriety work for rather than against it. In its advertising, the company asked the rhetorical question, 'Can a Movie Go <u>Too</u> <u>Far</u>?' then answered it in the following manner:

> *Many people who have gone to see the movie LAST HOUSE ON THE LEFT and many public officials contacted by outraged moviegoers believe the answer to this question is YES! Demands have been made to terminate the engagement of this movie immediately. WHY? LAST HOUSE ON THE LEFT relates to a problem and a situation that practically every teenage girl is vulnerable to and every parent lives in dread of. (Note: The movie is, in fact, a retelling of Ingmar Bergman's Academy Award Winner 'The Virgin Spring' in 1972 terms.) A young girl savagely brutalised, killed by a wanton band of degenerates. Revenge of the most horrible kind exacted by the parents of the dead girl—the killers are themselves killed. Yes, you will hate the people who perpetrate these outrages— you should! But, if a movie—and it is only a movie—can arouse you to such extreme emotion then the film director has succeeded. Violence and bestiality are not condoned in LAST HOUSE ON THE LEFT—far from it! The movie makes a plea for an end to all the senseless violence and inhuman cruelty that has become so much a part of the times in which we live. WE DON'T THINK ANY MOVIE CAN GO TOO FAR IN MAKING THIS MESSAGE HEARD AND FELT! This fact is already borne out by the number of parents who have taken their daughters to see the film. These parents regard this movie as a perfect deterrent to this type of behaviour.*

Proving once again that there is no such thing as bad publicity, *Last House on the Left* premiered to huge grosses in Boston, Chicago, Detroit, New York and Washington DC. Within just six months, the film had earned over $1.5 million. Over the next several years, it would become almost a permanent fixture at the nation's drive-ins; by 1977, it had earned some $4 million, plus an additional $10 million overseas.[2] 'It's a terribly disturbing piece of film,' Cunningham told *Fangoria*, 'but it plays and plays and plays...Perhaps some of the attraction is that most people feel they could make the same film themselves.'

Hallmark desperately wanted a sequel to *Last House*, but neither Cunningham nor Craven were willing to oblige. Undeterred, the company's creative advertisers

---

2 When submitted to the British Board of Film Censors in July 1974 by distributor Oppidan (UK) Ltd., *Last House* was refused certification for release in England. Its debut in the UK came in June 1982, when it was released on videocassette by Replay/VPD Video, although the film remained officially banned by the BBFC. Along with fifty-one other (mostly horror) titles, *Last House* was removed from the market in June 1983 at the direction of the Director of Public Prosecutions—this list of offensive movies came to be known as the 'Video Nasties'. In July 1984, Parliament passed the Video Recordings Act, which required all videocassettes to be certified by what was now known as the British Board of Film Classification. In February 2000, the Feature Film Company attempted to have *Last House* certified for DVD release in England but was refused; the same thing happened to Blue Underground in February 2002. *Last House* was finally passed that July with 31 seconds of cuts and was released to DVD by Anchor Bay Entertainment in May 2003. An uncut version was finally passed in March 2008 and was released to DVD by Metrodome Distribution that October.

simply made up a sequel by taking the old standby *Bay of Blood* and renaming it *Last House Part II* ('For those who survived the first!'), complete with a huge photo of Krug himself (David Hess) leering at a naked girl in agony. In June 1977, America was once again asked, 'Can a Movie Go <u>Too Far</u>?' but the word got out that the film was in fact a sham and it quickly disappeared from the scene.

In May 1985, Vestron Video released *Last House on the Left* to home video in America, while simultaneously announcing *Last House on the Left Part II* at that year's Cannes Film Festival ('The House That Set The Standard for Terror is Back!'). Scheduled to be directed by Danny Steinmann (who had just helmed *Friday the 13th Part V: A New Beginning*), the film was once again to have starred David Hess as Krug, who, despite the fact that he had been decapitated in the first film, now resides on an isolated island with a new bunch of cohorts who proceed to terrorise a group of young rafters. Needless to say, the film was never made and the property sat idle for nearly twenty years until the rights reverted back to The Night Company of Craven and Cunningham.

(2009)

We're not doing a watered-down version of the original. Some things are out, but I think it goes all the way. We had the opportunity to spend more money and time, and give more weight to the visuals and performances, while never holding back. It's a film that doesn't wuss out in any way.

—Dennis Iliadis, director

[Dennis and I] thought it was a core story that was so powerful, and was relevant way back then and it's relevant now, that I think we both felt like we weren't doing a remake so much as a re-imagination… which freed Dennis from having to think [that] I was worrying about how he was going to do my film. It was more like, do that story, but make it totally your own.

–Wes Craven, co-producer

Back in 1971, in Sean Cunningham's offices on West 45th Street in New York City, the organisation known as the Century Crime Company was formed between Cunningham and Craven for the purpose of making what they originally intended to call *Sex Crime of the Century*. When the title was changed during pre-production to *Night of Vengeance*, the Cunningham-Craven combine likewise changed its name to The Night Company, which went on to be the copyright holder for what was released as *Last House on the Left*. As a part of its contract with Hallmark Releasing, the Boston-based distributor—or its successors—would have control of the film for the next 30 years. And so The Night Company, for all intents and purposes, ceased to exist as Cunningham and Craven went their separate ways—until the year 2002.

'Sean Cunningham and I came back into ownership of the property after 30 years of it belonging to other people, which was the original contract,' Craven told Crave Online. 'Neither one of us ever thought…that we'd live that long. Then it was like well, we could do a remake. We own this…but how can we do one that we're really proud of? Let's do one where we get real filmmakers and somebody that we're really excited about and then tell them to go do their version without dictating what it has to be.'

But other matters had to be dealt with first: Cunningham was busy at last getting ready to shoot the long-delayed battle royal between his most famous creation—Jason Voorhees—and, in a great bit of irony, that of his ex-partner Craven. On September 9, 2002, cameras finally began rolling on *Freddy vs Jason*, a $30 million fanboy's dream-come-true that saw a $115 million worldwide gross when it was released the following summer.

Working in development on *Freddy vs Jason* for Cunningham was Mark Haslett, who had served in the same capacity on Cunningham's production of *Jason X* in 2000. In July 2005, Cunningham commissioned Haslett to write his first screenplay, a *redux* of *Last House on the Left*, with the intention that the film be made for New Line Cinema, which had backed Cunningham's last two productions.

In August 2006, it was announced that Rogue Pictures, the genre division of Universal-based Focus Features, had closed a deal with Cunningham and Craven to remake *Last House*. Rogue co-president Andrew Rona and Craven had forged a relationship while Rona was co-president of Dimension Films, where Craven made the *Scream* series. 'I'm far enough removed from these films that the remakes are a little like having grandchildren,' Craven said to *Variety*. 'The story, about the painful side effects of revenge, is an evergreen. The headlines are full of people and nations taking revenge and getting caught up in endless cycles of violence.'

LAKE
NDS IN THE
ROAD

That September, Craven, along with his long-time partner Marianne Maddalena, established Midnight Pictures, to be headquartered at Rogue and make horror films with budgets of under $15 million. It was agreed that the first film under the Midnight Pictures banner would be the *Last House* remake, to be possibly followed by remakes of the Craven films *Shocker* (1989) and *The People Under the Stairs* (1991), as both were owned by Rogue's parent company Universal.

Back in 2005, Craven and Maddalena had optioned the spec script *Home* by Adam Alleca. It told the story of an ex-con under house arrest in a cabin in the woods who struggles with his own psychological delusions. Alleca had also shown interest in scripting the proposed *People Under the Stairs* remake, but with *Last House* getting the green light first, Craven instead commissioned the young writer to revise Haslett's script.

Once Alleca turned in his draft, Craven felt it still needed more work and turned to Carl Ellsworth, who had written Craven's airplane thriller *Red Eye* (2005). 'The original movie is difficult to watch and is extreme for what I'm accustomed to,' Ellsworth told Shock Till You Drop. 'I went back and said, "What am I supposed to feel at the end of this movie?" When I go to the movies, I don't want to come out wanting to kill myself. But I don't always come out wanting a happy ending. So I told [Craven and Maddalena] my instincts tell me, first and foremost, that we have to be rooting for someone's survival here. They agreed to that premise. And that's where it started.'

While transferring convicted murderer Krug to prison, a police convoy is attacked by the crew of a station wagon and a pickup. All of the police are slaughtered and Krug is freed by his brother, Francis, and girlfriend Sadie. The next day, the Collingwood family—doctor John, real estate agent Emma and their seventeen-year-old daughter Mari—leave the city for a summer vacation at their lakeside home. Shortly after arriving, Mari heads into town for a reunion with her friend Paige Griffin, who works in her father's ice cream store. The two girls notice a fifteen-year-old boy wandering about aimlessly and begin to flirt with him. He invites them back to his motel room to smoke some marijuana; Mari is reluctant but Paige is insistent. The trio happily indulge until the party is crashed by Krug, Francis and Sadie—it turns out that the young man is Krug's son Justin. Because the story of Krug's escape—and his mug shot—is all over the news, the gang decides not to chance having the girls call the police. Paige tries to escape but is knocked unconscious by Francis. The gang and their captives pile into the Collingwood SUV and head out of town until the girls try to make an escape; in the ensuing melee, the SUV crashes in the woods. Paige makes a run for it, only to be caught by Francis and Sadie. While Krug taunts Justin with a challenge to rape the girls, Paige defies his authority and is the recipient of Krug's switchblade. As she bleeds to death in Mari's arms, Krug orders Mari to comfort her dying friend. When she fails

to do this to his satisfaction, Krug takes it as another act of defiance and brutally rapes Mari. Afterwards, she escapes to the nearby lake and begins to swim away; Krug repeatedly shoots at her before finally hitting her in the back. Leaving Mari for dead, the gang is forced by a thunderstorm to seek shelter at the nearest home, which just happens to be the Collingwood house. While John tends to Francis's broken nose, a lightning bolt knocks out the power, rendering the phone useless. With no way to call for transportation (their cell phones cannot get a signal in the wilderness), Krug and company accept the Collingwoods' offer to put them up for the night in their guesthouse. When he returns his coffee mug to the kitchen, Justin is startled to see a picture of Mari on the refrigerator. Guilt-ridden, the youngster places Mari's necklace on the mug for her parents to discover. Later that night, John and Emma hear a banging outside—investigating, they find their daughter, soaking wet and half-dead. John cauterises her gunshot wound and has to do a makeshift operation to relieve Mari's collapsed lung. Meanwhile, Emma finds the necklace, and when John happens to see Krug's face in the local paper, the couple put two and two together about their guests. Once Mari is stabilised, her parents begin a frantic search for the keys to their boat to get to the nearest house. Francis is awakened by the thunder and goes to the main house to get a beer and seduce Emma—she greets him with a wine bottle to the face and stabs him with a butcher knife while John hits him on the head with a claw hammer. John and Emma go to the guesthouse to get the boat keys—Justin is waiting and gives them Krug's gun. John shoots Sadie but Krug jumps out the window and runs to the main house. John and Sadie fight until Emma puts a bullet in her head. John goes to the house to confront Krug and the two get into a ferocious fight. Meanwhile, Justin finds the boat keys and brings them to Emma and Mari before going to the house to confront his father. He pulls the trigger but the gun is out of bullets; Krug attacks Justin but is intercepted by John and Emma, who knock him out with a fire extinguisher. John and Emma manage to make their escape with Mari and Justin. Some time later, Krug wakes up to find himself on a table in John's garage; he is unable to move because John has severed his spinal cord. Paige's father puts Krug's head in a microwave oven, then pushes the buttons—the killer's head explodes as the fathers leave.

'As much as you can say it's about the parents getting revenge, it's more so about survival,' remarked Ellsworth. 'It's a movie about a family doing what it takes to survive. And that is what got us going. We looked at the elements and chose which to use or not use from the original. There's a ticking clock to it too—having Mari show up alive you have the ticking clock of getting her to a hospital. The high concept for *Last House* is that what if this horrible stuff happens and just by happenstance the killers end up in the house where the parents live? That's what launched me. That's a great idea.'

'I try to always keep the audience in mind,' he continued. 'You want to surprise them, but it's a delicate balance of surprise and expectation. For this, I think the audience is more engaged if they have a rooting interest in the characters as opposed to leaving them in the darkness with a family who ends up in even worse shape at the end of a movie. This movie doesn't have a happy ending, but there is some hope. I couldn't be happier that, in the end, this is a good versus evil movie.'

JOHN
It's the last house on the left, in case you forgot.

MARI
It's the only house for miles, Dad.

JOHN
I was being ironical for God's
sake. I'm going back to sleep.

EMMA
Good, maybe you can dream
up some new material.

—From the original script,
shot but unused

In May 2007, *Variety* announced that Greek director Dennis Iliadis had been signed to helm the *Last House* remake on the basis of his hard-hitting prostitution drama *Hardcore* (2004). 'We were looking at all of the directors that had interesting films coming out,' Craven told the website FearNet. 'Mostly from Europe because they are unknown and somebody hasn't bought them up already. It was instant recognition with *Hardcore*—wow, this guy is a terrific filmmaker, [so] we met with him and...he was interested in doing something that was original.'

'We knew the remake would only work if we could find someone who could create strong characters while handling the more extreme moments,' co-producer Cody Zwieg told Movies Online. '*Hardcore* wasn't a genre or a horror film but showed completely believable characters in horrific, realistic situations. Many directors could handle the surface elements, the blood and shock moments of *Last House*, but Dennis proved that he could do it all without exploiting his characters and their situations.'

'It was a complex thing of updating,' Craven told Shock Till You Drop. 'How much of the Krug family

do you show? There were a lot of different ideas on that. What in the original do you keep or drop? Does Mari live or die? That was a discussion that went on for a long time. Do you have Junior, or the equivalent of Junior? Beyond that, there was a certain point where Dennis's sensibilities kicked in and we got in the ballpark and he went with it.'

'I've seen all of Wes's films and loved them,' Iliadis remarked to Movies Online. 'This film is based on a very archetypal...and primal story, which is a great foundation. I wanted to keep all the shock value and the power of Wes's film and develop the story in my own way [but] I didn't want to go sexy in a very superficial way and make the hard scenes titillating or enjoyable.'

With the mutual admiration society firmly in place, production finally began on the new *Last House on the Left* on March 24, 2008, in Cape Town and Helderberg Nature Preserve in South Africa. Craven had previously produced there in 2006 with *The Breed*, a horror film about killer dogs that marked the directing debut of Nick Mastandrea, who had frequently worked as Craven's assistant director. Zwieg and Craven's son Jonathan were the on-location producers for the $15 million *Last House*, as Craven was otherwise occupied on pre production of his latest film, *25/8*.

One of the criticisms that has plagued the original *Last House* over the years was the woefully out-of-place inclusion of so-called 'comic relief' in the person of two bumbling cops, played by Marshall Anker and future *Cagney & Lacey* star Martin Kove. Even Craven came to regret these asides and Iliadis was not about to make the same mistake, as he told Shock Till You Drop: 'I wasn't crazy about some of

the comedic elements [in the original]...The decision to inter-cut a rape with these comedic scenes was very weird...I think we tried to approach it [with] more consistency. Really trying to work the drama immediately and cut those diversions out...I wanted the movie to throw you into this scene with no place to cut away to. Because if you cut away, you have this feeling you're leaving the moment and things could turn out differently, but here, every second and every behaviour counted. That's why we made it a bit more dramatic and stayed [with it].'

One of the biggest changes from the original film was, of course, the fact that Mari (Sara Paxton) survives her ordeal. Now, instead of her parents taking revenge for her death, they are in a race against time to get their daughter to a hospital. Krug (Garret Dillahunt) and his gang are the obstacles to that goal. 'By having the daughter fighting to survive, it wasn't just about revenge,' said Iliadis. 'These parents are trying to protect their baby and they would do anything to keep her alive. It's a much more valid notion. There's this tendency now to go torture porn and all of that. I didn't like the idea of the parents devising torture tactics. It had to be this urgency. Our daughter is here, we have to keep her alive and no one is going to get in our way. By keeping this spirit alive, it's much more powerful.'

Revenge enters into the equation at the conclusion, however, and rather more sadistically than in 1972. Instead of killing Krug in the heat of the moment, as Mari's father did originally, John Collingwood (Tony Goldwyn) now returns to the home after his family has made their escape and methodically disables Krug so that both the doctor and Paige's father can exact their vengeance in a deliberate way.[3] 'You

---

3 The character of Paige's father—James Griffin—was dropped during shooting so that, in the film, only John takes revenge on Krug.

can argue that it's not such a heroic thing to do,' remarked Craven. '[John's] human, so it's not like we're trying to make these people heroic. You see them warts and all.'

As both perpetrator and, ultimately, the victim of violence, Garret Dillahunt's portrayal of Krug is the film's strongest point—far more menacing and less brutish than the infamous, over-the-top performance of David Hess, which, according to Iliadis, was seemingly everyone else's template: 'Everyone who came in before [Garret] was playing Krug with a squinty eye and raspy voice. What the hell? My feeling is, if you get the ambiguities right, he's much more terrifying. However evil Krug can get, he still has a sense of humour. He's supposed to be a father and Garret realised all of that, keeping those things alive.'

'I thought [Krug] was just a guy who's had some bad luck in his life and it really makes him angry, the way the world has treated him,' Dillahunt (who had previously played Jesus Christ in the controversial 2006 TV series *The Book of Daniel*) told Movies Online. 'He's just not responding to that bad luck in a healthy way. He's not seeking therapy or retraining. He's blaming everyone else, and he really can't let it go. He's physically incapable. It's everyone else's fault, and he gets obsessed with punishing them. He's meting out his own twisted justice.'

It was Krug's *way* of meting out that justice, particularly with regard to the rape of Mari, which caused problems with the MPAA Ratings Board. Long gone were the days when Craven and Cunningham could 'self-rate' their movie an 'R' by simply pruning the rating from another film print and splicing it onto theirs, as they in fact did in 1972. While the updated *Last House* is actually less gruesome than its predecessor (no one is eviscerated or chainsawed), in contrast, the rape of Mari is much more stark and prolonged. Given the subject matter of his previous film, it is not surprising that Iliadis should make the rape scene a graphic one, as he told Movies Online: 'To me making a good horror movie is...making the darkness inside everyone believable, so that when this darkness is expressed it's believable and it hits you even harder...But we've had a lot of problems [with the MPAA] and the basic thing they kept telling us is, it's too real.'

'Dennis had really strong feelings about the rape and the length it should go on,' Craven told FearNet, 'and that's one area the MPAA came in very insistently on and did cause us to shorten it...The funny thing is they said you don't need it because this is a marvellous film! It's really a "special" film and it's like wow, I've never heard that from the MPAA! It's both a good sign and a bad sign because it meant they were absolutely convinced you didn't need one more shot in the rape...I think because the film was so good they kept their hands off of most of it.'

Except for a scene of Mari showering after swimming in the lake and more fondling of the girls by the gang in the back seat of the Collingwood Suburban, the only major difference between the rated and unrated versions of the film is the rape scene, which was shortened by a minute. In both versions, two other scenes were shortened for time—Paige (Martha MacIsaac) teases Justin (Spencer Treat Clark) at the store when he tries to buy cigarettes and Emma (Monica Potter) goes through the guesthouse lighting candles for the gang—while one entire scene in the guesthouse was eliminated: when Krug goes to the bathroom, Justin enters the room his father is sharing with Sadie (Riki Lindhome) and takes Krug's gun, but is forced to put it

2: The Craven Connection

back and hide under the bed when Krug returns. Krug finds Mari's gym bag and lifts her barbells and wears her swim goggles to amuse Sadie before they make love, not aware that his son is underneath the bed.

Released on March 13, 2009, the new *Last House* was largely reviewed not with the utter contempt of its predecessor but with simple disdain. 'The original version... was vile but terrifying. This remake is merely vile (and dull),' was the verdict of *Entertainment Weekly*. 'The remodelled *House* is a mundane disappointment taken on its own and a deeply misguided refraction of the original,' said the *Los Angeles Times*. 'Steer as clear as you possibly can from *The Last House on the Left*. Not only is it plodding and completely predictable, the carnage is rendered slowly and quasi-reverently, making the whole brutal experience come off like torture porn,' warned *USA Today*. 'The low-budget grunginess that helped make Wes Craven's 1972 original...an unsettling memento of its era is wiped clean in Dennis Iliadis's remake—unnecessary on every level save the paramount commercial one,' was *Variety*'s judgment. 'This version...makes significant changes to the original plot, changes that water down the central idea, rendering it more palatable for mainstream audiences. In the end, like virtually every other remake that has been released recently, it's polished and predictable,' opined *The Washington Post*.

Even Roger Ebert, one of the original film's few defenders, could only muster half-hearted praise for this 21st century remodel: 'I wrote [the] original *Last House* review 37 years ago. I am not the same person. I am uninterested in being 'consistent'. I approach the new film as simply a filmgoer. I must say it is very well made. The rape scene appalled me. Other scenes, while violent, fell within the range of contemporary horror films, which strive to invent new ways to kill people, so the horror fans in the audience will get a laugh...Dennis Iliadis and his cinematographer Sharone Meir do a smooth job of handling space and time to create suspense. The film is an effective representative of its genre, and horror fans will like it, I think, but who knows? I'm giving it a 2.5 in the silly star rating system and throwing up my hands.'

There were a few exceptions to the brickbats, however. *The Boston Globe* felt that 'the Collingwoods' revenge, though preposterous in its thoroughness, makes more emotional sense than it did in 1972. Like the current hit *Taken*, *Last House* 2009 packs a vicarious jolt that might feel cathartic to certain moviegoers.' *The Hollywood Reporter* enthused: 'The refurbished *House* adheres sufficiently closely to the original template so as not to offend purists and manages to pack an intensely visceral punch of its own, most effectively in the extended setup.' And the *New York Times* commended, 'Replacing the earlier movie's more depraved sequences with sustained tension and truly unnerving editing, [Iliadis] proves adept at managing mayhem in cramped spaces.'

Last House debuted in the third spot in its opening weekend with $14.1 million, which, typical of many genre films, ended up being almost half of its entire domestic gross of $32.7 million, which it augmented with some $12.5 million overseas. While hardly spectacular, this nevertheless spelled a tidy profit for the low-budget film, which originally was intended as a straight-to-DVD release. Dillahunt speculated to the *Los Angeles Times*: 'There's something about [the] basic story that is speaking to people...people feel so powerless right now. People feel like they've been raped by—fill in the blank, the economy, 9/11...People are really responding to the film in a visceral way—and I think it gives them some release.'

THE HILLS HAVE EYES
(1977)

Peter Locke...told me for years that I should do another *Last House*, and I resisted his advice for as long a time as I could. I finally gave in and wrote *The Hills Have Eyes* when I ran out of money.

—Wes Craven, writer, director and editor

The good guys win in the end. I hope the picture will make me very rich.

—Peter Locke, producer

Those familiar with tall Scottish tales love to tell the grisly story of one Alexander 'Sawney' Beane, the legendary head of a clan in 16th-century Edinburgh that supposedly murdered and cannibalised over 1,000 people. Because the Beanes are meant to have lived in a coastal cave that was 200 yards deep and blocked during high tide, their existence went undetected for nearly 25 years. However, after scores of disappearances and discarded body parts washing up on beaches, King James VI of Scotland (who would later become James I of England) eventually led a regiment of 400 men that found the Beanes' cave, which was overflowing with human remains. The clan of fifty was captured and taken to Glasgow where they were publicly executed without trial; the men had their extremities cut off and bled to death, while the women and children were burned alive.

The lack of hard historical evidence (such atrocities, had they actually occurred, would surely have been documented properly), coupled with the fact that the primary source for the tale was the highly-sensationalised *Newgate Calendar*, have led most modern historians to seriously doubt the veracity of the Beane narrative. But, it certainly makes for good copy, and it caught the eye of Wes Craven when he visited the New York Public Library in early 1976 in search of inspiration for his third film project.

After the huge success and notoriety of *Last House on the Left*, Craven had tried to break out of the exploitation arena with 'important' projects that went nowhere, including a biopic of Colonel Anthony Herbert—who became a hero to the anti-war movement after being court-martialled for reporting alleged American atrocities in Vietnam. To support himself, Craven worked for a time in the porn business as both

an editor (*It Happened in Hollywood,* 1973) and a writer/director (*The Fireworks Woman,* 1975).

The man who had written and directed the former film and produced the latter was 33-year-old Peter Locke, who also directed another Craven editing job, the sex comedy, *The Carhops* (1975).[4] Locke was married to Liz Torres, an actress and stand-up comedienne who had an engagement in Las Vegas during the summer of 1976. Craven had actually written some of her material and, in taking advantage of opportunity, Locke invited Craven to write a script for a thriller set in the desert that the men could make while Torres was performing.

'[It] was originally written as a near-future drama, taking place during the 1984 presidential primaries,' Craven told *Fangoria.* 'People are all getting out of New York because it was too terrible to exist there anymore. You have to have a passport to cross the George Washington Bridge, you have to have state passports to go from one state to another, because everyone's trying to get to the Sun Belt; so this family has decided to sneak across through the back roads, through the hills to get to California, the promised land.'

Sometime in the near future, the Carter family load up their station wagon and camper trailer, leave behind the polluted, violence-ridden city that is New York and head for the supposed safe haven of California. Using the back roads so they will not be stopped by border guards, they break down in the Nevada desert outside Nellis Air Force Base. Completely isolated and off the beaten path, retired policeman 'Big' Bob Carter and his oldest daughter's scientist boyfriend, Doug Wood, decide to go in opposite directions to get help, leaving behind Bob's wife Ethel, Doug's girlfriend Lynne and their newborn Shanti, along with Bob and Ethel's teenage children Bobby and Brenda. The group also has two German Shepherds—Beauty and The Beast—the former of which goes running off on the trail of something. Bobby chases after her only to find her completely gutted; Lynne and Ethel try to raise help on their citizen's band radio but get only heavy breathing in response. The Carters are in fact being stalked by a feral family who live among the rock formations. As darkness falls, Doug returns from an unsuccessful expedition but Bob does not. Doug and Lynne retire to the station wagon, while the others rest in the camper. Bobby is lured outside by noises that seem to be coming from The Beast, which enables a 13-year-old savage named Pluto to invade and ransack the camper. A sudden explosion brings everyone running, save for Brenda, who is held at knifepoint by Pluto. The Carters are horrified to discover Bob, crucified and incinerated on a burning tree. With everyone distracted, Pluto's older brother Mars also enters the camper and interrupts Pluto's rape of Brenda with bad intentions of his own. When Lynne and Ethel arrive back at the camper, Pluto

---

4 On *Fireworks Woman*, Craven hid behind the pseudonym 'Abe Snake' while Locke used the *nom-de-plume* 'Carmen Rodriguez'.

comes bursting out with most of the family's provisions while Mars has their CB in one arm and Shanti in the other. Ethel attacks Mars with a broom and is shot, while Lynne stabs the savage in the ribs and thigh before he empties his pistol into her. Pluto and Mars bring Shanti back to the cave, where the baby is received by their teenage sister Ruby and their parents Ma Ma and Pa Pa, who has also brought back Bob's gutted corpse. Bobby tends to Ethel, who eventually dies of her wound. The feral clan turns out to be a large one as a procession goes into the woods to chop down a pine tree which they strip and bring back to the compound. Shanti is left with Ruby, who begins to bond with the baby. After raising the tree, the savages decorate it and then mount Bob's head at the top. They proceed to have a drunken, drug-crazed ceremony, wearing masks, costumes and head-dresses. The men cut themselves and pay homage to Ma Ma with their blood; soon an oiled, half-naked Ruby brings Shanti forth and places her on a sacrificial altar where she is sprinkled with chicken blood. After receiving word that one of their number has been killed, Pa Pa, Pluto and some others leave the ceremony to finish off the Carters. Warned by Doug that the savage posse is coming, Bobby and Brenda rig up an elaborate trap, with their mother's corpse as bait. Doug manages to steal a savage's costume and infiltrate the ceremony, where, with Ruby's help, he grabs Shanti and runs. Mars, meanwhile, has made a play for leadership of the clan by attacking and raping his mother, but his power grab is interrupted by the abduction of Shanti and the whole clan goes in pursuit of Doug and Ruby. Mars challenges Doug to a battle which Doug surprisingly wins, after which he castrates the would-be leader then throws his genitals at the mob, who retreat in shock. Bobby and Brenda, meanwhile, bag Pa Pa's posse by lassoing them with telephone wire and using their station wagon as a winch that drags the marauders through cactus before they are shot in the head by Bobby or hit with a baseball bat by Brenda. The two siblings then hightail it back to the trailer with Pa Pa in hot pursuit, not knowing that Bobby has rigged the camper to explode, which it does when Pa Pa opens the door. Not to be outdone, The Beast attacks Pluto and kills him by tearing out his throat. Doug, Shanti and Ruby join Bobby, Brenda and The Beast in the debris as an Army helicopter, alerted by the smoke, arrives on the scene.

What Craven initially called *Blood Relations: The Sun Wars* was a strange mix of *The Grapes of Wrath* and *Deliverance,* with a nominal dystopian setting for good measure (despite his comments, there is in fact no mention of 1984 or presidential primaries in Craven's script). It was also far too ambitious in scope for the $250,000 budget and 25-day schedule that Locke was to provide, which meant that the scenes in New York had to be dropped, the feral family was reduced in size to just six and the sacrificial ceremony (including Mars' rape of his mother) was eliminated.

The Hills Have Eyes (1977)

Between August and September, Craven and Locke scouted locations and finally decided on Apple Valley, California, in the Mojave Desert. The cameras started rolling in mid-October, and several changes were made to the script both before and during principal photography:

- The Carter family is now from Cleveland, although Doug (Martin Speer) and Lynne (Dee Wallace) live in New York. They are on their way to California for a vacation celebrating Bob (Russ Grieve) and Ethel's (Virginia Vincent) silver anniversary but are in the Nevada desert looking for a silver mine that was given to them by Ethel's aunt as an anniversary present.
- The opening scenes now feature the character of Grandpa Fred (John Steadman), who is the father of Pa Pa (James Whitworth) and runs a gas station in the desert.
- After breaking down, Bob returns to the gas station to find Fred hanging from a belt. Bob saves him, then Fred tells the ex-cop the whole story of how his murderous son went wild. Pa Pa (now known as Jupiter) suddenly crashes through the window, abducts Fred and impales him to the outhouse door.
- Bob pursues Jupiter but suffers a heart attack, after which we see Jupiter crucifying Bob on a Joshua tree.
- A scene was added where Jupiter eats Bob's corpse while haranguing the dead man for trespassing.
- As per the script, Doug and Ruby (Janus Blithe) retrieve the baby (now named Katy) and flee the scene with Mars (Lance Gordon) in pursuit. However, instead of Doug castrating Mars and throwing his genitals at the rest of the tribe, this was changed to Ruby snatching a rattlesnake and putting it on Mars' back before Doug stabs him to death.
- The climax was changed to have Jupiter survive the exploding camper. He dies only after being repeatedly stabbed with an axe by Brenda (Susan Lanier) and shot by Bobby (Robert Houston).

In 1973, following the release of *Last House on the Left*, the writer/ director of that film was committed for psychiatric observation. He was treated extensively with drugs, group therapies, electroshock programs and a final lobotomy. Despite these efforts at reform, Craven killed his nurse, Maura Heaphy, and escaped to the Mohave Desert. At the end of 1,000 days of meditation he was taken up by a jet-black saucer and trained in Secondary Media Infiltration and parametaphysical survival on the Planet Jupiter. Upon his graduation he was returned to the planet Earth at Exeter. This Film is his first since his return, and is respectfully dedicated to the memory of Maura Heaphy.

—Title crawl from the original script; unused

Originally, the film's climax was similar to the one in the script. However, Craven reversed the confrontations in the editing, making the climactic duel between Mars and Doug into the *denouement*, with the film ending on a freeze-frame of Doug stabbing Mars to death while Ruby screams for him to stop. The erstwhile civilised man has now become the savage, which was the message that Craven had been going for all along. 'The people outside the trailer and those inside are extremes,' he told the *Journal of Popular Film and Television*. 'But they merge...

The outsiders are one's darker side that one does not know or care to face. Although they are separate in the movie I'm really talking about the same people, two sides of the same coin.'

While Craven chose to cut the film's original, upbeat ending, which, like the script, has Ruby joining Doug and Katy in a reunion with Brenda, Bobby and The Beast, a number of other changes had to be made against his will to appease the MPAA when *Blood Relations* received an X rating. Jupiter's beating of Grandpa Fred with a crowbar and the old man's impalement were both shortened, as was the assault by Mars and Pluto (Michael Berryman) in the camper. Originally, Jupiter was clearly shown eating Bob's dismembered arm—which he then uses to poke the corpse in the eyes—but this was abbreviated so that it is only implied that he is in fact eating Bob's charred flesh. And it originally took more axe blows and bullets to put Jupiter down than are now shown. 'As they say in psychological circles, my family never got in touch with their rage,' Craven told the *Chicago Tribune*. 'So making movies—these awful horror movies, no less—was, I guess, my way of purging this rage.'

To produce the film, Locke had formed the one-shot Vanguard Releasing with partner Barry Cahn, and the two men decided on a new title for the film: *The Hills Have Eyes*. As with *Last House*, Craven was hardly enthused, but Locke made the most of the title's exploitability, spending much more to market *Hills* than he had to make it. With a 60/40 split between radio/television and print advertising, 'we go into each town on a big break,' Locke told the *Los Angeles Times*. 'Blue-collar workers in general are the bulk of our market, but in Detroit...black audiences certainly played a big part.'

In point of fact, the film's advertising was a masterpiece of misinformation. It proudly declared, '*The Hills Have Eyes* has been accepted for the film collection of the New York Museum of Modern Art as a TERROR CLASSIC!' This was totally untrue—as with *The Texas Chainsaw Massacre*, an unsolicited print of the film had been presented to MoMA by Cinema Shares (the movie's New York sub-distributor) and was accepted into the museum's study collection, which was a far cry from being invited for inclusion in the permanent archives. Likewise, the two rave reviews often cited in the print ads came with caveats: *The Hollywood Reporter* did indeed declare the film 'A terror classic...audiences will love it!' but this review was in fact written by Craven's long time friend (and New York School of Visual Arts professor) Roy Frumkes; the *Los Angeles Times*'s Linda Gross did credit *Hills* as 'a skilled example of well-sustained suspense and the evocation of an atmosphere of terror,' but this was only after warning, 'If there is any correlation between emotionally disturbed persons, the violence they reap and the films they see, *The Hills Have Eyes* could be a potentially dangerous film and should have been rated X (instead of R) for violence and sadism.'

The film premiered in Tucson, Arizona, in June 1977, then went on to a regional release; after its first three months, *Hills* had grossed $1.7 million in the southern and southwestern markets alone. Los Angeles and New York releases came in October, where *Hills* earned, respectively, $250,000 and $530,000 in its first two weeks. The film then experienced a hiatus until the spring of 1978, when it successfully bowed

in the Midwest and east coast before heading to Chicago that September, where it opened to a big $180,000.

There *was* some favourable critical reception for *The Hills Have Eyes,* particularly from *Cinefantastique* ('For his new film...[Craven's] work is better controlled, and because the whole has a sense of structure, the horror/suspense works more effectively') and *Variety* ('A satisfying piece of pulp with good drive-in and late-night prospects'). But Tom Allen—who would later champion *Halloween* and *Dawn of the Dead*—seemed to speak for the rest of the critical fraternity when he decreed that '*The Hills Have Eyes* has no class, and its writer-director Wes Craven is a devious scavenger...the most cynically evil film that I have ever seen from the Grand Guignol boondocks.'

In the exploitation business, however, the only verdict that matters is the one at the box office, and with *Hills* proving itself a solid performer, funding was soon forthcoming for Craven and Locke's proposed follow-up called *Deep in the Heart.* 'We already have a backer committed for our next film on the basis of how well *Hills* has done so far,' Craven told the *Los Angeles Times.* 'The violence in *Hills* is what you could call rough. On our next, we'd like to go more toward Hitchcock without getting artsy-craftsy to the point where we'd lose our market.'

'It would be fun to make a comedy or a love story,' added Locke. 'We'd love to, but with financing already promised for this genre, there's no reason to move away from it. Right now, we're going to keep our daily double going. We're not embarrassed about doing *Hills*. It's been compared to *Straw Dogs* and *Deliverance*.'

Like the promised financing, *Deep in the Heart* never materialised, and both Craven and Locke turned their separate attentions to television, where Craven directed the Linda Blair occult thriller *Stranger in Our House* (aka *Summer of Fear*, 1978) and Locke produced both series (*Just Friends*, 1979) and movies of the week (*A Gun in the House*, 1981) before joining forces with Donald Kushner in 1983 to form the Kushner-Locke Company. That same year Locke would reunite with Craven for a project five years in the making: *The Hills Have Eyes Part II*.

(2006)

We tried to keep [a] very realistic approach, even if we're doing a radioactive mutant cannibal movie.

−Alexandre Aja, co-writer and director

This is something I could control and guarantee it was the way I wanted. Artistically it made sense and financially it made sense, frankly. It was a chance to see some old piece of material that has a good set of legs remade by some young guy and just see what would happen. The horror genre has been blossoming, so it was a very easy sell.

−Wes Craven, co-producer

With the dawn of a new millennium, while most people were looking towards the future, a group of young filmmakers were harking back to the grit and gristle of the past: specifically, the graphically-violent and visceral horror films of the 1970s. They rejected the self-referential in-jokes of Wes Craven's phenomenally popular *Scream* trilogy (1996-2000), not to mention the outright parody of the *Scary Movie* comedies (2000-06). They also turned their backs on the successful but relatively benign PG-13 scares of remakes like *The Ring* (2002) and *The Grudge* (2004).

This new breed of directors, who would come to be dubbed 'The Splat Pack' by British film journalist Alan Jones, were practitioners of what became known as 'Torture Porn' or 'Gorno'—the main tenets of which came to be recognised thus:

- Hedonistic, self-absorbed protagonists (usually college students) are forced to commit barbarous acts to survive against primitive, psychotic predators.
- A morbid fascination with pain and suffering.
- A clinical obsession with anatomically-correct graphic violence.
- A decidedly non-politically-correct approach to women (who are almost always provocatively dressed and sexually available), drugs (one or more of the

protagonists smoke pot), profanity (everyone liberally drops the 'f'-bomb) and smoking (by men and women alike).
- Cruelty to animals is not taboo, especially dogs, as man's best friend often ends up gutted.

The first of the Gorno films was *House of 1,000 Corpses*, which sees four college kids unwittingly seek shelter at the house of a psychopathic family who subject the youngsters to systematic torture and mayhem. Written and directed by Rob Zombie, the film cost $7 million and was released by Lionsgate Films in April 2003, grossing $16.8 million worldwide. The next month saw the release of *Wrong Turn*, the story of six college kids stranded in the backwoods of West Virginia who run foul of a family of inbred, mutant cannibals. Directed by Rob Schmidt, the film cost $12.6 million and was released by 20th Century-Fox, grossing $28.6 million worldwide. In September came the release of *Cabin Fever*, about five college kids on

a weekend retreat in the woods who fall victim to a highly infectious flesh-eating virus that poisons the water. Co-written and directed by Eli Roth, the film cost $1.5 million and was released by Lionsgate, grossing $30.5 million worldwide.

But it was in October 2004 that Gorno saw its biggest success with the beginning of the franchise known as *Saw*, a reference to the film's terminally-ill 'Jigsaw Killer', who communicates through a ventriloquist's dummy. Said fiend is determined to teach the wayward the meaning of life by forcing them into sadistic games of survival. Despite being a rather unremarkable thriller—and bearing more than a passing resemblance to David Fincher's much better *Se7en* (1995)—the film was nevertheless a breakout hit for Lionsgate, which had already become the unofficial home of the Splat Pack. Co-written and directed by James Wan, *Saw* cost just $1.2 million but grossed $103 million worldwide. Lionsgate would subsequently release a *Saw* sequel every October between 2005 and 2010, earnings from which topped $750 million worldwide.

Both Zombie and Roth would follow up their initial efforts with even more extreme offerings (*The Devil's Rejects*, 2005, and *Hostel*, 2006, respectively), and their ranks were joined by Darren Lynn Bousman (who helmed three of the *Saw* sequels) and Australian Greg McLean, whose $1 million *Wolf Creek*, about stranded backpackers falling prey to a psychopath in the Outback, was released by Dimension Films in December 2005 and ended up earning $27 million worldwide.

It was two young Frenchmen, however, who would provide Gorno with its least successful, most derivative—but also most intriguing and shocking—film: *Haute Tension* (*High Tension*). The brainchild of 25-year-old writer/director Alexandre Aja (born Alexandre Arcady) and his long-time friend and partner Grégory Levasseur, *Haute Tension* follows two college girls, Alex and Marie, who go to Alex's

family farm in southern France to study for their upcoming exams. After they arrive, a psychotic truck driver invades the house, brutally murders the family and kidnaps Alex. Marie gives chase in a desperate attempt to rescue her friend. Obviously inspired by *Last House on the Left*, the film also bears similarities to early '70s British thrillers such as *And Soon the Darkness* and *See No Evil* and features a big, M Night Shyamalan-style twist-ending for good measure. But it is an undeniably *shocking* twist (not at all telegraphed), on top of a ferociously intense, graphic and high-octane saga that is well acted by the three principals: Cécile De France, Maïwenn Le Besco and Philippe Nahon.

Filmed in Romania and featuring gore effects from Italian *maestro* Giannetto De Rossi (veteran of many Lucio Fulci films), *Haute Tension* cost just $430,000 and was released in France in June 2003, where it earned over $500,000 and was pegged as being part of the so-called New French Extremity movement, which had

been heralded by the release of the highly controversial *Baise Moi* (*Rape Me*) in 2000. *Haute Tension* was picked up by Lionsgate after playing at the Toronto International Film Festival in September 2003 but was not released in the US until June 2005, when it grossed $3.6 million. Under the offbeat title *Switchblade Romance*, it was released in the UK in September 2004 and its final worldwide boxoffice take was just $6.2 million.

Many industry notables were impressed with *Haute Tension*, however, not least of whom was Wes Craven, who had seen the film in Toronto. In November 2003, he met with Aja and Lavasseur and made his pitch for a remake of *The Hills Have Eyes*, which was to have been part of his deal with Dimension Films. For Aja, the chance to work with Craven was a natural outgrowth of his previous film: 'We grew up with [Craven's] films,' he told *The Washington Post*, 'and *Last House on the Left* had a *major* influence on *High Tension*. When we started writing [*High Tension*], it was to relive this very specific spirit of the 70s, a very nasty, *savage* spirit.'

'We...came with the idea of bringing back the horror,' he continued to the *Los Angeles Times* 'Just scaring the audience as much as we can. Making movies that are not meant to be funny but make you as an audience member leave the movie as an experience. I think we managed to revive that intensity of the genre as it was at its most powerful in the '70s'. As one who had been there before, Craven saw a good deal of similarity between what had inspired him and what was now driving the young Gorno turks: 'The new films are very similar to those in the 1970s in that they are merciless with the audience,' he told the *New York Times*. 'I think they are a cultural way of coming to terms with the horrible realities of everyday life.' He then elaborated on that last point to the *Chicago Tribune*: 'I think films like these often happen during times of war, when very primal situations are going on. A bunch of teenagers in a van stumbling into some family that's totally different from them in the middle of nowhere isn't all that different from a bunch of American kids being thrust into the middle of Baghdad. The parable is quite germane during these times.'

With the signs of the times seemingly in bright neon, the notion of remaking *Hills* had been something Craven and Peter Locke had been actively discussing some time prior to Aja and Lavasseur's involvement. 'We both thought it would be interesting to try to redo *Hills*,' Craven told the website Cinematical. 'Part of it was that so many horror movies are getting remade, and we saw the field as wide open if we could do it in an unusual way...We were looking for a way to make it more original.'

'He asked us to come up with a way to remake the material; something to justify the remake,' Aja told the website Eat My Brains. 'We brought this nuclear testing background forward as a way of developing the characters and making it more real and more brutal. Wes offered us his trust. From the beginning he said, "Look, I did my movie and I want you to do yours." He was very supportive and very respectful; he was a perfect gentleman about that specific thing. So for a year we were writing and we were trading some e-mails with him. But he's not a teacher. He's not like, "I'm going to tell you how to do the best movie possible," he's not like that at all. He's much more respectful.'

Travelling through the New Mexico desert, the Carter family's SUV and mobile home hit a belt of spikes in the road and crash. Completely isolated and off the beaten path, retired policeman Big Bob Carter and his oldest daughter's husband Doug Bukowski decide to go in opposite directions to get help, leaving behind Bob's wife Ethel, Doug's wife Lynn and their newborn Catherine, along with Bob and Ethel's teenage children Bobby and Brenda. The group also has two German Shepherds—Beauty and Beast—the former of which goes running off on the trail of something. Bobby chases after her only to run into a deformed girl named Ruby. When she runs off, Bobby finds Beauty mutilated and a hideous figure named Goggle eating one of her legs. Bobby flees but stumbles and falls, knocked unconscious. Ruby saves Bobby from a rattlesnake, then watches over his immobile form. Meanwhile, Doug finds an atomic bomb crater full of abandoned vehicles before making his way back to the

trailer. As darkness falls, Brenda recovers Bobby while Bob arrives at the gas station the family visited earlier. Going inside, he finds old pictures of the station owner with his deformed children, along with aged newspaper clippings about nuclear testing and the forced eviction of local miners. More recent articles warn of mysterious disappearances in the area. Bob comes across the station owner who, in a drunken frenzy, blows his own head off. Bob tries to commandeer the man's pickup truck, but is attacked by a hairy beast known as Papa Jupiter and dragged into the mines. Some time later, Bobby is lured outside the trailer by noises that seem to be coming from Beast, which enables a young savage named Pluto to invade and ransack the place. A sudden explosion brings everyone running, save for Brenda, who is held at knifepoint by Pluto. The Carters are horrified to discover Bob, crucified and incinerated on a burning tree. With everyone thus distracted, Pluto's older brother Lizard also enters the trailer and interrupts Pluto's rape of Brenda with bad intentions of his own. When Lynn and Ethel arrive back at the camper, they find Lizard cradling Catherine and Pluto restraining Brenda. Both Lynn and Ethel attack Lizard but are brutally murdered for their trouble as he and his brother make their escape with Catherine. The next morning, Doug and Beast go into the mines after Catherine, only to discover a seemingly-abandoned town on the other side of the hills - it is in fact an 'atomic' village from the 1950s, populated with mannequins— and the rest of the irradiated family, including the misshapen Big Brain and the brace-wearing Cyst. Doug confronts Big Brain over the whereabouts of his daughter but is attacked by Pluto. The two have a violent confrontation that finally ends with a flag in Pluto's neck and an axe in his skull. Doug then kills Cyst before running off in pursuit of Ruby, who has escaped with Catherine to protect her from Lizard. Meanwhile, Papa Jupiter has come to the trailer to steal Ethel's body, which he begins to feast upon until Bobby lures him into a trap. Not knowing that Bobby has rigged the trailer to explode, Jupiter is killed when he opens the door. Doug finally catches up with Lizard, Ruby and Catherine, and after shooting Lizard repeatedly, Doug recovers his daughter when Ruby falls to her death from the clifftop, taking Lizard with her. Doug, Catherine and Beast subsequently join Bobby and Brenda in the smoking debris as someone watches the reunion through a pair of binoculars...

'I was really scared going into *The Hills Have Eyes* about the American system,' Aja admitted. 'That's why I fought for us to write the film. When you're writing you have a lot of control. But the reality was the opposite. I had exactly the same freedom as I had on *High Tension*, because of Wes, mainly. Wes was great on this film. He was happy with what we delivered.'

'Alex's concept is very different,' Craven remarked, 'with the miners being less

defined as a family, existing more as a pack. Alex builds his film like a good video game by continuously upping the ante as the movie goes on.'

'Bringing in the background of the nuclear testing we also did a lot of research into the effects of nuclear testing on humans,' said Aja. 'We found some absolutely awful, unwatchable, terrible stuff that we used as reference to create all of the designs. Big Brain was based on a picture that Greenpeace used for campaigning in Italy during the eighties...They are really freaks but at the same time they're based on the real footage we used in the opening credits. Realism was the key word... There were two ways to make the movie; one was, "OK, it's a radioactive mutant cannibal movie," and that was something else, and our way was, "Let's try to make *Deliverance*." That was the difference and we tried to stay as real as we could.'

Staying real apparently also involved 'borrowing' several elements from *Wrong Turn*, including the opening credits montage of deformity and news articles, the discovery of a mass of abandoned vehicles and making the marauders into inbred mutants as opposed to the original film's simple feral clan.

On Valentine's Day 2005, Aja and Levasseur handed in their final draft; just four months later the film was in production, although Craven had since upped sticks and moved to 20th Century-Fox. The Frenchmen had wanted to shoot *Hills* in Morocco, but co-producer Marianne Maddalena initially refused because of fears of terrorism. Instead, she had the duo scout locations in New Mexico, Mexico and Namibia before finally agreeing to Morocco, where *Hills* began filming at the CLA Studios in Ouarzazate on a $15 million budget.

'It's so insanely different than anywhere I had been before,' co-star Emilie de Ravin told the *Los Angeles Times*. 'We shot in a very small desert town with barely any water around. The cheat was so perfect for the desert here in the States. The hills are so huge, you are a little more frightened there for some reason. Everything is a little more scary.'

BOBBY
Have you seen her?

Ruby looks down. She knows something.

BOBBY (CONT'D)
Look at me, Ruby...Look at me...Where did you see my dog?

Ruby keeps looking to the ground. Bobby reaches under her chin to raise her head.
Instinctively, Ruby SCREAMS as she backs off, lifting her hands to protect herself.

HER HANDS LOOK LIKE CLAWS. DEFORMED AND MISSING FINGERS, THEY ARE NO LONGER HUMAN.

Frightened, Bobby takes a step back. The girl murmurs softly.

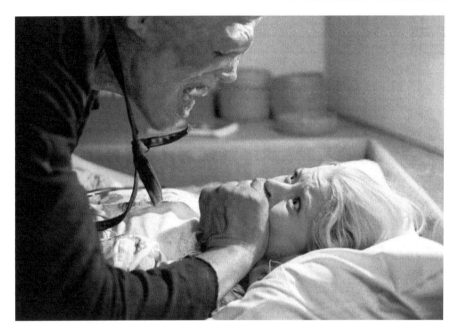

BOBBY (CONT'D)
What? I can't understand. What are you saying?

He comes closer trying to make eye contact as she continues to murmur the same thing. She too is terrified—

RUBY
(softly)
The hills...The hills have eyes...The hills have eyes...The hills have eyes...

—Unfilmed exchange, from the original script

While the above scene—along with one involving Ruby, her mother and Big Brain—was deleted before shooting, a number of others were added on location, including:

- Doug (Aaron Stanford) retrieves Catherine but is knocked out by Ruby's mother (Ivana Turchetto). He then wakes up in a meat locker full of dismembered body parts.
- Beast is mostly kept trapped in an abandoned car in the script but ended up being given a more active role in the film: he attacks Pluto (Michael Bailey Smith) during the latter's fight with Doug and also kills Big Brain (whose fate is left unresolved in the script).
- Doug is forced into not one but two confrontations with Lizard (Robert Joy) while trying to rescue Catherine.

- In keeping with the original film, Jupiter (Billy Drago) survives the explosion and meets his end when Brenda (de Ravin) puts a pickaxe through his skull.

Interestingly, some scripted scenes that were patterned as Craven homages and were in fact shot ended up being excised from the final cut:

- After Bob (Ted Levine) and Doug leave to find help, Ethel (Kathleen Quinlan), Lynn (Vinessa Shaw) and Brenda have a conversation that tells where the family hails from (Cleveland) as well as Bob's propensity for shortcuts.
- Ruby (Laura Ortiz) traps a rattlesnake to keep it from attacking Bobby (Dan Byrd).
- After radioing for help on the CB, Ethel and Lynn get a response that sounds like heavy breathing.
- Doug and Lynn make love in the back of the SUV, unaware that Pluto is siphoning gas outside. Ironically, this was the first scene shot with make-up effects.
- Big Brain (Desmond Askew) tells Doug that Catherine 'is in the last house on the left...'

These were of course voluntary deletions, whereas two minutes had to be cut from the film at the MPAA's insistence in order to avoid an NC-17 rating. The deleted footage included:

- Lizard draining the blood from the Carters' dead parakeet into his mouth.
- Close-ups of Bob burning and his eyes turning white.
- A close-up of Lynne being shot in the head by Lizard.
- A shot of Lizard pointing a gun at Catherine.
- Half a minute of Brenda's rape scene.
- A close-up of Cyst (Greg Nicotero) with a pickaxe in his skull.
- An extra shot of Papa Jupiter eating Ethel's heart.
- Doug's second fight with Lizard is shortened from seven strikes and three gunshots to five strikes and two gunshots.

'I tried to explain to [the MPAA] that there are two kinds of violence, the one that is very seductive, very attractive and the one that's very repulsive,' Aja reasoned to the website Zap2It. 'I found out something which is funny—when your acting is bad, really bad, you can really go as far as you want, because they think it becomes like a joke. If you have a very realistic approach of acting and if it's as real as you can, as I think we did in *Hills Have Eyes,* it becomes much more tricky to have them let you go through.'

Hills was released by Fox Searchlight Pictures on March 10, 2006, to a $15.7 million opening weekend, on its way to a cumulative American box office take of $41.7 million, with an additional $27.8 million foreign gross. It was well received by both *The Boston Globe* ('*Hills* is surprisingly artful and, believe it or not, about as much fun as a grisly horror movie can be') and the *New York Times* ('*Hills* confirms

the promise of *High Tension*...No one else under 30 makes movies this savage—and disturbingly symptomatic').

The vast majority of critics, however, were put off by the film's Gorno style. '*The Hills Have Eyes* should not be rated R,' declared the *Chicago Tribune*. 'It should be rated NC-17, or ITTS-OW, which stands for Is This Thing Sadistic, Or What?' *USA Today* was totally dismissive: 'Nothing is right about this ridiculous horror schlockfest...Don't expect logic, coherence or even resolution here,' while *Variety* warned that 'the audience will feel bloodied and bruised by the end credits.' 'This remake of the 1977 Wes Craven alleged classic has one very disturbing quality: It's too damned good,' remarked *The Washington Post*. 'It establishes what we already knew...the presence in a substantial percentage of our species of a morbid imagination, which is provoked by images of carnage and violence.'

Aja and Levasseur went on to make the Kiefer Sutherland thriller *Mirrors* (2008) as well as the much-maligned, all-star 3D remake of the New World cult film *Piranha* (2010). Craven, however, would take a much more active role in the next *Hills* excursion.

THE HILLS HAVE EYES PART II

(1984)

The reason I did *Hills 2* is because I was dead broke and needed to do any film. I would have directed Godzilla Goes to Paris. It got me going again, and got me some money in the bank, and it got my confidence back a little bit.

—Wes Craven, writer and director

The flashback by the dog was genius...I think that scene is fantastic.

—Peter Locke, co-producer

After two years (1979-80) writing and preparing a Colombian drug-smuggling movie that never got made (*Marimba*), Wes Craven directed his first theatrical feature in four years, Polygram's *Deadly Blessing,* about murders in a Hutterite community. Released in August 1981, the film was a minor success (an $8 million gross on a $2.5 million budget) and led to his bid for mainstream acceptance, the $3 million comic book adaptation *Swamp Thing*. Despite some good notices, the film nevertheless got lost in the shuffle during the 1982 buyout of Avco Embassy Pictures by Norman Lear and Jerry Perenchio and floundered, earning just $2 million in rentals. In the succeeding years it developed a cult following, resulting in a 1989 sequel (*The Return of Swamp Thing*) and a cable TV series that ran from 1990-1993.

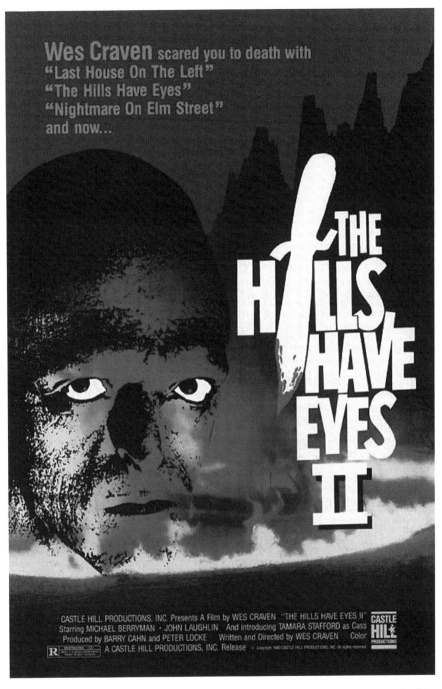

After the failure of *Swamp Thing*, Craven and Peter Locke were approached by Adrienne Fancey and Guy Collins— heads of, respectively, New Realm Entertainment and Video Tape Centre—concerning a sequel to *The Hills Have Eyes*. New Realm had released *Hills* theatrically in England in February 1979, while VTC had made a fortune from releasing *Hills* on videotape there in 1981-82. 'They had done so well with the sales of the *Hills Have Eyes* cassette…that they were in a position to finance a sequel,' Craven told *Fangoria*. 'They pursued us on the matter for about a year and a half, telling me that any time I wanted to write a sequel to *Hills*, I could do it.'

With nothing else on the front burner, Craven decided to oblige Fancey and Collins and knocked out a quick draft of what he originally called *The Night of Jupiter*. 'They liked it so well that they immediately gave us the money,' said Craven. 'I had written that first draft pretty quickly, over a period of about two weeks; I then sat down and wrote a really good revision of it—and then they got *really* excited about it.'

Eight years after his experiences in the desert, Bobby Carter is plagued by nightmares and is seeing a psychiatrist. Now the owner of a successful Yamaha dealership in Los Angeles, he sponsors a motocross team and has developed a special, high-octane racing fuel. Bobby's business manager—and his wife—is none other than Ruby, the formerly feral daughter of Papa Jupiter who is now reformed and goes by the name of Rachel. Bobby's racing crew includes two riders (Roy and Harry), two mechanics (Foster and Hulk) and girlfriends Cass (who is blind), Julie and Sue. A big race is being held in the Mojave Desert, but because of its proximity to the events of eight years ago, Bobby cannot bring himself to go along, so Rachel goes instead. On the way, the group picks up Bobby's Alsatian, Beast, from a stud farm. The race is being held on the first Sunday in April, which is the start of daylight savings time, but since no one remembers this fact, the group is an hour behind. To make up time they decide to take a shortcut through the desert, despite Rachel and Cass's protests. Their bus hits a rut and ruptures the gas tank, forcing the group to stop outside a seemingly-abandoned mining compound. While exploring the camp, Rachel is attacked by her still-wild brother Pluto—whom she thought dead—who ends up stealing one of the team's motorbikes. Roy and Harry give chase but Harry is knocked off his bike by a tripwire and crushed by a falling boulder. Roy catches up with Pluto before being attacked by a huge wild man called the Reaper, who drags Pluto away, then comes back for Roy. The youngster tries to get away but is caught in a net and knocked out by the giant. When Roy and Harry fail to return, Hulk and Rachel head out to look for them but Hulk is caught in a trap and speared by a crossbow. After getting into a fight with Sue, Foster goes to the bus where he finds a huge knife in the dirt; before he can pick it up, he is dragged underneath the bus, castrated, has his fingers cut off and is partially devoured. While exploring the compound, Jane and Cass find a caravan that is full of blood, bones, pinups, knives and debris—Jane also finds Foster's body stuffed in a wardrobe before

she is attacked and mutilated by the Reaper, who later on stabs Sue to death for good measure. Wandering back to camp, Rachel is once again attacked by Pluto, who is then attacked by Beast. Pluto runs off with Beast in pursuit. Rachel soon finds herself hunted by the Reaper until she falls into a pit lined with spikes and is impaled. While chasing Pluto, Beast finds Roy and revives him; Pluto arrives to kill Roy but Beast attacks and pushes him off a cliff and he falls to his death. The Reaper attacks Cass but she manages to get away, running to the caravan where a refrigerator leads to a mineshaft. She goes down into a vast underground cavern that is full of meathooks, knives, saws, old clothes and cleavers: a slaughterhouse that also contains the bodies of Hulk and Sue. The Reaper goes into the cavern after Cass but she finds another shaft and begins to climb up the rope before being pulled to safety by Roy, who has heard her cries for help. The two use the tank of super fuel to make the bus into a trap for the Reaper. Acting as bait, Roy entices the Reaper to an area outside the bus before the two are encircled by fire; Roy escapes by being pulled through the flames by a tow-cable attached to a mine car. The Reaper goes into the bus to escape the flames but the lake of super fuel underneath the bus causes a massive explosion. Thinking themselves to be safe, Roy and Cass enjoy a brief celebration before the Reaper, now charred and disfigured, comes charging again at the couple. They manage to sidestep the giant's assault and send him plunging into a mineshaft.

With Craven's script in hand, Fancey and Collins went to the 1983 Cannes Film Festival, where they also showed prospective buyers a promo reel containing highlights of the first *Hills*. Thorn EMI Screen Entertainment ended up acquiring the world rights, which put the picture in profit before it was even made. On a budget of $700,000, what became known as *The Hills Have Eyes Part II* went into production at 29 Palms, Joshua Tree, Pioneertown and Yucca Valley, California that September. 'We figured, let's have some fun and do it,' Craven reasoned. 'So we're going to go out and have a rip in the desert. I know there's a certain amount of snobbery about a director doing a sequel to his own film. But screw that!'

SERGEANT
One pole here. Another here, then a chain between. Make it good and sturdy—I don't wanna have to go in there lookin' for no more asshole offroaders.

PRIVATE
They really lose another bunch last week?

SERGEANT
Damn right. Bunch of kids snuck in to look for an old gold

mine or somethin', and just goddamn disappeared. Same shit
as always. We send in patrols, and the patrols don't find
nothin', just like always.

PRIVATE
Been going on for ten years. 'Bout time they closed the
damn place off and left it to the snakes.

—Unfilmed exchange, from the original script

Whatever conceits Craven may have had about making a sequel to his own movie
were soon dispelled by the criminally-low budget (the director's smallest since the
first *Hills*) and breakneck shooting schedule (just 24 days) that made it next to
impossible to film the script as written:

- The script begins with a nightmare sequence where Bobby awakens to find
Pluto standing over him with a pistol. He puts the gun in Bobby's mouth and
pulls the trigger—the gunshot bringing Bobby back to reality. He is comforted
by Rachel, whom we are meant to recognise as Ruby from the first film, and it
is revealed that the two are now married. The film eschews all this and simply
starts with Bobby (Robert Houston) at the psychiatrist's office.
- After the bus gets off the main road, the script features a scene with an army
patrol where the squad fixes the fence that is supposed to block the short cut and
the exchange highlighted above takes place. None of this was shot.
- The motorbike chase between Roy and the Reaper was written to be fairly long
and witnessed by the rest of the racing crew. As shot, it is almost comically brief,
which is not helped by the obviously undercranked film when Roy (Kevin Blair)
is caught in the Reaper's (John Bloom) net.
- In the script, both Foster and Jane are brutally mutilated by the Reaper.
This was changed to Foster's (Willard Pugh) death being off-camera while Jane
(Colleen Riley) is merely crushed to death in the Reaper's arms.
- In Rachel's (Janus Blythe) second confrontation with Pluto (Michael
Berryman), a line was added during shooting where she identifies the Reaper as
'Papa Jupe's big brother'. This makes no sense in light of the feral clan's history
from the first film and was not in the original script.
- After being struck by Hulk's lifeless body, the script has Rachel fall backwards
into a pit lined with spikes and impaled. This was not shot and she merely
stumbles and hits her head on a rock instead. Her character is then absent from
the rest of the film.
- The script features a scene where Cass confronts the Reaper and tricks him
into throwing a spear at the camp's generator, which explodes. She then grabs
the wooden handle and lunges at the Reaper with the hot spear, seriously
wounding him in the process. None of this was shot.
- The Reaper was meant to have survived the bus explosion and come after Roy
and Cass a second time before plunging to his death in a mineshaft. The film

does not give him such recuperative powers, and the Reaper simply dies in the explosion.

'It was a much better script, I think, than the movie turned out to be,' Craven confessed to Kim Newman. 'It was an important film for me to do, just to get the momentum going again, but it was very underfunded. The movie was originally budgeted on the first draft of the script, and the producers said they thought it should be expanded, so I wrote a much better and bigger script, but the budget stayed the same. It was a real nightmare to shoot.'

Post-production was taken over by co-producers Barry Cahn and Jonathan Debin since Craven had moved on to direct the TV movie *Invitation to Hell* (in which *All My Children*'s soap queen Susan Lucci plays the devil) and answer the green light that he had finally gotten from Robert Shaye's New Line Cinema to put his long-gestating script *A Nightmare on Elm Street* into production. Before Craven knew it, *Hills Part II* was being screened at the 1984 Cannes Film Festival. 'It was not intended to be released as it was,' he revealed. 'It was not completed, and I had an agreement that when we'd finished the initial shoot the producers would cut it together and we'd see what we needed. Then we'd go shoot for another five or six days. That was agreed upon but they decided to make an answer print. Suddenly they were acting as if that was the finished film.'[5]

'Wes needed money for re-shoots and I wasn't able to get him the money...so we had to finish the movie prematurely,' Locke told Kamera Film Salon. 'It was not ready...to be shown.' When the film was finally put on limited release by Castle Hill Productions in August 1985, those few critics who managed to catch it found themselves in total agreement with Locke: 'Craven's sequel to his earlier film lands with a resounding thud...[the] ludicrous screenplay is so bad that even the derogatory laughs aren't there' (*Cinefantastique*); 'This movie is so shallow and pointless that it goes beyond the usual horror idiocy and enters the realm of anti-humanity. Its plot is so simple I couldn't even follow it' (*Philadelphia Daily News*); 'Craven...shows his contempt for the project in one very funny scene: after numerous flashbacks by characters recalling the first film's events (and padding the running time with old footage), Craven runs out of survivors so suddenly the dog...has a flashback of its own!' (*Variety*).

It is the latter scene that is actually the sole surviving trace of any inspiration left in a project that was obviously rushed and patched together with scenes and music that look and sound like out-takes from the latest *Friday the 13th* movie (not surprisingly, as *Friday the 13th* composer Harry Manfredini did the score for *Hills Part II*). Because of its name recognition, *Hills Part II* did end up being a home video success, but for Craven, the film was merely a way-station as he advanced towards the *Nightmare* that lay ahead.

(2007)

Sometimes experimenting means going back to the roots. And maybe you don't do it different...to the horror genre [in general], but

---

5 Thorn EMI Screen Entertainment submitted *Hills 2* to the British Board of Film Censors for certification in April 1984, when it received an 18 rating with no cuts required. Thorn EMI released the film directly to video in the UK in January 1985.

different to what the horror genre right now looks like…and trying to be more true to the roots and going back to the classics.

—Martin Weisz, director

I found that making sequels to my old films is a fun way to make films with young directors and keep it all in motion. This particular cycle of horror is not going to last forever, so we just try to make films and keep them interesting.

—Wes Craven, co-writer and co-producer

With *The Hills Have Eyes* remake pulling in nearly $70 million worldwide, it was inevitable that there would be a *Hills Have Eyes 2*. Craven's original concept for *Hills 2* was much like that of his own 1984 sequel: namely, that one of the survivors (in this case, Brenda) would end up returning to the desert to face the mutants once again. However, instead of being on a motocross team, young Brenda would now be part of a National Guard unit that is called upon to rid

the hinterlands of Papa Jupiter's family of freaks. With that premise in mind, Emilie de Ravin was scheduled to reprise the role of Brenda, while Englishman Michael J. Bassett, the writer/director of the World War I horror film *Deathwatch* (2002), was recruited to write and direct the sequel.

Unfortunately, Craven ended up losing both of them to scheduling conflicts: de Ravin was on the hit TV series *Lost* and Bassett went to work on the script for the Robert E Howard adaptation, *Solomon Kane*.[6] If *Hills 2* was going to happen, it was clear that it would take Craven's direct involvement. 'I offered to write it and I invited [my son] Jon to come with me,' he told the Canadian website Horror-Movies. 'The first draft had to be finished in a month, so we basically checked into a hotel for the month of May [2006] and came up with what we thought was a really good script. And in all honesty there were parallels between the National Guard out in the desert up against terrible threats, and so there seemed to be a certain relevance to it as well.'

'We've been at war for over five years,' observed Craven, 'with people who are unidentifiable from innocent civilians, there are people who are willing to climb into a truck and blow themselves up and how do you deal with that, how do you wrap your head around that, and part of the spine of writing this

The Hills Have Eyes II (2007)

---

6 Bassett probably ended up wishing he had stayed on *Hills 2*. Despite delivering the *Solomon Kane* script in August 2006, the film did not enter production until January 2008 under Bassett's direction. It then sat on the shelf for two years before finally being commercially released in Europe. To date, the $40 million film has not been released in America.

script was, "Let's take some National Guardsmen who are just kids and they're in this situation where you can't even believe what these people are doing and could be done by a human being, and smart human beings.'"

'It certainly was a great process for me,' said Jonathan Craven, who would also co-produce the film. 'Having ideas and bouncing them off someone you know so well is a great experience...anyone who has ever written with someone in a room, it's really hard to get along and add to that the explosive potential elements of family, but we actually got along really well.'

In the top secret Sector 16, located in the mountains of Yucca Flats, Nevada, two civilian scientists and a Special Forces officer are running tests in an old 1950s command centre housed in a deserted mine. Suddenly, they are attacked by the scaly Snake and the hump-backed Stabber, two mutated monstrosities. Nearby, a National Guard unit training for deployment to Afghanistan is called to deliver equipment to the encampment. Nine soldiers—Delmar, Missy, Spitter, Amber, Crank, Mickey, Stump, Napoleon and Sergeant Millstone—arrive to find Sector 16 seemingly deserted. A walkie-talkie suddenly sputters to life with a call for help, followed by flashes of light from atop the mountain. Millstone orders the group into rescue mode, and stages a climbing assault, leaving Napoleon and Amber behind to wait for help. Napoleon goes to use the latrine but a hand thrusts up from underneath and grabs him. He calls to Amber and the two pull an injured Dr Wilson from the muck—he is covered with cuts, infected by the waste, from which he soon dies. Napoleon and Amber then discover their vehicles on fire. Amber begins to go up the hill to find

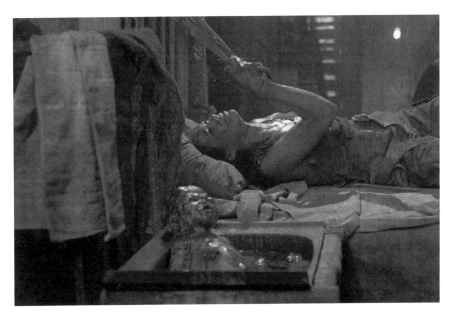

the rest of the unit when the skeletal mutant Letch emerges from a hole and grabs her. Before he can put an axe in the young soldier, the mutant is shot by Mickey—injured and returning for treatment—and retreats back to his hole. A second mutant, Grabber, reaches out and forcefully pulls Mickey into a hole that is too small for him, ripping him apart in the process. Meanwhile, the rest of the unit finds the half-naked body of Dr Han, strung up and eviscerated. Millstone is stabbed by Chameleon, a rock-contoured mutant, then accidentally shot by Spitter; Napoleon and Amber scale the mountain and join the rest of the unit, now gripped with fear and shock. They try to lower down Spitter and Millstone's body, but the rope is cut and Spitter falls to his death. On the descent, they come across the battered and bloody Colonel Redding, who shoots himself just before falling off the cliff. The unit uses Amber and Missy as bait, luring out Letch before killing him. Missy goes off to urinate but is kidnapped by Chameleon; the unit is in hot pursuit as she is dragged into the mine. Exploring through the seemingly-endless maze of tunnels, Amber and Napoleon are suddenly sucked down a flooded shaft. Delmar and Crank work to get down to them, almost dying in the process. Missy is bound and gagged and laid in front of Spitter's corpse. Chameleon tries to rape her, sticking his abnormally long tongue down her throat. She bites it off and then uses Spitter's detached leg to impale Chameleon in the genitals. Turning to escape, she runs right into the massive Uncle Hades, dragging an unconscious Stump behind him. Hades kills Stump and beats Missy mercilessly. Chameleon attacks Napoleon and Amber but the two soldiers get the better of him and Napoleon ends up smashing the mutant's head in with a rock. About to be attacked by Grabber, Amber and Napoleon are rescued by the hulking but childlike mutant Hansel. Crank and Delmar run into Grabber, Missy, Hades and Snake—Grabber and Snake are killed in the ensuing firefight but Hades escapes with Missy. Hansel leads the four soldiers through a labyrinth of chambers, passageways and a makeshift slaughterhouse where they find the half-eaten bodies of Millstone and Mickey. Delmar suddenly dies from gunshot wounds he suffered in the fight with the mutants. The remaining trio make their way to the old command centre but Napoleon and Amber decide to go back for Missy, with Hansel in tow. Crank finds an old case of dynamite and accidentally ignites it, killing himself and injuring the others. Recovered, the trio set out to find Missy but run into Stabber, who is himself stabbed to death by Amber. She and Napoleon finally find a battered and barely conscious Missy, then have a brutal, bloody battle royal with Hades, which ends with the giant being felled. Hansel then leads the exhausted survivors to what they presume is safety but in fact is another mine—with another group of mutants waiting for them...

The Cravens delivered their script on June 16. With production scheduled for September, it was imperative that a director be found. Wes Craven's partner Marianne Maddalena had just seen and been impressed by the German film *Grimm Love* (2006), which was inspired by the actual Armin Meiwes cannibal-murder case. It follows an American graduate student writing her thesis on a notorious cannibal killer who actually found a willing victim via the internet. The movie was the first feature for 40-year-old Martin Weisz, a veteran of music videos (for such artists as Brandy, Fuel, Korn, Puff Daddy and Sisqo) and hundreds of commercials, and whose debut won him Best Director at the Sitges Fantasy Film Festival. 'Marianne...had seen *Grimm Love* and spoke with the other producers about me,' Weisz told Bloody Disgusting. 'I was sent the script, read it and went to a meeting with Marianne, Wes and some others. Then Wes saw *Grimm Love* and knew I could go to very dark places. We had another meeting and I had the job.'

The Hills Have Eyes 2 began filming on September 11, once again at the CLA Studios in Ouarzazate, Morocco on a $15 million budget. 'Even though we didn't shoot at any location used in the last one,' Weisz told the website RadioFree, 'it was obviously the same kind of vast desert field. And they also had the stages from the last time that we used for the interiors and the mines...And they all knew, I guess, what to budget with and everything, because they had the experience from the last time.'

NAPOLEON
Look!

He points, incredulous—

IN THEIR POV—SPITTER'S BODY, no, Spitter himself is twitching—no, moving! He reaches an arm out—miraculously alive after the fall—

AMBER
He's alive!

They're delirious—yelling his name!

ALL
Spitter! Hang on!

Spitter looks up—then his whole body lifts off the ore car—levitating!

Their jaws drop open. Then, with the light just right, they see the RUSTY OLD CABLES tied to Spitter's wrists and ankles—cables that run up to another hole in the rock face, not that different from their own!

CRANK
Fuckers!

He unleashes at the opening—three bursts that rock the tunnel and smack into the opposite hole with high-velocity slugs. There's a HOOT of surprise or injury or maybe mockery—hard to say which—and the cables are dropped.

Spitter's body crashes back into the ore hopper like a sack of rocks. It lays there lifeless, as in fact it always was.

−Unfilmed scene, from the original script

Despite having such a short window between script delivery and the start of production, and regardless of the fact that Craven *père et fils* wrote and produced *Hills 2*, a number of scenes were nevertheless cut from their script:

- Napoleon and Amber almost fall to their deaths after they hit the drop off while chasing Chameleon and Missy. They are saved by Crank.
- Cornered inside the mine by the squad, Chameleon uses Missy as a human shield and makes a getaway.
- Chameleon causes a cave-in on Amber and Napoleon when he pulls down a rotten beam.
- Hansel's room is covered with chalk drawings of soldiers killing mutants.
- Hansel takes the squad to a burial chamber where hundreds of bones are all that is left of his people.
- The squad finds Millstone's mutilated body hanging on a meat hook in a makeshift slaughterhouse.
- After the dynamite explosion, Napoleon, Amber and Hansel return to the hub room and find Crank's head, still wearing an expression of shock.
- Amber tries to get Napoleon to leave without her, but he refuses.

As with the previous *Hills* excursion, several things were added or changed on location in the desert, to include:

- A title sequence was added involving a 'breeder' giving birth to a stillborn mutant baby.
- A third scientist named Dr Foster (Philip Pavel) is now on the scene, only to be killed by Stabber (Tyrell Kemlo).
- Missy was meant to awaken in Hades' lair and find herself lying next to the remnants of Spitter's corpse. This was changed to her finding the dead baby in a sink (a scene that did not make the final cut).
- Stump's death was changed from being killed by Hades to having him fall to his death when Stabber amputates one of his arms.
- In a scene not in the script, Hades (Michael Bailey Smith) brutally rapes Missy (Daniella Alonso).
- Originally, Hades is killed when Napoleon impales him while he strangles Amber. As shot, Hades revives after this and it takes a sledgehammer to the groin from Missy and a bayonet in the mouth from Napoleon (Michael McMillian) to put the main mutant down for good.
- In the script, Hansel leads Amber, Napoleon and Missy to what they think is safety but is actually another trap. This was changed to the trio escaping the

mine only to find Hansel (David Reynolds) outside gnawing on a corpse and grinning. This was in turn changed in post production to the trio escaping the mine but being watched on thermal imaging by an unidentified mutant.

In conferring with his cinematographer Sam McCurdy, Weisz sought a visual style that harked back much further than the Alexandre Aja/Gorno love of the '70s aesthetic. 'We wanted to go back to the roots, and watched old classics,' said Weisz. 'And we watched a lot of new films. I mean, we took like ten horror films and [noticed] there is one thing that's actually common to all of them—they all look very glossy, very manufactured. And they're just very translated into the pop culture of Generation X nowadays. But there is such a big genre following out there that we said, "They all still love the classics. Why don't we, besides watching the new stuff, watch the old stuff and see what's different really?" And you see some differences, like you're lingering on shots a little bit longer, you stay more with the character...And that's kind of what we tried to do. And so in a way, I think that sets us a little bit apart, because it's not just a normal popcorn ride."

While Weisz was allowed some leeway as to the style and pace of the film, Jonathan Craven was on set for the entire three-and-a-half month shoot to ensure that his father's franchise was safeguarded. Wes Craven showed up for the final two weeks of shooting, both to work with the lagging second unit and to solve a labour dispute that threatened to derail the production. 'The crew didn't want to work anymore,' Weisz revealed to Bloody Disgusting. 'They stopped working. They thought they were getting screwed. During the last week of shooting, the producers renegotiated and got things up and running again...[but] I loved the crew and had a great time working with them. Like the previous film, it was a very international crew—people from England, Italy, Ireland, Morocco, everywhere.'

With only three months allocated to post-production, Weisz was forced to rely more on old-fashioned prosthetic effects than the now-standard CGI technology. 'We tried to stay a lot [with] practical [effects] just because of turnaround,' he admitted to RadioFree. 'We had a very tight turnaround, a very tight schedule in terms of post, so we tried to shoot a lot of stuff in-camera.' According to the director,

the hand of Wes Craven was heavy during the editing process: 'He's a producer, so you're always going to be doing his cut. And he has final cut, so it's always going to be his last word, of course.'

Hills 2 was released on March 23, 2007, to a $9.6 million opening weekend, which accounted for roughly half of its cumulative American box-office take of $20.8 million, with an additional $16.6 million earned overseas. It received guarded endorsements from both the *New York Times* ('Gleefully sensationalistic and paced like an adults-only shoot-em-up video game, it's ultimately less interested in subversion and subtext than in making viewers squirm, shriek and throw up into their popcorn bags') and *Variety* ('The politics of *Hills 2* won't enlist any new converts to the horror ranks, but existing fans will be drawn to the combination of visceral tension, violent payoff and the patented Craven gift for innovative gore'). As with its predecessor, however, most of the critics were quick to dismiss *Hills 2*. *Entertainment Weekly* wrote it off as 'A retro horror-comedy featuring quick deaths and cheapo-looking gore, with a few dorky laughs and gross-outs but not so many scares.' The *Los Angeles Times* judged, 'It turns out to be at best uninteresting and at worst as offensive as the rape scene that's been woven into the mix.' The *New York Daily News* opined: 'On the whole, this is an awfully long slog through very arid terrain, in which generic soldiers track, fight and try to escape from generic villains (you'd be surprised at how uninteresting mutant flesh-eaters can be).' And

Premiere magazine advised: 'the atmosphere for horror movies might be better if moviemakers stopped making ones like this.'

Hills 2 was the first in-house release for Fox Atomic, which had been created in late 2006 as parent company 20th Century Fox's attempt to have a low-budget, comedy/horror division akin to Sony's Screen Gems or The Weinstein Company's Dimension. Its inaugural release was the horror film pickup *Turistas* in December. *Hills 2* came next, followed by the horror sequel *28 Weeks Later* in May 2007 and the sports comedy *The Comebacks* in October. None of these films were successful in relation to their cost.

In January 2008, Fox Atomic scaled back its production operations and shut down its marketing division, with all of its productions now being released either by the parent company or the Fox Searchlight division. In April 2009, Fox Atomic was closed down entirely, with its remaining productions—*12 Rounds, I Love You Beth Cooper, Post Grad* and *Jennifer's Body*—being unloaded during the rest of the year.

Fox Atomic had a comic book division, and in July 2007 it published the graphic novel *The Hills Have Eyes: The Beginning* by Jimmy Palmiotti and Justin Gray. A prequel to both 21st century *Hills* films, it relates the backstory of the miners who refused to leave their small New Mexico town once the US government began above-ground atomic testing. Spanning multiple generations, it is revealed how the once-normal citizens slowly devolved into murderous mutants. The comic was one of only four published by Fox Atomic (*28 Days Later: The Aftermath* and two volumes of Thomas Ligotti's *The Nightmare Factory* being the others) before the demise of the company.

A NIGHTMARE ON ELM STREET

(1984)

I really feel this will be a landmark film for me, my watershed film. It's not an ordinary, run-of-the-mill little film. There's really something quite extraordinary about it. It's going to be a nice piece of work.

—Wes Craven, writer and director

I like the movie a lot, but I would have liked to have seen Freddy as more than just a personification of abstract evil.

—Robert Englund, 'Fred Krueger'

After the failure of *Swamp Thing* and the debacle of *Hills Have Eyes Part II*, Wes Craven desperately needed to get back on track. Salvation, appropriately enough,

A Nightmare on Elm Street (1984)

would come in the form of a nightmare: 'I had always had dream sequences in my movies,' he told the *Chicago Tribune*. 'Then I conceived the idea of doing an entire film as a dream but I couldn't figure out a way to do it. Then I read several stories in the *Los Angeles Times*. They were about healthy young men in their 20s who died during nightmares. They would try to stay awake, and they would describe the nightmares to their families. Finally there would be a scream and the guy would be dead. Death by nightmare...I thought it was perfect set-up for a horror film.'

Unfortunately, no one else thought so, and Craven's script *A Nightmare on Elm Street* bounced from studio to studio until it landed at Robert Shaye's New Line Cinema in 1982. For the next two years Shaye attempted to get financing for the film while Craven kept himself busy at the typewriter, telling *Fangoria*: 'I wrote about twelve different full-length treatments for various projects; re-writes for people, script doctoring, and several things of my own.'

However, he never lost hope that he would get to make his most offbeat, challenging script: 'It was the first thing I wrote that I wasn't commissioned to write. It was a departure for me. This movie is not based on everyday reality; it has a prosaic quality. I'm standing conventional scenes on their heads. A lot of scenes start off normally and then, all of a sudden, you don't know what the hell to expect next. It takes place as much in dreams as it does in reality.'

Tina, Rod, Nancy and Glen are two high school couples who share similar nightmares about a horribly-scarred man in a worn fedora and dirty red and yellow sweater who comes after them using a taloned glove, which he scrapes menacingly against metal. During a sleepover, Tina is suddenly and viciously attacked in her bedroom by an unseen force while Rod watches on helplessly. He flees the scene before Nancy

and Glen break into the room to find it covered in blood and Tina's lifeless body on the bed. Assuming Rod to be the killer, Lt Donald Thompson—Nancy's father—arrests the boy even though he denies perpetrating the crime. The next day at school Nancy falls asleep in English class only to be lured by Tina—in a body bag—to a boiler room where she is attacked by the nightmare killer. Burning herself on a hot pipe, she wakes up screaming, with the burn mark still on her arm. That night she falls asleep in the bathtub and is almost drowned when she is pulled into what seems like a bottomless well. Later on, Nancy dreams that Rod is being attacked in his cell by the fedora-wearing fiend. She and Glen rush to the police station, only to find that Rod has seemingly hung himself. Nancy's mother Marge takes her to the UCLA Institute for the Study of Sleep Disorders where her nightmares register off the chart; Marge and the doctor are stunned when Nancy awakens, now clutching the killer's hat. Inside the hat is embroidered a name: Fred Krueger. This revelation sends the alcoholic Marge on a bender—in a drunken rage she slaps Nancy and then has bars put on all the windows of the house. Taking Nancy to the basement, Marge shows the girl Krueger's taloned glove and tells her the whole story. Krueger was in fact a child murderer who escaped justice on a technicality. Enraged and fearing for their children's safety, a citizens' group (including Nancy's parents and those of her friends) took it upon themselves to trap and murder Krueger. He died in a fireball, vowing revenge on the mob's children. That night Glen falls asleep, only to be dragged into his bed and vomited out in a geyser of blood. With her friends all dead, Nancy resolves to bring Krueger into the real world, where he can be arrested by her father.

She rigs the house with booby traps and sets her alarm clock. Falling asleep, her dream takes her back to the boiler room where she finds Krueger and leads him to her house where she grabs onto him just as the alarm rings. Now in the land of the awake, Krueger chases Nancy through the house of traps until she is able to set him on fire. A walking inferno, Krueger decides to take revenge on Marge—Nancy and her father find them wrestling on the bed. After extinguishing the burning bodies, only Marge's corpse is left before it sinks into the bed and vanishes. Krueger returns one last time but Nancy is ready for

him—she denies his existence and orders him to return things to the way they were. With no more fear to fuel him, Krueger disintegrates. The next morning things are apparently restored—Marge pledges to quit drinking and sees Nancy off to school. But as Nancy walks into an unusually thick fog, some girls skipping warn her with a song:
One, two, Freddy's coming for you
Three, four, better lock your door
Five, six, get your crucifix
Seven, eight, gonna stay up late
Nine, ten, never sleep again...

In March 1984 it was announced that *A Nightmare on Elm Street* would finally go into production as a $2.5 million co-venture between New Line and two British companies, Smart Egg Pictures and Video Tape Centre (VTC), the latter of which had just co-financed Craven's *Hills Have Eyes* sequel. VTC ended up dropping out at the last minute, however, and was replaced by the American video company Media Home Entertainment, a division of Heron Communications.

With a start date pencilled in for May 1, Craven set to work casting his latest picture. The pivotal role of dream slayer Fred Krueger went to 36-year-old Robert Englund, who had begun his career in the mid-1970s with bit parts in studio films like *Hustle, St Ives* and *A Star is Born* before gaining notice for his portrayal of the sex-crazed Buck in Tobe Hooper's *Eaten Alive* (1976). Englund then became a guest player on numerous TV series including *Charlie's Angels, CHiPs, Police Woman* and *Soap,* while continuing to show up in drive-in movies like *The Great Smokey Roadblock* (1977) and *The Fifth Floor* (1980). In the early 1980s, he returned to the horror genre with memorable appearances in *Dead and Buried* and *Galaxy of Terror* (both 1981) before winning his biggest role yet, that of Willie, the lizard alien with a conscience in the TV mini-series *V* (1983) and *V: The Final Battle* (1984).

'I started by looking at big stunt guys who could do the stunts,' Craven told Shock Till You Drop. 'Then we looked at old men for the 'old man' element. Those that were alive had reached a certain gentleness. The stunt guys have a totally different mentality. They don't want to go someplace dark and creepy. Robert Englund wanted to. You need an actor who can bring a complete sense of commitment to that character without making it silly and not be afraid to go in there to the point where someone might say, "Oh, you got bad in you?" You have to be brave enough and mature enough to know we've all got it, and you're not afraid of putting it out there.'

'I didn't know exactly what the Fred Krueger character was to be,' Englund explained to *Fangoria*, 'so I went into the interview looking as punk-rocked, psychoed-out as I could with a four-day beard growth...I let Wes do all the talking while I stared at him with my Lee Harvey Oswald stare and I got the part!'

After the notional heroine, Tina (played by *Fast Times at Ridgemont High*'s Amanda Wyss), is killed off *Psycho*-style in the first act, her place is taken by Nancy Thompson, played by 19-year-old Heather Langenkamp, whose only previous experience had been Francis Ford Coppola's *The Outsiders* (1983)—where her scenes ended up on the cutting-room floor—and the little-seen John Gardner adaptation

Nickel Mountain (1984).[7] Nevertheless, she was optimistic about *Nightmare* being a film apart from the average teen slice-and-dicer: 'The kids have a real relationship with one another and a real care about what happens to the others. And it *is* one of those movies where the parents are sort of the bad guys and the kids are the good, heroic, virtuous people.'

The part of Nancy's boyfriend Glen Lantz went to a complete unknown who would subsequently go on to become one of Hollywood's biggest stars: 20-year-old Johnny Depp. 'I always thought it would be real cool to act and I was always intrigued by it,' he said. 'My friend, Nicolas Cage, tried to talk me into it, but I said "Nah". Finally, I was walking down Melrose Avenue looking for a job with a friend and we ran into Nick and his agent. Three days later I met Wes and got the part.'

Elm Street finally entered production on June 11, on a $1.8 million budget, and Englund under some eight pounds of makeup. 'Wes wanted me to get outrageous at times and he would have me do scenes two or three takes because I tended to underplay it. I thought the elaborate makeup would do most of that for me.'

Craven himself got a bit carried away with the surrealist theatrics of the piece—almost to the detriment of his life and that of his crew during the scene where Glen is sucked into his bed and becomes a geyser of blood. 'The weight of the fluid was so great that the room began to tip the other way and the water immediately rushed in that direction,' Craven related to *Cinefantastique*. 'The whole room just went spinning out of control like a giant carnival ride with fluid flying every which way. The cameras were drenched and we were almost killed. All the lights shorted out. By the time they got us down we were soaked.'

In fact, the logistical problems of engineering the film's nightmare effects bogged Craven down to the point that his old friend Sean Cunningham was called in to lend a hand. 'Cunningham [came in] on the very last day,' Langenkamp told *Fangoria*, 'and he was 180 degrees different from Wes...Wes is a lot more soft-spoken, while Sean gestured much more and was much more *emphatic* about everything...I guess it was necessary because we were really running out of time and we needed a good second-unit director.' However, the actress was quick to add that *Elm Street* had not been a *total* nightmare to shoot: 'There's a lot of humour in this movie. Wes has such an incredible sense of humour that, if you're really looking for it, you'll find it in every scene.'

NANCY

So he's alive?

MARGE smiles grimly.

MARGE

He wouldn't've stopped. The bastard would've got more kids first chance he got—they found nearly ten bodies in his boiler room as it was. But the law couldn't touch him.

---

7 Langenkamp beat 200 other actresses—including then-unknowns Courteney Cox, Jennifer Grey and Demi Moore—to land the role.

At the mention of 'boiler room', NANCY gives a shake. MARGE misses this, too busy taking a pull on the bottle that's never left her hand.

> MARGE (CONTD)
> What was needed were some private citizens willing to do what had to be done.

She reels slowly, looking at NANCY in defiance.

> NANCY
> (HUSHED)
> What did you do, mother?

MARGE cradles the bottle.

> MARGE
> Bunch of us parents tracked him down after they let him go.
> Found him in an old boiler room, just like before. Saw him lying there in that caked red and yellow sweater he always wore, drunk an' asleep with his weird knives by his side...

> NANCY
> (DREADING IT)
> Go on...

MARGE reaches over and taps a dusty two-gallon jug of gasoline near the lawn mower.

> MARGE
> We poured gasoline all around the place, left a trail out the door, locked the door, then...

She mimes striking a match—

> MARGE (CONTD)
> WHOOSH!!!

Her arms shoot up and her eyes go wide with the light of that fire. There's awe in her voice. Then she drops her arms.

> MARGE (CONTD)
> (HUSHED, REMEMBERING)
> But just when it seemed not even the devil could live in there any more—he crashed out like a banshee, all on fire—swinging those

fingerknives every which direction and screaming he...he was going to get us by killing all our kids...

She stops with a sudden quake and drinks for a long moment. But the intake doesn't hide the image. Her face bathed in tears, she looks at her daughter and shakes her head.

MARGE (CONTD)

There were all those men, Nancy, even your father, oh yes, even him. But none could do what had to be done—Krueger rolling and screaming so loud the whole state could hear—no one could take your father's gun and kill him good and proper except me.

She sweeps her hand across the air in a terrific slash, then stops, her hand shaking, her voice hoarse and terrified. She looks at her daughter, begging.

—Unfilmed exchange, from the original script

Despite the fact that the *Elm Street* script was Craven's pride and joy, he was nevertheless forced by time constraints and logistics to trim a number of scenes, including:

- After making love, Rod and Tina were to be shown covered in a dirty red and yellow blanket that matches Krueger's sweater.[8]
- After Nancy nearly drowns in the bathtub, Marge was to put her to bed and give her a sleeping pill, which the girl promptly spits out when her mother leaves the room.
- Several of the exchanges between Dr King and Marge at the sleep lab were dropped, including King telling Marge about Filipino refugees in California dying in their sleep from nightmares.
- When King tries to awaken Nancy, we were meant to switch to her POV and see Krueger dressed in the doctor's clothes. She then hits King and knocks him off his feet.
- We were meant to see the crew putting bars on the Thompson house, which ends with Marge accusing the foreman of ripping her off.
- Desperate to save her daughter, Marge was to get in the middle of the climactic battle between Krueger and Nancy and prevent him from slicing her with his knives. In a rage, Krueger knocks Marge across her bed and is poised to strike before Nancy hits the monster in the kidneys and sends him sprawling.
- At the scene of Glen's murder, the coroner was to find one of Krueger's knives and give it to Donald, forcing him to finally believe that the dream demon is real.

---

8 Whereas in the script, Krueger's sweater was red and yellow, Craven changed it during filming, having supposedly discovered in a magazine article that the two most contrasting colours to the human retina were red and green.

Subsequently, in cutting the film down to 91 minutes, Craven was also forced to drop several scenes that had been shot:

- In her fatal dream with Krueger, Tina picks up a garbage can lid, only to find her hands are covered in worms.
- When Nancy first comes to visit Rod (Nick Corri) in jail, she tries to convince her father of his innocence, to which Donald (John Saxon) replies, 'I know, thanks to your testimony, that he was locked in a room with a girl who went in alive and came out in a rubber bag.'
- At Rod's funeral, Marge (Ronee Blakley) tells her ex-husband, 'This reminds me too much of ten years ago' and Donald responds with, 'Let's not start digging up bodies just because we're in a cemetery.'
- The revelatory exchange between Nancy and Marge (cited above) about what happened to Krueger was greatly abbreviated and changed during shooting to include the following twist: Nancy and all of her friends had brothers and sisters they never knew about that were killed by Krueger. This was apparently considered too convoluted and was dropped from the final cut.
- After Glen's death, his father tells Donald that Glen was killed by Krueger.
- In escaping the boiler room and returning to Elm Street, Nancy was supposed to be shown tumbling in the sky over the San Fernando Valley. Tests were done in front of a blue screen for this effect, but it was scrapped.

In addition, the ending was the source of some consternation between Craven, who wanted to shoot the epilogue as written, and Robert Shaye, who wanted a 'twist' that would leave the door open for future sequels. In Craven's words to *Cinefantastique*: "Bob Shaye said to me, 'Wes, I gave you this film when nobody else would. Just give me this one thing'...The ending as written was she just comes out the front door, and her mother's alive and there's a tremendous fog...she was supposed to walk off into the mist, and that would be it—which to me was a lot cleaner."

Nevertheless, Craven agreed to Shaye's request and rewrote the ending: Tina, Rod and Glen pull up in Glen's convertible and Nancy gets in—only to realise that Krueger is driving! As she tries to escape, the top comes crashing down, trapping her and her friends as the car drives off into the fog. But when it came time to shoot the scene, Craven decided to give himself some options. Four separate endings were filmed: the first was just as originally scripted; the second was as originally scripted but with the added 'Gotcha!' of Krueger suddenly dragging Marge through the front door window after the kids are gone; the third was according to the rewrite, but with the added shock finale; and the fourth was the same as the third, only without Krueger driving the car. It was the fourth ending that made the final cut.

As far as Englund was concerned, Craven should have gone with his initial instincts: 'They go through all this soft-focus stuff,' the actor told *Fangoria*, 'and you figure to yourself that it was only a dream. You pat yourself on the back for thinking that. To have had the original ending, it would have been a classic *Twilight Zone*-like ending where yes, it was a dream, but the dream never stops.'

Released in Los Angeles and New York on November 9, *Elm Street* made $1.2 million in its opening weekend. Within a month, it had broadened its release and grossed $6.5 million. By January 1985, it had grossed $9.5 million and won Best Film and Best Actress at the Avoriaz Fantastic Film Festival. The film would go on to take a total of $25.5 million at the box office—a personal best for Craven.

Just as *Elm Street* gave Craven the biggest box office of his career, so too it gave him his best reviews ever. 'The best horror film to come this direction in many a full moon,' praised *The Baltimore Sun*. '*Nightmare on Elm Street* is juicily Freudian; that's why it's potent,' analysed *The Boston Globe*. 'The slasher stuff will satisfy those who ask only blood from this genre. But it's the Freudian psychodrama embedded in the acting-out of the nightmares that makes *Nightmare on Elm Street* interesting.' 'An effective little scare piece that does well in sustaining its creepy mood,' commended *Cinefantastique*. *Variety* evaluated it as 'a highly imaginative horror film that provides the requisite shocks to keep fans of the genre happy,' while *The Washington Post* lauded: 'A Nightmare on Elm Street is halfway between an exploitation flick and classic surrealism...Craven's slasher is the most chilling figure in the genre since The Shape made his debut in *Halloween*.'

There were, of course, some who were determined to rain on Craven's parade, including the ever-antagonistic Gene Siskel, who asked his readers, 'What could be more depressing than to spend Thanksgiving morning in a movie theatre with five other adult males watching a teenage girl terrorised for 90 minutes by a phantom killer with a molten face and knives for fingers?' Kevin Thomas likewise posed the question, 'When a film is designed to drench the screen in blood—with maximum violence directed, as usual, mainly toward women—rather than to give a good, fun fright, what does it finally matter how well it was made? There does come a point when form cannot sustain or justify content, and it arrives very early in this film.' The *Village Voice* felt that Craven had definitely bitten off more than he could chew:

'*Elm Street* has so much in it that Craven has to screw it up; he's like a fisherman who hooks a whale and then cuts his line for fear it will dismantle his boat and chomp him in half. He solves the mystery; he explains what's going on; he spells out his themes in clumsy, stilted dialogue; and his actors, except for the courageous Heather Langenkamp, let him down.'

With its success at the box office and sales of videocassettes topping 100,000, Shaye was eager for another trip to *Elm Street*. Craven, however, had already contracted to write and direct an adaptation of V C Andrews's 1979 supermarket gothic *Flowers in the Attic* for New World Pictures.[9] Undaunted, Shayne pressed ahead, and *A Nightmare on Elm Street Part II*, budgeted at $3 million and written by New Line branch manager David Chaskin, began shooting under New Line trailer editor Jack Sholder in June 1985 and was rushed into cinemas that Halloween. 'We intend to establish a thriller tradition in the manner of *Friday the 13th* and *Halloween*,' Shaye told *Variety*. How right he was.

Elm Street II, subtitled *Freddy's Revenge*, earned $30 million. *A Nightmare on Elm Street 3: Dream Warriors*, co-written and co-produced by Craven, earned $45 million. Between 1988 and 1991, three more sequels were released, for a combined total of over $100 million. In 1994, Craven unsuccessfully tried to revamp the series by writing and directing the horror-movie-within-a-horror-movie *New Nightmare*, which grossed only $18 million. Freddy was then laid to rest until being resurrected in 2003 for the hit terror-titan face-off *Freddy vs Jason*.

Thanks largely to the *Elm Street* franchise—which included the *Freddy's Nightmares* TV series (1988-90) and a ton of merchandise—New Line Cinema went on to become the biggest independent in the business before being bought by Ted Turner in 1993 and becoming a part of the Time-Warner media empire three years later. With the subsequent *Austin Powers, Lord of the Rings* and *Rush Hour* film trilogies, New Line was one of the hottest studios in town before merging with parent company Warner Brothers in 2008.

Often referred to as 'The House that Freddy Built', New Line's success did not trickle down to Wes Craven's bank account. As he told Digital Spy: '[*Elm Street*] was one of my better ideas and better films, but the fact is that, because I was completely broke [when I sold the script], I completely sold the rights to it.'

After the success of *Elm Street*, Craven directed several television movies (*Chiller, Casebusters, Night Visions*) and episodes of the revived *Twilight Zone* series (1985-86), as well as creating two short-lived TV shows: *The People Next Door* (1989) and *Nightmare Cafe* (1992). Beginning with *Deadly Friend* in 1986, he also wrote and/ or directed several critically-acclaimed but commercially unsuccessful horror films, including *The Serpent and the Rainbow* (1988), *Shocker, The People Under the Stairs* and *Vampire in Brooklyn* (1995). He hit the jackpot with the *Scream* trilogy,

---

9 Initially scheduled to begin shooting on a $4 million budget in May 1985, *Flowers* was put on hold, while Craven's script—deemed too graphic by the producers—was rewritten by Hilary Henkin. This version too was rejected, and Craven was replaced on the project by Jeffrey Bloom (*Blood Beach*). Shot in the fall of 1986, *Flowers* was beset by production problems (both Bloom and star Victoria Tennant walked off the film) and not released until November 1987, when it was greeted by bad reviews and mediocre box office. Until *Rain* in 2006, it was the only one of Andrews's novels to be filmed.

featuring the now-famous 'Ghostface' killer, the success of which (over $500 million worldwide) allowed him to make his first non-horror film, *Music of the Heart* (1999), which garnered an Oscar nomination for star Meryl Streep. That same year he published his first novel, *The Fountain Society*, a cloning thriller.

Craven's status in the genre has allowed him to help other directors get their start, and he has served as a producer for Joe Gayton (*Mind Ripper*, 1995), Adam Grossman (*Carnival of Souls*, 1998), Robert Kurtzman (*Wishmaster*, 1998), Patrick Lussier (*Dracula 2000*, 2000), Robert Harmon (*They*, 2002), John Gulager (*Feast*, 2005), and Nicholas Mastandrea (*The Breed*, 2006).[10]

Craven returned to directing horror in 2003 with the werewolf movie *Cursed*, which he followed up in 2010 with *My Soul to Take* (aka *25/8*), a failed attempt at revisiting some of the themes of *Nightmare on Elm Street*.[11] His stock seemed to be due for an increase with the April 2011 release of *Scream 4,* but it ended up being the lowest-grossing entry in the series—the first to make less than $100 million worldwide.

(2010)

This is a movie that you can mention to people and their jaws drop. And not because I'm redoing it, but because…that character had a profound effect on their childhood. And not just for horror fans. I hear things like, 'Freddy scared the hell out of me.' I think what I want to do and what everyone involved wants to do is re-invent the character for a new generation. I think I'd be happy if people welcome this and at the same time see we're going off on a slightly different path, but if you follow the DNA…it goes all the way back to the first movie.

—Samuel Bayer, director

Robert Englund's done an amazing job over the years playing Freddy. Everybody that's a fan of the *Nightmare* loves Robert, so that's a challenge when you've got to step in a big man's shoes like that. It's scary, but it's also exciting. You can't please everybody. All I can do is really just try to work from the heart and do the best job at playing Freddy that I can and hope for the best.

—Jackie Earle Haley, 'Freddy Krueger'

---

10 *Mind Ripper* (aka *The Outpost*) was originally written by Jonathan Craven as *The Hills Have Eyes Part III* but was rewritten by Phil Mittleman to have no connection to the previous films.

11 *Cursed* was a very troubled production that was initially shot in March-August 2003 but had to be largely rewritten and reshot in November 2003-January 2004. It was not released until February 2005. Many actors who worked on it—James Brolin, Illeana Douglas, Omar Epps, Corey Feldman, Scott Foley, Robert Forster, Heather Langenkamp, Mandy Moore, and Skeet Ulrich—subsequently found themselves on the cutting room floor.

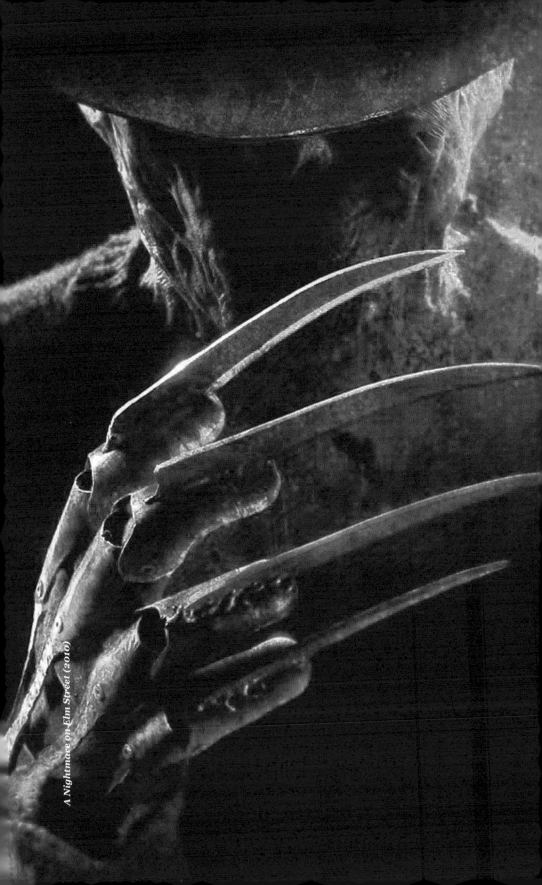

A Nightmare on Elm Street (2010)

After their successful 'reimagining' of *The Texas Chainsaw Massacre* (q.v.) and with their reboot of *Friday the 13th* (q.v.) about to enter production, *Variety* reported in January 2008 that Michael Bay's Platinum Dunes production company would be joining forces for a third time with New Line Cinema to revive New Line's signature film series *A Nightmare on Elm Street*. Platinum Dunes co-founder Brad Fuller was quick to emphasise that their version of *Elm Street* would take the series back to its roots. 'It's like what we're doing to *Friday the 13th*,' he told Shock Till You Drop. 'It's not Freddy cracking jokes. We want to make a horrifying movie. The concept is so scary: don't fall asleep or you'll die. This guy gets you when you're most vulnerable, in your sleep. We love that. That's the basis of the movie. It'll be most similar to the first one but in terms of kills and dreams we'll borrow from the entire series.'

'I just think there's something incredibly ingenious and universally frightening about Wes Craven's idea for Freddy Krueger,' Toby Emmerich, New Line's production chief, told the *Los Angeles Times*. 'The *Nightmare* films are profoundly disturbing on a deep, human level because they're about our dreams. It's why we thought that we could reach an especially broad audience with a new film...The whole idea was to find a way to reinvent the series and use contemporary filmmaking and storytelling to bring the series into the modern era.'

New Line had originally intended that Krueger return in a sequel to *Freddy vs Jason*, but ended up being persuaded by Platinum Dunes that bringing the series full circle would be a better approach. 'New Line thinks that this is like their Batman, and Freddy Krueger is very important to them,' Fuller told Shock Till You Drop. 'We were trying to get these rights before *Friday the 13th* and feet were dragging for a long time. It really wasn't until *Friday the 13th* was done and in the can that they felt positive about it and they finally decided, "Yeah, let's go with these guys"...It was not a rights issue as much as "Whose hands are we going to put this in?" And we had to prove to them that we were the best guys for the job.'

While Platinum Dunes had enjoyed the cooperation of original directors, Tobe Hooper and Sean Cunningham, on their previous New Line forays, this time they would find Wes Craven conspicuous by his absence. 'I don't know what happened there,' Fuller said. 'I can certainly empathise with the fact that he created it and has nothing to do with it and that's not something that we feel good about. As producers and horror fans, Wes Craven is one of our heroes in the respect that he's made movies that we all love and we love to make movies that are similar to those. Sometimes it works great in these situations. We had a great relationship with Sean Cunningham...[but] with Wes we never had an opportunity to have that.'

In the summer of 2008, Emmerich hired Wesley Strick (*Cape Fear, Wolf*) to write the script for the new *Elm Street*, the New Line executive having admired Strick's unproduced screenplay for a prequel to *Se7en*.

High school senior Kris goes to a graduation party at her friend Dean's house. After things slow down, she heads upstairs, only to find Dean struggling on his balcony with an unseen assailant. Suddenly four parallel slashes rip through his shirt and he plunges to his death. At Dean's funeral, Kris sees a five-year-old girl with a

ripped dress who is grabbed by a charred hand from the open grave. Kris awakens with a start, then goes to the wake, where childhood photos of Dean reveal the same little girl from Kris' daydream—which is actually Kris herself at a young age. Strangely, Kris does not remember knowing Dean before high school. Unable to locate any early childhood photos of herself in the family albums, Kris heads to the attic, where she finds the torn dress from her daydream and has an encounter with a hideously-burned, talon-gloved man before waking up screaming. The next day, Kris falls asleep in class, only to find herself in a charred, smouldering classroom with the same deformed man now standing where her teacher had been. He attacks her and slices a lock of her hair with his glove, which she finds on her history book when she wakes up screaming. That night, with Kris' flight-attendant mother gone, ex-boyfriend Jesse sneaks over to comfort her and ends up sleeping over. Kris has a nightmare about meeting her younger self and friends at an old preschool and playing hide-and-seek from the gloved monster, who now wears a fedora. As Kris struggles with the man in her dreams, she is literally ripped apart in reality before Jesse's horrified eyes. Fleeing the scene, Jesse briefly takes refuge at the house of Kris's artist friend Nancy, who just happens to be painting a scene of four parallel slashes made by a taloned glove. Jesse swears that he had nothing to do with Kris's death and that the actual killer is the same person who has been haunting their dreams. Hearing sirens, Jesse flees, but is caught by the police. Nancy and her friend Quentin, who hosts a podcast called 'Insomnia Radio', meet at the local bookstore to discuss their nightmares and the meaning of the name 'Freddy'. Meanwhile, Jesse struggles to stay awake in his holding cell, only to fall asleep and dream of his father being eviscerated by the maniac's talons before he finds himself back at the preschool with his childhood friends, all once again playing hide and seek with the madman. Jesse runs into a boiler room where he sees the strung-up bodies of Dean and Kris, right before he himself is cut to shreds by the bladed glove and bleeds out all over the jail cell. That night Nancy falls asleep in the bathtub and finds herself walking in the snow outside the preschool where she is met by the killer, who taunts her with his blades until her cell phone wakes her up. Hunting in her mother's home office, Nancy and Quentin find a class picture from preschool that shows the two of them, Dean, Kris, Jesse—and a fedora-wearing handyman named Fred Krueger. Confronted by her daughter, Nancy's mother Gwen tells the tale: Krueger was in fact a paedophile who abused and violated the children, especially Nancy. However, before the parents could take action, Krueger supposedly skipped town and was never seen again. Gwen assures Nancy and Quentin that their nightmares are just repressed memories and cannot harm them. That afternoon at swim practice, Quentin falls

asleep in the pool and finds himself at an abandoned factory, where Fred Krueger suddenly appears, running for his life from a group of enraged parents—including Quentin's and those of his friends—who corner the child molester in a small containment building. Vigilante justice prevails as the mob sets fire to the building and Krueger is consumed by flames, burning alive inside the upper level of a boiler room. Now armed with the truth of what happened, Quentin and Nancy confront the boy's father, who admits to acting rashly and not investigating the validity of the children's claims of abuse. Believing that closure can only be found at the abandoned preschool, Quentin and Nancy—both now suffering the delusions of 'micronaps' from lack of sleep—make their way there, only to discover evidence in Krueger's old basement room that everything the children said about the man was true, and worse. Nancy decides the only way to make the nightmares stop is to somehow bring Freddy back into the real world. She falls asleep and finds herself in the boiler room, where Freddy taunts her with images of her younger self pleading for help against the pervert who is stalking her. Attempting a mock seduction, Freddy caresses grown-up Nancy with his knives, but the girl grabs his hand and plunges the blades into his gut. Unaware that Nancy has woken up, Freddy is now back to his pre-immolated state and in the basement of the preschool. Suddenly, Nancy is upon him with a baseball bat, beating the child molester with savage fury. As he crashes to the floor, Krueger smashes into a gas lamp and is once again on fire—a fire that Nancy inflames with a canister of oil. With Krueger apparently now dead for real, Nancy and Quentin are rescued from the burning preschool and put into an ambulance. On the way to the hospital, Nancy hears the eerie whistling of the driver, then looks up to see Krueger's fedora in the rear-view mirror...

With script in hand, two important holes needed to be filled. First, a director needed to be found. Bay strongly advocated hiring 46-year-old Samuel Bayer, an award-winning music video and commercials director (best known for directing the

groundbreaking video for Nirvana's 1991 hit 'Smells Like Teen Spirit', as well as countless other artists like Aerosmith, David Bowie, Sheryl Crow, Metallica, The Rolling Stones and Justin Timberlake) but with no previous feature film experience. Platinum Dunes had originally approached Bayer about directing both their *Chainsaw Massacre* and *Amityville Horror* remakes, but he had turned both down. He did, however, agree to direct the company's proposed remake of Kathryn Bigelow's 1987 vampire road movie *Near Dark*, but the project was dropped for fear of competing with the *Twilight* juggernaut.

Fuller and partner Andrew Form tried to interest Bayer in the *Elm Street* remake instead, but the director initially fell back on principle and refused. This time, however, Bay intervened directly and decided not to take no for an answer. 'Michael sent me an e-mail and made a lot of sense,' Bayer told Shock Till You Drop. 'Just talking about the business and why this was a good movie to make. There were a lot of opportunities in doing this that might not have happened with another film. I think what he said made a lot of sense and I think it's hard to argue with the richest guy in Hollywood...I thought whatever that first film was going to be, it better be the right one. Michael said I could wait forever and it might not ever happen. He definitely got my appetite whet and the more I thought about what could be done with this franchise, the more excited I got.'

Bayer was determined to make his own mark on the *Elm Street* franchise, particularly when it came to the trademark surrealistic set pieces. 'I look at the old movies and I think the dream sequences aren't that interesting,' the director told Bloody Disgusting. 'I think they feel like bad Broadway musicals or something, like with steam and smoke and they're not scary, they're not beautiful, they're not interesting. I've looked at everything from German expressionistic film to Tim Burton movies to all kinds of disparate influences and the one thing this movie is going to have [is] a vision when it comes to the dream sequences...beautiful and macabre and scary.'

The second piece of the puzzle was the casting of Freddy Krueger. The decision had been taken from the off not to rehire Robert Englund—who was now in his 60s—and instead go with an unknown, and Emmerich had been impressed by the actor who had played paedophile Ronnie McGorvey in Todd Field's *Little Children*, an art film that New Line released in 2006. The performance was recognised as the Best Supporting Actor of the Year by the Chicago, New York and San Francisco Film Critics Awards and was nominated as such by both AMPAS and the Screen Actors Guild.

Jackie Earle Haley was born on July 14, 1961, in Northridge, California, and had achieved fame in the 1970s as an up-and-coming teenage actor in films like *Day of the Locust* (1975), *The Bad News Bears* (1976) and its two sequels, *Damnation Alley* (1977) and *Breaking Away* (1979). Haley's career had stalled in the 1980s, however, and he became stuck in guest spots on TV shows such as *MacGyver* and *Murder She Wrote* and direct-to-video schlock like *Dollman* (1991) and *Maniac Cop 3* (1993). His last appearance came in the 1993 TV movie *Prophet of Evil: The Ervil LeBaron Story* before he effectively retired from acting, moved to Texas and worked as a commercial director, limousine driver, furniture refinisher, security officer and pizza deliverer.

In 2004, Haley got a call out of the blue from writer/director Steven Zaillian (*Schindler's List, Gangs of New York*), who remembered the actor from his 70s work and wanted him for the role of bodyguard Sugar Boy in the adaptation of Robert Penn Warren's novel *All the King's Men* that he was filming in Louisiana. Critics were quick to take note of Haley's comeback performance in the otherwise-failed film and he was immediately cast in *Little Children*, which he then followed with a tour-de-force performance as the masked antihero Rorschach in Zack Snyder's comic book adaptation *Watchmen* (2009). It was Rorschach that led to Freddy Krueger.

'We got our hands on a screen test for Rorschach that [Haley did] that was unbelievable,' Bayer enthused to Shock Till You Drop. 'It blew my mind. He's the real deal. He becomes that character. I appreciate his craft and how much he cares

147

about what he does. You have got to convince someone that you're a psychopathic character with a burned face and a claw. I don't know how much research you can do for that, but you've got an Academy Award-nominated actor that has to go deep to find that and not do it in a silly way...We did a couple of scenes with him and Nancy [Rooney Mara] where he's threatening her...and it's just creepy.'

Haley was game for the part, even though he knew the risks involved in stepping into another actor's shoes: 'I definitely had to think about it. It just kind of boiled down to: How do you not play Freddy Krueger? It's just such a cool project. Such an iconic character and such a cool challenge. Clearly, I wasn't thinking about all of this shit glued to my head, but it was too cool not to do, man.'

'Jackie was so on top of everything that this character did, and gave it so much thought,' Fuller praised to Bloody Disgusting. 'He committed totally to this. And he had a ton of time every day to really think about how he could be as evil as humanly possible, because his makeup took between 3½ and 4 hours a day. And I think that he would just sit in the chair, like, "What is the scariest possible thing that I can do?" And in four hours, you can come up with a lot of stuff.'

Haley elaborated on the Krueger transformation to Shock Till You Drop: 'It's torturous for me. It's just a long time in the chair. Wearing this stuff, my ears are killing me and it pulls down on the back of my neck. I have to eat Advil, but, at the same time, it's kind of odd, man. It's like the best Freddy research and motivation shit I could do is sit in that torturous chair for three and a half hours and I'm ready to throw the glove on and start slicing just about anybody. It's almost like I'm wondering if I can even play this character if [the make-up] wasn't on.'

Kris gets off the bed and backs along one wall, looking up at the small air duct from which she fell.

No one else drops in. Kris takes in the room a bit more, her focus landing on

THE FEDORA resting on the toy chest.

Kris picks it up, aware she's seen it before but unable to know why it's familiar.

FREDDY (O.S.)
Your mother gave me that...

Kris whirls around—No sign of Freddy. Stepping more into the center of the room, in search of the voice...

FREDDY (O.S.) (CONT'D)
For when I worked out in the sun...

Whirling around again...But he's not there.

FREDDY (O.S.) (CONT'D)
So I wouldn't burn my face.

Spinning around a third time and this time he's standing right there—

And now Freddy's face comes into full view. Raw, exposed muscle clings to his jaw-line like overlapping rubber bands. Eyes with no eyelids, ever staring. The teeth of a skull, with a gum-line pulled back so far even a smile is a sneer.

—Unfilmed scene, from the original script

Apparently feeling that Strick's draft was not sufficiently geared towards young audiences, Fuller and Form turned to Eric Heisserer for a rewrite. Heisserer had created the popular online epistolary *Dionaea House* in 2004, a series of linked internet pages about a man searching for answers as to why an old friend committed a double murder/suicide. Optioned by Warners a year later, it was intended for filming in 2007 but was never made.

Heisserer's main contribution to the *Elm Street* script was the almost wholesale revision of Strick's dialogue. Most of the exchanges between the teens were changed, and the whole notion of a 'nightmare map'—the locales that manifest themselves in the teens' nightmares—that was an important part of Strick's third act was dropped. As originally written, Nancy was to discover the nightmare map on a video blog of one of her former schoolmates; she and Quentin then use the map to locate the abandoned preschool. On the way there, Quentin sees Freddy hitchhiking, and then he is suddenly in the backseat. Before Quentin can act, Freddy traps Nancy with her seatbelt and impales her with his glove. Quentin's car then hits a tree, the airbag deployment jarring him back to reality. This was all greatly simplified in the rewrite: Nancy and Quentin Google the preschool, get directions, drive out, encounter Freddy on the way and run off the road into a ditch.

Likewise, Freddy's final pursuit of Nancy was markedly different between the two scripts. In Strick's version, Nancy runs from the boiler room only to find herself in a corridor with a tall mirror. Suddenly, in the mirror, Nancy sees her preschool self, who pleads for help from the pursuing Fred Krueger, who implores little Nancy not to tell anyone about how he has violated her. At the same time, Freddy Krueger advances behind teenage Nancy, confronting her about her having told her mother about the abuse. As Freddy prepares to strike Nancy, the ringtone of Quentin's cell phone suddenly jars the girl back to reality, and as she plunges Freddy's glove into his gut, the surroundings change to the real world of the preschool basement.

Conversely, Heisserer's rewrite is more of a *redux* of the original film, with Freddy pursuing Nancy in a nightmare version of her house—complete with sinking into the floorboards (instead of the stairs, as she did in Craven's film). Pinned to her

bed and wearing the dress she wore as a little girl, Nancy is taunted by Freddy until Quentin injects the sleeping Nancy with a shot of adrenaline, after which she is able to pull Freddy back to the preschool basement.

Before bringing Nancy back to the land of the awake, Quentin was meant to have a nightmare on his own. After falling asleep in the basement, he finds the whole place tipping sideways and he slides into the door that leads to the boiler room, which slams shut after him. In Heisserer's script, this was changed to Quentin finding himself in an abandoned cathedral with Freddy, dressed in a monk's robes, beckoning him to be a sacrifice. Just as Freddy is about to kill Quentin, Nancy arrives on the scene and the killer changes quarry.

Instead of the 'quiet' twist ending that Strick had come up with—which was to have Freddy drive the ambulance—Heisserer again decided to go with the familiar, specifically a reprise of the original film's shock coda. Arriving home from the hospital, Gwen orders Nancy upstairs to bed, but before she can heed her mother, Freddy reaches out from a mirror and thrusts his gloved talons through Gwen's eyes before pulling her inside.

With the explicit references to Fred Krueger as a paedophile, the minds behind the new *Elm Street* sought to give the character a back story and a motive for pursuing the teenagers which had not previously existed in the franchise. 'We've gone in a slightly different direction with our take on Freddy and I like that,' said Bayer. 'We delve a little deeper into him as a person. How he became the thing he was. That's certainly attracted me to this character. He's not a mindless guy with an axe. He's a thinking, talking, psychologically disturbed character.' Added Fuller: 'Our Freddy is definitely...not a child killer. He probably has killed, but that's not our angle. Our angle is more of the molestation. And that makes it different and more horrifying.'

Filming on the new-and-supposedly-improved *Nightmare* began in Chicago on May 5, 2009, on a 46-day shooting schedule, at an estimated cost of $27 million. When production wrapped on July 10, Bayer waxed philosophical to Shock Till You Drop: 'I think we made an intelligent horror movie...you can either pretend and try and put style into something, or your style speaks for itself and you're not pretending. That's where I am. If anyone does know me or my music videos, you'll see this movie is connected to that style. The way I see the world is part of this movie.'

Unfortunately, the preview audience that saw the first cut of the film that November was not overly impressed with Bayer's vision of life on Elm Street. The decision was taken to completely reshoot the opening and the ending. Now instead of opening at Dean's (Kellan Lutz) party, the film would begin in a diner, where Dean is plagued by visions until he is forced by Freddy to cut his own throat as Kris (Katie Cassidy) and Nancy look on in helpless terror. Similarly, the ending was reshot to be a more physical confrontation between Nancy and Freddy (who is now kept in his nightmare guise), thanks to the last-minute contributions of famed stunt coordinator Brad Allan.

Another reshot scene was Quentin's (Kyle Gallner) nightmare. The test audience did not go for the Gothic approach, and the scene in the cathedral was dropped in favour of a new one in which Quentin encounters Freddy in the same boiler room as the other teenagers. In the same vein, a scene in which Jesse (Thomas Dekker) leaves his jail cell and finds himself back in his childhood bedroom was dropped. The scene shows Jesse watching his younger self tell his father about Fred hurting him. Suddenly, Freddy appears behind Jesse's father and kills him as both Jesses watch helplessly.

All the post-production tinkering added an additional $8 million to the tab and pushed *Elm Street*'s release back to April 30, 2010, where it earned $33 million in its opening weekend. That was enough to rank it in first place, but the film took a whopping 72% drop in its second weekend and ended up grossing just $63 million total; with roughly $32 million in rentals, its US haul did not even cover the film's revised budget. *Elm Street* earned an additional $52.5 million overseas, but when one considers that DreamWorks' horror pickup *Paranormal Activity* (2009) made nearly $200 million worldwide and cost a miniscule $15,000, it is difficult to see Bayer's 'reimagining' as anything but an expensive failure.

To add critical insult to box office injury, the reviews were almost universally negative. 'I stared at *A Nightmare on Elm Street* with weary resignation,' wrote Roger Ebert. 'The movie consists of a series of teenagers who are introduced, haunted by nightmares and then slashed to death by Freddy. So what?' *Entertainment Weekly*'s verdict was that 'the new *Nightmare on Elm Street* is a by-the-numbers bad dream that plays a little too much like a corporately ordered rerun. One, two, Freddy's coming for you. Three, four, we've been there before.' 'This *Nightmare* is mostly stale goods,' judged the *Los Angeles Times*. 'You'd think Bayer's music video background would jibe well with the playful surreality of Craven's premise. But when not paying homage...Bayer surprisingly traffics in factory-level horror atmospherics and loud, saw-it-coming shocks.' The *Chicago Tribune*'s Michael Phillips admitted, 'I've seen far worse horror remakes, but let's not grade on too much of a curve: This *Nightmare* offers dutifully grinding thrills of a routine sort.' *Rolling Stone*'s Peter Travers noted: 'The new *Elm Street* marks the feature-directing debut of music video whiz Samuel Bayer...But it's the Bay touch you feel in the way actors register as body count, characters go undeveloped, and sensation trumps feeling. A nightmare, indeed.' *The Washington Post* summed up the majority opinion: 'Unfortunately, in the remake of 1984's *Nightmare on Elm Street*—don't call this a reimagining, people, because imagination is the last thing at work here—good ol' Fred loses any sense of playful shock he once possessed and turns into a generic figure meticulously manufactured to simultaneously gross and freak us out. It doesn't work.'

For his part, Wes Craven was not terribly disappointed at his lack of involvement in the project, remarking to the website MovieWeb: 'I have no ownership in it. The original people I did it with are all gone. If you have no control or ownership when it comes to those things, and it's being taken over by other people, you tend to lose interest. There are much more creative situations that I can get myself into, rather than a situation where I would be working for someone else who is exploiting something I created. It wouldn't be a very happy situation.'

154

THE ROMERO REVIVAL

NIGHT OF THE LIVING DEAD

(1968)

We made it as our first picture and our friends in distribution circles told us to make something exploitive because it's safer. So we decided to do a horror film. Now when we did it, we said, we're not just going to do a horror film, we're going to really 'go out' with it and try and make it 'gutsy'.

—George A Romero, director, co-writer, cinematographer and editor

I think the film is an attempt to make money. And it's an attempt to tell a good, honest, emotionally involving story. A lot of the critics have jumped off the deep end in likening the ghouls to the silent majority and finding all sorts of implications that none of us ever intended. I think George wants to encourage that kind of thinking on the part of some critics. But I'd rather tell them that they're full of shit.

—John Russo, co-writer

In 1954, at the age of 14, George Andrew Romero got busted by the cops. Being a teenager in the Bronx, this was hardly a newsworthy event, but in Romero's case, it was prescient: he was shooting his first movie, *The Man from the Meteor*, and he had thrown a burning dummy off a rooftop for effect.

Such antics aside, the teenage Romero was already making a name for himself—he was the head of a young filmmakers' co-op called Herald Pictures and he would win an award from the Future Scientists of America for his senior science project, a geology documentary called *Earthbottom*. The summer before he left New York to study at Pittsburgh's famed Carnegie Institute of Technology (soon to become Carnegie-Mellon Institute), he was employed as a production assistant on the 1958

James Stewart-Kim Novak witchcraft comedy for Columbia Pictures, *Bell, Book and Candle.*

Romero's time at college was highly unproductive academically—he spent five years there without graduating—but he honed his dramatic and filmmaking skills thanks to YMCA summer theatre and a two hour-plus 16mm experimental film he directed called *Expostulations*, produced for a mere $2,000 in 1960. It was through these activities that Romero made the acquaintance of his future business partners, Russell Streiner and John Russo.

In 1962, with a Bolex camera and $500 borrowed from Romero's rich doctor uncle (who had also bankrolled some of his nephew's earlier endeavours), Romero and Streiner set up a studio in the South Side of Pittsburgh called The Latent Image. Rent was $65 a month and work was scarce, as Romero remarked to the *Village Voice*: 'We did everything from communion photographs to whatever would make people walk in off the streets. Some weeks, we made more money on bets on a miniature hockey game in the window than from our work.'

Latent Image's big break came in the form of a commercial for the local planetarium, produced for just $1,600 and featuring not-so-special effects involving a model rocket, sugar, saltpetre and a clay moonscape. But as they were soon to demonstrate on a bigger scale, what Latent Image lacked in funds they made up for in creativity and sweat equity. The spot turned heads, and the Romero-Streiner combine began to take off.

By 1965, Latent Image was solvent enough to secure a small business loan of $30,000 (once again underwritten by Uncle Monnie), to move to a bigger studio in downtown Pittsburgh and to hire Russo. Over the next few years, Latent Image produced commercials for everything from grills and cake mixes to Iron City Beer and Calgon Detergent, winning a number of regional and national awards along the way. But making pickle and beer spots was hardly an artistic enterprise, and Romero and his co-workers longed for something more: feature films. After being in business for five years, they had both the equipment and the know-how; the only thing they did not have was the money. So they did what any group of enterprising,

hard-working, visionary Americans would do—they begged off their family and friends.

In January 1967, the production company Image Ten was formed, with a $600 initial contribution each from Romero, Streiner, Russo, Vincent Survinski, Streiner's brother Gary, Richard and Rudy Ricci, Karl Hardman, Marilyn Eastman and David Clipper, who served as legal counsel for the whole enterprise. Each investor was in turn required to bring in another investor, also at $600 a pop, so that Image Ten (or Twenty, at this point) would have $12,000 in cash to get things moving.

In the delegation of tasks, it was Romero who took the lead as writer, director, editor and cinematographer. Russ Streiner was to produce, and Russo would help with the script and serve as an assistant cameraman.

Survinski would be the production manager, Gary Streiner would be the soundman; Hardman would co-produce and Eastman was a production assistant. The latter two were partners in Hardman Associates, a sound studio specialising in industrial shows and radio commercials, which would end up providing all of the stock music and sound effects for the film.

For reasons of cost and exploitability, the decision was taken to make a black-and-white 35mm horror film—in fact, the pre-production title was simply *Monster Flick*. With things on the move, it fell to Romero to come up with some kind of screenplay, and he claimed some lofty ideas to the *Pittsburgh Press*: 'The inspiration...had been Richard Matheson's [1954 novel] *I Am Legend*. It got me thinking in terms of a socio-political allegory of a revolutionary society overthrowing the operative society.' However, according to Bill Cardille (known as 'Chilly Billy'), the local host of the then-popular Saturday night horror show *Chiller Theatre*, the genesis was much more pragmatic, as he told *Fangoria*: 'They were watching Vincent Price in *The Last Man on Earth* [a low-budget 1964 version of Matheson's book], and they said, "Let's make a *Chiller Theatre* movie. We can make a movie that's better than what they have on the air."'

157

Whatever the true nature of the muse, Romero began typing away at what would come to form the first half of the script...

Johnny and Barbara come to a deserted cemetery to lay a wreath on their father's grave. Barbara is suddenly attacked by a ghoulish man who kills Johnny after the latter comes to his sister's defence. Barbara flees the scene, making her way to an abandoned farmhouse, still pursued by the attacker, who in turn is joined by other anonymous assailants. Exploring the darkened abode, Barbara discovers a half-eaten corpse upstairs and runs outside, only to be stopped dead in her tracks by the arrival of a pick-up truck. The driver, a blue-collar type named Ben, ushers her back inside the house before doing battle with the small group of marauders outside. Once the attackers are vanquished, Ben enters the house and begins to fortify it against attack. Through radio broadcasts, it is learned that the phenomenon of assault by unidentified assassins is worldwide in scope and that the killers actually eat the flesh of those they murder. As more and more members of this ghoulish mob assemble outside the farmhouse, Ben and Barbara discover there are other people hiding in the basement: Harry and Helen Tinsdale and their son Timmy, who has been immobilised by a bite from one of the aggressors, and Tom Ryan, the cemetery caretaker.

While additional funding was being secured, casting began taking place from amongst the members of Image Ten. Russ Streiner would play Johnny, while Harry and Helen would be portrayed by Hardman and Eastman, who in turn knew stage actress Judith O'Dea and recommended her for the role of Barbara. As for the truck driver Ben, it was thought that Rudy Ricci, a long-time friend of the Latent Image gang and a budding novelist, would play the part. However, a 31-year old black actor named Duane Jones, a Pittsburgh native currently studying at the famed Actors Studio in New York, won the role when everyone, including Ricci, was astounded by his audition. The final bit of casting came when nightclub singer Keith Wayne, a friend of Ricci and Russo's, was given the role of Tom.

Romero had written the first part of the script solo, but demands on his time for commercial projects necessitated that the rest of the screenplay be written as a collaboration, as Russo told *Cinefantastique*: 'Karl, Marilyn, George and I, together, figured out an action outline of what should happen [with the rest of] the script. Then, sort of by default, I ended up writing the screenplay we began shooting with. I took the work George had written and all the notes from our discussions and came up with the finished script. The screenplay itself was a community effort.'

Harry and Ben immediately set to arguing about whether to stay upstairs or retreat to the basement; Harry returns downstairs while Tom decides to stay upstairs with Ben and Barbara. However, once a TV set is found, Helen convinces her husband to let them join

the group. Through Civil Defence broadcasts, it is learned that the army of attackers are actually the recently deceased, inexplicably reanimated and searching for living victims. Rather than wait for an uncertain deliverance, the group decide to make their way to a rescue station in a nearby town using Ben's truck. Through a tragic mishap, Ben and Tom's attempt to get fuel for the truck results in the escape vehicle being blown up, Tom being killed by the zombies and Ben running for his life. He fights his way back into the house and the remaining survivors decide to wait out the long night. Helen goes downstairs to find that her son has died and come back as a ghoul who murders his mother with a knife. Suddenly, the living dead besiege the house and finally gain entrance. In the resulting melee, Harry makes his way to the cellar only to become entangled with his dead son; while trying to kill Timmy, Ben accidentally shoots Harry instead. Ben and Barbara enter the cellar only to encounter an undead Helen. Ben's rifle blows her across the room; he and Barbara make their way downstairs where the rifle is called on again to make short work of a newly-revived Harry. The next morning, a sheriff's posse arrives outside the house, mistakes Ben for a zombie and kills him. Barbara, now the sole survivor, is rescued.

The script for what was to be known as *Night of the Flesh Eaters* was finished and all of the lead roles had been cast, save one: the farmhouse. As luck would have it, such a place was scheduled for demolition in Evans City, just 40 miles from Pittsburgh. The owner, Ken Gass, agreed to rent the farmhouse to Image Ten for $300 a month for the duration of the shoot, but since the basement was unsuited to filming, a set was constructed in the basement of The Latent Image building instead. Cameras finally began rolling on July 7, 1967, but there would be some major differences between the script and the film being shot, mainly involving the character of Ben.

Ben had been written as a redneck truck driver trying to make it back to his unattended children, as evidenced by this monologue from the original draft:

TRUCKDRIVER

I'm just...I got kids, you know...And...I guess they'll do all right... They can take care of themselves...But they're still only kids...And I'm bein' away and all...And...I'm just gonna do what I can...And I'm gonna get back...And I'm gonna see my people...And things is gonna be all right...I'm gonna get back...

However, once Duane Jones was aboard, Ben's lines were redone on location to accommodate an erudite black man, though his actions remained largely the same. Over the years, many have read great meaning into Jones's casting, but the part was clearly not written to give the film any kind of racial subtext, as Russo insisted at the time to the Associated Press: 'It is one of the few films, if not the only one, where the male lead is played by a Negro, who doesn't have to be a Negro. Duane

kept suspecting we were going to make him an Uncle Tom or something. It wasn't until we were halfway through that he was convinced he was going to be a hero.' 'He would have gotten the part if he were an Oriental or an American Indian or an Eskimo,' Streiner told *Cinefantastique*.

While not as radical a departure as Ben, the character of Tom Ryan was changed as well, as he went from being a middle-aged cemetery caretaker to a college-age free spirit; again, reflective of the casting of Keith Wayne. Tom was also given a love interest—his girlfriend Judy—who was played by Latent Image's secretary Judith Ridley. The tragic fate they share—being incinerated and having their remains devoured—was originally supposed to play out with Tom jumping clear of the burning truck, only to fall into the waiting arms of zombies, who tear him apart.

There were other changes as well: the Tinsdales became the Coopers and their son Timmy became a daughter named Karen, mainly so Hardman's own daughter Kyra Schon could play the part. But the biggest change of all was the ending, where the decision was taken not to have *anyone* survive the night, as Barbara is dragged into the mass of flesh-eaters by her zombified brother. 'Most people like the uncompromising ending,' Russo told *Cinefantastique*. 'They say they don't like it, but it creates what we wanted to create. They're just totally wiped out by the whole thing.'

They were also wiped out by the amount of graphic violence in the picture, rivalled only by fellow Pittsburgher Herschell Gordon Lewis and his drive-in Grand Guignols like *Blood Feast* (1963) and *Two Thousand Maniacs* (1964). As Romero would write in the preface to Russo's novelisation of *Night*, 'I directed for naturalism and saw no reason to cut away for reaction shots when the ghouls began devouring

the flesh of their victims. In fact I was delighted when one of our investors, who happened to be in the meat-packing business, turned up on the set with a sackful of animal innards which made the sequences seem so real, never realising the extent of taboo-breaking the scenes would achieve.'

Since the film could only be shot on weekends and in between commercial assignments, principal photography was not completed until November 1967, with the opening cemetery scenes being shot last. The final cost of the film came to $70,000, not including nearly $44,000 in deferred salaries for cast and crew. Next came several months of editing and sound mixing, until finally a rough cut was assembled and shown to the Image Ten principals in March 1968. 'When we saw a relatively complete edit it just smacked us in the eyes,' Russo told *Cinefantastique*. 'Karl jumped up and said, "Goddamit! We've got it! We have a movie!" We knew then that it was a good horror film. All of us felt that way. And we knew it was capable of making some kind of splash, at least with horror film fans.'

The first splash it made, however, was with a rival company—Vulcan Productions, the producers of the film *The Flesh Eaters* (1964)—who threatened to sue Latent Image if they released the movie under its present title. The film was hastily renamed *Night of Anubis*, a reference to the Egyptian god of death. On April 4, 1968 (the same day as Martin Luther King Jr's assassination, which could not have been seen as a good omen), Romero and Streiner loaded the trunk of their car with cans of the finished print and headed for New York in the hope of finding a distributor for their feature. Their first stop was Columbia Pictures, who held Image Ten on a string for some time before finally turning the picture down on the pretext that it was not in colour. Then American International Pictures made an offer, but only if the ending were reshot so that Ben would survive, a condition Romero refused.

Frustrated at their lack of success in securing distribution, Image Ten turned *Anubis* over to former distributor-turned-producer's representative Budd Rogers, who managed to get an offer from Continental Film Distributors, the motion picture arm of the Walter Reade Organisation, one of the east coast's premiere theatre chains. Founded in 1954 primarily as an outlet for foreign films, Continental came to release some of the most important films of the British New Cinema, including *Room at the Top* (1959), *The Entertainer, Saturday Night and Sunday Morning* (both 1960), *A Taste of Honey* (1961) and *The Loneliness of the Long Distance Runner* (1962). They also released domestic art films from directors like John Cassavetes (*Faces*, 1968), Frank Perry (*David and Lisa*, 1962) and Joseph Strick (*The Balcony*, 1963). Continental was not *totally* highbrow, however. They had also released *Pretty Boy Floyd* (1960), *The Hands of Orlac* (1961), *Dr Who and the Daleks*, *Ghidrah the Three Headed Monster* and *Godzilla vs. the Sea Monster* (all 1966).

On the morning of June 6, the top brass from Walter Reade gathered to see *Anubis*. Unfortunately, their minds were elsewhere, as former Continental executive Arthur Rubine told *Andy Warhol's Interview*: 'The screening for the whole company was the morning Bobby Kennedy died. You can imagine how much we were into it. When Duane hit the guy in the head with the [tyre iron]—Well, at that point we just said, "Fuck this. Who wants to sit through this? Bobby Kennedy just died." We'd all sat up all night listening [to the news].' Nevertheless, the company did see some potential for exploitation, and a deal was struck between Continental and Image Ten on June 10 that was a 50/50 split on the profits after prints and advertising were deducted. However, Continental thought that *Night of Anubis* was too esoteric a title, so the more proletarian *Night of the Living Dead* became the picture's official moniker. Unfortunately, an oversight on the new title card left off the copyright notice: a mistake which would inadvertently place the film in the public domain and cost millions in lost revenue in the decades to come.

The picture was premiered before an invited audience of 1,000 at Pittsburgh's Fulton Theatre on October 1, 1968, and received a standing ovation. Cast, crew and friends then partied until midnight in the grand ballroom of the swank William Penn Hotel. The next day the film went into general release at 11 theatres in the Pittsburgh area, where it made an astounding $75,874 in its first week. The local reviews were impressive as well, with KDKA-TV proclaiming the movie to be 'More terrifying than Hitchcock's *Psycho*' and the *Pittsburgh Press*'s Thomas Blakely declaring, 'In case anyone has the idea that Pittsburgh's first full-length motion picture, with a complete, all-district cast, is on the amateurish side in comparison with Hollywood's horror science fiction films, he is forewarned here to be ready for the shock of his life. *Night of the Living Dead*...shook up the hardiest of chiller-thriller fans. Some of the scenes are so grisly that—well suffice to say that it's a gourmet session for those followers of macabre, grotesque situations.'

Continental was caught totally off guard by the film's runaway success. President Jerry Pickman told the *Pittsburgh Post-Gazette*, 'We figured that it was a novelty that might make a good program filler and get us a few bucks and Image Ten off the hook for their investment and maybe show a small profit for them, too...we never expected in our wildest dreams anything like this. Continental would be willing to pay Image Ten between $250,000 and $500,000 right now for their interest in *Night of the Living Dead* but they'd be out of their minds to take it.'

Excited by *Living Dead*'s prospects, Continental hastily arranged a press screening of the film in New York on October 10, to be attended by Streiner, Russo, Jones, Pickman and Harold Marenstein, Continental's general sales manager. One of those invited was Lee Beaupre, a critic for the *Variety* trade paper. Unfortunately for those involved, Beaupre had an axe to grind with Continental over their lack of press screenings in the past and apparently decided to take out his frustration on its latest release. His damning review appeared in the October 16 issue: 'Until the Supreme Court establishes clear-cut guidelines for the pornography of violence, *Night of the Living Dead* will serve nicely as an outer-limit definition by example... this horror film (pun intended) casts serious aspersions on the integrity and social responsibility of its Pittsburgh-based makers, distrib Walter Reade, the film industry as a whole and exhibs who book the pic, as well as raising doubts about the future of the regional cinema movement and about the moral health of filmgoers who cheerfully opt for this unrelieved orgy of sadism.'

When *Living Dead* actually premiered in New York on December 4, it was greeted not with moral outrage but simple disdain by Vincent Canby: '*Night of the Living Dead* is a grainy little movie acted by what appear to be non-professional actors, who are besieged in a farm house by some other non-professional actors who stagger around, stiff-legged, pretending to be flesh-eating ghouls. The dialogue and background music sound hollow, as if they had been recorded in an empty swimming pool, and the wobbly camera seems to have a fetishist's interest in hands, clutch, wrung, scratched, severed and finally—in the ultimate assumption—eaten like pizza. The movie...was made by some people in Pittsburgh...' Not that Canby's opinion mattered to the grindhouse crowd, who swarmed the New Amsterdam Theatre on 42nd Street as well as the 39 other theatres showing the film and gave *Living Dead* its highest first week gross of $177,130.

The next major market release was Chicago on December 27, where the picture saw an opening week's gross of $110,580. Roger Ebert happened to catch *Living Dead* at a forty-cent Saturday matinee that was mostly attended by unaccompanied children. Because the Motion Picture Association of America's rating system did not take effect until after *Living Dead*'s premiere, the picture was unrestricted, despite its violent content. Also, Continental had oddly chosen to double book Image Ten's decidedly adult production with the British kiddie sci-fi film *Dr Who and the Daleks*. As a result, the children were totally unprepared for the violence and nihilism they were about to witness. On January 5, 1969, Ebert's review appeared, and he described in stark detail what he witnessed when the lights came up that Saturday afternoon:

The children in the audience were stunned. There was almost complete silence. The movie had stopped being delightfully scary about halfway through, and had become unexpectedly terrifying. There was a little girl across the aisle from me, maybe 9 years old, who was sitting very still in her seat and crying. I don't think the

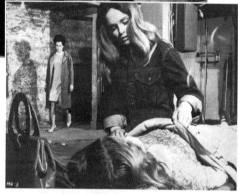

younger children really knew what hit them. They were used to going to movies, sure, and they'd seen some horror movies before, sure, but this was something else. This was ghouls eating people up—and you could actually see what they were eating. This was little girls killing their mothers. This was being set on fire. Worst of all, even the hero got killed. It's hard to remember what sort of effect this movie might have on you when you were 7 or 8. But try to remember. At that age, children take the events on the screen seriously, and they identify fiercely with the hero. When the hero is killed, that's not an unhappy ending but a tragic one: Nobody got out alive. It's just over, that's all. I felt real terror in that neighbourhood theatre last Saturday afternoon. I saw children who had no sources they could draw upon to protect themselves from the dread and fear they felt...Censorship isn't the answer to something like this. But I would be ashamed to make a civil libertarian argument defending the 'right' of those little girls and boys to see a film which left a lot of them stunned with terror. In a case like this, I'd want to know what the parents were thinking of when they dumped the children in front of the theatre to see a film titled Night of the Living Dead...[the movie] was produced before the MPAA code went into effect, and so exhibitors technically weren't required to keep the children out. I suppose the idea was to make a fast buck before movies like this are off-limits to children. Maybe that's it, but I don't know how I could explain it to the children who left the theatre with tears in their eyes.

Ebert's review appeared in newspapers across the country, and was also reprinted in the June 1969 edition of *Reader's Digest* magazine. For his part, Streiner answered Ebert's criticism this way in *Cinefantastique*: 'I can't help thinking that when you drop your kid off in front of the show and the marquee says *Night of the Living Dead*, you should know it isn't going to be a Disney film or *Hans Brinker and the Silver Skates*. So, if you don't want your kids to see a film with that title and you have some suspicions as to what it might be, then don't take them.'

There is no such thing as bad publicity, however, and the notoriety *Living Dead* was getting only spurred its grosses. Premiering on January 10, 1969 in Los Angeles, the film earned $157,420 in its first week as well as its first rave from a major paper, when Kevin Thomas bucked the trend and judged the movie 'a genuinely scary little horror picture...*Night of the Living Dead* is taut and uncompromising, ending on a note of bitter irony. Performances are adequate and often better, especially in the case of Jones, who clearly has what it takes to go on to bigger things.' Bigger things in this case came just a few months later, when *Living Dead* was shown that June at the prestigious Edinburgh International Film Festival.

Between 1968 and 1970, the film earned $1.6 million in rentals—an enormous return on a modest investment—and Continental seemed satisfied to let the film play itself out. 'We figured what we had was a programmer,' Rabine told *Interview*. 'You know, you bring it into town, you run a big ad the day it opens and you say "Scream-your-guts-out-scare-yourself-to-death" and that's it.' But an entirely new audience—different from the grindhouse and drive-in thrill seekers—was about to give the *Living Dead* a new lease on life.

In the spring of 1970, *Living Dead* was shown in an SRO screening at New York's Museum of Modern Art as part of their annual Cineprobe series. At the same time, the film received praise from the influential film journals *Cahiers du Cinema* and *Sight and Sound*. Now that the *cinéastes* had got hold of it, the race was on to define *Living Dead* in terms other than just an effectively scary horror movie. The most common subtextual reading of the film was as a metaphor for Nixonian America, with either the ghouls or the ghoul-hunters (depending on whose interpretation you read) representing the so-called 'silent majority' that supported both Nixon and the war in Vietnam and were too busy living their law-and-order lives to bother with protests and the like. In this interpretation, *Sight and Sound*'s Elliott Stein took the lead: 'Who are these ghouls...all of them so horrifying, so convincing, who mow down, defoliate and gobble up everything in their path? In the film a local TV station sends out a warning message: "The ghouls are ordinary people...but in a kind of trance." Many of these ordinary people, in all the trance-like security of their 'silent majority' can be seen these days…cramming their popcorn in front of a large Broadway screen where Fox's *Patton* is doing land-office business.'

The Washington Post's Kenneth Turan saw the silent majority too, but in a different guise: 'There appears to be a layer of socio-political allegory to the film, an uprising by monsters who "look like ordinary people," and scenes of equally repulsive vigilante bands set to destroy them seemingly have 'silent majority' written all over.' The fact that *Living Dead* was written and filmed before Nixon was even elected did not deter Stein, Turan or many others from sharing either this contextual viewpoint or the one that said the zombies were in fact America's war dead returning for revenge.

Despite having such lofty pretensions harnessed to it, *Living Dead*'s second life did not really start until May 1971, when it began to be shown on Fridays and Saturdays at midnight at Walter Reade's Waverly Theatre in Greenwich Village. The phenomenon of so-called 'Midnight Movies' traced its origins to the late-night showings at New York's Elgin Theatre of Alejandro Jodorowski's surreal western, *El Topo*, beginning in December 1970. Previously screened only at the Museum of Modern Art, *El Topo* became such a *cause célèbre* that it played at the Elgin for two years, until one of its biggest fans—John Lennon—had manager Allen Klein buy it for wider distribution. Playing during normal hours, the film was a total flop, and was taken out of circulation entirely for several years.

It was at the Waverly that the so-called 'cult' of *Night of the Living Dead* was born, as described by the *New York Daily News*'s Ernest Leogrande: 'Every Friday and Saturday night for the last month, a line of eager, smiling young faces has stretched along the block in front of Greenwich Village's Waverly Theatre, waiting with restrained impatience to be admitted for the midnight showing.' Howard Smith, columnist for the *Village Voice*, attended one of the screenings, and like Roger Ebert before him, wrote about the experience, though his judgment on the film was much different:

As the film opens, the obligatory guffaws and verbal macho-tactics start up, but they give way almost immediately to an uneasy silence as genuinely frightened people begin screaming and pleading with the mockers to shut up. Soon almost everyone watching the film is terrified; the fright builds so quickly because, unlike most horror films, this one is totally unrelieved by those 'human interest' themes that are meant to augment tension but usually just dilute the tale's terror. By the time the real action of the film is underway, most of the all-adult, typically Village sophisticated audience was shrieking and groaning. Many people hid their heads in their hands and refused to do more than glance furtively at the screen. Only occasional bursts of nervous laughter marred the mood and diverted the dread. The state of shock continued right through to the surprise ending…directors of the new high-budget horrors would do well to study the honest brutality and unrelieved gruesomeness of Night of the Living Dead; they might learn the difference between what makes people giggle nervously and what makes them scream in terror.

Several other New York critics joined in the chorus of praise, including *Newsday*'s Harry Pearson ('Quite simply the most gruesome and frightening film ever made'), Rex Reed ('One of the best examples of quintessential horror. It is unthinkable for anyone seriously interested in horror movies not to see it') and *Newsweek*'s Paul Zimmerman ('The packed houses of young people...shriek and groan with the frenzy that only a true horror classic can conjure'). *Living Dead*'s first run at the Waverly ended in October 1971, when it was replaced by the stop-motion fantasy *Equinox*. However, it was enjoying late night success in other cities as well, with long runs in places like Boston, Chicago, Los Angeles and Philadelphia. By January 1972, *Living Dead* was showing on no less than four screens simultaneously in New York (including repertory theatres and midnight shows) before returning home to the Waverly in June and settling in for a 13-month run.

In the two years since *Living Dead* had been taken off the first-run circuit, it had made over $1 million, largely at midnight shows. Unfortunately, very little of that— or of the entire gross, for that matter—had been seen in Pittsburgh. In February 1972, Image Ten filed suit in Pittsburgh Common Pleas Court for the return of *Living Dead* from Walter Reade, along with some $1.3 million in arrears. The lawsuit would drag on for four years until Image Ten won a $3 million judgment against Reade in the Pennsylvania Supreme Court. Unfortunately, Reade filed for bankruptcy in January 1977 and Image Ten had to console itself with the $500,000 it had collected up to that point. It was not until January 1980 that Image Ten finally reclaimed ownership of *Living Dead*, the same year the film was acquired by the Museum of Modern Art for its permanent collection.

Desiring to move on to other types of films, Romero was initially dismissive of *Living Dead*, remarking to *Cinefantastique*, 'Often times I laugh about some of the interpretations read into it. We've had some outlandish things said about it...There are so many things in the film that I consider to be bad. There's so much terrible dialogue and there are several really poor performances. Technically, the film is not that bad, but Christ, our commercial work is better than that!' Apparently, Streiner and Russo were not best pleased with their colleague's attitude towards the film that put their company on the map, and with two follow-on efforts—a *Graduate*-style comedy called *There's Always Vanilla* and the suburban witchcraft drama *Jack's Wife*—having failed to light any fires, push finally came to shove. In January 1972, the Streiner brothers and Russo left Latent Image and, together with Rudy Ricci, formed their own company, New American Films. One of their first projects was a sequel entitled *Return of the Living Dead*, which they announced just as the third wave of appreciation for the original film was about to kick off.

Between 1972 and 1975, retrospectives on *Night of the Living Dead* appeared in such diverse magazines as *Andy Warhol's Interview*, *Cinefantastique*, *Filmmakers Newsletter* and *Take One*. In 1973, the film began showing on late-night television, thus giving its ghouls exposure to a broad new audience, albeit in a truncated form. For those who wished to see the *Living Dead* in print, Russo's novelisation was published as a mass-market paperback by Warner Books in 1974.[1] But perhaps

---

1 The novel takes several liberties with the screenplay: Ben is a widower with two young sons who are under the care of their grandmother while their father is away; the corpse upstairs in the farmhouse is that of a Mrs Miller—the body of her 11-year-old grandson Jimmy is never found; Barbara, Tom and Judy are all teenagers; and Sheriff McClellan's posse is encamped just a few miles away while the Miller farmhouse is under siege.

the greatest testament to *Living Dead*'s staying power was when Romero's long-awaited follow-up, *Dawn of the Dead* (q.v.), entered production at the Monroeville Mall outside Pittsburgh in November 1977.

When New American was unable to mount its own sequel, Russo instead turned it into a novel, which was published by Dale Books in September 1978, just one month before Romero secured a judgment against Chicago distributor William Links for re-releasing *Messiah of Evil* (1973) as *Return of the Living Dead* and copying the *Dawn* tag-line, 'When There's No More Room in Hell, The Dead Will Walk the Earth'. Russo's *Return of the Living Dead* takes place ten years after the events in *Night*, when people drive spikes into the heads of the recently-deceased to prevent their revival. A bus accident leads to a new outbreak of the living dead, and *Night*'s Sheriff McClellan is called back into action to combat the ghouls...

In November 1980, it was announced that *Return* would be made as a feature film under the auspices of former Chicago investment banker-turned-film financier Tom Fox, with Streiner producing a script by Russo and Edmondo Raphael that Russo would direct. Filming was set to take place in Pittsburgh in March 1981 on a budget *Variety* called 'considerably less than $1 million', and Orion Pictures contracted to take the foreign rights. The start date came and went, however, with no film being exposed.

Over the next two years, the project went through major changes. Russo and Streiner were bought out for $250,000 by Fox, who brought in *Alien* scribe Dan O'Bannon to completely overhaul the script. About the only thing O'Bannon kept was the title, turning a rather straightforward sequel into a postmodern, punk-rock comedy that took as its premise the notion that *Night of the Living Dead* had been based on actual events, subsequently covered up by the government, and that the Army was keeping the zombies in cold storage. Two bumbling stockmen accidentally release the ghouls, thereby starting the whole cycle of carnage anew. In March 1983 it was announced that the film would be made in 3D, directed by *The Texas Chainsaw Massacre*'s Tobe Hooper, and the budget would be in excess of $4 million. Orion would now be the domestic distributor, with foreign rights handled by the British Hemdale Leisure Corporation.

Filming was scheduled to begin in Los Angeles that May; however, Romero persuaded the Motion Picture Association of America to block production on the grounds of unfair competition—contending that the movie's title was muddying the waters for his own, third *Living Dead* movie, *Day of the Dead* (q.v.), which was scheduled for production in 1984. For his part, Fox stated that when he paid New American for the rights to *Return* he had also acquired the 'quit claim' that Romero and his former partners had each given the other, effectively freeing the parties to make their own *Living Dead* sequels. By the time the MPAA arbitration board ruled in Fox's favour in March 1984, Hooper had moved on to direct the $25 million *Space Vampires* for Cannon Films (also written by O'Bannon). O'Bannon took over the director's chair on *Return* and production finally began (in 2D) on July 9, 1984.

When it was released in August 1985, *Return* ended up following in the wake of both *Space Vampires* (released as *Lifeforce* in June) and *Day of the Dead* (released

in July), but received better reviews and higher box office than both ($6 million in rentals vs $5 million for *Lifeforce* and $2 million for *Day*). The film was actually followed by a sequel-cum-remake in 1988 and three other name-only sequels in 1993 and 2005.

By the 1980s, with the explosion of the home video market, it was estimated that *Night of the Living Dead* had made somewhere between $30 and $50 million worldwide, although an exact accounting was virtually impossible given the film's status as a public domain title. Despite an aggressive effort on Image Ten's part to reassert its claim of ownership (including formally copyrighting of the film when the laws changed in 1978), it had so far only been able to return just $1.5 million to *Living Dead*'s investors. Faced with such a shortfall, Image Ten agreed to license the film to Hal Roach Studios in 1986 for the controversial colourisation process. Broadcast on Halloween of that year, this new version of *Living Dead* scored nice ratings for syndicated stations and was a big seller on videocassette as well.

In February 1987, Russo announced that he was discussing remaking the film with Romero, who was at that time involved in a proposed remake of *War of the Worlds* at Paramount. When the project stalled (eventually being made for the studio in 2005 by Steven Spielberg, at a cost of $132 million), Romero was able to give serious consideration to Russo's idea. The catalyst for a remake came on the scene in February 1989, when Menahem Golan, chairman of Cannon Films, sold out to Italian financier Giancarlo Parretti and started a new company, 21st Century Film Corporation. On the lookout for low-budget projects with name recognition,

Golan immediately agreed to finance a new, $4 million *Night of the Living Dead*, which was formally announced at the 1989 Cannes Film Festival.

Romero would update the original script and serve as co-executive producer with Golan, while fellow Image Ten partners Russo and Streiner would produce the film. Directorial chores went to Romero's long-time make-up effects man Tom Savini, here making his feature-directing debut. Production was scheduled to begin outside Pittsburgh in November, but Romero's co-directing of the Edgar Allan Poe film *Two Evil Eyes* with Dario Argento pushed the *Living Dead* into the new decade. On April 23, 1990, filming began in Washington, Pennsylvania, on what would be the old Latent Image group's first movie together in almost 20 years. Romero's reasoning for doing the remake was simple: 'There probably isn't a week that goes by that the original isn't playing somewhere in the world,' he told the *Los Angeles Times*, 'and I can tell you that I have no idea who's seeing that revenue.'

Making the most of the opportunity, Romero and company worked some nice twists on the story, while still keeping the claustrophobic setting of the original film. The main change came in the character of Barbara, who instead of slipping into catatonia slips into overalls and combat boots and becomes a tough survivalist. In fact, Barbara emerges as the last one standing (as she was originally intended to do), though the ending is hardly a happy one. There are plenty of sly winks to the audience, such as Barbara and Johnny being accosted first by a confused old man and *then* by a zombie (as opposed to just the ghoul), or when the zombie daughter goes to kill her mother and we cut to a trowel hanging on the wall—which is what the child used to hack her mother to death originally.

But while Romero's script contains its share of references, it is also filled with constant profanity and an unwise desire to make literal what was implied in the original film—namely, people's callousness and stupidity make them worse than the zombies. Here it finds its expression in the gun-toting, slimy rednecks who pile kills in their pick-up trucks and mercilessly taunt captured zombies instead of putting them out of their misery. This dubious social commentary reaches a level of the absurd when zombies are strung up and shot repeatedly like gulag prisoners and Barbara remarks incredulously, 'They're us. We're them and they're us.' Whatever.

Given Romero and Savini's reputations for over-the-top gruesomeness by this point, *Living Dead*'s gore quotient is surprisingly low—less even than its predecessor—as the movie focuses more on action and dark humour. 'This is not a splatter movie,' Savini told the Associated Press. 'It's like film noir—but it's in colour.' Makeup effects supervisor John Vulich elaborated: 'We're using the idea that less blood is worth more. I think a film's more scary if it's realistic—like the girl next door coming after you.'

Moviegoers did not appear to agree. Despite a major release—just two weeks before Halloween—via Columbia Pictures, the updated *Night* was a box office disappointment, earning just $6 million. Critics were unimpressed as well, such as *Entertainment Weekly*'s Owen Gleiberman: 'In the history of bad ideas, George Romero's decision to produce a colour remake of his disturbingly frenzied 1968 zombiefest...has to rank right up there with New Coke.'

Incredibly, Russo and Streiner were not through trying to wrangle yet more blood from the gravestone. In 1998, they shot 15 minutes of new scenes—including a prologue, epilogue and insert material—to be mixed with existing footage and added a brand new score for a special 30th anniversary edition of *Night*. 'If the people love a movie, they're entertained by seeing improvements and variations on it,' Russo told the *Pittsburgh Post-Gazette*. 'We were painstaking, we used the same lenses, the same film stock, lighting techniques, the same lab to process the film.' This new version was premiered at the American Film Market in February 1999 and released on DVD by Anchor Bay that August to almost universal scorn. The popular web site Ain't It Cool News concluded its acerbic rant against the picture this way: 'Do not order it. Don't buy it for a dollar...50 cents or even a penny. That shiny coppery Lincoln will be worth more someday than this.'

The sting of such gross opportunism did find a balm that November, however, when *Night of the Living Dead* was added to the National Film Registry of the Library of Congress, along with *A Streetcar Named Desire* (1951), *The Ten Commandments* (1956), *The Wild Bunch* (1969), *Raiders of the Lost Ark* (1981) and twenty others. For Romero, whose opinion of the film has seemingly corresponded with its ever-increasing status, *Night* holds a unique place in his resume: 'It's the only scary film I've made,' he told *The Washington Post*. 'It's really more of a traditional nightmare. Zombies just keep coming. You kill one, and two take its place. There is no way out.'

(2006)

I never set out to remake *Night of the Living Dead*. To be honest, it is not one of my favourite horror films...They came to me and offered me the film—including bringing me on as the sole producer and also the director, so I didn't have to answer to anybody and I had total freedom, a bigger budget and a longer shooting schedule than I had ever had before.

—Jeff Broadstreet, producer and director

Jeff was disturbed—he thought he was going to end up being the director of Cheech and Chong vs the Living Dead—but I thought I could do something that was at least semi-serious.

—Robert Valding, writer and editor

In 1989, Jeff Broadstreet, who had broken into the film business via Charles Band's Empire Pictures, found himself at the helm of his first feature. At the age of 35, he was directing one of executive producer Fred Olen Ray's innumerable direct-to-cable/video cheapies, *Sexbomb*—a supposed 'send-up' of the low budget movie business. The movie had a typically eclectic Ray cast, including Parisian model-turned-Penthouse Pet Delia Sheppard, scream queen Linnea Quigley, porn starlet Veronica Hart (under one of her many aliases), bodybuilder Spice Williams and

Night of the Living Dead (2006)

former AIP horror star Robert Quarry. Despite boasting such a diverse group of players, the film received little play (it was never released to video) and slipped into oblivion until its DVD resurrection in 2003.

Broadstreet's career took much the same path. With the exception of the *faux* documentary *Area 51: The Alien Interview* (1997) and the comedy short *Megalomania* (2000), he did not direct another feature until 2002, with the horror film *Dr Rage* (aka *Nightmare Hostel*), which had the dubious distinction of sitting on the shelf for three years before being pawned off on DVD, and then only in England (it was subsequently given the rather benign title of *The Straun House* for its 2006 US DVD premiere).

Undaunted by his lack of success, Broadstreet searched the public domain listings for his next project, deciding on the Stephen King favourite *I Bury the Living* (1959). He then pitched the idea to German producer Ingo Jucht of Lux Digital Pictures, who took things in an entirely different direction: 'He said, "Well I'm not interested in that title but if you bring me a title that has some brand name value I would finance *that*,"' Broadstreet told The Horrorworks. 'So I said, "I think *Night of the Living Dead* is in the public domain" and he said, "No, it can't be." We did some due diligence on it and it [turned] out that the title was in the public domain, so that set the wheels in motion.' In actual fact, their so-called 'due diligence' was scanning the Amazon.com listings and marvelling at how many unlicensed DVD copies were available.

Given the sudden popularity of 3D films, Jucht had the brainstorm of doing a 3D remake of *Living Dead*. Curiously, Broadstreet's lack of experience with the format did not seem to bother his producer: 'Even though I hadn't made a film in 3D, I had come close a couple of times,' Broadstreet told the website 411 Mania. 'It was his decision. I didn't particularly want to make the film in 3D, because we didn't have a huge budget...[and] I knew the kind of complexity and difficulty that [3D] would bring to it.'

For Broadstreet and his writer Robert Valding, the edicts from Germany kept coming: 'We knew we were going to be [remaking] *Night of the Living Dead*,' Valding told The Horrorworks, 'and then we found out we were going to be doing it in 3D—and then we found out that the farmhouse...was now going to be the home of pot farmers and we were going to have pot humour. This was imposed upon us [but] I thought I could run with it.' Jucht also wanted the picture filmed under the false title of *The Undead 3D*, lest someone else steal their thunder.

> **Arriving at their aunt's funeral, Barbara and her brother Johnny are attacked by zombies. Johnny escapes in the car, leaving Barbara to fend for herself. On the run, she is picked up by motorcyclist Ben and taken to the Cooper ranch, a marijuana farm. Once inside, Barbara and Ben try to convince Henry Cooper that the dead are coming back to life and are on their way to the farm. Henry scoffs at their claim until zombies begin attacking the place and killing the inhabitants. Soon after, Gerald Tovar Jr, the proprietor of the local mortuary, arrives and confesses that he is responsible for the undead plague. Because of pyrophobia, he has not cremated either cadavers or so-called 'medical experiments' for the last two years, and the contamination of one has led to the reanimation of the other.**

While the characters and situations were ostensibly *Night of the Living Dead*, the

film's central gimmick—toxic waste spawning zombies—was straight out of Dan O'Bannon's version of *Return of the Living Dead*. 'We decided, since the original film is out there and had already been remade once...let's not do a note-for-note remake,' Broadstreet told 411 Mania. 'Let's try to take it in some new and interesting directions...If we're gonna remake the film, let's try to make it a little bit different. So, what we tried to do was give you familiar elements and then just when you started to feel comfortable, we kind of go off in a different direction. We kind of keep you on edge a little bit...And then just when you thought you start to see where it was going, we kind of veer back and come back into familiar territory.'

The one novel addition to the mix was the Gerald Tovar Jr character, which was based on mortician Ray Brent Marsh, who was sentenced to two prison terms in 2004 for failure to cremate over 300 bodies at the Tri-State Crematory in Georgia. The bodies were found intact and decaying on the crematorium's grounds, and the ashes that had been returned to the families were not in fact human remains; they were made of wood and concrete dust. The role of Tovar had been specifically written for cult actor Sid Haig, whose work Broadstreet had admired in Rob Zombie's *House of 1,000 Corpses*.

With a budget of just $750,000 and a tight, 20-day shooting schedule (June-July 2005) in and around Los Angeles, Broadstreet and his cinematographer Andrew Parke nevertheless sought to break new ground in the third dimension: 'We had two lightweight custom rigs built specifically for this film,' said the director. 'This is the first 3D film to feature extensive hand-held and Steadicam photography... I wanted this film to be a bit more realistic than a lot of the zombie films, so I tried to keep the 3D kind of organic. I didn't want it to be obtrusive, so I tried to work the 3D elements organically into the story so things don't constantly jump off the screen.'

While there are in fact several gimmicky effects (a huge joint is held out; a pot-head blows smoke rings at the camera; a slow-motion bullet fires through a window; a shovel is thrust forward), the picture does achieve a depth-of-field that is

uncommon to most 3D films while also delivering some genuinely startling images, such as a group of zombies reaching toward the camera to claim another victim. A tip of the hat to the original *Living Dead* provides another impressive effect, when the familiar title of the first film suddenly floats off a television screen and becomes the new title: *Night of the Living De3D* (this self-reflexivity continues at the Cooper farm, where everyone is gathered around the television watching their movie's predecessor).

After a very lengthy post-production period, *Night of the Living De3D* finally premiered at midnight, September 8, 2006, at the opening of the World 3D Film Expo II at Grauman's Egyptian Theatre in Hollywood. The film's 3D engineer, Daniel Symmes, told the website 3D Moving Pictures: 'It looked fabulous...My goals were met in having 3D interface with production with the least impact on the crew and production schedule. And more importantly, we achieved natural 3D with no eyestrain—something seemingly impossible for the big budget films.'

Unfortunately, the film's distributor—Midnight Movies, an offshoot of Lux Digital—was unable to get *Night of the Living De3D* much of a release. It opened in just 145 theatres (80 of which were in Los Angeles) on November 10, and grossed a paltry $215,300. The picture was then pulled until the spring of 2007, when it was reissued for midnight screenings only, giving it an additional gross of just $55,700.

The film's fortunes were hardly helped by an internet backlash against remaking Romero's classic (the website Bloody Disgusting scolded, 'To be blunt *NOTLD3D* is a travesty. Shot on a non-existent budget, this has to be the worst 'reimagining' of a movie since 2001's *Planet Of The Apes*') as well as a rash of bad reviews. 'Even for ultra-low-budget, grade-Z horror movies, this is a truly incompetent film,' said the Los Angeles Times. 'No wonder it carries a disclaimer that George Romero, king of the zombies, had nothing to do with it. That doesn't stop the new edition from cannibalising the original, resulting in food poisoning-like symptoms for the viewer.' Variety asked rhetorically: 'What is the point of a 3D zombie movie when the story and the scares have zero dimension to begin with? This and other pressing questions remain unanswered with...a juiceless quasi-remake of George Romero's 1968 classic

that, cardboard glasses aside, brings absolutely nothing new to the party.' Vue Weekly observed: 'What makes [it] so disappointing is not the badder-than-bad acting or even excruciatingly terrible dialogue, it's the completely missed opportunity to use its selling feature (3D) to any effect whatsoever. I mean, would it have killed Broadstreet to have at least one zombie come out of the screen at his audience?'

Defenders were a distinct minority, but they did appear in the form of LA Weekly's Luke Thompson ('As a 3D zombie flick on the big screen, it offers something new and fun: Zombies, breasts and copious joint-passing coming right out of the screen') and Ain't It Cool News's Run-and-Gun ('The 3D was awesome...If you get a chance to see it in 3D, I definitely recommend it'). The film had a limited run overseas, earning $1.2 million in places like Japan and Russia (where it actually placed in the Top 10 earners three weeks in a row). Lux Digital was able to secure an American DVD release through indie heavyweight Lionsgate in October 2007, which issued the film in both 2D and 3D versions.

For Broadstreet and Valding, the experience did not deter their desire to play with fire. Their prequel *Night of the Living De3D: Re-Animation*, featuring Andrew Divoff in the Gerald Tovar role, is due for DVD/Blu-Ray release in August 2012.

Just as the dead refuse to die, so too does *Night of the Living Dead*. In 2009, over 100 artists, animators and filmmakers from around the globe contributed to *Night of the Living Dead: Reanimated*, a mixed media celebration of the original. Various scenes have been redone, using puppetry, CGI, hand-drawn animation, illustration, acrylics, claymation and even animated tattoos. After playing several festivals, including the San Diego Comic Con, the film was released to DVD in August 2010.

At the same time, a more ambitious commercial project, *Night of the Living Dead: Origins 3D*, began production in 2012 under the direction of Zebediah de Soto

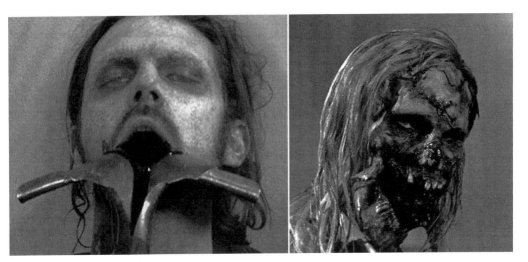

and producer Simon West (director of *Lara Croft: Tomb Raider* and the *When a Stranger Calls* remake). The film was shot as a computer-animated feature in a style de Soto calls 'American-style anime.' It takes the original characters and relocates them to New York City, post-zombie apocalypse. Two members of the 1990 remake are reprising their roles—Tony Todd and Bill Moseley—and Danielle Harris from the Halloween films and Joe Pilato (*Day of the Dead*) are also in the cast.

THE CRAZIES

(1973)

I don't consider *The Crazies* being a horror film, really. It's science fiction to the extent that Fail Safe was science fiction...It isn't really fantasy.

—George Romero, director, rewriter and editor

We went through rewrite after rewrite until it was decided that 'the kid' didn't make it as a screenwriter, and the scripting chores were passed down the line.

—Paul McCollough, original writer

After graduating from Penn State University with a degree in journalism, Paul McCollough joined The Latent Image in October 1968, just after *Night of the Living Dead* had knocked 'em dead in Pittsburgh, making George Romero and his associates the talk of the town. The offices at 247 Fort Pitt Boulevard were abuzz with success: what to do for an encore?

At first there was thought of making another genre film, tentatively titled *Horror*

Anthology. But Romero and John Russo wanted to show that they were not just horror movie mavens, and thought there might be something more to be gleaned from a half-hour short Latent Image had made earlier that year. Rudy Ricci was tasked with expanding his script into a feature, to once again star local actor Ray Laine and *Living Dead* alumnus Judith Ridley, who had since married Russ Streiner. The idea was to make a youth-oriented film along the lines of *The Graduate*, which had become the top box office attraction of 1968.

With Romero directing and Russo and Streiner producing, *At Play with the Angels* went into production in January 1969 on a $100,000 budget and a 10-week shooting schedule. When interviewed by the *Wall Street Journal*, Romero falsely boasted that *Angels* cost $450,000, would 'look like $1.6 million' and predicted it would gross 'between $15 and $30 million, depending on how it's promoted.' The ensuing tribulations would make a mockery of such ill-advised bravado.

McCollough, who worked as assistant cameraman on *Angels*, wrote in *Take One* magazine, 'An unbelievably uncoordinated production schedule, coupled with a talkative, amorphous script soon sealed the doom of *Angels*. For the next two years and some odd months, between shooting commercials, between long periods of limited cash for the project, Romero ground away at the picture.' After finally being finished and retitled *There's Always Vanilla*, the film was sold to Lee Hessel's Cambist Films, which gave it a Pittsburgh world premiere in March 1972, after which the picture closed in just two weeks. That summer, Hessel retitled the film *The Affair* and tried a sexed-up 'testimonial' campaign that borrowed from Sean Cunningham's *Together*—without much success.

In 1971, Romero had hired Alvin Croft, an advertising executive who worked with Romero's wife Nancy, to handle the commercial end of Latent Image, which resulted in immediate clashes with Streiner and Russo. Nancy Romero joined the company at the same time, and in August she ended up producing her husband's newest film, *Jack's Wife*, a contemporary drama about witchcraft in suburbia. The movie was supposed to be the first of three Romero films a Pittsburgh brokerage firm had committed to back at $250,000 a piece. On the strength of the agreement, Latent Image secured a bank loan of $100,000 to begin production, only to have the brokerage firm go out of business in the middle of shooting, effectively leaving Romero and company holding the can. The film was eventually finished and bought by producer/distributor Jack H. Harris (*The Blob*), who cut out 40 minutes from its two-hour-plus running time and retitled it *Hungry Wives* ('Caviar in the kitchen... Nothing in the bedroom'). Given an abortive April 1973 release, the picture effectively vanished until 1982, when it was reissued as *Season of the Witch* (the Donovan song of the same name is heard on the soundtrack) to cash in on the release of *Halloween III: Season of the Witch*.

In the four years since *Night of the Living Dead's* release, Latent Image had gone from being a hot property to a hot potato no one wanted to touch—including Streiner and Russo, who left the company in 1972. Desperate for the hit he needed to pay off Latent Image's mounting debts, Romero swallowed his pride, accepted $225,000 of Lee Hessel's money and agreed to make another *Living Dead*-type thriller. Fortuitously, he did not have to look very far for a story.

While McCollough had been working his way up to the position of key grip in Latent Image's commercial unit, he also had aspirations of being a screenwriter. To that end, he had written something called *The Mad People* in the fall of 1970. His

plot concerned a group of five people who attempt to escape a military quarantine after their town's water supply is contaminated by a chemical weapon that induces madness. The twist is that all the members of the quintet have also been exposed, and are slowly going berserk even as they try to flee to safety. After typing up his maiden effort, McCollough submitted *Mad People* to Latent Image, where it was promptly shelved.

When Hessel came calling, Romero dusted off *The Mad People*, sent it to New York and got back an affirmative—so long as it could be rewritten. McCollough tried and failed to tailor the script to Hessel's satisfaction and had to contend himself with being involved in the casting in New York, where he discovered *The Mad People*'s prospective producer was a bit mad himself. McCollough wrote, '[Hessel] rose from his chair, stretched and reached for his briefcase which he snapped open. He pulled out a 38-calibre pistol with holster and strapped it on under his coat. As I naively asked why he was doing that, he patted his gun and said that a fellow can't be too sure these days. Then we went to lunch next door, braving the adversities of New York street life for maybe ten or fifteen seconds.' It mattered little, in any event: the only casting choice to come out of the sessions was Hessel's girlfriend Lane Carroll, who got to play the leading lady.

Not surprisingly, it fell to Romero to refashion the script, giving him yet another opportunity to exercise his literary pretensions: 'Again, that film, as an original story, was written as a pure allegory,' he told *Cinefantastique*. 'The basic premise being that everyone in the world is operating at some level of insanity...The device that was used in the story...enabled us to look at people really operating, that is to crystallise this operation of different types of people at varying levels of insanity.'

An army plane carrying a biological weapon known as Trixie crashes outside of Evans City, Pennsylvania. The virus contaminates the local water supply and begins making the citizens either delirious or homicidal. The army arrives and quarantines the town, forcibly relocating everyone to the local high school. Pitched battles erupt between the frightened citizens and the white-suited, gas-masked soldiers. A quintet of people—firefighters David and Clank, David's pregnant fiancée Judy, widower Artie and his teenage daughter Kathie—manage to escape army custody and make their way to the perimeter of the town, where three of them begin to show signs of

infection. Meanwhile, Dr Watts, one of the scientists who developed Trixie, desperately searches for an antidote in the high school chemistry lab, only to have his potential cure destroyed when he is carelessly tossed in with the crazed mob.

Hessel was pleased with Romero's rewrite, but McCollough was not: 'I quit my job after the script was rewritten in a fashion so ruthless to my original intentions that only my characters' names were retained. Instead, the Army came out both villain and hero, and my poor beleaguered protagonists were reduced to simps.'

Retitled *The Crazies*, filming began in mid-March 1972, the eight-week shoot being the smoothest of Romero's feature career, though not exactly trouble-free. '[Evans City] shut us down for a week because of the incest scene [between an infected Artie and Kathie] which wasn't at all graphic, but they shut us down,' Romero told *Andy Warhol's Interview*. 'They saw it in the script. They locked us out of the high school.' Said high school being Seneca Valley, which ended up not only as a location, but a casting centre as well: 'A lot of the soldiers [in the film] are ROTC kids. [Their commander] said, "Well, I really don't like the idea of the film, but sometimes we have to look aside. And my boys, I like to get them off to camp every summer and they could use a contribution..." And so that's the way it worked out.'

The film is entirely reflective of where Romero was at that point in his life—rapid-fire editing, overlapping sound, cramped spaces and organised chaos all work to give a distinct sense of dislocation and despair. As he himself would write in Paul Gagne's book *The Zombies That Ate Pittsburgh*, 'I was frantic at the time (personal and financial pressures) and I see the film, in retrospect, as being too frantic. Its scale was too big for its budget, it was rushed, the cast was weak in part, and yet it came close to representing, for the first time, my filmmaking personality.'

While *The Crazies* certainly had more commercial potential than either of his previous two efforts, Romero was unfortunately about to endure yet another failure. This time, however, it had less to do with the content of the film itself than the lack of know-how on the part of its distributor, Hessel's Cambist Films. 'They thought they had a smash,' Romero told *Starlog*, 'so they talked themselves out of opening wide with it and decided to spend big money on a New York opening [in March 1973], which they didn't really know how to handle. Instead of treating it carefully, they spent their money on 50-foot high statues of the soldiers in Times Square. Hessel even refused to promote the fact that I had directed *Night of the Living*

Dead. He literally said, "Why should I make money for Walter Reade?" He didn't understand the film, and in essence he blew his wad. It didn't even survive a week.'

The initial critical response was tepid as well. Vincent Canby declared it 'An inept science fiction film...shot near Pittsburgh with a bunch of actors who perform with the kind of hysterical enthusiasm I haven't seen in 30 years, not since viewing a grade-school production.' *Cinefantastique* damned with faint praise: 'It is well-constructed symbolically, despite some lapses in believability and a generally poor script.' 'Overall technical deficiencies and script inadequacies make *The Crazies* an unlikely bet as a solo feature click,' *Variety* judged.

After playing a week at three theatres, *The Crazies* left New York, apparently destined for the same oblivion that had greeted *Vanilla* and *Jack's Wife*. However, Ernest Leogrande, who had already noted the 'cult' appeal of *Living Dead*, once more proved an astute prognosticator: 'George Romero did it again. Once more he has unleashed a snarling movie on an unwitting world...*The Crazies* slipped in and out of town last month like a cockroach hitting the kitchen sink in between lights out and sunrise, but if you think that's the end of it, you don't know cockroaches or horror-action movie fans. I predict *The Crazies* will return.'

It was not long before Romero's latest film began to make waves, first by being selected as the opening film for the 1973 Edinburgh Film Festival, where *The Scotsman's* Nicholas Fuller raved: 'Romero's work can be placed in the great tradition of the American science fiction film...*The Crazies* works on many levels. It is a contemporary critique of militarism, but at the same time is concerned with the most basic mechanisms of the unconscious. If it is not what is generally considered to be a 'festival film', we should rethink our conception of film festivals.' In August, Cambist changed the title to *Code Name Trixie* and gave the film some additional exposure, though not enough to suit Romero, who bought the picture back from Hessel. In February 1975, *The Crazies* enjoyed a brief midnight stint at the original Midnight Movie theatre, New York's Elgin, as a dry run for its re-release via Ben Barenholtz's Libra Films in April 1976. Playing in Boston, Los Angeles, New York and Washington DC, *The Crazies* benefited immensely from the publicity surrounding a nationwide outbreak of swine flu, which had the side effect of making the film topical. In May, it was shown for three consecutive nights at the Seattle Film Festival, the only film to be shown more than twice.

While *The Crazies* was hardly the box office success Romero so desperately needed, it did pay unexpected dividends. In April 1973, *Filmmakers Newsletter* sent Richard Rubinstein to interview Romero for an article on the picture, and out of that meeting a new partnership was born. Also, the film made news in Italy thanks to what seemed like divine intervention: 'The movie opened [in Italy] just as an earthquake hit, wiping out an entire town except for a single wall that was left standing,' Romero told the *Pittsburgh Post-Gazette*. 'The poster advertising our film was on that wall, and the Italian title for *The Crazies* was *The City That Died at Dawn*. The news media took a picture of that wall and it went out on the wire all over Italy. All the newspapers and magazines ran it and we benefited from this tragic publicity.'

Ironically, it was a combination of Rubinstein and three Italian producers that would soon give rise to the biggest hit of Romero's career—the film that would rank as his masterpiece. It was time to resurrect the living dead; *The City That Died at Dawn* became, appropriately enough, the forerunner for *Dawn of the Dead*.

(2010)

[Romero's] involvement was primarily at the beginning...Making the deal, coming up with the basic concept, stuff like that. Once I was there, his view was that I should make the movie and do my own thing. When it was done, we set up a screening and showed him the movie. I called him up after, and he had positive things to say about the movie--he was quite excited about it.

—Breck Eisner, director

It was very important to Breck that these crazies have their own signature look...Basically, the approach is to take it [to] the opposite of death...too full of life. Which really fit in with all the characteristics of the diseases we're trying to mimic, which is tetanus, jaundice, a little bit of rabies. So your face, your body, your extremities are sort of blistered, and veins are starting to pop because you have too much blood in you, too much serum, too much everything.

—Robert Hall, make-up effects designer

The Crazies (2010)

Much like Romero's career itself, the proposed remake of *The Crazies* spent several years in development hell, beginning in June 2004 when producers Michael Aguilar (formerly of the Donner Company, where he had worked on the *X Men* films) and Dean Georgaris (writer of *Paycheck* and *The Manchurian Candidate* remake) first optioned the rights directly from Romero, who would serve as a *de facto* executive producer. With a deal set at Paramount, the partners then engaged writer Scott Kosar—who was a hot commodity, given his scripts for *The Texas Chainsaw Massacre* remake (q.v.) and *The Machinist* (2004)—to pen a draft. The following year, it was announced that Kosar's nomination for director, *The Machinist*'s Brad Anderson, had been accepted.

For the next three years nothing happened, the project ultimately ending up in the studio no man's land known as turnaround. In February 2008, it was rescued by Rogue Pictures, the genre division of Universal (responsible for such films as *Seed of Chucky* and *Shaun of the Dead*), who signed Breck Eisner (son of studio executive Michael Eisner and director of the 2005 megaflop *Sahara*) to direct. One of the first things Eisner did was to engage Ray Wright (who rewrote Wes Craven's script for the 2006 thriller *Pulse*) to overhaul Kosar's script. 'The first draft followed the structure of the original film a little more closely,' Eisner told FearNet. 'The original and the first draft both had this bifurcated view: the movie was half from the point of view of the military and half from the point of view of the townspeople. I felt that by putting...in the military's point of view, it turned the movie more towards action and less towards horror. I worked with the writers and we excised the military's point of view and focused on the point of view of the hero and the townsfolk. I think it makes the movie...a darker, more mysterious journey.'

In the small town of Ogden Marsh, Kansas, Sheriff David Dutton is forced to kill a local pig farmer when he wanders onto the high school baseball game, brandishing a shotgun. The next night, a dairy farmer locks his wife and son in a closet, dumps gasoline all over the house, lights it and sits outside watching his home and family burn. Along with his deputy Russell, Dutton discovers a military transport plane has crashed in the local bog, the pilot long since dead. The bog feeds into the town's water supply—and the outlying farms are the first customers. To his horror, Dutton realises that whatever the plane was carrying has somehow infected the town's drinking water. Suddenly, all the lines of communication in town are rendered inoperable—prelude to the arrival of soldiers in white biohazard suits, who forcibly corral the town's residents into a makeshift prison at the ball field. With methodical coldness, they separate the infected—including Dutton's pregnant doctor wife Judy—from the crowd and send them to the high school, which is now an infirmary of the crazed. Dutton and Russell manage to rescue Judy and her office worker Becca and set out on foot, following the highway. Forced to take refuge from helicopter gunships inside a car wash, Dutton's group is attacked by maniacs who kill Becca. Later, Russell causes a

passing military SUV to crash, and the intelligence officer inside tells the group that the town is infected with an enhanced strain of rabies from a biological weapon. Obviously crazed, Russell shoots the man dead. After two confrontations, Dutton disarms Russell, who realises that he is going mad and volunteers to distract the soldiers at a checkpoint so Dutton and Judy can escape. While Russell is shot dead, Dutton and Judy make their way to a truck stop, only to find it abandoned except for three refrigerated trailers full of executed townspeople. After eluding three crazed hunters, the sheriff and his wife abscond with a big truck. On the road to Wichita, the military radio they confiscated begins a countdown—when it reaches zero, a blinding nuclear blast illuminates the night sky: Ogden Marsh is no more.

Unfortunately, Eisner would run into the same mindset at Rogue that had stalled the project at Paramount: '[They] decided that they needed this flick to be populated by young characters...and that just wasn't acceptable,' he told the website Dread Central. 'Spooky stuff happens to adults, too, and when an adult sees these things going on, it's even more intense because now we're dealing with a character [who]... has more life experience than a teenager.' Once again, *The Crazies* was in limbo.

But not for long. That October, it was announced that Overture Films had taken over Rogue's option on the project, with CEO Chris McGurk feeling it was a good fit for the company's expanding slate. 'We've been trying to move into horror fare that is clever and smart,' he told *Variety*. After several modestly-performing movies (*Mad Money, Sunshine Cleaning, Traitor*), they were also looking for something with more breakout potential.

With a $20 million budget, Overture decided to spread the risk by co-financing *The Crazies* with Participant Media, producers of the Edward R Murrow biopic *Good Night and Good Luck* (2005) and the Oscar-winning documentary *An Inconvenient Truth* (2006), and the Abu Dhabi-based Imagenation. 'This is their first genre movie,' Eisner told the website IGN. 'So, clearly, there's a message in there. They saw it and I see it as well. Romero made his movie in the shadow of Vietnam; it was a time of war and a time of economic strife, and I think it's a pretty similar era that we're existing in right now... It seemed to me that the time was right for this movie, and for this idea.'

With *The Crazies* finally about to become a reality, Eisner next set his sights

on how exactly to portray the titular characters: 'The very first thing I did was go through books and online research and medical libraries and just kind of pulled all of the potential diseases that it could really be,' he told Dread Central. 'I was able to

kind of pick and choose what we wanted. The idea was that I was bio-engineering a weapon that took the three best, or worst, infections out there and combined them into a cocktail of sorts. What would the results look like? So in the end we kind of mixed together the greatest hits of awful diseases and added an accelerant.'

To make his concepts a reality, Eisner turned to Robert Hall of the Almost Human special effects company, which had been responsible for TV shows like *Angel*, *Buffy the Vampire Slayer*, *Firefly* and *Terminator: The Sarah Connor Chronicles*. More importantly, they had just done the effects for the film *Quarantine* (2008), which was very similar to the refashioned *Crazies*. Eisner and Hall referenced actual diseases such as Tetanus, Ebola and Rabies in an effort to come up with something unique: 'The first pass on the design ended up looking too much like a zombie,' said Eisner, 'then on the third or fourth try we discovered that what we needed to do was avoid decaying colours and go for more red and bloodshot colours as if the blood was really pumping. There would be no facial decay because not enough time would have passed, so we turned to this kind of enhanced veining and a neck piece which was inspired by tetanus, which causes an extreme tightening of the muscles in the face, neck, and body...Once we had all of these elements, it kind of cued the rage that that these characters were in.'

Despite the fact that he was occupying Romero country, Eisner was adamant that *The Crazies* not be confused with anything else that had borne the legendary director's moniker: 'It's definitely not a zombie film,' he insisted to FearNet. 'That's one of the things I like about it...Zombies are—in theory—undead human beings who are decaying. They all have a collective conscious. They all want to eat brains or infect, and they all act as one. The concept of the infected in *The Crazies* is that they all maintain some sense of their deep psyche. They all act differently, and they may act out based on their own deep-seated desires. That is what keeps it distinctly different from zombies.'

Filming on interiors for *The Crazies* began on March 5, 2009, in Perry, Georgia, while exteriors were shot over two weeks in Lenox, Iowa beginning on April 14. Despite the script being set in Kansas and location scouting that took them all over the Midwest and Canada, the tax breaks that Georgia and Iowa offered were too good to pass up. Iowa also offered the *mise-en-scène* that Eisner desired: 'I really wanted the wide open plains,' he told Dark Horizons. 'I wanted this idea that our heroes are not trapped in small boxes, but open spaces that go on for miles and miles and miles. There's literally nowhere to hide.'

In contrast to the wide-open plains, however, was the town of Ogden Marsh

itself, a tight-knit community that is violently invaded by outside forces, both seen and unseen. 'To me, the small town design of the movie was crucial, one that I embraced from the very beginning of the movie,' Eisner told the website Collider. 'Because oftentimes horror films exist in worlds that are already kind of horrific, whether it's an urban environment or a dark, scary underground environment, or just a world that is already set up to be horrific. I wanted *The Crazies* to be one that exists in a world that, although not perfect, was one that was at peace, and one which was containable and one which can have an identity in the movie that can be summed up quickly and simply and cohesively...the town is pretty much a character in the film at the beginning and then as the military comes in and the disease takes over and the violence grips this small town, you see the whole world is literally turned on its side.'

Scheduled for release in September 2009, *The Crazies* was pushed back into the new year, eventually opening on February 26, 2010, to a $16 million first weekend, on its way to a final domestic gross of $39 million, with an additional $15 million gross overseas. To promote the film, Overture and its parent company Starz Media went all out, including the release of a four-part comic book from Top Cow, a motion comic series downloaded from Amazon, iTunes or Playstation, two games on Facebook—*The Crazies Tower Defense* and *Battlemail*—and the iPhone application, *Beware the Infected*.

Critical response was evenly divided, with *The Boston Globe* praising, 'The *Crazies* does what an exploitation movie should: It gets in, it scares you silly, and it gets out, all while playing fair by the audience.' The *Chicago Tribune* raved, 'One of the year's nicest bloody surprises...*The Crazies* must be approached with the proper expectations. It should not be judged for what it is not. But nearly everything about it works.' *USA Today* advised, 'The *Crazies* is familiar B movie fare, but it's also lively fun and presented with well-paced flair. Be sure to watch it in a safe and contained area.'

Not everyone felt the same, however, including the *Los Angeles Times*, which dismissed *The Crazies* as 'The latest in jacked-up horror remakes that replace iconoclastic chills with paint-by-numbers shocks.' Similarly unimpressed were the *New York Times* ('The filmmakers seem so determined to make a serious, respectable horror movie that they have only the bare minimum of fun. The occasional out-pops-a-homicidal-maniac jolts are too well telegraphed to be very scary, and the denouement manages to be both apocalyptic and anticlimactic') and *The Washington Post* ('The *Crazies* delivers some satisfying scares but skims blithely over the darker ramifications of its story...Breck Eisner's remake nods to contemporary anti-government sentiment, but its military villains are as faceless as the virus that turns the residents of Ogden Marsh into blood-spattered psychopaths— and substantially less scary').

It was in the 'apocalyptic and anticlimactic' denouement that in fact the biggest change occurred between script and screen. As written, the film ended with Dutton and Judy arriving in Wichita, where they stop at a diner for water. The local news is airing the 'official version' of events in Ogden Marsh, which was supposedly destroyed in a chemical plant blast. As he reaches for the check, Dutton notices a red spot, which turns out to be from his bloody nose—he is infected. In contrast, the film simply ends with the couple on the outskirts of Cedar Rapids, Iowa, when the military's 'Eye in the Sky' suddenly breaks in with the directive to start the containment procedure all over again.

Apparently following suit is Eisner, who at the time of writing is attached to not one but three remakes—*The Brood*, *Escape from New York* and *Flash Gordon*. Time will tell if he can parlay the success of *The Crazies* into a niche like Michael Bay's Platinum Dunes company.

DAWN OF THE DEAD

(1978)

It's much more open, more of a high action film, which is why I resist calling it a sequel. It's not so much that as Part 2 of a conceptual trilogy. The zombie phenomenon continues, but it is much bigger. *Night of the Living Dead* is a '40s horror film, made in the '60s. *Dawn of the Dead* is a '60s film, made in the '70s.

—George A Romero, writer, director and editor

George left *Night of the Living Dead* open, that although the main characters themselves didn't make it, human society appeared to be in control, the sheriff was out there cleaning things up. This one will leave you feeling not really sure...that society is even operative any longer.

—Richard Rubinstein, producer

In April 1973, Richard Rubinstein, a 25 year-old with an MBA from Columbia University, was working on Wall Street as a consultant to a brokerage firm that made investments in feature films. His interest in videography had led to a sideline as a columnist for *Filmmakers' Newsletter*, on whose behalf he met and interviewed George Romero. It turned out that each man was what the other had been looking for: Rubinstein wanted to leave Wall Street and get into film production; Romero needed someone to get him out of the financial hole he had dug. The two decided to resurrect an old shell company Romero had set up previously—Laurel Tape & Film—which was rechristened the Laurel Group. 'We had a sense that we didn't want each other's jobs,' Rubinstein told *Cinefantastique*, 'but we had synergistic talents that, when put together, could make more than each of us could do alone. He's 80 percent director and 20 percent a businessman. I'm 20 percent director and 80 percent business. That's enough overlap so that we talk the same language.'

In Laurel's beginnings, however, it was money that talked—and Rubinstein was determined that the new company not repeat Romero's past mistakes. He effectively shut down Latent Image, firing most of the staff, and expressly forbid Romero from making any more films until, Rubinstein told the *New York Times*, 'We had the financial ability to walk away from a bad deal.' Gaining that ability would take three years (in fact, it was not until 1980 that Romero was debt-free), during which time Laurel became a diversified company, producing 15 sports documentaries, placing 23 foreign films with distributors and placing 38 books by authors like Anthony Burgess and JB Priestley with publishers. All of which, Rubinstein told the *Village Voice*, 'built us a business to operate from. [It] gave us a corporate structure, money in the bank, and a professional credibility on a national level. [It] gave us a head start.'

Laurel took its first tentative steps towards feature filmmaking in August 1976, when filming began on *Martin*, a modern vampire story written and directed by Romero. Made on a budget even lower than *Night of the Living Dead* ($100,000, raised from a group of Pittsburgh businessmen), *Martin* nevertheless won raves at the 1977 Cannes and London Film Festivals. The film was put on limited release by Libra Films (who shared an office with Rubinstein in New York) at midnight shows in July 1978—most notably at the Waverly, *Living Dead*'s old stomping ground—where it ran for eleven months. While it never caught on with the general public, *Martin* enjoyed critical acclaim and won second prize at the first-ever US Film Festival in Salt Lake City, Utah (forerunner to Sundance) that September.

With his credibility as a feature filmmaker restored, Romero was at long last able to mount his eagerly-awaited sequel to *Living Dead*. 'I spent five years avoiding making the sequel and another five years trying to put [it] together,' he told the *Winnipeg Free Press*. 'Basically I was afraid that making the two pictures back to back would not be artistically satisfying. I could have produced a carbon copy of the original or something at the other end of the spectrum. I think waiting has allowed me to make a movie that's different but still relates to the original premise.'

What was first known as *Dawn of the Living Dead* had its origins in 1974, when Romero toured the five-year-old, $30 million Monroeville Shopping Mall outside Pittsburgh and had a brainstorm. 'I know the people who own it,' he told *Rolling Stone*, 'and I went through the mall, empty, one time and I said, "Holy shit! That's the *perfect* place for the fulcral episode where we can show the false security of the whole consumer America trip"…I'm really surprised no one else picked up on the idea, because now there are these shopping developments where you can live on top and work and shop down below and never have to leave the building. That's a *trip*. In this film, the mall becomes the *cause*. The four heroes get in there to get some Civil Defence water and food and then they rack out and this consumerism, it's too tempting for them to resist. They arm themselves heavily; they become banditos fighting for all that stuff.'

Romero wrote an 80-page treatment and showed it around. There was some excitement, particularly from American International Pictures, but AIP wanted to cast OJ Simpson, and although Romero had made a documentary on Simpson, he was not interested in making a movie with him. In 1976, Italian producer Alfredo Cuomo (*Tepepa*) showed an interest in the project, but on the condition that Franco Nero (*Camelot*) star. Romero was no more interested in Sir Lancelot than he was in The Juice, however, and talks broke down.

In February 1977, Italian turnstiles were sent spinning by the decidedly gory and surreal horror film *Suspiria*, which ended up grossing $1.4 million worth of *lire* before banking an additional $1.8 million in rentals for US distributor 20th Century Fox that summer. The film's writer and director, 36 year-old Dario Argento, had been responsible for several *giallo* thrillers, including *Four Flies on Grey Velvet* (1971) and *Deep Red* (1975)—and he was also a huge fan of *Night of the Living Dead*. When he learned from Cuomo that Romero had an idea for a sequel, Argento arranged to meet Laurel's main men at their headquarters in New York, where he

Dawn of the Dead (1978)

heard Romero's pitch. Intrigued, he flew with Romero back to Pittsburgh to look at the Monroeville Mall and was hooked. While at the 1977 Cannes Film Festival for the premiere of *Martin*, Romero finalised plans for *Dawn of the Living Dead* as a co-production between Laurel, Cuomo, Argento and his brother Claudio. In exchange for all rights in non-English speaking countries—with the exception of Latin America—Cuomo and the Argentos (backed by Goffredo Lombardo's Titanus Distribution) agreed to put up half the film's budget.

After Cannes, Romero went to Rome for two weeks to collaborate with Argento on the script. 'Before we wrote I travelled around the Caribbean islands to study the stories of the zombie legends and myths,' Argento told *Fangoria*. 'George works the American way, I the European way, but together we worked very well...[we] had a wonderful time.' As far as Rubinstein was concerned, however, the collaboration was less an artistic one than a formality, as he told Gagne: 'Since [the Italians] were co-financing it was a way for them to see what was being done...[George] was basically there as their guest to further the political relationships.' Nevertheless, all the parties concerned had to initial every one of the 253 pages of the working draft to keep their lawyers happy, with Romero getting sole credit as screenwriter while Argento was listed as 'script consultant'.

At a television station in Philadelphia named WJAS, chaos reigns.[2] An inexplicable national phenomenon has caused the newly dead to rise again and seek human victims; law and order is breaking down as a result. Helicopter pilot Stephen Andrews, traffic reporter for WJAS, and his pregnant fiancée Francine, another WJAS employee, decide to steal the helicopter and flee from the pandemonium that is engulfing the city. Meanwhile, two SWAT team members—Roger and Peter—participate in a raid on a ghetto tenement that results in carnage; Roger asks Peter to join him in escaping the horror. The two meet up with Stephen and Francine and the four journey several hundred miles before landing on the roof of an abandoned shopping mall. They discover a storage room filled with Civil Defence rations; gaining entry, they hole up to eat and rest. While Stephen sleeps, Roger and Peter decide to make an excursion into the mall to get a radio, TV and supplies. Stephen awakens and joins the other men downstairs, where the trio manage to battle past hordes of the undead and bring their booty back up to the makeshift apartment. Because of its abundance of supplies—and, unspoken, its consumer appeal—the decision is taken to remain at the mall and wait out the zombie apocalypse. The men block the entrances with trucks, but Roger is bitten by zombies in the process and begins to get sick. The four manage to close off the mall and exterminate the zombies inside before Roger becomes the last undead casualty of the campaign. From news reports, the survivors learn that the situation has become

2 The station's call letters were changed in the film to WGON when WJAS, an actual Pittsburgh radio station, refused permission to use its call-sign.

unmanageable and civilisation has largely broken down; soon, the TV and radio go dead. Stephen, Francine and Peter make a comfortable life for themselves in the mall (which includes Stephen giving his lover flying lessons) until a large gang of motorcycle thieves arrive on the scene, determined to loot the place. The gang breaks in and engage in a gun battle with Peter and Stephen, while also fighting off the undead legions that have regained access to the mall. In the resulting melee, Stephen is shot and then attacked by zombies; he dies, only to revive and lead a group of zombies upstairs to the apartment. Peter is waiting for him, however, with a high-powered rifle greeting. Peter then ushers Francine to the helicopter and holds off the zombies before shooting himself in the head. Knowing she cannot make it alone, Francine starts the helicopter and thrusts her head into the spinning blades as dawn breaks on the horizon.

With the initial draft written, it fell to Laurel to come up with the remainder of the film's budget. A variety of sources were tapped: New York film handlers Herbert R Steinmann and Billy Baxter, best known for importing Lina Wertmuller's films, took a 32% stake, Pittsburgh insurance broker Alvin Rogal put up 12.5%, and Romero, Rubinstein and their relatives provided the rest. Various reports put the budget at anywhere from $400,000 to $1.5 million (the most commonly quoted figure), but the actual cost was $650,000, which was kept under wraps in order not to prejudice potential distributors.

Filming on the newly-titled *Dawn of the Dead* began at the Monroeville Mall on November 13, 1977. Because of his personal relationship with the mall's owners, Oxford Development, Romero was able to obtain the use of the mall at a bargain price—$40,000 and a percentage of the profits. Of the 143 stores located therein, only thirteen refused to give their permission to be used in the film. However, because of store operations, shooting could only be done late at night and early in the morning. 'That meant often we couldn't get our equipment set up and start shooting until 1:30 am,' Romero told Newhouse Newspapers. 'Then we had to be out of there by 7:30 am. We shot on Sunday mornings, too, because the mall doesn't open until noon on Sunday. The mayhem that went on in the parking lot as we were pulling out and the customers were driving in was scarier than anything in our movie.' Rather than trying to shoot around the mall's Christmas decorations (which would have been a continuity and logistical nightmare), *Dawn* relocated during the month of December to downtown Pittsburgh, where the opening scenes in the TV station and housing project were filmed. Production resumed at the mall on January 3, 1978 and finished on February 10. On February 25, *Night of the Living Dead* debuted on Pittsburgh television. Hosted by George Anderson, the *Pittsburgh Post-Gazette* drama critic, his guest was none other than the film's director, who took the opportunity to also show clips from *Dawn* for the first time.

STEVE
Don't ya wonder what the archaeologists are gonna think...guys in

> the future...diggin' the place up. Imagine all the stuff in these boxes... jewellery...maybe they'll figure it's all some kind of offering to the gods...like in the pyramids...a burial chamber.

> **PETER**
> **That's exactly what it is now...**

> *–Unfilmed exchange, from the original script*

With a shooting script that was roughly half the length of Romero and Argento's original Roman draft, it was natural that several things on the page either did not make it to the screen or were substantially altered, including:

- Access to the mall is much less involved, eliminating Roger (Scott Reiniger) and Peter (Ken Foree) winding their way through several different offices, including that of the mall president, who has shot himself.
- Stephen (David Emge) is only attacked by one zombie, instead of the original three, on his way down to the mall.
- Besides the Hare Krishna zombie that attacks Francine (Gaylen Ross), there was originally a scene with another zombie trying to invade the survivors' apartment after the men have returned from their raid.
- Peter and Stephen are unmolested when they raid the gun shop, whereas in the script they must fight off zombies to get to the weapons.
- Roger's corpse is buried in one of the gardens, whereas originally it was just dumped on a heap with other dead zombies in a bank vault (which was also changed to a meat locker).
- In the script, Francine takes care of the animals in the mall's pet store and adopts a puppy that ends up being killed by the zombies (off-screen). None of this was shot.
- Originally it was intended that Peter be the aggressor in defending the mall from the motorcycle gang, whereas the film has Stephen in that role.

As with *Night of the Living Dead*, the biggest difference between the script and film of *Dawn* was the ending, although this time it was changed to something more hopeful. Despite having shot the scripted ending, Romero decided instead to allow Peter and Francine to escape in the helicopter. 'I really pulled toward the tragic ending,' the director told Gagne, 'but then I couldn't decide whether I was doing it just because I wanted a family resemblance to the first film. I really got lost in what I wanted. Also, the effect didn't work great—it would have been spectacular to have [Francine] stand up into the blades, and I'm sure that had the effect been wonderful, I would have kept it that way. I was really on the fence with it, right down to the last. Then I just woke up one day and decided to let them go simply because I liked them too much.'

On March 31, it was announced that *Dawn* would be shown to prospective buyers at the 1978 Cannes Film Festival. Romero had locked himself in the editing room and was feverishly cutting away to make the May deadline, finally getting *Dawn*

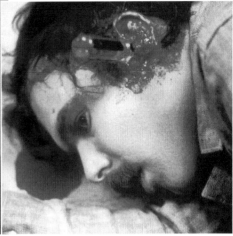

down to 139 minutes. Several major international distributors were duly impressed and signed up for the film, including Germany's Neue Constantin Film and Japan's Nippon Herald Films. The biggest coup came in the form of American major United Artists, which, though refusing to distribute the film in the US due to its violent content, had no such compunction about releasing it in South America and Australia. As a condition of the co-production agreement, Argento had the right to re-edit *Dawn* as he saw fit for foreign consumption. In September 1978, his version, titled *Zombi*, was released in Italy to huge business, eventually earning $3 million, though that total was somewhat tainted by controversy after Titanus raised ticket prices 20% on the film. Critical response was strong, with Rome's *Il Messaggero* raving, 'This impressive effort of Romero should not be missed!' The Venetian paper *Il Gazzettino* judged *Zombi* 'An extremely rich and opulent—we would even say high-class—product' and Milan's *L'Europeo* advised its readers, '*Zombi* may be read as a catastrophic allegory on the end of capitalism. Try seeing the film if you are brave enough.'

Zombi was very different from the version of *Dawn* that had been shown at Cannes, starting with its soundtrack. Whereas Romero had used largely stock music, Argento had commissioned an original score from the Italian rock group Goblin (who had also scored *Deep Red* and *Suspiria*) and mixed it extremely loud, rendering much of the dialogue inaudible. To make matters worse, Argento's version used the original location recordings, meaning natural sound instead of sound effects and the original dialogue instead of a cleaner, post-synchronised track.

Many scenes were deleted as well, giving *Zombi* a running time that was over 20 minutes shorter than Romero's initial cut. Some of the things left out of this version included:

- Stephen and Francine's encounter with a group of phoney cops at the Philadelphia Police Dock.
- The exchange between Francine and Peter in the helicopter where he tells her about his family.
- The zombie that gets the top of its head cut off by the 'copter's blades.
- Roger and Peter's first excursion into the mall.

195

- Roger and Peter's first run at blocking the mall entrances with trucks.
- A montage of Stephen, Francine and Peter shopping after Roger's death.
- Interludes such as Francine pitifully eyeing a zombie in a baseball uniform or her asking Stephen and Peter 'What have we done to ourselves?' when their complacent existence gets on her nerves.

In addition to some added dialogue and a few extra shots of gut-munching and dismemberment, Argento did include one scene that Romero saw fit to eliminate, when Stephen, Roger and Peter, relaxing after their raid on the mall, listen to the radio and hear the news that communication has been lost with Philadelphia:

STEVE

I know GON's out by now. That place is a madhouse back there. People are crazy...if they'd just organise. I can't believe they let it get this bad...I can't believe they couldn't handle it! Look at us; look what we were able to do today. Knocked the shit out of 'em...they never even touched us. Not really.

PETER

They touched us good, flyboy. We're lucky to get out with our asses— you don't forget that. You underestimate those suckers and you get eaten. They got one big advantage over us—they don't think. And that bunch out there, that's just a handful. And every day there's gonna be more.

STEVE

But those things can be stopped so easily! If people would just listen; do what has to be done...

PETER

How 'bout it, flyboy? Let's say the lady gets killed. You be able to chop off her head?

To prepare for its imminent release in America, St Martin's published a hardback novelisation of *Dawn of the Dead* in December. It would be the second such adaptation by Susanna Sparrow after *Martin* the previous year, which was published as a paperback from Stein & Day. The St Martin's book is actually Romero's original script in narrative form, with most of the dialogue and scene descriptions reproduced verbatim. Sparrow does add some back story to each of the characters—we learn, for instance, that Francine (Parker) is a 23-year-old divorcee who got married too young then 'found herself' and became WGON's assistant station manager—and a much broader description of the mall itself (including its billionaire owner, CJ Porter). Unlike the script, the book mirrors the upbeat ending Romero chose for the film (doubly so, since Francine's puppy also escapes in the helicopter).

The Hills Have Eyes (2006) / INSET: Wes Craven

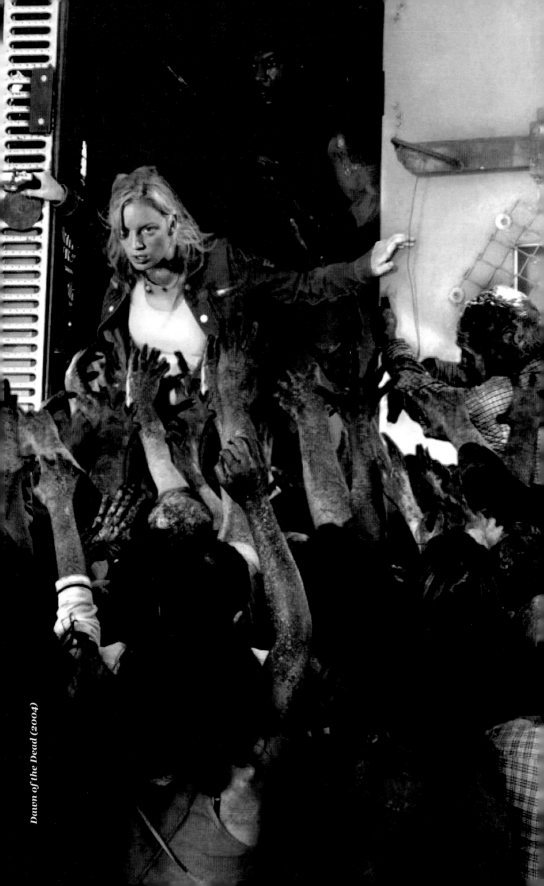

Dawn of the Dead (2004)

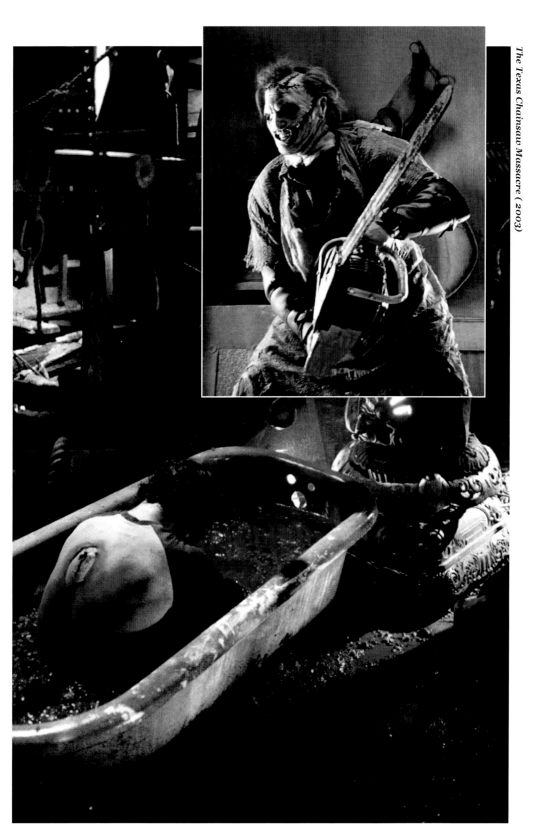

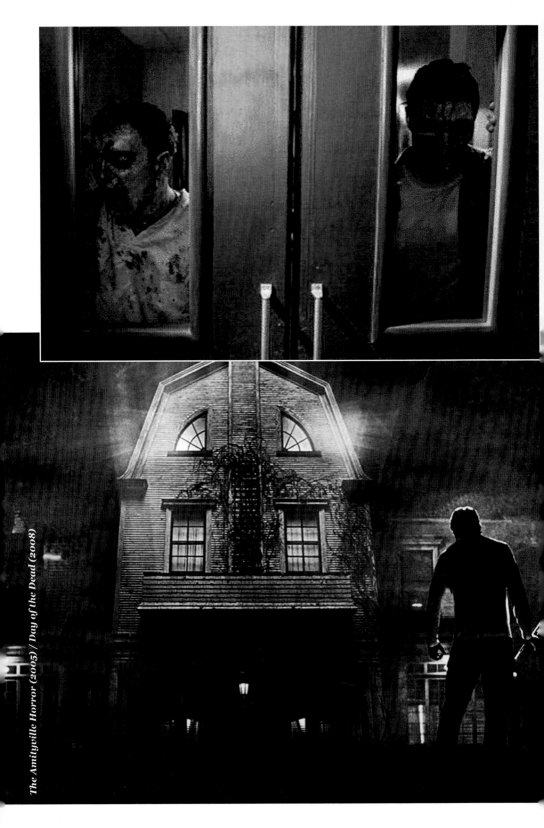

The Amityville Horror (2005) / Day of the Dead (2008)

My Bloody Valentine 3D (2009) / When a Stranger Calls (2006)

When it came to assembling his final, 126-minute version of *Dawn* for domestic release, Romero apparently took his cues from Argento and made several changes from his initial cut, including:

- Using less stock music and more of Goblin's original score.
- Deleting shots of Roger shooting zombies in the tenement cellar.
- Greatly shortening Stephen and Francine's encounter with the phony cops at the Philadelphia Police Dock.
- Eliminating the exchange between Francine and Peter in the helicopter where he tells her about his family.
- Deleting Roger and Peter's first excursion into the mall.
- Eliminating an exchange between Stephen and Francine where they debate about staying at the mall.
- Deleting a montage of Stephen, Francine and Peter shopping after Roger's death.
- Shortening the biker gang's assault on the mall and battle with the zombies.

One thing Romero did not alter, however, was the extremely violent content of the film, courtesy of 31-year-old make-up effects whiz Tom Savini. Heads are blown up and chopped off, people are ripped apart and eviscerated and zombies feast on various body parts—all in full light and Technicolor, as if Sam Peckinpah himself had been turned loose on the horror genre. 'The explicit violence is necessary because it's partially what the film is about,' Romero told *Starlog*. 'There's a violent under-bed in America, and violence is certainly an integral part of any revolution. Having it there in such abundance is almost easier to take than an occasional isolated moment. It becomes texture—it's constantly threatening and you don't know when it's going to unleash...I'm kind of playing around a little bit to see if the violence can be that dominant a factor in the film and still enable the audience to get past it and experience the storyline and the allegory.'

The allegory to which Romero was referring was as much a part of *Dawn*'s conception as the horrific violence. Conspicuous consumption is just as big a threat to the lives of our four survivors as being eaten by zombies, and the mall is the ultimate temple of materialism, as evidenced by how it is described in the original script:

Stores of every type offer gaudy displays of consumer items. Everything from clothing to appliances. Photo equipment; audio and video outlets; sporting goods and weaponry; gourmet foods and natural organic foods...And at either end of the concourse like the main Altars at each end of a Cathedral, stand the mammoth two storey Department Stores; great symbols of a consumer society...The images are all too familiar, but in their present state they appear as an archaeological discovery revealing the Gods and Customs of a civilisation now gone. The ghosts of a civilisation, however, are not figments in the mind. They are quite real. And they walk below in the aisles of the great Cathedral.

Romero was nothing if not direct, and even he had some regrets about whether the

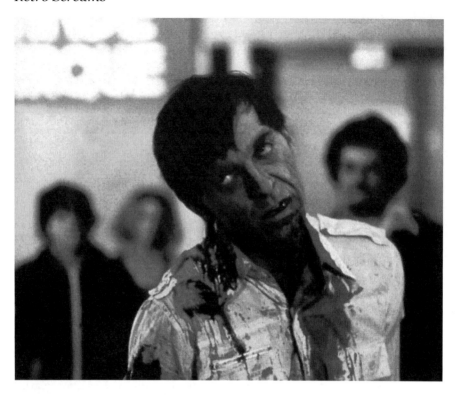

'message' might get in the way of the experience: 'As for the jibes at the consumer society,' he told the *Winnipeg Free Press*, 'I'm not entirely convinced they're successful. I felt that placing the action in the shopping mall offered an extra dimension to the tension. But I'm afraid that sometimes I've been too obvious about my sentiments.'

For prospective American distributors, however, it was not the sentiments that caused the problem—it was the violence that most saw as excessive and Romero's unwillingness to cut the picture down to qualify for an R rating. When *Dawn* was submitted to the Motion Picture Association of America, Laurel was told that the MPAA did not have a computer big enough to list all the changes necessary in order to avoid an X rating, something that, by then, had an unwanted stigma attached to it. 'The X is not a patented trademark,' Romero pointed out to the *Los Angeles Times*. 'X used to mean adult—remember *Midnight Cowboy* [1969] was originally an X—but now it means sleaze and porn. X is a symbol and not an abbreviation, like R, PG and G. Anyone who went out and made a motel movie could advertise it as a triple X.' Because of this, Romero and Rubinstein proposed the rare and highly risky step that *Dawn* be released *without* an MPAA rating. 'We're all generally supportive of the rating system,' Rubinstein told *Variety*, 'but felt that since there is no classification for an adult feature that happens not to have sexual content, we didn't want the misconception—or the economic sanctions—of an X rating.'

Serious consideration was given to *Dawn* by AIP, Warner Brothers and United Film Distribution, the motion picture arm of United Artists Communications (a distant cousin to the United Artists film studio), which was at that time the second largest theatre owner in the country. Given his experience with Continental and Walter Reade, Romero could be forgiven his lack of enthusiasm for UFD, but they were the only company willing to release the picture unrated—and had the theatres to book it in. 'A lot of theatres resist playing an unrated picture,' Rubinstein told *Cinefantastique*, 'some newspapers won't take ads, and you can't buy commercial time before 11 pm. But we felt that to cut the picture to get an R rating, we'd destroy it. George and I were in perfect synch. I thought we'd make more money leaving it uncut, and he wanted to leave it uncut because it was his baby. We both got our satisfaction.'

UFD arranged a series of previews for *Dawn*, beginning in New York on February 8, 1979, then Los Angeles on February 17, and a special midnight screening at the LA International Film Exposition on March 17. The film's biggest pre-release exposure came at the USA Film Festival in Dallas on April 7, where it had been invited by, of all people, Roger Ebert—the critic who had lambasted *Night of the Living Dead*. 'The festival asked four film critics to invite new American films and discuss them, and *Dawn* was one of my choices,' he wrote. 'It was also the most controversial film: after one screening a shouting match developed between audience members who asked, "What kind of sick mind could make a film like this?" and others who called it the best film in the festival.'

'In Dallas, in such a conservative setting, we had about 20% of the audience walk out,' Romero told the *Pittsburgh Post-Gazette*. 'Then it turned into a real scene when some of the people who stayed started hissing some of the people leaving. Roger Ebert...was to appear with me on stage after the screening. "I'm willing to get up there if you are," I told him. The question session was really good, though.'

The first American print review of *Dawn* appeared in the *Dallas Times Herald* by critic CW Smith, whose verdict was seminal: '*Dawn of the Dead* is without any doubt the most horrific, brutal, nightmarish descent into Hell (literally) ever put on the screen, and its power can be gauged by the peals of maniacal laughter bursting forth from many of us who survived the movie's first few moments. The film gave me nightmares so severe that I awoke afraid to return to sleep; its frames are burned forever on my consciousness in an indelible way.' The official American premiere of *Dawn of the Dead* was at the Gateway Theatre in Pittsburgh on April 12. It carried the following warning: 'There is no explicit sex in this picture. However, there are scenes of violence which may be considered shocking. No one under 17 will be admitted.'[3] While the film was a hit with hometown audiences, earning over $55,000 in its first week at three theatres, it did not sit well with local critics. Donald Miller of the *Pittsburgh Post-Gazette* lambasted, 'The opening scenes were confusing for the viewer to understand exactly what was happening. Later when we know what is happening, we could use some relief. The real point to this picture seems to be to see how far its makers went to make a low-grade horror flick horrible.' Much more thoughtful was Ed Blank of the *Pittsburgh Press*, whose analysis was astute: 'By no means lavish, the film is orchestrated like a coherent bad dream set in a sterile neon wonderland. It's filled with revolting

---

3 This was changed to 'Prohibited to anyone under 17 unless accompanied by a parent or guardian' for *Dawn*'s west coast release.

sights, yet it isn't a nightmare. It can't be. At least one of the leading men behaves anti-heroically—taking astonishing pleasure in pulverising and blowing apart the zombies. The effect on an even slightly sensitive audience is distancing. The human characters, by looting and enjoying violence so much, forfeit some of the empathy that otherwise would be theirs. They also push *Dawn* beyond the routine perimeter of horror films—past the 'nightmare' conflict of human and non-human—into a sphere in which humanly evil people take on the helplessly once human.'

Blank's real objection to the movie, however, had more to do with its effect on the audience: 'Nothing in the movie is quite so disturbing as last night's audience reaction. Clearly *Dawn* was appreciated. There was plenty of positive reaction: rooting, laughing and gasping. One can, with reservations, understand the glee with which some of the gruesome action is watched; it's visceral and gaudy. But when they cheer looting and applaud anti-heroic violence, they create a horror more real than any in the movie.' Romero actually came to agree, telling *Starlog*: 'What bothers me most about the movie is that I've seen audiences get off on the idea of having possession of the mall. That's a dangerous fantasy...I don't think the picture will cause anybody to go out and shoot someone—but it just might cause somebody to try to break into a shopping mall.'

Upon its release in New York on April 20, *Dawn* proved to be a surprise hit, grossing nearly $1 million in its first week alone. In the coming months of national release, *Dawn* would earn over $16 million at the box office. In addition, it enjoyed unprecedented critical acclaim for a so-called 'splatter' film. Tom Allen placed *Dawn* among his Top 10 Films of 1979, predicting, 'I think it's going to be the biggest cult blockbuster of all time...While there's no denying the exploitative frissons of violence driven past unchartered limits of exaggeration, the film also throbs with sardonic commentary and a compulsive inner logic. A comic apocalypse has come to maul the becalmed 70s.' Ebert championed the movie as 'Brilliant filmmaking that inspires extreme reactions...Is the film a scathing social satire or a wallowing in violence and depravity? This debate alone is what makes *Dawn of the Dead* an extraordinary film—hard to take, impossible to forget.' Kevin Thomas proclaimed, '*Dawn of the Dead* is one of the most genuinely original American movies of this or any other year' while *Playboy*'s Bruce Williamson evaluated Romero as 'An audacious, stunningly talented filmmaker, a visionary who happens to view the world through garishly tinted glasses.'

For some critics, however, Romero's glasses were *too* garishly tinted. Janet Maslin of the *New York Times* told her readers, 'Some people hate musicals, and some dislike westerns, and I have a pet peeve about flesh-eating zombies who never stop snacking. Accordingly, I was able to sit through only the first 15 minutes of *Dawn of the Dead*.' After receiving a fair amount of heat for printing a review of a movie that Maslin did not actually see, the *Times*' senior critic Vincent Canby stepped in and dismissed *Dawn* as 'Fake mayhem and not worth getting exercised about. If simulated cannibalism is your dish, then go and enjoy it. If not, stay away.' Gary Arnold seemed to agree: 'Witty as they sometimes are, Romero's ironies aren't subtle or devastating enough to justify lengthy contemplation. *Dawn* seems like a good 80-minute horror premise stretched out at least half an hour too long.'

Internationally, *Dawn* amassed some $40 million, including $3 million from Japan and $5 million from Germany. It also inspired a raft of mostly Neapolitan rip-offs, the first of which, Lucio Fulci's *faux* sequel *Zombi 2* (aka *Island of the Living Dead*), went into production in April 1979 and premiered in Italy just four months later. Such was the speed of the Italian copy machine that Fulci's film (retitled *Zombie Flesh Eaters*) actually beat *Dawn* to British screens by some five months in 1980 (though *Dawn* had been shown at the 1979 London Film Festival).

As a testament to Romero's newfound success, a week-long retrospective of his work was held in July 1980 at New York's Harold Clurman Theatre, including three screenings each of *Night of the Living Dead* and *Dawn of the Dead* and the New York premiere of *Jack's Wife*, nine years after its production. In addition to

continuous midnight shows around the country, *Dawn* would receive three major national re-releases: in March 1980, May 1982 (on a double-bill with *Mother's Day*) and May 1983. (The latter release endured a backlash from fans when *Dawn* actually sustained some 50 cuts to qualify for an R rating so it could be released with Romero's *Creepshow*; 1982. UFD subsequently pulled the edited version, surrendered the rating and vowed never again to release *Dawn* in a truncated form.) While UFD and others were anxious for an immediate follow-up to Romero's biggest-ever money-maker, the director was not to be rushed. 'Everyone wants to do the third part of the Living Dead Trilogy,' he told the *Los Angeles Times*, 'but I don't want to do that right now. All I have is a sketch for it. I'm threatening to do a *Zombies at Home*, a kind of *My Three Sons*, nonviolent and totally boring.' Instead, Romero went in a totally different direction, retelling the Camelot story as a modern-day parable on motorcycles called *Knightriders*, which was released by UFD in April 1981 to the kind of lacklustre business that reminded one of the bad old days back at Latent Image.

(2004)

I think *Dawn of the Dead* as a project is inherently cool. Zombies are inherently cool. There's nothing you can do to get away from that. People have gravitated toward zombies for a variety of reasons and for me, it is mostly [because] you can kill them with impunity. There's no moral imperative.

–Zack Snyder, director

The story benefits from a larger canvas, and the fact that malls have changed so much. There are all kinds of things we can use, down to the food courts. George did a lot with a pedestrian mall...where the only real highlight was a hockey rink.

–Richard Rubinstein, co-producer

In June 1985, just prior to the release of *Day of the Dead*, George Romero left the Laurel Group and Richard Rubinstein carried on alone until merging with the Aaron Spelling Entertainment Group in 1988. He saw Laurel through two more mergers (with Blockbuster in 1992 and Viacom in 1994) until he decided he had had enough of the corporate revolving-door and left Laurel in 1995 to start a new company, New Amsterdam Entertainment. Everything Laurel had produced remained with Viacom, with the exception of Romero's movies, two of which Rubinstein had tenaciously held onto—even setting up a separate company, the MKR (Messina-Kolbert-Rubinstein) Group, to control the rights to both *Martin* and *Dawn of the Dead*.

Over the years, many had tried and failed to convince Rubinstein to allow them to remake *Dawn*, but a pitch from Beacon Pictures' president Marc Abraham

finally got his attention. 'Growing up, I had always loved [zombie] movies,' Abraham told the website About.com, 'but *Dawn of the Dead* was my favourite. There were always other zombie movies around, but *Dawn* felt to me like the one movie that stood out from the rest. I feel that the genre has not received the attention it deserves in this generation.' Rubinstein evidently agreed, and signed off on a new *Dawn*—with the proviso that he would be one of its producers.

In August 2001, it was announced that the script was being written by James Gunn, who had got his start at New York's infamous Troma Entertainment, where he co-wrote and executive-produced *Tromeo and Juliet* in 1996, as well as co-authoring (with Troma president Lloyd Kaufman) the book *All I Need to Know About Filmmaking I Learned from the Toxic Avenger*, a reference to the studio's franchise movie series. After leaving Troma he headed west to Warner Brothers, where he wrote two adaptations: the first being *Mad* magazine's *Spy vs Spy* comic strip (which did not get made) and the second being Hanna-Barbera's popular cartoon *Scooby-Doo* (which did, in 2002). After being hired by Beacon to work on *Dawn,* Gunn gleefully told *Variety,* 'It combines my two all-time favourite things, flesh-eating zombies and shopping.'

Everett, Washington, north of Seattle. Nurse Ana Cortez and her husband Luis are awakened early by their neighbour's girl, who appears to be injured. But when Luis goes to help her, she suddenly attacks him, ripping out his throat. Ana is unable to stop the bleeding and the 911 lines are busy; Luis dies. Ana has no time for mourning, however—Luis is soon revived and trying to kill her. Ana flees the house to find Everett in chaos as people are being attacked everywhere in an orgy of violence. After wrecking her car, she meets policeman Kenneth Robeson and the two journey on foot together until they encounter the trio of black gangbanger Randall 'Peacock' Bryant, his pregnant girlfriend Luda Chernyak and their companion Michael Shaunessy. The quintet decide to take refuge in the nearby Crossroads Mall, as Michael had got the keys to The Gap store from a neighbourhood kid. Once inside, they are attacked by zombies and Luda is bitten. They make their way to the upper level, only to be confronted by three security guards: Terry, E-Bomb and their hot-headed leader CJ, who disarms the survivors and treats them like prisoners on work detail. A confrontation erupts when an eighteen-wheeler arrives on the scene with 12 more refugees and CJ refuses them sanctuary; the other men immobilise CJ and E-Bomb and put them in a holding cell. The group of mall-dwellers swells to 20, with the addition of truck driver Norma, her teenage daughter Nicole (and her dog Captain Amazing), yuppie Steve Markus and his socialite girlfriend, Irish Catholic priest Glenn O'Ryan, Goth-girl Celeste and six others who either end up dying or becoming zombie food. For the next week, the rest of the survivors make a life for themselves inside the mall until the power goes out. Kenneth, Michael, CJ and E-Bomb descend to the parking garage to activate the generators when they are attacked by zombies; E-Bomb is killed. Meanwhile, Norma enters Randall and Luda's store to check on them, only to find Luda, dying, has given birth to an undead foetus. Luda revives, but before Norma can shoot her, Randall and Norma shoot each other; a dying Norma sees Luda feast on Randall while the zombie baby scurries away. Ana and the others come upon the grisly scene and have to do battle with their former comrades turned monsters. Realising that the fuel for the generators will not last, the remaining survivors decide to flee the mall using two parking shuttles, which they will take to the marina to use Steve's boat for an exodus to the San Juan Islands, off the coast of Puget Sound. Predictably, the escape goes awry, and only a few make it to the marina, where Michael is forced to stay behind because of a zombie bite. As he commits suicide on the shore, Ana, Kenneth, Nicole, Terry and Captain Amazing sail off to an uncertain future.

In May 2002, Abraham decided to leave Beacon and form a new company called Strike Entertainment, to be headquartered at Universal Studios, where he had a four-year distribution deal. He took two of his Beacon associates with him—CEO Thomas Bliss and development head Eric Newman (son of film composer Randy Newman)—as well as the script for *Dawn of the Dead*. After producing the hit action film *The Rundown* (2003), Strike turned its attention back to remaking Romero's classic. In March 2003, they signed Zack Snyder, a 37-year-old TV commercial veteran with no feature film experience, to direct *Dawn*. 'There was no question after meeting him that this was a guy who was going to bring every ounce of his heart and soul and viscera to the movie,' Abraham told the *Los Angeles Times*. Like Romero himself, Snyder was fascinated by what the zombies could represent, as he admitted to About.com: 'They present like an anonymous enemy that doesn't rely on politics or skin colour to make you think, "Oh, that's the bad guy." They are clearly that – and they are everyone. I think that's one of the reasons [to do this film]. It allowed me to make a movie that in a lot of ways verges on cult status, and that's what I wanted to do.'

A DECAPITATED HEAD plummets through the hole in the truck and lands beside the jostled Citizens. The Head, still alive, looks around and gnaws helplessly at the air. Steve Markus's SOCIALITE GIRLFRIEND, a pretty, somewhat bimboesque young woman, and a HEAVYSET MAN freak out.

SOCIALITE

Somebody kill it!

HEAVYSET MAN

Don't touch it! It's diseased!

—From Gunn's original draft; unused

When *Scooby-Doo* became a surprise hit, Gunn found himself immediately writing a sequel (*Scooby Too*) and was unavailable when his *Dawn* script needed reworking. Michael Tolkin, Oscar-nominated writer of Robert Altman's *The Player* (1992), was brought in to do a complete overhaul.

Tolkin started with the characters: eliminating some peripheral, unnamed parts ('Heavyset Man', 'Fanatic', 'Socialite Girlfriend'), expanding others ('Farmer Brother' became Tucker, 'Goth Chick' became Monica, 'Tall Man' became Frank) and drastically changing the rest (Randall went from being a stereotypical black punk to a more generic character, Father Glenn became an atheist church organist named Bruce, CJ started off as an antagonist but became a hero). Nearly all of the dialogue was changed and several of Gunn's more outrageous notions were dropped as well, including a severed head that uses its tongue to move (shades of John Carpenter's *The Thing*), an undead foetus that 'scurries like a crab' before being blown to pieces (*a la Aliens*) and two scenes that actually prefigure the 2007 remake of *I Am Legend*, when zombies use abandoned trucks and ladders to assault the mall and a pack of zombie dogs attack Captain Amazing.

BRUCE

All of these people, the people here, the people outside, they used to be alive. We loved them, we hated them, but they were alive, the way we're alive now. And after this, there's eternity. It's a mystery, but we'll get there.

—From Bruce's eulogy in the Tolkin rewrite; unused

Still dissatisfied with the results, Strike and Snyder hired another Oscar nominee, Scott Frank (*Out of Sight*), to take a third pass at the script. The biggest change was to accommodate the casting of Mekhi Phifer (*ER*'s Dr Gregory Pratt); as a result, Randall Bryant was now the black Andre, who is very similar to the way that the character was originally outlined in the Gunn draft. Three major scenes were also completely reworked: the arrival of the refugees in the truck (the Gunn-Tolkin scripts have them arrive in a semi that crashes through the garage, almost killing Michael and Randall, then jams in the entrance; Michael and Randall have to back the truck out into the parking lot, swing it around, and back into the loading dock for the passengers in the trailer to exit); the survivors' dinner before the power goes out (the Tolkin script sees Michael and Ana and Terry and Nicole respectively pair off and confess their feelings for each other); and the burial where the decision is made to leave the mall (the Tolkin script has Bruce the organist deliver the eulogy before everyone realises that the fuel for the generators will not last and a plan to escape must be made). In Frank's version, the rescue is much less involved, the dinner is a group affair where Michael talks about his jobs and family, and the funeral is presided over by Kenneth after the (now gay and renamed) Glen denies a belief in God. Likewise, the reasoning for the escape now has less to do with practicality and more a desire not to die in the mall like the others.

With a budget of $26 million, production began on June 2, 2003, at the Thornhill Square Mall in Thornhill, Ontario, Canada, which had been scheduled for demolition. It was renovated under the direction of production designer Andrew Neskoromny, and several fictitious stores (Case Hardware, Hallowed Grounds Coffee, Reflex Sports, etc.) were created when real companies like Starbucks Coffee refused to lend their support. Changing the setting from Washington to Milwaukee, Wisconsin, was Snyder's idea: 'I was born in [Green Bay] so I thought it would be fun,' he told the website UGO. 'We knew we were going to shoot in Toronto so I wanted a US city that would be similar to the landscape.'

Snyder also sought to pay homage to Romero's film in many ways: one of the mall's stores is called 'Gaylen Ross' (after the actress who played Francine); two of the original film's stars have cameos—Scott Reiniger as a general and Ken Foree as a televangelist (who gets to utter his classic line, 'When there's no more room in hell, the dead will walk the earth')—as does Tom Savini (who plays a sheriff), the WGON traffic helicopter flies by when Ana is making her escape, and BP Trucking once again supplied the rigs outside the mall. However, unlike the original *Dawn*'s beginning *in medias res* (we are told that the zombie phenomenon has been happening for weeks), Snyder's version sees the catastrophe happen literally overnight: 'We got to

see the fall of society, because that's what I'm into and I was into having it happen really fast. I have a feeling that our whole way of life is like an eggshell that we think is so impervious, but once you put a crack in it comes apart pretty quickly.'

Quickness came to differentiate this new take on *Dawn* in regards to the zombies as well. Unlike Romero's shuffling, leaden-footed hordes, Snyder's zombies are nimble and energised. 'When I first heard they moved fast, I was a bit disappointed,' co-star Sarah Polley told *USA Today*. 'I like the idea of the zombies being the hapless enemy, loping, dumb and hilarious. But now I'm sold. It really does add a caffeinated feel to the film. Besides, we live in a fast-paced, cutthroat culture. Monsters have to be fast, too.' Snyder was also quick to label his version of *Dawn* as a 're-envisioning' rather than a remake, as he told About.com: 'I think re-envisioning is when you take an idea and sort of make it your own. Remaking is when you say, "Okay, I want that movie experience again." I don't know...I think there's arguments for both. [But] I like the original so much that I couldn't have [just remade it].'

Any film with the name *Dawn of the Dead*, however, would have to meet certain audience expectations, not the least of which was graphic gore and intense action. Snyder undoubtedly sensed this and was refreshingly old-school when it came to execution, not relying totally on CGI effects or flashy technique. 'I wanted to do a make-up based movie with a lot of violence,' he told UGO. 'It would be scary when it should be. I'm a director/cameraman in the commercial world and everything I do is pretty slick, but I really had fun letting it go and making something a little less polished and organic.' In this, Snyder clearly felt he was on to something, as he told *USA Today*: 'There is a bubbling groundswell for these kind of films that don't feel like a Hollywood movie exactly, one that puts the cult experience back in.'

Apparently so; 2002-03 would see the release of two zombie films based on popular video games: *Resident Evil* (to which Romero himself was once attached to direct but was replaced by Paul WS Anderson) and *House of the Dead*. The former was a huge success, the latter was not, but the tipping point for the genre came with the release of the low budget ($8 million), shot-on-digital video British thriller *28 Days Later*, which follows a small band of survivors who trek through a devastated England after a mysterious virus turns the population into homicidal maniacs. Heavily inspired by Romero's zombie movies and *The Crazies* (as well as a healthy dose of John Wyndham's *Day of the Triffids*), the film was released in the UK in November 2002 and in America seven months later. It received near-unanimous critical acclaim, grossed over $82 million worldwide and beat Snyder to the punch when it came to introducing so-called 'running zombies'.

Filming on the *Dawn* retake ended on August 22, 2003, but as it turned out, this was not the end of shooting. The film's original conclusion was the same as that in the script—with the survivors sailing off into the sunrise—but audiences at test screenings in January 2004 were not satisfied with this reprise of the original's 'hopeful' ending. As a result, additional footage was hastily shot, both off the coast of Catalina Island in California and at Universal Studios, showing Ana (Polley), Kenneth (Ving Rhames), Nicole (Lindy Booth) and Terry (Kevin Zegers) on their sailing journey and winding up docking at an island that turns out to be infested with zombies. The entire sequence is shot POV with a hand-held video camera and ends with a crowd of ghouls attacking and (presumably) killing the remaining foursome. Snyder then interspersed the footage with the end credits, giving audiences a reason to stay in their seats. While this revision is indicative of the postmodern, anti-romantic mentality that seems to inform 21st century horror movies (in both tone *and* technique), it nevertheless renders the film dramatically inconsistent, as it makes meaningless the self-sacrifice of two of the main characters, including Ana's second love, who die so that the others might escape.

While making additions to the film's coda, Snyder conversely eliminated over 20 minutes' worth of material from the rough cut, including:

- The whole sequence of Ana, Kenneth and the rest actually entering the mall and having to battle zombies on their way inside.
- A heated exchange between Michael (Jake Weber) and Andre (Phifer) about who should be in charge.
- A scene with Andre and Michael getting the loading door open for the refugees and having to shoot a legless zombie before opening the back of the truck.
- Terry and Ana joking about old headlines while he makes lattes.

- Michael and Ana's budding romance, including an exchange after she comes down from the roof and a passionate embrace inside one of the getaway trucks.
- Glen (RD Reid) telling a captive CJ (Michael Kelly) and Bart/E-Bomb (Michael Barry) about his first homosexual experience.
- Glen refusing to give the eulogy at the funeral for Andre, Luda (Inna Korobkina) and Norma (Jayne Eastwood).

Other cuts were made as well, in order to qualify for an R rating. These included CJ's shooting of the eviscerated zombie in Reflex Sports, multiple gunshot impacts when the men make their way to the gun shop (including an exploding zombie head) and the propane explosion that roasts several zombies when the group make their way back to the mall.

With the film finally in the can, *Dawn of the Dead* had its world premiere at a shopping mall in Beverly Hills on March 10. Then, in an unprecedented marketing move, Universal chose to air the film's ten-minute pre-title sequence unedited on the USA cable network four days before the film's opening on March 19. It seemed to do the trick, as *Dawn* unseated Mel Gibson's blockbuster *The Passion of the Christ* to become the top film in the country with a tremendous opening weekend gross of $26.7 million. Business dropped off a whopping 60% the following weekend, however, and *Dawn*'s final take was $59 million, with an additional $43 million earned overseas. Critical reaction to the film was mostly negative, with the *New York Times* ironically commenting, 'Mr Snyder's blood feast is strictly by the numbers: this second-rater could be the world's most expensive Troma film.' *The Chicago Tribune* decried it as 'a blood-spattered zombie of a picture, almost as violent, soulless and drenched with gore as the undead mob that keeps trying to break into the movie's super-mall to kill the clichéd characters inside.' *The Boston Globe* remarked, 'George Romero's gruesome and acutely intelligent do-it-yourself freak-out is now a loud, glossy horror show for people who think the movies began with *The Breakfast Club*.' And Roger Ebert, one of the original film's staunchest defenders, was able to give this new version only a lukewarm endorsement: 'The contrast between this new version...and the 1979 George Romero original is instructive in the ways that Hollywood has grown more skilful and less daring over the years. From a technical point of view, the new *Dawn* is slicker and more polished, and the acting is better, too. But it lacks the mordant humour of the Romero version, and although both films are mostly set inside a shopping mall, only Romero uses that as an occasion for satirical jabs at a consumer society.'

Though defenders of *Dawn of the Dead* were few, they were nevertheless enthusiastic, such as *Entertainment Weekly* ('Zack Snyder, making a killer feature debut, trades homemade cheesiness for knowing style, revels in the sophistication of modern special effects, and stomps off with the best remake of a horror classic in memory') and the *Los Angeles Times* ('Good zombie fun, the remake of...*Dawn of the Dead* is the best proof in ages that cannibalising old material sometimes works fiendishly well').

For his part, Romero found himself with mixed feelings about Zack Snyder's remake of *Dawn of the Dead*, confessing to *Time Out*, 'It was better than I expected. I thought it was a good action film. The first 15, 20 minutes were terrific, but it sort of lost its reason for being. It was more of a video game...There was nothing going on underneath.'

Regardless of Romero's verdict, *Dawn* proved to be a launch-pad for Snyder's career, which would see him added to Hollywood's A-list of directors with such movies as *300* (2006), *Watchmen* (2009) and *Legend of the Guardians* (2010). At time of writing, he is directing Warner Brothers' $175 million *Superman: Man of Steel*, set for release in June 2013.

DAY OF THE DEAD

(1985)

I sat on my ass for the three years between *Creepshow* and *Day of the Dead*. And I think that, had I been an individual facing the problems that faced me with the first script for *Day of the Dead*, I would have told them to shove it. Because of the responsibility that I had to Laurel's stockholders, I wasn't able to do that, couldn't take that kind of a chance.

–George Romero, writer and director

I fought for George's original version as long and as hard as I could until the last possible moment before losing credibility from a business standpoint. We had a deal with UFD, and we knew what the budgetary parameters were. We had given our word, and I was not prepared to back out of that.

–Richard Rubinstein, producer

With the success of *Dawn of the Dead*, Laurel and United Film signed a five-year, three picture deal in February 1980 to include the modern-day Camelot tale *Knights* (a co-production with United Artists Pictures), the sci-fi comedy *Shoo-Be-Doo-Be-Moon* and, of course, the final film in Romero's zombie trilogy, *Day of the Dead*. The first film entered production in May 1980 as *Knightriders* (it turned out that John Boorman had already optioned the title *Knights* for what was to become *Excalibur*) and was released the following year to critical praise and total audience indifference. *Shoo-Be-Doo-Be-Moon*—from a script by Romero's old friend Rudy Ricci—was retitled *Invasion of the Spaghetti Monsters,* but its wacked-out story of aliens who use spaghetti-like sexual surrogates to impregnate Earth women and proposed $6.5 million price tag led to UFD passing on the project. With *Day of the Dead* a good three to four years away from production, another film was needed to plug the hole in the Laurel-UFD deal.

At the same time as they were linking up with UFD, Laurel had also entered into a development deal with Stephen King; the author and Romero had been introduced by Warner Brothers when it was trying to get King's 1975 novel *Salem's Lot* made into a feature film. When a deal was finally done to make it into a two-part TV movie instead, Romero bowed out, being replaced by Tobe Hooper. King then offered Romero his choice of any novel not already optioned; being the cautious soul that he was, Romero immediately chose King's biggest, most unfilmable book, *The Stand* (1978). While King toiled away at trying to condense his 800-page novel into a manageable screenplay, he also wrote a five-part anthology horror film as an homage to the EC Comics of the 1950s: *Creepshow*.

What was originally intended as a 'tune up' for the much higher-budgeted *The Stand* (which was projected to be in the $15-$20 million range) instead became Romero's biggest film to that time, with a $7.2 million budget and a name cast, including Adrienne Barbeau, Hal Holbrook, Viveca Lindfors, EG Marshall, Leslie Nielsen and Fritz Weaver, along with Stephen King himself (and his son) and a pre-*Cheers* Ted Danson. The film was financed by UFD (in place of *Spaghetti Monsters*) and originally scheduled for release in July 1982, but the teaming of Romero and King had too much marquee value for the majors to resist and after a bidding war between Paramount, Universal and Warners, *Creepshow* ended up going out under the Warner's shield that November, grossing $25 million, which is still the highest-ever domestic total for a Romero film.

Richard Rubinstein had taken Laurel to the market in June 1980, raising over $2 million in development capital; with that seed money and the success of *Creepshow*, it seemed that making *The Stand* a reality would not be too difficult, provided one of the majors came on board. Unfortunately, after three drafts, King still could not get the script down to less than 200 pages, and no studio was interested in financing a three-hour horror movie. While *The Stand* struggled to stand on its feet, Romero found himself behind a typewriter, grinding out scripts.

Between 1983 and 1984, Romero wrote both *Mongrel: The Legend of Copperhead* (aka *Hero of the Century*), a proposed co-production with Marvel Comics about a Philadelphia sheriff in the not-too-distant future who becomes a superhero, as well as a new take on Mary Shelley's *Frankenstein*. He also adapted five more Stephen King stories into *Creepshow II*. *Mongrel* and *Frankenstein* never made it off the drawing board, *Creepshow II* sat in limbo for three years before losing two of its stories and half its budget, and Romero was announced to direct a version of King's 1983 novel *Pet Sematary*, a project that got no further than *The Stand*.[4] Given all

---

4 Laurel finally produced *Pet Sematary* in 1989 for Paramount Pictures with Mary Lambert (*Siesta*) as director. It likewise finally produced *The Stand* as an 8-hour miniseries that was aired on ABC in May 1994 to huge ratings and Emmy awards. Produced on a budget of $28 million, it was directed by Mick Garris (who had previously directed King's screenplay *Sleepwalkers*) from a King teleplay.

of this, Romero should not have been surprised when his last-produced script for Laurel became the biggest disappointment of them all.

As we CUT IN CLOSER we see that the three slumped figures are ZOMBIES. They are wearing khakis and they are armed with RIFLES AND PISTOL BELTS. Their HELMETS have been painted an identifying bright RED and they wear slipover vests dyed the same bright colour. All the others in the platoon are humans. They, too, wear vests but theirs are not red but WHITE, WITH LARGE ORANGE CIRCLES emblazoned front and back. Two of the men wield LONG ELECTRIC CATTLE PRODS for use should the ZOMBIES misbehave, but the creatures, amazingly, are shambling along with the rest of the platoon voluntarily, cooperatively, even somewhat excitedly... the kind of excitement seen in a puppy that's just learned a new trick.

CHICO

It can't be. Are we truly in hell?

—From Romero's original draft of Day of the Dead

Romero had been thinking about *Day of the Dead* for a long time. Back in 1979, he told *Film Comment*, 'I have this vision of a layered society where the humans are little dictators, down in bomb shelters, and they fight their wars using zombies as soldiers. The operative humans have to be out feeding the zombies, controlling them and keeping law and order. In that layer of society we'll ultimately get our hope; those are the characters we'll be able to care about. It's a return to what the zombie was in the beginning: Lugosi always lived in a castle while the zombies went out to pick the sugar cane [referencing 1932's *White Zombie*].'

After the completion of *Creepshow* in early 1982, Romero finally put his *Day* in writing. He clearly had *The Stand* on the brain: the resulting draft was a sprawling, 204-page epic that effects maestro Tom Savini described as '*Raiders of the Lost Ark* with zombies.'

Florida, 1987—five years since the dead first walked. A quintet of guerrillas—Tony, Miguel, Maria, Sarah and Chico—arrive in Fort Myers to find the city totally deserted except for thousands of zombies. After a gunfight with a rival group of desperados and some encounters with the living dead, only Miguel, Sarah and Chico make it to a nearby island where Miguel—infected from a zombie bite— begins to go mad. The group's plight turns worse, however, when they come to find that the island is inhabited by something they never could have imagined: a corps of corpses that are under the control of a dictator named Gasparilla (formerly Floridian governor Henry Dickerson) and his band of paramilitary thugs, the most sadistic of whom is Captain Rhodes. With the help of a scientific team led by Dr Mary Henried, Gasparilla's men have trained a group of the living

dead to be soldiers—nicknamed Bluto, Grumpy, Tonto, Samson, Fatso and Bub—who are sent on search and destroy missions against other zombies. Chico is killed by Rhodes' platoon, and Sarah falls in with a group of revolutionaries led by John, a West Indian. Along with Toby Tyler, a soldier exiled from the bunkers beneath the island to the concentration camp called 'Stalag 17' above, the group plots to overthrow Gasparilla and end Rhodes's reign of terror.

Over the years, Romero's original vision has gained the reputation of a lost masterpiece, but in fact it is simply a wallow in degradation. Just as the zombies are more decayed and disgusting than ever before, so too are the people, who run the gamut from the cold-hearted to the perverse to the truly wretched. Characters are religious fanatics, alcoholics, military goons, megalomaniacs, insane butchers or just plain subhuman. Their profane exploits continue on for page after page, along with a milieu that is literally covered in sweat, grease, grime, blood, guts, bile, saliva and rot. This reaches its apex when Romero spares no detail in describing the Stalag 17 concentration camp:

PEOPLE wallow in the mud. ONE MAN has just taken a shit and is wiping his ass. Nearby A DRUNK lies unconscious. SEVERAL MEN are fighting. It's a brutal fight with BOTTLES AND PIPES AND LENGTHS OF CHAIN. The men are really hurting each other. PEOPLE SMOKE AND SNORT AND SHOOT UP in wide open disarray.

A HUGE PREGNANT WOMAN plants herself right in TOBY'S path.

PREGNANT WOMAN
How 'bout it, baby? I'm big but I'm beautiful.

TOBY pushes past her and bumps into A SURLY DRUNK.

DRUNK
Hey, you fuck! You fuck!

He grabs TOBY and flings him violently against an upright on one of the long huts. THE OTHER TWO PRISONERS move on, abandoning TOBY, disappearing into the crowd. THE DRUNK pulls A RUSTED, HOMEMADE KNIFE.

DRUNK
I oughta slice you up, you fuck! You can't push me around like... push me around...like...

Suddenly VOMIT rises in the man's throat and he doubles over.

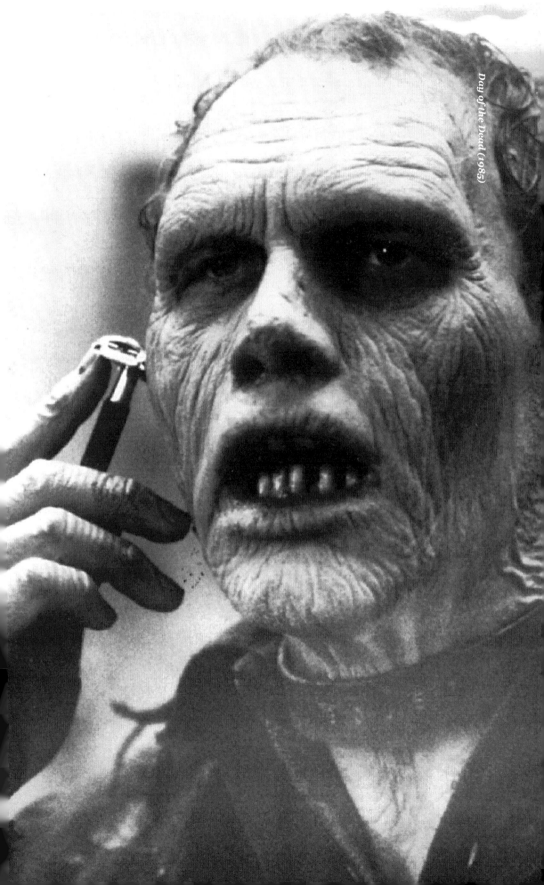

Day of the Dead (1985)

TOBY is aware of SOUNDS behind him. At his back, in the hut, A HAIRY FAT MAN, still wearing his boxer shorts and his muddy boots, is wham-bam-bamming A WHORE, who is wearing everything but underwear and boots. There are needle tracks on the woman's arms and her face looks as though she's been beaten brutally. She purses her deep red, damaged lips and blows TOBY a kiss that's meant to be seductive.

Unlike *Dawn of the Dead*, where the violence served the story, here the plot seems to exist solely to move from one gross-out set piece to another, including a bag of living decapitated heads, a hospital full of diseased and dying patients who are decapitated or trepanned, a deaf mute girl who has vials of nitroglycerine inserted all over her body, and a climax of such grotesque proportions that Romero describes it as 'The gross finale. The intestine-tugger. The zombies get their supper. They feast among the pillows, like Romans at an orgy.' In fact, the scope of the make-up effects was so vast that even Savini was overwhelmed: 'It was just incredible,' he told Gagne. 'George and I had a meeting to discuss the individual effects, and about halfway through it, we were tired of talking!'

Romero's desire to go over the top, while not commendable, is perhaps understandable since he quite obviously intended for *Day of the Dead* to be a grand finale. At the conclusion, John baptises the survivors (for good measure, the script is full of Judeo-Christian symbolism, too) and watches over the corpse of a comrade who, miraculously, has not revived. Apparently, the zombie plague is finally over:

JOHN
Satan ain't sent this man back. Not yet, anyway. So we all hopin' that maybe he's up there with you, Lord. This might be the first decent soul we been able ta offer ya in quite a few years. That's a fact. We just gonna... pray, Lord. We gonna pray that what seems ta be happenin' here...is really happenin'...and I'm gonna take the chance and speak these words that I ain't been able ta speak for so long...May he rest in peace.

'Because the heroes had found salvation,' Romero told *The Washington Post*, 'found the strength to do this and redeemed themselves, the dead stopped coming back to life.' To prove the point, the script ends with.. 'the movement of red letters that spin up off the head of the corpse and settle before our eyes. The letters read: THE END (I PROMISE).'

'UFD was ecstatic over [the script],' Romero told Gagne. 'But we were all deluding ourselves. It wasn't until we came down to it that we discovered what the real budget was.' To film *Day of the Dead* as Romero had originally written it was estimated to cost around $6.5 million, a figure UFD was simply unwilling to bankroll on an unrated film. While *Dawn of the Dead* had been successful, UFD had only seen $7 million of the box office take in rentals and that was *without* any investment in the film itself. Now they were being asked to foot the entire bill for a film that was not likely to make much more than its production cost back at the box office. That was a risk United Artists Theatres was unwilling to take, and Laurel did not have the option of shopping the film around to other distributors—they were contractually obligated to deliver it to UFD, and the deadline of 1985 was getting closer.

Romero rewrote the script twice in an effort to get the cost down, and while he eliminated nearly 100 pages, the budget was still in the $5 million range. UFD's position was firm: $3.5 million for an unrated movie; $6.5 million for an R-rated one. Since both Romero and Rubinstein knew that *Day* would never make it past the MPAA, there was only one option left—completely rewrite the script to meet the $3.5 million budgetary parameters. I had absolute, consummate faith that George would be able to sit down and do a very, very good script within the resources that we had,' Rubinstein told *Cinefantastique*.

With production of *Day of the Dead* set for the fall of 1984, Romero bit the bullet and, in just three weeks, retooled his vision. He kept the original opening (more or less), some of the characters, the underground facility and the gory denouement, but greatly streamlined the plot, locations, cast and effects.

> **After waking up from a nightmare, Sarah finds herself in a helicopter circling Fort Myers, Florida, along with a soldier (Miguel), the radioman (Bill) and the pilot (John). They land to look for survivors— but all they find is a ruined city populated by thousands of zombies. They return to their underground shelter, an abandoned storage facility now co-habited by three scientists, seven soldiers, two civilians and several captured zombies. The mad Dr Matthew Logan is determined to domesticate the zombies—who he has calculated outnumber the living 400,000:1—while the sadistic Captain Rhodes simply wants them destroyed. A power struggle predictably ensues, the powder keg finally being lit when the military discovers that Logan's chief experiment—a docile zombie nicknamed 'Bub'—has been rewarded for good behaviour with the remains of dead soldiers. Rhodes kills Logan and another scientist, then sends Sarah and Bill, unarmed, into the corral where the zombies are kept. In the meantime, Miguel—driven mad from a zombie bite and amputation— has gone to the surface and allows the zombie hordes entry into the complex. John rescues his friends and they make it to the helicopter as a complete bloodbath engulfs the soldiers trapped underground.**

'It was really difficult,' Romero told Gagne. 'The first week I sat there with those conditions was awful. I've never had that imposed on me.' Indeed, Romero took his frustrations out on the script, since nearly every page is laced with sarcastic comments like:

- 'A matte painting, if affordable, could augment the actual shot of the city here, making it appear worn and devastated.'
- 'It takes SARAH a moment to shake off the startle. (Let's hope we all drop our Necco Wafers on that one, kiddies.)'

- '(This zombie's name is BUB...we'll see more of him later...those of us who don't walk out of the theatre, that is.)'
- 'There are ZOMBIES, lots of them, fifty (or more, if we can afford it), pushing in through the trees, moving through the open gate.'
- 'McDERMOTT stops as well...and ANOTHER ZOMBIE looms up behind him. (This is gettin' to be a regular Laff-in-the-Dark, kiddies.)'
- 'BUB, noticing the weapons, seems to smile. Strange but true. You saw it here first, folks.'
- And it gets worse. Yep, this is it, kiddies...the stomach-churning finale, the gore fest we've all been waiting for, those of us still in our seats. THE ZOMBIES extract intestines and livers and hearts...they munch on fingers and ears and.. well, you get the picture, I'm sure.'

Production began on October 22, at the Wampum Industrial Facility, a 125-acre former limestone mine-turned-underground storage facility just north of Beaver Falls, Pennsylvania. Working 14-15 hour days, six days a week, many of the cast and crew came down with 'mine fever' from being in the damp, chilly environment for weeks on end. According to Savini, however, the production itself was cold: 'I felt like there had been a major change in the way the Romero 'family' works,' he told *Fangoria*. 'I felt that I was being picked on in some little ways; it was almost like I was working with total strangers.' He later elaborated to Gagne: '*Day* was strictly business. You had to go through six people just to get a message to George. I didn't enjoy it, personally.'

One of the things Romero had carried over from his original draft of *Day of the Dead* was the notion of trained zombies. While the first version had a half-dozen such creatures, the movie as shot had only one—Bub, the 'star pupil' of Dr Logan. Bub was played by Chicago mime Howard Sherman, who managed to take a rather unlikely concept and turn it into the film's only real standout performance. 'Bub wasn't supposed to be a regular zombie,' he told the *Chicago Daily Herald*. 'He had personality and was intended to be the hero of the story. This was the challenge—to take a dead creature that craves human flesh and turn him into a sympathetic character. To me, that was a piece of work worth tackling.'

After two weeks of location photography in Florida in early December, the production returned to Wampum and wrapped in mid-January 1985. *Day of the Dead* premiered in New York on July 3, to an $825,000 opening (second only to *Back to the Future* and *Cocoon*) and a review from the *New York Times*' Janet Maslin that seemed an attempt to make up for her earlier negligence: 'Greatly admired in some circles as the horror film sardonic enough to let its zombies go shopping, George A Romero's *Dawn of the Dead* had a central metaphor Mr Romero may never top. His use in that film of an immense, all-American mall, complete with fountains and muzak, as the site of vicious fighting between the blue-faced dead and the living made *Dawn of the Dead* at least as ingenious as it was stomach-turning. *Day of the Dead* has a less startling setting...But it still affords Mr Romero the opportunity for intermittent philosophy and satire, without compromising his reputation as the grisliest guy around.'

As it turned out, Ms Maslin would be in the minority once again. Whereas she had missed the critical boat on *Dawn*, she would now be one of the few critics to give a positive notice to its successor. As *Day of the Dead* broadened its release, the bad reviews came pouring in: 'One of the most ridiculously acted, poorly written and stagnantly directed movies of the year' (*Boston Globe*); 'You might assume that it would be impossible to steal a scene from a zombie, especially one with blood dripping from his orifices, but you haven't seen the overacting in this movie. The characters shout their lines from beginning to end, their temples pound with anger, and they use distracting Jamaican and Irish accents, until we are so busy listening to their endless dialogue that we lose interest in the movie they occupy' (Roger Ebert); 'Let's hope [Romero is] not tempted to go for a quartet, for at this point sheer gruesomeness overwhelms his ideas and even his dynamic visuals. He would, in fact, have been better off not having tried for a third instalment' (Kevin Thomas); 'Instead of providing a spectacular climax...*Day* seems to be merely vamping until a payoff in a potential part four' (*Variety*); 'Romero...seems bored by the whole enterprise, less interested in the story than in sausage-making' (*Washington Post*).

Not only was the film a critical flop, but a commercial one as well, earning just $5 million at the box office—its $2 million in rentals not even enough to cover the reduced budget.[5] This can partly be laid at the feet of UFD's haphazard distribution (*Day* did not play in Los Angeles until three months after its premiere) and the foolish decision to open the picture in the middle of summer. '[UFD] can never be competitive with advertising,' Romero told *Cinefantastique*, 'partly because it's unrated and partly because UFD is such a small company—they can't compete with Paramount; the big boys. So I don't know how long the film can survive against big product.'

Where *Day* really failed to connect with an audience, however, was in its total lack of sympathetic characters (save for Bub). As Ebert noted, 'In the earlier films, we really identified with the small cadre of surviving humans. They were seen as positive characters, and we cared about them. This time, the humans are mostly unpleasant, violent, insane or so noble that we can predict with utter certainty that they will survive.' Ironically it was Savini, whose effects work dominates the picture, who seemed clued in to what turned people off, telling *Fangoria*: 'In this film, it's not a hideous monster lurking behind closed doors...it's the people that are the monsters, for the most part...a lot of the strongest effects came in for what people were doing to zombies.'

Obviously demoralised by the whole experience, Romero himself seemed uncertain as to whether or not he would attempt another zombie movie. He first told the *New York Daily News*, 'You can beat a dead horse into the ground...I truly have no plans for any more,' then later contradicted himself to *Cinefantastique*: 'The phenomenon is not over with this film. But as for a fourth picture, I might not be able to finance it unless something happens with the rating system.'

In June 1985, after 12 years of partnership with Rubinstein, Romero left the Laurel Group. 'I want to be able to do my own projects, take my own risks, without

---

5 *Day of the Dead* was eventually profitable, earning an additional $29 million for itself overseas.

that kind of fiscal responsibility,' he told *Fangoria*. 'What I am doing is buying myself a certain amount of freedom; the ability to go out and do other projects.' But, without Rubinstein's business acumen, Romero struggled and only made a handful of films (*Monkey Shines, Two Evil Eyes, The Dark Half*) before finally returning to the zombie genre exclusively with *Land of the Dead* (2005), *Diary of the Dead* (2008) and *Survival of the Dead* (2010).

In contrast, Rubinstein thrived at Laurel, first by producing two syndicated TV horror shows, *Tales from the Darkside* (1984-88) and *Monsters* (1988-90), then by turning Stephen King into a company franchise, producing both feature films based on King's work (*The Night Flier, Pet Sematary, Thinner*) as well as miniseries (*Golden Years, The Langoliers* and *The Stand*). Since forming New Amsterdam Entertainment in 1995, Rubinstein has switched from King to Frank Herbert, producing both the *Dune* (2000) and *Children of Dune* (2003) miniseries aired on the Sci-Fi Channel.

(2008)

The idea was to do...an action zombie movie in the sense that you use the form of an action movie with zombies in it.

–Steve Miner, director

I originally pitched a story that was a lot closer to the original, but in the dreaded development process it got further and further away. So I look at it as a fun movie...where zombies attack a small town, and no one will compare it to the original.

–Jeffrey Reddick, writer

In 1987, United Artists Theatres formed a new company, Taurus Entertainment, as a successor to United Film Distribution. The company released mostly cheap horror films (*Retribution, Slaughterhouse Rock*) but did attempt to go mainstream with the John Belushi biopic *Wired* and the martial arts film *Best of the Best* (both 1989), both without much success. Taurus effectively folded in 1991, sitting dormant until it was bought by Robert and James Dudelson in 1998. Undoubtedly, part of the appeal of Taurus was it being the rights holder for George Romero's *Creepshow, Day of the Dead* and *Knightriders*. In April 2004, James Dudelson and his wife/partner Ana Clavell began production on *Day of the Dead 2: Contagium*, a totally unrelated 'sequel' that concerns the accidental release of a bacteriological weapon that turns people into zombies (sound familiar?). Released to DVD in October 2005, the film was met with complete disdain, but this was not enough to dissuade Dudelson and Clavell from making another bogus sequel, *Creepshow 3* (2006).

Having seen the returns on Zack Snyder's *Dawn of the Dead*, as well as the same year's British sleeper *Shaun of the Dead* and the hit sequel *Resident Evil:*

Apocalypse, Dudelson knew his ownership of *Day of the Dead* could pay off big. He subsequently approached Randall Emmett and George Furla of Emmett/Furla Films, one of the producers of the 2003 *Amityville Horror* remake, with the idea of remaking Romero's third zombie film. Emmett/Furla jumped at the chance and, in conjunction with its frequent partner, Avi Lerner's Millennium Films (purveyors of countless direct-to-video action movies), a new version of *Day of the Dead* was announced in May 2005.

That November, it was also announced that veteran horror director Steve Miner (*Friday the 13th Part II* and *III, Halloween: H20, Warlock*) had been signed to the project, along with screenwriter Jeffrey Reddick (*Final Destination*). 'I was nervous about doing it,' Reddick told UGO, 'then I found out that Steve Miner would be directing, and that they would definitely be making it one way or another! I went in and pitched a couple of ideas and at first they wanted someone to write the script in two weeks...I said, "I can't do that!" It was Steve who fought to keep me on and fought to have the time to actually write the script.'

'He told me he wanted to make this more of an action movie, and that that was important to him,' Reddick continued. 'And we talked about the military, and we were originally going to have the military folks be older in the first few drafts of the story. But we'd seen so many movies...where you have these hardened military guys going up against some kind of monster. We said, "Well, why don't we make them reservists?" You know, none of them know when they're called in that everyone is going to turn into a cannibal. They're not ready for that when they get there!'

Edgewater, Colorado. Army reservists—including local girl Sarah Bowman—are called in to enforce a 24-hour quarantine of the town after what seems like an outbreak of the flu. Sarah and her fellow reservist Bud Crain go to the Bowman house to get her brother Trevor,

Day of the Dead (2005)

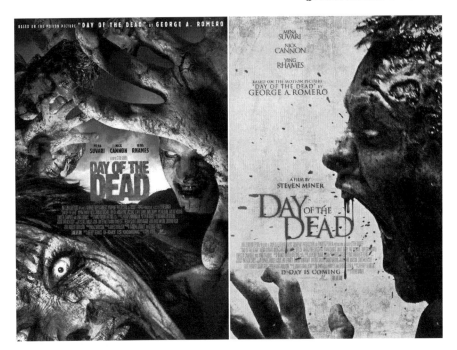

his girlfriend Nina and Sarah's seriously ill mother. They drive to the hospital, only to find it overwhelmed with patients. Suddenly, all the infected go rigid and are cold to the touch. But only momentarily—for they are soon attacking their loved ones and the hospital staff, taking bites out of exposed body parts. Trevor and Nina escape to a nearby radio station while Sarah and Bud are trapped in the hospital, along with another reservist named Salazar and a doctor named Logan. The four manage to escape, but not before Bud is bitten and Logan takes off. After arming themselves at the local gun store, the soldiers make their way to the radio station to pick up Trevor and Nina. Bud has turned, but is strangely unaggressive. The group seeks shelter at an abandoned Nike missile site in the mountains, where they find an underground bunker that is mysteriously outfitted with all the latest equipment but is ransacked. Hiding in the file room is Dr Logan, who turns out to be one of the scientists on The Omega Project, a covert bioweapons program designed to paralyse enemy soldiers. But the virus has mutated and instead causes death, reanimation and a reversion to primal instincts. Two infected scientists are still in the bunker and attack the survivors, killing Logan and Salazar. The male scientist (Dr Engle) allows an army of zombies into the bunker, then captures Sarah in an effort to lure out Trevor and Nina. As Engle tortures Sarah, Bud reappears on the scene and begins shooting at the zombies' leader. He misses, then picks up Salazar's flamethrower and roasts the zombies around him.

Sarah then leads Engle and other zombies on a mad chase to the trap Trevor and Nina have set up—using old missile propulsion rockets as makeshift flamethrowers. As they enter the Jet Propulsion Testing Room, the zombies are incinerated. Driving away from the base, Sarah turns on the radio and hears a broadcast from a nearby town about another flu epidemic before noticing that Nina has a bite mark on her arm...

'Steve Miner and I have really worked hard to create a story that is definitely respectful of the original,' Reddick told interviewer Russell Trunk, 'whilst telling a new zombie story for our generation. George Romero was very good about framing his movies in the time that they were set. What I want to do is set this movie in the here and now, the culture that we live in, and the fears that we have about our national security and things like that. And so I wanted to take those things that George Romeo did and put my stamp on it.'

Blood is still fountaining from the stump of MIGUEL'S arm. SARAH slaps the flaming end of the rifle onto the stump. There's A SIZZLING SOUND as the raw flesh there cooks. The pain reaches MIGUEL even in his unconscious state. He starts to breathe heavily. His head shakes from side to side, silently pleading 'NO, NO, NO.' The flames do their job. The flesh crusts over and the bleeding stops. MIGUEL'S shirt catches. His eyes pop open and he screams like the man on fire that he is.

−Romero's 1984 script

The shower of flames has started to die down. Tears well up in Sarah's eyes as she pulls up Salazar's wrist...which continues to spout crimson. She puts the dying flame to the bloody stump. It begins to sizzle and burn. Salazar almost passes out from the pain. He thrashes and screams like the man on fire that he is. But the flames do their job. The flesh blackens and crusts over. The bleeding stops. Salazar is in unbelievable agony.

−Reddick's 2006 script

Nowhere is this sentiment more obvious than with the character of Private Salazar, Reddick's version of the original's Miguel Salazar, who is Sarah's lover and suffering a nervous breakdown. Conversely, Reddick's Salazar is cocky and gung-ho, proving himself quite adept at zombie-killing; that is, until he gets his fingers bitten off. Like her Romero namesake, Sarah amputates the infected area and cauterises the stump in an effort to save Salazar's life. He will ultimately return the favour by sacrificing himself so that Sarah can get away from Dr Engle.

With an $18 million budget, the film began a six-week shoot in Sofia, Bulgaria,

on July 17, 2006, on sets left over from Millennium's recently-completed Brian De Palma film *The Black Dahlia*. In keeping with the recent trend in zombie movies, Miner wanted his ghouls to be supercharged, even having zombies crawl on the ceiling and leap out of buildings. 'We had a guy fly out to teach us how Steve wanted the zombies to move and act, so it was much different from the original,' co-star Christa Campbell told FearNet. 'The way you move your body you're supposed to be stiff, but they're not too stiff because they are sort of superhuman. When they're fast, it helps with the action and becomes a full-on action film, which is really cool. You're on the edge of your seat the whole time, freaking out.'

Miner's *Day* would break new ground by being one of the first zombie movies to rely as much (or more) on CGI effects than standard make-up prosthetics or pyrotechnics, especially when it came to bullet hits, decapitations, explosions and the like. Nikolay Gachev's Worldwide FX group engineered 400 computer-generated effects shots to augment the practical effects that were handled by Dean and Starr Jones, who had also done the zombie effects on *Night of the Living De3D*.

Miner faithfully adhered to Reddick's script, but apparently decided that the amputation scene was too literal an homage and eliminated it. He did, however, keep Salazar's sacrificial death. But test audiences enjoyed rapper-turned-actor Nick Cannon's performance so much that Salazar's death scene ended up being reshot so that he could escape and rejoin Sarah (*American Beauty*'s Mena Suvari), Trevor (Michael Welch) and Nina (AnnaLynne McCord) as they head back to town. Ultimately, Miner decided to buck the audience anyway and keep Salazar's demise intact.

Scheduled for theatrical release in April 2007 via Millennium's distribution arm

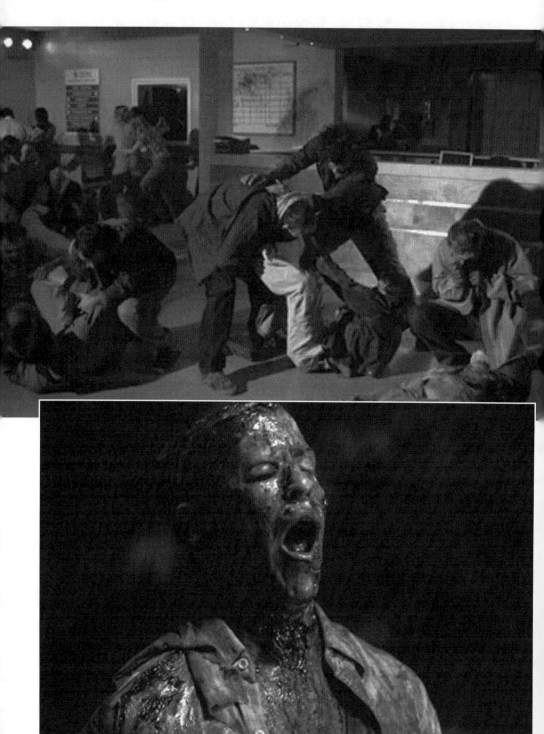

First Look Studios, the film instead sat on the shelf for a year before being released directly to DVD. It found a mixed reaction on the various websites that reviewed it, with Crave Online advising its readers, 'Forget it's called *Day of the Dead*, forget it's allegedly a remake, and just bow your head and power on through and what you'll find is a zombie flick that's so bad it's...well, it's quite good.' Dread Central gave a qualified recommendation—'Once you realise how absolutely ridiculous this whole affair is, you may even start having fun just by seeing how far into the realm of idiocy the filmmakers are prepared to go'—while UGO enthused, 'This movie mercifully delivers what many horror films and most straight to video flicks lack: Good scares, competently delivered.'

Ain't It Cool News did not agree—'This movie has no good parts in it. It does not capture a single thing that's good about the original. It doesn't improve on a single weakness of the original. It doesn't add a single worthwhile new thing to the story or the genre'—and neither did Real Movie News: 'A quick cash-in flick that comes out of nowhere and will return just as quickly to that void. It is a remake in name only and a defanged one at that'.

The refashioned *Day of the Dead* did not partake in the box office bonanza that the living dead have reaped in recent years—but amazingly enough, neither has the man who started it all. George Romero's long-awaited return to the genre, *Land of the Dead*, only made $46 million worldwide, as opposed to movies like *Zombieland* ($102 million) or *Resident Evil: Afterlife* ($296 million). In fact, Romero's last two zombie movies—*Diary of the Dead* and *Survival of the Dead*—received only token releases before going straight to DVD. In terms of profitability, however, Romero may indeed have the last laugh: both *Diary* and *Survival* cost less than $5 million to make, whereas the latest *Resident Evil* chapter's $60 million production cost means it will not show a profit until after the first $120 million in box office receipts (since roughly half of the gross stays with the exhibitors). And if his first three zombie movies are any indication, time is most definitely on George Romero's side.

228

RETRO SCREAMS
NEW MILLENNIUM

THE PLATINUM DUNES PROGRAMME

THE TEXAS CHAIN SAW MASSACRE

(1974)

The idea actually came from a doctor I knew. I remembered that he'd once told me this story about how, when he was a pre-med student, the class was studying cadavers. And he went into the morgue and skinned a cadaver and made a mask for Halloween. We decided Leatherface would have a different human-skin mask to fit each of his moods.

—Tobe Hooper, co-writer, producer and director

We had no budget, we had no cast, and [our] last picture had not been successful. What do you do? Horror films is about it.

—Kim Henkel, co-writer and associate producer

Christmas 1972. Tobe Hooper, a 29-year-old aspiring film director, was waiting in line at the Montgomery Ward department store in Austin, Texas, when his frustration at the mass of shoppers turned into a flash of inspiration, as he would later tell *Texas Monthly*: 'There were these big Christmas crowds, I was frustrated, and I found myself near a display rack of chainsaws. I just kind of zoned in on it. I did a rack focus to the saws, and I thought, I know a way I could get through this crowd really quickly. I went home, sat down, all the channels just tuned in, the zeitgeist blew through, and the whole damn story came to me in what seemed like about thirty seconds.'

Hooper's 'whole damn story' had actually been brewing since the age of three, when he first experimented with his father's Bell & Howell 8mm home movie camera. Throughout his childhood, Hooper made a multitude of home movies—pressing his family members and friends into service as actors—and even converted his class projects into excuses to make movies. In 1962, he enrolled as one of the inaugural two students in the University of Texas at Austin's newly-founded Department of Radio-Television-Film. He left after two years, finding work in commercials and utilising the contacts he had made with the local public television station to make two documentaries: *Down Friday Street* (1966), about the destruction of local landmarks, and *The Song is Love* (1969), a touring chronicle of the folk trio Peter, Paul and Mary.

In 1969-70, with $40,000 invested by a Houston businessman, Hooper wrote, directed, produced, shot and edited his first feature, *Eggshells*. His idea was '..to show the end of the Vietnam War, with the troops coming home, but tell it through the eyes of a commune,' but the film was largely an improvised mess, with a ghost in the basement to no apparent purpose but Hooper's own amusement. Nevertheless, the hippy time capsule won a gold medal at the 1971 Atlanta International Film Festival and played briefly in Texas theatres in May 1972 before being relegated to a tax write-off and forgotten.[1]

One of the actors in the film was Kim Henkel (using the pseudonym Boris Schnurr), an illustrator by trade who struck up a friendship with Hooper that turned into a collaboration on writing a modern version of Hansel and Gretel. For inspiration, the two Texans looked to the real-life case of Edward Gein, a handyman from Plainfield, Wisconsin, who was arrested in 1957 for the murder of two women. When the authorities searched his house, they found the grotesque results of nearly ten years of grave robbing, as well as a female corpse hanging in his barn, field-dressed like a deer. Gein, who apparently had a mother fixation and liked to don suits made of female body parts, was declared insane and spent the rest of his life in asylums. Author Robert Bloch based the character of Norman Bates in his 1959 novel *Psycho* on Gein, although Bates came to be associated in the public's mind with actor Anthony Perkins after Alfred Hitchcock's 1960 film version.[2]

'I'd walk over to Tobe's house after supper,' Henkel told the *Los Angeles Times*. 'The criteria for acceptance was, if Tobe chuckled when he read the pages I'd hand him, then we knew it was all right. We intended to scare people, but it had to be funny.' Within six weeks, Hooper and Henkel had their script, which they called *Leatherface*.

In a beat-up van, bra-less blonde Sally, her handicapped brother Franklin and boyfriend Jerry are joined by another young couple

---

1 The film was considered lost for nearly 40 years until a print was uncovered and shown in March 2009 at the South by Southwest Film and Media Conference in Austin. Hooper was in attendance and introduced the screening.

2 Gein's story was unofficially told in *Deranged* (1974) and then officially as *Ed Gein* (2000) and *Ed Gein: The Butcher of Plainfield* (2007). The character of Buffalo Bill in Thomas Harris' 1988 novel *The Silence of the Lambs* and its 1991 film version is also said to be based on Gein.

(Pam and Kirk) in making their way back to Houston from a skiing trip in Colorado. They stop to pay their respects at the grave of Sally and Franklin's grandfather, only to find the cemetery full of locals and reporters because of a spate of grave-robbing. Moving along, the group picks up a hitchhiker, which they come to regret after the grungy nutcase uses a straight razor to attack Franklin. Shoved out of the van, the hitchhiker marks it with his blood. The kids next stop at the abandoned stone house of Sally and Franklin's grandfather, where Pam and Kirk go in search of a swimming hole. What they find instead is an old barn full of abandoned cars and a weathered farmhouse. Upon entering, Kirk is assaulted by a huge man wearing a leathery mask, who pummels the youth to death with a sledgehammer. When Pam comes looking for Kirk, she finds the house is full of bones—both human and animal—before being captured by the fiend in the mask and hung on a meat hook. From there, she watches as 'Leatherface'—whose mask is made of human skin—goes to work on Kirk with a chainsaw. Jerry is the next visitor to the charnel-house when he comes looking for his friends; after discovering Pam barely alive in a freezer, Jerry is also pummelled to death by Leatherface. As darkness falls, Sally and Franklin decide to go looking for their friends, only to be met in the woods by Leatherface, whose chainsaw passes straight through Franklin and into his wheelchair. With her brother now dead, Sally frantically makes her way to the nearby farmhouse, not realising the fate her friends have met there. Upstairs, Sally encounters a near-cadaverous man in a rocking chair who does not respond to her pleas for help; she is cornered by Leatherface and forced to jump out a window into the meadow below. With Leatherface in pursuit, Sally makes her way to the cook's shed of a closed general store, begging the old man inside for help. What she gets instead is beaten, bound and put in the front seat of an old pickup, which takes her straight back to the house of horrors. Coming up the driveway is the deranged hitchhiker—the old cook berates him for being so reckless in digging up bodies at the cemetery. Once inside, the hitchhiker and his brother 'Bubba' (Leatherface) bring their grandfather—the decrepit old man that Sally found earlier—down from the attic. They cut Sally's finger and let the living corpse suck at the blood. The horror of her new surroundings causes Sally to pass out. When she comes to, she finds herself at the dinner table, which Leatherface—now wearing a female mask—has stocked with fresh cold cuts and 'headcheese'. The brothers want a demonstration of their grandfather's legendary slaughterhouse skills; to that end, they put Sally over a galvanised washtub and give grandpa a hammer to pummel her with. After repeatedly missing his target, Sally takes advantage of a respite to once again jump out a window, with the brothers on her heels. She runs to the highway,

The Texas Chain Saw Massacre (1974)

where a cattle truck barely misses her and runs over the hitchhiker instead. The driver gets out but flees from Leatherface's chainsaw while Sally puts herself in the path of an oncoming truck. She jumps in the back and narrowly avoids the saw before the stalled truck finally recovers and speeds off, leaving a frustrated Leatherface to slash the dawn sky with his power tool.

William Jay Parsley was the vice president of financial affairs for Texas Tech University, and a good friend of Governor Preston Smith, and both men shared more than a passing interest in motion pictures—Smith because he owned a chain of theatres; Parsley because he fancied himself as a movie producer. Along with oilman RB McGowen, Parsley had already financed three films: *Mark of the Witch* (1970), *Quadroon* (1972) and *Fox Style* (1973).

Parsley was also well known to Warren Skaaren, who at the time was the head of the newly-formed Texas Film Commission. In the early summer of 1973, Hooper and Henkel took *Leatherface* to Skaaren in the hopes of securing Film Commission support. Skaaren in turn contacted Parsley, who shortly thereafter met with Hooper and Henkel and told them he would raise a $60,000 operating budget in exchange for 50% interest in the picture. Parsley put up $40,000 of his own money, while the remainder came from the rather odd combine of Parsley's attorney Robert Kuhn, marijuana smuggler Richard Saenz and Henkel's sister.

Parsley immediately took a hands-on approach to the project by casting the lead role of Sally. A frequent patron of Austin's Villa Capri cocktail lounge, Parsley had taken a shine to one of the waitresses there, 21-year-old Marilyn Burns. She was a drama student at the University of Texas and happened to be the only actress serving on the Texas Film Commission, despite the fact that her sole professional engagement had been a bit part in Robert Altman's *Brewster McCloud* (1970). Nevertheless, she had the physical qualities that Hooper was looking for, as Henkel told *Texas Monthly*: 'Tobe always liked busty women and Marilyn is a busty woman, and, well, he was enchanted.' Apparently so was Parsley. When he had Kuhn draw up the papers for the company investing in the movie, he named it MAB Inc. A lot of people, including the actress herself, believed the 'MAB' stood for 'Marilyn A Burns'.

The other pivotal role in the film, that of the title character Leatherface, went to six-foot-four Scandinavian Gunnar Hansen, who was working as a carpenter and a bartender, but happened to know Robert Burns (no relation to Marilyn), who was serving as *Leatherface*'s art director. 'I was sitting in Bob's office,' said Hooper, 'and I saw Bob bringing him across the street. He got the part before he came through the front door.'

Shortly before dawn on July 15, 1973, principal photography began outside the tiny town of Round Rock, Texas. According to Dottie Pearl, wife of the film's cinematographer Daniel Pearl and who also served as *Leatherface*'s make-up artist, the shoot was unbelievably gruelling: 'It was 105 or 110 degrees every day,' she told the *Los Angeles Times*, 'with 98% humidity, blazing sun, bugs, mosquitoes, ants, poor working conditions, one toilet for 40 people, maybe a dozen workers doing the job of a 50-person crew. One day we shot for 22 hours straight with only one meal.'

Hooper shot seven days a week, twelve to sixteen hours a day. To create a realistic slaughterhouse atmosphere, Robert Burns had rounded up the carcasses of cows, deer, goats and chickens, not to mention inundating the farmhouse with the skeletal remains he had purloined from a veteranian's stockpile. To make matters worse, since the whole story takes place in a 24-hour period, the cast had to wear the same clothing for five weeks straight.

'The heat was unbearable,' co-star Edwin Neal (the Hitchhiker) told the *Village Voice*. 'It was 95 plus *before* they hit the lights, and sometimes there were two and a half hour waits for individual shots. They mixed molasses with the stage blood to keep it fluid, and it would just melt all over people's bodies...The animals on the table were filled with formaldehyde, and they were literally rotting under the lights. There was a doctor giving antinausea pills, but they didn't help. As soon as they'd yell 'Cut', we'd run to the windows and throw up. For 36 hours straight!' The charnel-house atmosphere was not helped by the gross inexperience of all involved. 'Tobe really did have a vision,' Ronald Bozman, the film's production manager, told *Texas Monthly*. 'He knew exactly where we were at all times. But the rest of us were flying blind. I had never managed a movie. We had no prop man, so I found the props. We didn't even have a chainsaw. I found one...I had to take the teeth out of it so it wouldn't hurt anyone.' But the sheer physicality of the film meant that injuries were par for the course, as Hooper himself told the *Village Voice*: 'Everyone was injured at one time or another. Everyone got sliced, or cut, or was bleeding. Leatherface got hurt a lot of times, falling with the chain saw. His mask had no peripheral vision, so he'd run into doorsills and crack his head.'

Parsley was not best pleased with what he saw as a group of amateur hippies crashing into walls and wasting his money, and his constant presence on the set became a source of tension, especially when it came to his ingénue Marilyn Burns, who got to cool off in her beau's air-conditioned red Cadillac while everyone else suffered with the heat. 'I don't think they knew how mad he was,' she claimed. 'I calmed him down. I convinced him that maybe things would go smoother if he didn't show up so much. He thought the movie was a catastrophe, and he wanted to step in and take it over.'

During the last three days of filming, Burns earned the respect of her peers by giving an exhausting performance while drenched in Karo syrup, glycerine, red tempera paint, vegetable colouring and Hershey's chocolate syrup. 'She was covered head to toe, not one inch of flesh showing,' Pearl told the *Los Angeles Times*. 'It was 110 degrees and she was sticky and covered with flies. Then the stuff hardened.' Burns elaborated: 'One time I was covered with blood when [my] mother came to visit. I was just sitting in the tub crying while she was trying to get it off me.'

THIN MAN
They done found two more empty graves.

RED
(Shakes head in righteous disgust)
Must be somebody escaped from the state hospital.

THIN MAN
They say it's got to be somebody from these parts. They just taking bodies

ain't been in the ground more than a day or two near as they can figure.

WOMAN
Mrs Culpepper said she seen some lights moving around out here not more than a week ago.

OLD MAN
It don't come as no surprise to me.

RED
What are you talking about old man?

OLD MAN
They's just some things happened in my time not many can tell about.

—Unfilmed exchange in the Newt cemetery, from the original script

Because of the tight, 32-day shooting schedule, a number of elements in Henkel and Hooper's script did not make it into the film, including:

- A longer diatribe from Pam in the van about the mysteries of the planets.
- The scene at the Newt graveyard was to have contained a lot of interaction amongst the townsfolk before Sally and her friends get there, giving the recent history of grave-robbing in the area.
- In the van, the kids and the hitchhiker were meant to have more interaction, telling him where they are from and about their families.
- On their way to the farmhouse, Kirk and Pam find the remains of a campsite with all the gear still there, rusting. This was actually shot but did not make the final cut.
- Leatherface was originally given gibberish lines ('Aba de ah du o day; erik beaka obida tey') but it was decided to have him make animal-like noises instead.

Once filming was complete, Hooper would spend the next eight months working first with editor Larry Carroll and then with his replacement Sallye Richardson to piece together a rough cut of *Leatherface*. By the spring of 1974, however, the initial $60,000 investment was gone and Hooper was unable to pay the lab bills. He and Henkel went back to Parsley, asking him to buy 19% of Vortex, the company they had set up to represent their half-share in the movie. Parsley, who was by then convinced that the film was a lost cause, curtly refused, and reminded the filmmakers that they were contractually obligated to deliver a completed picture—if they could not, Parsley would own it outright and could do anything he wanted with it.

Just when it looked like *Leatherface* might become the tax write-off that Kuhn had originally predicted, another eclectic group of investors (including William Wittliff, who would go on to write and/or produce such films as *The Black Stallion, Raggedy Man, Legends of the Fall* and *The Perfect Storm*)—mostly friends from a weekly poker game—answered the distress call and, after seeing a 12-minute highlight reel, agreed to put up $23,532 in exchange for 19% of Vortex. This new investors corporation, like Parsley's, chose an acronym: PITS, meaning 'Pie in the Sky'.

Hooper finally finished *Leatherface* in late summer, but not before taking Skaaren's advice and changing the title to the more hard-sell *The Texas Chain Saw Massacre* and adding an opening narration by a then-unknown John Larroquette (who would achieve small-screen fame in the 1980s on the TV comedy *Night Court*). In exchange for a $5,000 fee, 15% of Vortex and 3% of *Chain Saw*'s gross profits, Skaaren agreed to become a producer's representative and find a distributor for the film. Finding no takers among the majors, Skaaren screened the film for several independents before finally receiving an initial offer of $100,000 from a relatively new film company called Bryanston Distributors.[3]

Bryanston had been formed in New York in July 1971 by brothers Louis and Joseph Peraino as a sister company to Damiano Film Productions, the company co-founded by Louis Peraino and hairdresser-turned-filmmaker Gerard Damiano to make porn movies. In January 1972, Peraino put up $22,000 for Damiano to make the fellatio-themed *Deep Throat* which, on its release that June, became a national phenomenon that would go on to earn millions at the box office. With his two-thirds ownership in the picture, Peraino ploughed the profits from *Deep Throat* into legitimate film production through Bryanston, which opened offices in Hollywood in September 1973.

March 1974 saw Bryanston's first major release, *Andy Warhol's Frankenstein*, which earned $25 million, followed that August by Bruce Lee's *Return of the Dragon*, which returned $20 million to the company. At the same time, a print of *Chain Saw* had been sent to New York for Peraino's viewing. Convinced that he had another smash hit on his hands, Peraino upped the Bryanston offer to $200,000. On August 9, 1974—the day Richard Nixon resigned the US presidency—the deal was struck between Bryanston and Vortex/MAB/PITS for $225,000 + 35% of the gross box-office profits.

On October 11, Bryanston released *Chain Saw* to 230 theatres across Texas, seeing an astounding four-day gross of over $600,000. Later that month, the film was released nationally, from which it would earn $20 million over the next year. Critical response was mixed, with strong endorsements from Vincent Canby ('[Hooper] displays the kind of Grand Guignol sense of humour that effectively separates his film...The intelligence at work within it transforms the second-rate into an unexpectedly provocative entertainment'), Rex Reed ('Run, don't walk, to see the sleeper horror movie of the year...Makes *Psycho* look like a nursery rhyme and *The Exorcist* look like a comedy. It is a horror movie to end them all!') and the hometown *Texas American-Statesman* ('The most significant horror movie since *The Exorcist* and the most important since *Night of the Living Dead*').

But those critics who disliked the film—and there were many—*really* disliked it. '*The Texas Chain Saw Massacre* is as violent and gruesome and blood-soaked

---

3 In the 1980s, Skaaren became one of the highest-paid screenwriters in Hollywood (*Beverly Hills Cop II, Beetlejuice, Batman*) before dying of cancer in December 1990 at the age of 44.

as the title promises,' remarked Roger Ebert, 'a real Grand Guignol of a movie. It's also without any apparent purpose, unless the creation of disgust and fright is a purpose...I can't imagine why anyone would want to make a movie like this.' The *Los Angeles Times*'s Linda Gross dismissed *Chain Saw* as 'a despicable film... Torture and gruesome death through a filtered lens are still ugly and obscene. Craziness handled without sensitivity is a degrading, senseless misuse of film and time.' Writing in *Harper's* magazine, Stephen Koch lambasted the film as 'A vile little piece of sick crap...It is a film with literally nothing to recommend it: nothing but a hysterically paced, slapdash, imbecile concoction of cannibalism, voodoo, astrology, sundry hippie-esque cults, and unrelenting sadistic violence as extreme and hideous as a complete lack of imagination can possibly make it... We are here discussing something close to the absolute degradation of the artistic imagination.' *The Washington Post*'s Tom Shales was quick to agree: '*Texas Chain Saw Massacre*...is the latest discouraging entry in a horror movie subgenre that might be called gorenography—films that strive not so much to shock or frighten as merely to sicken...For what it is, it is well done, but it's hard not to find what it is lamentable and what it represents cause for despair.'

Despite the critical brickbats, Bryanston managed to get a lot of mileage out of the fact that they had made a gift of a perfect print of *Chain Saw* to the film collection of the Museum of Modern Art in New York and had also gotten the film accepted by the Director's Fortnight section of the 1975 Cannes Film Festival. What they failed to mention was that *Chain Saw* had not been neither solicited nor accepted into

MoMA's permanent film collection and that the Director's Fortnight was in fact an out-of-competition sideshow for offbeat films.

However, *Chain Saw* did indeed find an audience outside of the drive-in, when it became an invited entry at the 1975 London Film Festival—despite being banned for theatrical exhibition in the UK by the British Board of Film Censors—as part of MoMA's 1975 ReView Series and winning the critics' prize at the Avoriaz Fantastic Film Festival in 1976. For those involved in the making of *Chain Saw*, there had never been any expectation of greatness, as Neal expressed to *Fangoria*: 'There was no doubt in our minds that the thing would show at about three drive-ins in south Texas, and that'd be the end of it, and we'd all have a good laugh over it when we got old.' However, when the dollars and laurels began rolling in, those who had worked for peanuts on the film began to wonder when they would see the percentages of the movie's profits that they had been promised in lieu of salaries (most of which ranged from a paltry $50 to $125 for the entire shoot). 'Everything was fine till the film began to appear on the *Variety* charts,' Hooper told the *Village Voice*. 'Then, people began to have expectations of sugar plums. They were unfamiliar with the industry, and they didn't realise there was a group of investors who had to be reimbursed.'

What they also did not realise was how *many* investors there were—35 in all, counting the members of cast and crew who also had points in the film. They were further startled to discover that Vortex—the company in which they had shares— only owned half the movie, which meant that their 1% in the movie's profits was actually only 0.5%. Not that Hooper and Henkel fared much better, as they each wound up owning only 7.5% of the movie they created.

The breaking point was reached when Bryanston was not forthcoming with the Texans' share of the profits. Despite earning $6 million in rentals (plus an estimated $5 million overseas), Bryanston had only remitted a comical $5,734 of *Chain Saw*'s profits to Vortex. In the fall of 1975, Henkel, Kuhn, Parsley and Skaaren went to New York to personally meet with Peraino and demand a full accounting of *Chain Saw*'s revenues. 'Skaaren and I went over to [Bryanston's] offices,' Kuhn told *Texas Monthly*. 'Henkel and Parsley stayed in the hotel. We waited a long time, and then Lou Peraino invited us into his office. On either side of him were two great big guys who looked like stereotypical thugs. We sat down and said, "We're here to audit the books." He said, "You're not gonna audit the books." I said, "In that case we would have no choice but to sue you." He looked at me and said, "You don't have enough balls to sue me."'

What the Texans did not know about the Perainos was their connection to the Colombo crime family, which was about to become public that October with stories in the *New York Post* and *New York Times* linking Bryanston to organised crime. Louis Peraino—whose nickname of 'Butchie' should have been a dead giveaway— was also one of several individuals indicted in August 1974 by a federal grand jury in Memphis for trafficking in pornography by distributing *Deep Throat*, a case that came to trial in March 1976 and became a *cause célèbre* in Hollywood as a litmus test for the First Amendment.[4]

In May 1976, Kuhn filed a lawsuit on behalf of Vortex and others for breach of contract against Bryanston, but the Peraino-owned company folded the same month, apparently in hock to the Internal Revenue Service and companies all over the world. Kuhn was able to reach an out-of-court settlement with Bryanston in February 1977, when it agreed to pay the Texans a lump sum of $400,000 and to return all prints of *Chain Saw* to Vortex. The money and the prints were never collected, however, as they were superseded by claims from various creditors and sub-distributors who had their own scores to settle with Peraino. In fact, Bryanston

---

4 The trial lasted 14 weeks and cost over $4 million. Louis Peraino was sentenced to a year in prison and fined $10,000. His conviction was overturned and the case was retried in September 1978, at which time his conviction was reinstated. Over the next three years, Peraino appealed his case all the way to the US Supreme Court, but he was refused a hearing. In February 1982, he was sentenced to an additional 6 years in prison as a result of the FBI's MIPORN sting operation in Miami, Florida. Peraino died of lung cancer in April 1999 at the age of 59.

did not even own *Chain Saw* anymore—Peraino had assigned the domestic rights in the picture to another New York-based distributor, Joseph Brenner Associates, back in May 1976 in return for a $10,000 payment on Bryanston's behalf to the National Film Service.

Leaving the increasingly-thorny business to the lawyers, Hooper and Henkel had gone Hollywood, moving into an office on the back lot of Universal Pictures in July 1976, where a contract for their next five pictures (including an original screenplay called *Bleeding Hearts* and a remake of the 1951 sci-fi classic *The Thing*) had been secured with the backing of *Exorcist* director William Friedkin. But nothing came of the deal and when the contract expired, Hooper struggled to find work while Henkel returned to Texas, where he wound up teaching film at Texas A&M University.

In June 1978, Brenner Associates' ownership of the *Chain Saw* rights expired and Kuhn and Parsley began negotiating a distribution deal with Robert Shaye's New Line Cinema, distributors of foreign films by the likes of Pasolini and Wertmuller as well as such midnight movie hits as John Waters's *Pink Flamingos* (1972) and *Female Trouble* (1974). The two men did not deign to inform Hooper or Henkel of this, however—nor of the fact that Kuhn had transferred the copyright into his name—which resulted in Henkel and Hooper filing suit in a Texas court against Kuhn and Parsley. For the next two years, *Chain Saw* sat in limbo as the Texans engaged in an intramural battle over who would control the film. Things got so messy that a federal judge in Austin ordered that all revenues from the film be deposited with the court and appointed a third party to preside over the awarding of US distribution rights for the film.

Thanks to the efforts of Shaye, New Line was successful in gaining the domestic distribution contract on *Chain Saw* in mid-1980. 'It was an extremely arduous process of contacting all of [the interested parties], setting up a meeting and outlining our proposal,' Shaye told *Fangoria*. 'They came to New York and we showed them our operation. Basically, I think one of the things that most determined our ability to get the movie was our assurance that we would treat them fairly.'

The Texas Chain Saw Massacre had its New Line premiere on November 21 in Memphis, where it earned over $100,000 in its first three weeks. The film went into general re-release in May 1981, and earned over $6 million, of which $1 million was deposited in the Austin federal courthouse. That year, the lawsuit between Henkel, Hooper, Kuhn and Parsley was finally settled in Hooper and Henkel's favour. Kuhn and Parsley had supposedly discussed a *Chain Saw* sequel with New Line (to be written by Skaaren)—as did Hooper, Henkel and writer/director John Milius—but it turned out to be nothing more than talk.

   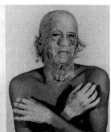

'We never did a sequel to *Chain Saw* due to legal problems,' Henkel told the *Chicago Daily Herald* on the occasion of the original film's re-release. 'Now, it'd be difficult to follow the original since it became such a cult classic. Tobe and I decided to just leave it alone and go on to other things.' For Hooper, that meant directing the Steven Spielberg-produced blockbuster *Poltergeist* (1982) and two big-budget sci-fi flops for the Cannon Group: *Lifeforce* (1985) and a remake of the 1953 classic *Invaders from Mars* (1986). Henkel preferred to stay close to home, however, writing and producing Eagle Pennell's low budget cult film *Last Night at the Alamo* (1983).

In May 1986, Tobe Hooper finally returned to where it all began when he produced and directed *The Texas Chainsaw Massacre Part 2*, the final film in his three-picture deal with Cannon. This time the script was written by LM 'Kit' Carson, best known for co-writing Wim Wenders's highly acclaimed *Paris, Texas* (1984) with Sam Shepard. Despite his now-advanced pedigree, *Chainsaw 2* marked a distinct step back for Hooper—a $5 million budget, 8-week shooting schedule and only 7 weeks of post-production before the guaranteed release date of August 22.

With a decided emphasis on black humour (as well as Tom Savini gore effects that earned the film an X rating; it was released unrated), *Chainsaw 2* nevertheless failed to find its audience, earning just $8 million at the box office, although it did become a success on home video. Two years later, Hooper sought to interest New Line in another *Chainsaw* sequel, but he soon exited the project in favour of making *Spontaneous Combustion* (1989). New Line, however, picked up the option and hired 'splatterpunk' writer David Schow to come up with a third chapter in the series. Under the direction of Jeff Burr (*From a Whisper to a Scream, Stepfather II*), *Leatherface: The Texas Chainsaw Massacre III* went into production in July 1989 on a $3 million budget. The film ended up being re-edited by the studio and had much of its violence cut to avoid an X rating. Its release was delayed until January 1990, when *Leatherface* met with critical disdain and audience indifference, and New Line abandoned its plans for further sequels.

In the summer of 1993, one-time legal enemies Kim Henkel and Robert Kuhn joined forces to make the $600,000 sequel *Return of the Texas Chainsaw Massacre,* with Henkel serving as both writer and director. The film would star Texas natives Matthew McConaughey and Renee Zellweger, who had both just appeared in Richard Linklater's coming-of-age movie *Dazed and Confused.* This latest *Chainsaw* chapter had its world premiere at the South by Southwest Film and Media Conference in Austin in March 1995, then was test-marketed that August. It caught the attention of Columbia Pictures, which acquired the picture for distribution, cutting it by 15 minutes and retitling it *Texas Chainsaw Massacre: The Next Generation*. It was then scheduled for release in early 1996, but the sudden interest in both McConaughey (for the John Grisham thriller *A Time to Kill*) and Zellweger (for the Tom Cruise vehicle *Jerry Maguire*) caused Columbia to hold back, supposedly under pressure from Creative Artists Agency, which felt that the film might hurt its clients' blossoming careers. Henkel's sequel ended up receiving only a token release in August 1997 before being pawned off to video a year later. In keeping with *Chain Saw* tradition, Henkel and Kuhn filed suits against CAA, Columbia and McConaughey but the action went nowhere.

For his part, Hooper has spent the past two decades directing for TV series like *Masters of Horror, Night Visions* and *Nowhere Man,* as well as direct-to-video horror movies like *Night Terrors* (1993), *Crocodile* (2000), *Toolbox Murders* (2004) and *Mortuary* (2005). In 2003, Hooper wrote an article in the *Los Angeles Times* in which he summed up *Chain Saw*'s appeal after 30 years: '*Chain Saw* was more complex than it seemed. It worked because it had three narratives. One was the framework that the story hangs on, another was what you learn in the interchange between the characters, and the third is the visual that stands on its own. As the three weave together, the story forms in your imagination...The construction of *Chain Saw* was like this throughout, and it was *what you didn't see* that had the strongest impact.'

(2003)

I'm a man out of time. I really identify with the '70s filmmakers. I guess I have a lot of chutzpah, so I'm proud to carry the torch.

–Marcus Nispel, director

I have always been fascinated by Leatherface—he's a very iconic figure. He has a niche, he's the guy with the saw, and the saw is very powerful. The saw wields great influence. Few things are as intimidating and infamous as the roaring power tool with sharp teeth...It's a horrifying prospect to be chased by an insane, towering brute with a chainsaw...And that's why I dig it.

– Andrew Bryniarski, 'Leatherface'

The Texas Chain Saw Massacre (2003)

Despite the bad fortune that had constantly befallen the *Texas Chain Saw Massacre* franchise, people kept trying to make lightning strike twice. In November 1998, Unapix Entertainment, producers of direct-to-video fare like *Devil in the Flesh* and *Legend of the Mummy* (both 1998), announced that they were the latest to write a cheque to Charles Grigson—the trustee for the owners of *Chain Saw*—to make yet another chapter in the life of Leatherface. This time, however, the project would coincide with the 25th anniversary of *Chain Saw*'s release and would be known as *The Texas Chainsaw Massacre: TX25*. Unapix was planning a summer or fall 1999 release and was supposedly negotiating with Tobe Hooper to write and direct the latest instalment, but the standard excuse of 'script problems' pushed the project into the new millennium—now with the title *TX2000*—and finally into oblivion.

Unapix's loss would prove to be Michael Bay's gain. The 37-year-old Bay had been an award-winning director of commercials and music videos before making the switch to feature films with the hit Will Smith-Martin Lawrence buddy-

cop vehicle *Bad Boys* in 1995. Bay's status as one of Hollywood's hottest directors was solidified with a string of big-budget blockbusters, including *The Rock* (1996), *Armageddon* (1998) and *Pearl Harbor* (2001). In November 2001, Bay, along with Andrew Form and Brad Fuller, formed the company Platinum Dunes with the express purpose of hiring new directors for so-called 'high concept' commercial projects in the under-$20 million range. 'The philosophy of the company is to tap first-timers who have directed in other mediums and have set experience and savvy,' Bay told *Variety*.

In January 2002, it was reported that the Platinum

Dunes' inaugural production would be a remake of *The Texas Chain Saw Massacre*, in conjunction with Radar Pictures and Next Entertainment. Tobe Hooper and Kim Henkel were said to be writing a draft script, but their involvement proved to be extremely limited. 'We got paid for writing a script but there was never any intention to even look at that script,' Henkel told author Stefan Jaworzyn in his 2003 book, *The Texas Chain Saw Massacre Companion*. 'In fact, we didn't get paid for writing the script until they were already in pre-production.'

To drum up interest in the remake, Bay himself shot a promotional reel to be used as a sales tool at the upcoming American Film Market. Just 90 seconds long, the short is mainly sound against a black screen as a woman is trying to hide from Leatherface inside a house. Suddenly, the chainsaw carves shafts of light into the picture, revealing Leatherface's trademark mask. Bay's gimmick worked a treat, as some 40 companies worldwide snapped up distribution rights to the film, which still had no writer, director or cast. New Line Cinema, which already had extensive experience with Leatherface, wound up paying between $5 and $7 million for the North American and Italian rights to the remake, outbidding Dimension Films, Paramount and Screen Gems. New Line owner Robert Shaye told *Variety* the new *Chain Saw* would be 'an original, fresh and thrilling postmodern' take on the original film. Studio president Toby Emmerich added: 'My sense from Bay is that he will not so much look at the previous *Chainsaw* movies as look back to the original, real stories that informed [them].'

In March, it was announced that Bay's good friend, 38-year-old German Marcus

Nispel—another veteran of countless music videos and commercials—would be making his feature debut with the film. 'I knew about [the original] but I was not in a country where it was as well received as it was here where it really broke all the rules, where it became this monolithical cult,' Nispel would later tell DVD Empire. 'So I didn't have that reverence to it. Then you sign on and you look at...what a sacred cow this really is and then you start to take this really damn seriously and say, "You know what? I don't care what's being said. When it's done I want to make sure I don't turn off those people that pay their hard-earned money to see this type of a movie." And our big mantra was, "Let's keep it in the seventies." That's one first step towards authenticity because that's maybe the last time that truly authentic movies were done on a regular basis...[plus the fact] a story like this with modern day kids wouldn't even be possible because they'd all have cell phones.'

At the same time, it was announced that another rookie, Scott Kosar, would write the film; Kosar's UCLA graduate screenplay *The Machinist* (which was produced in 2004) had generated a lot of buzz. 'I couldn't possibly say no to my first big break,' Kosar told Dread Central, 'and I also thought it was such a thrill and an honour to have my first job be a remake of *The Texas Chain Saw Massacre*. I also knew that we were dealing with one of the seminal works of the genre and it was a thankless job and no one in the world could make a better version of Tobe Hooper's film...So in the beginning when I had my story meetings with Platinum Dunes that was very much part of the discussion. "Look, let's not try to compete with the original." It was a very different movie made under very different circumstances...I have nothing but love for the movie so it was challenging and very daunting to take it on.'

Nispel was very much in agreement, telling Bloody Disgusting: 'We couldn't sell the same thing twice. We had to do new things. We tried not to think of it as a remake of Tobe Hooper's *Texas Chain Saw Massacre*. We're doing a remake of Hansel and Gretel. It's basically the same story. The story that it's based on, Ed Gein's story, is truly frightening...So, I had other goals than paying homage to the first *Texas Chain Saw Massacre*. I think, actually, the script brought us much closer to the movie *Deliverance*. The movie I also had in my head...was the movie *Alien*. That style, that type of pacing. It's more than just a remake, it's storytelling in general.'

Like the original, this new *Chain Saw* would be filmed on location in the summer, but unlike his predecessor, the new Leatherface would supposedly enjoy a budget of between $13 and $19 million. After working for three months, and with some uncredited help from screenwriter Eric Bernt (*Virtuosity*, *Romeo Must Die*), Kosar delivered his final draft on June 5...

August 1973. Police pull the remains of 33 murder victims from a farmhouse in Travis County, Texas. Later that day, two detectives go back to film the crime scene, but they are attacked and killed by Thomas Brown Hewitt—aka the butcher Leatherface. Soon after, a man believed to be Hewitt is killed by police but a shotgun blast to the face prevents positive identification. However, the killings stop. Thirty years later, an interviewer tries to get the story from an anonymous 'only known survivor' of the murder spree, but he cannot

be seen and does not speak. The interviewer also talks to a woman in her 50s named Erin—incarcerated in an asylum—who claims that the wrong man was killed and that Leatherface is still alive. She then recounts what happened to her and her friends that August...

Erin and her boyfriend Kemper, along with Andy, Pepper and Morgan, are in their customised van on the way to a Lynyrd Skynyrd concert in Dallas. They pick up a catatonic hitchhiker—a teenage girl who mumbles about everyone being dead. She then pulls out a .357 snubnose and blows her brains out in front of the shocked stoners. Now saddled with a suicide, the gang stops at a general store for help, where the female owner, Luda May, calls Sheriff Hoyt and tells the incredulous kids to meet him at an abandoned cotton mill. While they wait, they encounter a strange young boy named Jedidiah, who tells them that the sheriff lives nearby. Erin and Kemper decide to make their way to the sheriff's house while the others stay with Jedidiah at the mill. The couple find a farmhouse with an invalid named Old Monty inside, but no sheriff. While Monty distracts Erin by pretending to fall in the bathroom, Kemper is attacked and butchered by Leatherface, a huge man with a blood-stained apron, a dirty black wig and a mask made of human flesh. Meanwhile, Sheriff Hoyt arrives at the mill, wraps the corpse in cellophane, puts the body in the trunk of his car and simply drives off without taking any statements. Erin returns to the mill, expecting to find Kemper waiting with their friends, when suddenly a blaring car horn brings the group to a junkyard full of abandoned vehicles. There they find a family photo that includes the suicidal hitchhiker. Erin decides that Kemper must still be back at the farmhouse and gets Andy to come with her. Upon entering, they are attacked by Old Monty and Leatherface—Erin gets away but Andy has his leg chopped off and is hung on meat hooks in the basement. Erin rejoins Pepper and Morgan at the van but before they can take off, they are intercepted by Sheriff Hoyt, who proceeds to mentally and physically torture the trio. Sheriff Hoyt takes Morgan to the farmhouse, leaving Erin and Pepper to be attacked by Leatherface, now wearing a Kemper mask. Pepper is killed but Erin makes her way to a lonely trailer, where she is taken in by the dowdy and obtuse Henrietta, who talks about how mistreated Thomas Hewitt was as a child because of deformities caused by skin cancer. Erin discovers that Henrietta has kidnapped a baby, but before she can act, she succumbs to the drugged tea that Henrietta has given her. Erin awakens at the farmhouse in the midst of a family reunion—Henrietta and the baby, Sheriff Hoyt, Old Monty, Luda May, Jedidiah and Leatherface. She is thrown into the basement, where she finds Andy barely alive on the meat hooks and ends his torment by putting a butcher's knife through his sternum. She also finds a badly-beaten Morgan—wearing Leatherface's old mask—before the two are ushered into a secret passageway by Jedidiah which takes them to an underground tornado shelter. With Leatherface in pursuit, Erin and Morgan pop the hatch and make a run for it, seeking shelter in an abandoned prairie house. Its thin walls are no match for Leatherface, however, who carves up the place before sawing Morgan in two. Erin makes her way to a nearby slaughterhouse for a final confrontation with Leatherface that sees the fiend lose an arm and his chainsaw before giving up the chase. Erin is picked up by a passing truck, but when the driver takes her back to the general store, she steals Henrietta's 'adopted' baby and Sheriff Hoyt's car—running the crooked cop over in the process. With her story complete, Erin tells the interviewer that the man who was mistaken by police for Leatherface had two arms. Only then does the interviewer realise that the silent man in the shadows had only one arm...

Filming began on July 22 on a greatly-reduced $9.5 million budget and a 40-day shooting schedule. The cast was primarily young TV stars, including Eric Balfour (*Six Feet Under*), Jessica Biel (*7th Heaven*), Erica Leerhsen (*The Guardian*) and Mike Vogel (*Grounded for Life*), who willingly exchanged their cushy day jobs to endure much the same torment as had their predecessors 30 years earlier. 'It's the hottest day, the hottest time, shot in the middle of the summer, in a little van,' Nispel told DVD Empire. 'You have to turn off the air conditioner, you have to close the windows because cells are flapping, and you're not popular. And then suddenly you look at the cast and they're acting from the inside out. They're putting their heart and soul in it. They're really suffering. When Vogel is hanging on that hook he's in tremendous pain and everybody knows it. When Jessica is acting it's not Visine in her eyes, she's really crying her eyes out and she's keeping herself in that mode 24 hours a day...So these kids were everything that I had. I had nothing else, and they became the barometer of [professionalism], so I can't say enough good things about them.'

From Biel, cast in the lead role of Erin, came the determination to play the tough survivor and not just another pretty young victim. 'To me it was, how am I going to make this real?' she told IGN. 'How am I going to make this scary? How am I going to make women who watch this movie not go, "Oh God, another girl running around in her little blond panties and falling and tripping and running to the second floor"... From the beginning I was like, I'm not interested in making a silly horror movie. I'm really interested in making this a serious movie with a strong lead character that's really going to make women, men, whoever, just go, "Rock on girl!" That was important to me.'

The archetypal role of Leatherface went to 34-year-old Andrew Bryniarski, a six-foot-three former bodybuilder who had already appeared in a dozen films and almost as many TV shows. He knew Bay from working on *Pearl Harbor* and, as the story goes, approached the producer at a Christmas party and insisted that he be cast as Leatherface. Bay obliged, as Bryniarski's physical stature was exceeded only by his self-confidence, which the actor expressed to Bloody Disgusting: 'I raised the bar, which I am totally capable of doing because I am [a] very intense, very

professional, and very accurate individual...Once I decide that that's what I am going to do, with passion and conviction, then I can arise to that challenge and supersede everyone's expectations...That motivates me greatly, to do a great job...

There was a lot that I had to prove in this movie...A lot of people were looking to me to deliver this performance because, really, it's the key to delivering this franchise back to its rightful spot on top of the horror food chain.'

Nispel also felt that the portrayal of Leatherface was the key to this version's success: 'When I saw the mask, I thought to myself, "He looks like a monster, but it's really the guy next door." That's why I put in the scene where I made him take off his mask briefly, to remind us of two things: a) that this is a human being under the mask; and b) that he has some serious problems, there is skin cancer under the mask. He is the object of ridicule. This explains to us why he wears the masks of other kids' faces. They represent the kids that ridiculed him. The way Bryniarski went about it, he played down the human oafishness of [Gunnar Hansen's] Leatherface, and he brought much more stealth to the part.'

FLASH TO—ROGER CHURCH, 50s, retired Police Officer. Bloodshot eyes, leans against police car.

ROGER CHURCH
Yeah, we botched the case. Anybody with half a brain knew the crime scene wasn't sealed properly.

FLASH TO—FRANKLIN NASH, unfazed.

FRANKLIN NASH
I lost two guys down there...

FLASH TO—PHOTOS of a POLICE FUNERAL, POLICE TOMBSTONES and OFFICERS lined up in FULL DRESS.
FRANKLIN NASH (VO) (CONT'D)
But we tracked the killer down...

FLASH—PHOTO—a MAN slumped to the side of the steering wheel, blood everywhere—his face has been obliterated.

FLASH—TO FRANKLIN NASH, folding his hands over his desk.

FRANKLIN NASH (CONT'D)
...and while attempting to escape, Mr. Hewitt took a shotgun blast to the face. And that day, the State of Texas won.

FLASH TO—newspaper headlines: 'MADMAN GUNNED DOWN BY POLICE'... 'TEXAS HOUSE OF HORRORS COMES TO END'.

–Unfilmed montage, from the original script

As written, this *Chainsaw* was supposed to have bookends that spoke to Leatherface's supposed death and the failure of law enforcement to positively identify him. The script called for documentary-style interview footage with Cook County Supervisor Franklin Nash and retired detective Roger Church, talking about the case and how Leatherface was supposedly killed while trying to escape from the police. This was replaced by the film shot by detectives investigating the house. The parenthetical interviews were in fact shot, with a reporter named Randy Fletcher (the film's actual first assistant director) attempting to interview an unseen, obese survivor who says nothing while munching on chocolates. Fletcher then interviews an older Erin in an asylum, who relates the narrative as a flashback. After her story, Erin tells Fletcher that she knows the man who was killed was not Leatherface because he had two arms, whereas Leatherface only has one. It suddenly occurs to Fletcher that the person he previously interviewed only had one arm. We then cut to a phalanx of SWAT and FBI agents raiding the unseen survivor's home, but he has already left. This was all replaced by returning to the film shot by detectives as they are attacked by Leatherface.[5]

'Our big question was, "How do we approach it?" and I really felt it had to be like a snuff film,' Nispel told DVD Empire. 'What really was guiding me was not the commercial style but the fact that horror and violence can have something incredibly poetic about it and I haven't really seen that yet. It's something that, when it happens, makes people very uncomfortable.'

As it turned out, the MPAA was certainly made uncomfortable and, failing to see the poetry in all the bloodletting, slapped *Chainsaw* with an NC-17 rating. To appease the Ratings Board, two scenes had to be altered to obtain a more marketable R rating. The Hitchhiker's already-graphic suicide originally featured a grotesque aside, as one of her disembodied ears lands on Pepper and is quickly brushed to the floor, where it is the subject of a close-up. This was eliminated. Likewise, the original cut had Leatherface saw upwards into Morgan's groin, followed by a rush of blood and intestines. These shots were replaced by cut-aways of Erin screaming and running out. 'It's funny, when you do this kind of a movie, you don't really know if it's scary,' Nispel confessed to Bloody Disgusting. 'You've pushed all the buttons, you know what's working, but you haven't really seen it with an audience. You're not quite sure. The film editor was having me watch scenes that we were working on, towards the end of the film. But he didn't tell me about some certain shots he had inserted. So we're watching it, and I am completely jumping out of my seat! I thought, My God, if all the scenes are as scary as this one, I'm really a lucky dog.'

Originally scheduled for a January 2003 opening, New Line decided to hold off until Halloween, releasing the film on October 17. The new *Chainsaw* enjoyed a $28 million opening weekend, on its way to a domestic gross of $80.5 million, with an additional $26.5 million earned overseas. The picture met with a few positive reviews, notably from the *Chicago Tribune* ('Lays out enough fright and carnage to revitalise a horror trove that was becoming dangerously cartoonish...the new *Texas Chainsaw Massacre* has no pretensions about sneaking up on you—it simply charges, motor

---

5 A scripted subplot involving Erin's pregnancy and her discussions with Kemper about marriage was also shot, but was eliminated from the final cut for fear that it got in the way of the action.

humming and blades flying, carving the spot where masochism and entertainment meet') and the *Los Angeles Times* ('At once more broadly comic and more overtly sadistic... the new *Massacre* works hard to scare the pants off the audience and mostly succeeds through slamming edits, loud noises and lots of realistic-looking blood'). But as with his previous outings, Leatherface was not well received in most circles. 'The new version of *The Texas Chainsaw Massacre* is a contemptible film,' declared Roger Ebert. 'Vile, ugly and brutal. There is not a shred of a reason to see it.' 'Everything that made the original *Chainsaw* a classic is ground into the dirt in this new version,' observed *Film Threat*. 'This new *Chainsaw* takes $20 million [sic] to emulate the original, which had less than one percent of this budget, and it's still just a cheap imitation.' *The New York Times* felt likewise: 'With a budget many times that of the 1974 drive-in classic on which it is based, Marcus Nispel's *Texas Chainsaw Massacre* delivers proportionately fewer thrills and no discernible suspense. It is, instead, a long march to the slaughterhouse that seems to take forever to get going and, once it does, goes nowhere that hasn't been visited before by more talented filmmakers.' 'There's no denying the technical skill displayed by Nispel,' admitted *Time Out*, 'but he has no feel for narrative rhythm, cumulative tension or raw terror. The best one can say is that his version is not slavishly in thrall to Hooper's: boring, fright-free and pointless, maybe, but not craven.'

Despite his marginal participation, Hooper (who, along with Henkel, received a co-producer's credit) came out in support of the remake, telling About.com: 'I created Leatherface and the original *Chain Saw* and so there was a certain truth in that that I feel has been fused into this quite nicely. It's still my baby. I mean, it's Leatherface and in the history books you can't separate Tobe Hooper and Leatherface. I'm happy to see my little boy back at it.'

In October 2005, production began on Platinum Dunes's $16 million *Texas Chainsaw Massacre: The Beginning*, a prequel scripted by Sheldon Turner, who had done an uncredited rewrite on the companies *Amityville Horror* remake (q.v.) as well as penning the remake of *The Longest Yard*. It covered Thomas Hewitt's birth and adoption by the psychotic Hewitt family, his troubled upbringing and employment at the local meat-packing plant. After the facility is closed, Hewitt goes over the edge and becomes the cannibalistic Leatherface, and the Hewitt family once again plays grisly host to two road-tripping brothers and their girlfriends.

With Nispel otherwise engaged on the adventure movie *Pathfinder* (which was shot in 2005 but not released until 2007), Jonathan Liebesman (*Darkness Falls*) took over the director's chair, with Bryniarski reprising the role of Leatherface, along with returning cast members R Lee Ermey (Sheriff Hoyt), Terrence Evans (Old Monty), Kathy Lamkin (Tea Lady) and Marietta Marich (Luda May).

Released by New Line in October 2006, *The Beginning* met with universally negative reviews and a gross almost exactly half that of its predecessor ($39.5 million domestic; $12.2 million foreign), which led to the Hewitt family relocating away from Platinum Dunes. Leatherface's option was soon picked up by the folks at Twisted Pictures, producers of the *Saw* series, who in October 2009 announced that they had acquired the rights to once again 'reboot' the *Chainsaw* franchise. The plan was to make a modern-day Leatherface story and shoot it in 3-D, with a script from Stephen Susco, late of *The Grudge* and its 2006 sequel.

The next two years saw some internal wrangling at Twisted, with production president Carl Mazzocone leaving the company and taking *Chainsaw* with him. In May 2011, Mazzocone announced that he would be producing *The Texas Chainsaw Massacre 3D* in a joint venture with Nu Image and Lionsgate Films, with John

Luessenhop (*Takers*) as director. An eclectic group of writers have since taken a crack at the script, including Kirsten Elms (*Banshee*), Adam Marcus (*Jason Goes to Hell*) and actress Debra Sullivan. The latest Leatherface adventure, which features a cameo by Marilyn Burns, is due for release in January 2013.

THE AMITYVILLE HORROR
(1979)

Whether or not this is true is not germane. To me as a director the important thing is—does it work and is it entertaining?

–Stuart Rosenberg, director

I simply ask why would George Lutz move out of his dream house, abandon a business which had been in his family for three generations and flee to San Diego with his wife and three children for nothing? Just to have a book written about it?

–James Brolin, 'George Lutz'

In the early morning hours of November 13, 1974, the quiet South Shore village of Amityville, Long Island (population 10,700) was the scene of an almost unbelievably gruesome murder. Ronald DeFeo Jr, then 23 years old and known to his family as 'Butch', had executed his parents and four siblings with a .35 calibre rifle while they slept in their three-story Dutch colonial home. Initially, he told police that his family were the victims of a Mob slaying, but when all the evidence pointed back to him, DeFeo changed his story at the behest of his attorney, William Weber. DeFeo now claimed that demonic voices had ordered him to commit the murders. The jury did not buy DeFeo's claims of supernatural possession and found him guilty on six counts of second-degree murder. On December 6, 1975, DeFeo was sentenced to six life terms in prison.

Twelve days later, newlyweds George and Kathleen Lutz bought the house for $80,000 and moved in with Kathleen's three young children. Just twenty-eight days later, on January 14, 1976, the Lutzes supposedly fled the house in fear for their lives, leaving all of their worldly possessions behind. Little more than a week after that, the Lutzes contacted Weber, as the lawyer would later recall for the TV documentary *Amityville: Horror or Hoax* (2000): 'When I first met with the Lutzes, they told me a story about incidences that occurred to them and their children...and they wanted to know if I had any evidence during the trial or during my investigation that could help them. I didn't believe ninety percent of what they were saying, but admittedly

The Amityville Horror (1979)

I was interested in writing a book on the case. The book we were contemplating had three parts to it: whether DeFeo was a cold blooded killer; whether he was criminally insane; and whether he was possessed by some supernatural forces. The reader was going to be left to decide.'

Weber wanted to publish the Lutzes' story as part of his book, which he had already commissioned Paul Hoffman to write, and felt that some preliminary publicity would be a great way to kick things off. On February 16, Weber's office played host to a press conference where George and Kathleen Lutz publicly claimed that, while living at 112 Ocean Avenue, they and their children were the victims of malignant poltergeist activity. According to Kathleen, however, it was a forum that was forced upon them: 'Weber [wanted] a press conference, which was something I didn't really want to do. And he said if we didn't meet with him, that he would send the reporters to the school where the children were going and they would get the information from the children. And under that threat I agreed to the press conference.'

Weber subsequently drew up a contract whereby the Lutzes would tell their story to Hoffman in exchange for a share in the profits from the book. The Lutzes initially agreed, then withdrew once they discovered that one of the partners in the project was a convicted murderer. George Lutz stated, 'The idea that Ronnie DeFeo was going to receive monies from this enterprise was just not something that made any sense to us to even consider.'

Lutz took it upon himself to contact Stephen Kaplan, founder of Long Island's Parapsychology Institute of America, to see if he would investigate the Amityville house. Kaplan agreed, but just days later, Lutz called things off: 'When [Kaplan's] credentials wouldn't check out and I found out he was a vampirologist, we told him…we would have no more to do with him.' The very next day, Kaplan told Long Island *Newsday* that he believed the Amityville case to be a hoax. For the next 20 years, Kaplan would insist that the Lutzes' story was a fraud, culminating in the book *The Amityville Horror Conspiracy*, published in 1995, the year Kaplan died of a heart attack at the age of 54.

The Lutzes subsequently met Laura Didio, a 19-year-old intern with New York's Channel 5 television station, who in turn introduced them to paranormal investigators Ed and Lorraine Warren. On February 24, the Warrens, accompanied by a Channel 5 crew, investigated the abandoned Lutz home. While inspecting the basement, Ed Warren claimed to have encountered a terrifying presence. Days after their first visit to the house, the Warrens met with the Lutzes' priest, Father Ralph Pecoraro.

At the Lutzes' request, the Warrens and a team of experts returned to the house in Amityville on March 6, for a night of séances that were recorded for the benefit of Channel 5. Despite their best efforts, nothing untoward happened for the cameras, although a series of time-lapse photographs was taken, one of which allegedly shows a preternatural spirit manifesting itself as an eyeless young boy. The Warrens came to the conclusion that the house was possessed by evil spirits and would have to be exorcised by a high-ranking Anglican or Catholic priest.

In the early weeks and months after fleeing the house, George and Kathleen recorded a series of audio tapes in an attempt to chronicle their experience. Shortly before moving to San Diego that spring, the Lutzes were introduced to Tom Mosman, an editor for the publishing firm of Prentice-Hall. Mosman was intrigued by their story and recommended hiring Jay Anson, 54, a former New York reporter who had worked for Professional Films since 1967, scripting promotional featurettes for Hollywood films. A 50/50 deal on the book's profits was worked out between Anson and the Lutzes, although the writer never personally met with George and Kathleen, basing his work on their tape-recorded recollections. Through his friend Rev John Nicola, technical advisor for *The Exorcist,* Anson supposedly gained access to Father Pecoraro, who, under the name 'Father Mancuso', is also victimised in the book by rampant demonic activity.[6] It was Anson who came up with the title *The Amityville Horror*, and Rev Nicola provided the introduction. Anson also used his connections with Professional Films to negotiate the movie rights to the book, with he and the Lutzes each receiving 1.25% of the profits from the proposed film.

Anson claimed that, while writing the book, those connected with it suffered supernatural attacks, including his own cardiac arrest. On *The David Susskind Show*, Anson told the host, 'After I finished the manuscript, I turned it over to my editor to take back to New Jersey. His car caught on fire...I gave a copy of the manuscript to another friend, and there was a rainstorm and he went through...a pothole. And his whole car sank. It was total wreck. The only thing that was dry in the whole car was the manuscript...I had given the first two chapters to a friend of mine...She took it home and she died in a fire that night. She and [her] two daughters were killed.'

On July 18, an article on the Lutzes' experience entitled 'Life in a Haunted House' appeared in the *New York Sunday News*. The by-line was that of Paul Hoffman, who was evidently trying to get a jump on the Anson-Lutz tome as he was contractually obligated to deliver his own book to Weber by December 31. When it became obvious that the Lutzes would get their book out first, however, Weber cancelled the deal with Hoffman and went with professional ghost hunter Dr Hans Holzer, who had been inquiring about writing a book on the DeFeo murders. On January 13, 1977, Holzer and spiritual medium

---

6 Pecoraro left Long Island in May 1978 for 'personal reasons' and went to the Diocese of Oakland, California before apparently giving up the priesthood. He died in 1987.

Ethel Johnson-Meyers entered 112 Ocean Avenue. Meyers claimed that the house had been built over an ancient Indian burial ground and the angry spirit of a Shinnecock chief named Rolling Thunder had possessed DeFeo, driving him to murder his family.

That April, just as the Amityville house was once again inhabited, this time by Jim and Barbara Cromarty (who paid just $55,000 for the place), the Lutzes' story received national attention when Hoffman's article—now retitled 'Our Dream House Was Haunted'—was reprinted in *Good Housekeeping* magazine. Since neither the *Sunday News* article nor the *Good Housekeeping* reprinting had been done with the Lutzes' permission, George and Kathleen filed a $4.5 million lawsuit that May against Hoffman, Weber, *Good Housekeeping,* the *Sunday News* and the Hearst Corporation. The couple alleged invasion of privacy, misappropriation of name for trade purposes and mental distress. In retaliation, Hoffman and Weber each filed a counterclaim against the Lutzes for $2 million, claiming fraud and breach of contract. Judge Jacob Mishler dismissed the claims against the various publishers but allowed the rest of the suit to go forward.

In September, *The Amityville Horror* was published in hardback, selling 250,000 copies. Two months later, attorneys for the Diocese of Rockville Centre (which oversaw Amityville) prepared a list of 'numerous inaccuracies, factually incorrect references and untrue statements regarding events, persons, and occurrences that never happened' and submitted it to Prentice-Hall. Undaunted, Bantam went ahead and published the book in paperback in August 1978. It would go on to sell 6 million copies, becoming the longest-running bestseller since *The Exorcist*.

In February 1978, Professional Films entered into a co-production deal for a film of *The Amityville Horror* with American International Pictures[7] and a prolonged game of round-robin ensued with the screenplay. Anson wrote a first draft, which was promptly rejected. AIP hired Laird Koenig (*The Little Girl Who Lives Down the Lane*) to rewrite Anson, then decided to go with a new script altogether, written by Canadian physician-turned-television writer Sandor Stern (*The Strange and Deadly Occurrence, Where Have All the People Gone*). Stern's script was in turn rewritten by newcomer Alison Cross (who went on to win Emmys for the TV movies *Roe vs Wade* and *Serving in Silence*), whose work went uncredited.

Newlyweds George and Kathleen Lutz and her three children move into a Dutch colonial house in the Amityville district of Long Island, where just a year before a deranged young man had murdered his entire family. When the Lutzes' priest, Father Delaney, arrives to bless the house, he is overcome with illness, assaulted by flies and hears a voice telling him to 'Get out!' Later, when Delaney tries to call Kathy, static interrupts the line and his hand is covered in boils. George begins to succumb to the house's malevolent influence— waking up every morning at 3:15am (the time of the murders),

7 The film was originally scheduled to be made as a TV movie for CBS, which agreed to relinquish its claim on the property in exchange for broadcast rights to the theatrical feature. When the film of *The Amityville Horror* became a smash hit, CBS was able to acquire it for only $1.75 million. Airing in March 1981, it was a Top Five ratings success.

constantly complaining of the cold and allowing himself to physically deteriorate. The couple's young daughter Amy begins playing with an imaginary friend, 'Jody', who turns out to be not so imaginary. Father Delaney and his associate Father Bolen try to visit the Lutz house but on the way their car careers out of control, almost killing them. Afterwards, Delaney holds a meeting with his superiors where he tries unsuccessfully to convince them of supernatural happenings at the Lutz house. That night, George is awakened by the sound of buzzing and finds the sewing room full of flies, just as the front door is ripped off its hinges by an invisible force. Convinced that something is dreadfully wrong, George goes to the Amityville Historical Society, where he steals a book on the town's history. Meeting his partner Jeff and Jeff's girlfriend Carolyn at a bar, the trio read that the Lutz house was built on the site of an old Indian exposure pen for the insane. The land was subsequently used by the Salem warlock John Ketcham for satanic rituals. That night, Kathy interrupts Amy and 'Jody', only to see two red eyes staring at her from outside the second-story window, followed by the grunting of an animal. George, Jeff and Carolyn arrive at the house and, with Kathy, go to the basement, where they find a hollow space behind one of the walls. George grabs a pickaxe and begins to chop away at the panelling until the wall caves in, revealing an entire room painted in red. Suddenly, Carolyn begins to speak in Father Delaney's voice, telling the astonished crowd that the room is the 'back door to hell' and that they must find and cover a well to stop the passage of demons. After finding their decorative crucifix hanging upside down and soot-black, the couple use Kathy's necklace and holy water to bless the house. While chanting the Hail Mary prayer, Kathy's cross is ripped from her and she begins to break out in large welts. Meanwhile, Father Delaney says a mass for the Lutzes but is assaulted by psychic forces that leave him blind. That night, George is awakened by the sounds of a marching band traipsing through the house. Going downstairs to investigate, he is seemingly attacked by a ceramic lion. George and Kathy have an argument that flares into violence, with each striking the other. Kathy goes to the offices of Long Island Newsday and begins searching through the records to find out what happened the previous year. To her horror, the photo of the murderer is identical in appearance to George. Rushing home to save her children, she finds George on the rampage with an axe as blood seeps from the walls and the house fills with noise. Kathy's screams bring George back to sanity and the couple determine to rescue their family; with the animalistic 'Jody' in pursuit, the Lutzes flee the house only to realise that their dog Harry is still trapped inside. Despite Kathy's pleading, George returns to the house, falling through the basement stairs and into the red room, now full of black muck. He recovers, grabs Harry and is forced to escape through one of

the windows when the house itself bars the front door. Making his way to the van, George shoves Harry inside and takes off in the nick of time. A title card tells us that the Lutzes never returned.

Between September and October, the script went through five revisions (the last one just three days before shooting), with the following changes/additions made to the original draft:

- The parts of Sgt Lou Vito (originally Sgt Al Gionfriddo) and Father Bolen were expanded.
- After getting his hand slammed in a window, Greg Lutz is taken to the hospital, where the family is amazed to find that he has no broken bones (this was carried over from the book).
- A strange man shows up at the Lutzes' door, supposedly as a welcoming committee, then mysteriously disappears (ditto).
- The meeting between George and Jeff was changed to a confrontation.
- The meeting between George, Jeff and Carolyn was changed and ends with Jeff and Carolyn offering to babysit the Lutz kids so that George and Kathy can have a night out.
- Jeff and Carolyn go to the basement first and it is Carolyn who begins pounding out the wall to the red room.

While the majority of the supernatural incidents in the script are translated from the book, the Stern/Cross screenplay does take creative license with George's obsessive axe-chopping, the attack of flies on Father Delaney, the babysitter's ordeal in the

closet, George's refusal to leave the house, and his possessed attack on his family. Conversely, the script leaves out a number of the book's more harrowing episodes, including Kathy's repeated levitations during her sleep, she and George finding Jodie's cloven hoof prints in the snow and the family's escape being blocked by a towering, hooded figure in white. Co-producer Ronald Saland told the *Los Angeles Times*: 'We want to reach a broader audience than those who read the book and options have been made which will, hopefully, make a more credible story.'

Seven weeks of filming began on October 23, with a budget of $7 million. Because of all the adverse publicity Amityville had suffered, the town was not about to let the film be shot there, and the production had to settle for Toms River, New Jersey, instead, where a Dutch colonial was rented for $12,000 and a boathouse was constructed for $31,000. 'The Amityville authorities didn't want anyone to know [about the movie],' star James Brolin claimed. 'Apparently they've been overrun with tourists ever since the book came out. They wouldn't even cooperate with us in getting things like the Fire Department uniforms right. I don't blame them, really. It seems that every sign that had Amityville on it has long since been stolen for people to hang over their bars.'

Director Stuart Rosenberg, late of *Cool Hand Luke* (1967) and *Voyage of the Damned* (1976), had another reason for not filming in the actual locale, telling Rex Reed: 'We couldn't use the actual house because of credibility. People would say, "If it's a true story, then how did they make a film with evil spirits there?"'

Reed also talked to Brolin, who told the critic what attracted him to the project: 'I read the book, and I identified with George [Lutz] right away. I feel I know this guy. He's not all that different from myself. In my discussions with Stuart he was telling me what he thought George Lutz was and I was, and I was telling him he was wrong. I told Stuart I thought I had George Lutz nailed, and in the end that's what he wanted to hear. As long as I felt I was sure and secure in who I was playing. At first I thought they were going to keep George kind of straight and let the spirits be the drama, but they're doing it the way I hoped. They're really going all the way with the guy.'

'A lot of the things in the book don't quite meet,' Brolin said in a separate interview with UPI columnist Vernon Scott. 'Sceptics say it's hokum. I'm not superstitious. I've never had an occult experience myself. But I have an open mind about what happened in that Amityville house.' Co-producer Elliot Geisinger continued on this theme with the *Los Angeles Times*: 'We're operating in the realm of the possible. These events may be true or imagined. But this world is a strange place, with lots of strange events, and we hope people will at least feel this.'

INT. DELANEY'S ROOM—THE RECTORY—NIGHT
Delaney sits on the edge of his bed. His fists are digging into his thighs... his eyes staring into space... and he is rocking ever-so-slightly, perhaps tottering. This is his side of the exchange experience. The TELEPHONE BEGINS TO RING... and RING... and RING.
The sound slowly penetrates Delaney's disconnected consciousness. He reaches for the phone.

                    DELANEY
                    (TIRED)
Hello?

                    GEORGE (VO)
                (FILTERED; ANXIOUS)
Father Delaney?

                    DELANEY
                (STARTING TO FOCUS)
Speaking.

                    GEORGE (OS)
                (EDGING TOWARDS PANIC)
This is George Lutz...We need help, we can't do it by ourselves!

STATIC suddenly hits Delaney's eardrum, and painfully. He jerks
the phone away and stares at it with anger and frustration. We can
HEAR the PHONE continuing to SCREECH.

INT. KITCHEN—NIGHT
Carolyn has just thrown up in the sink. Kathy is holding the woman's

shoulders supportively as she runs the tap water to wash away the vomit. Reaching for a paper towel, she wets it quickly and wipes Carolyn's white, perspiring face while she guides her over to a kitchen chair. Carolyn has begun to cry. Jeff looks shocked and convinced. George is hanging up the telephone.

GEORGE
(TENSE)

Static cut us off.

Hysteria is rising in Carolyn.

CAROLYN

They've even got the phone! They're in the phone!

—Unfilmed scene, from the original script

While a nightmare sequence where Kathy (Margot Kidder) finds George murdering the children before turning the axe on his wife was added during shooting, there were a number of scripted scenes that did not make it off the page, including:

- Father Delaney, who has been jogging, gives CPR to a young boy who has been electrocuted.
- Before their car accident, Father Bolen tries to persuade Delaney not to go back to the Lutz house.
- As the Lutzes leave her brother's wedding reception, their new sister-in-law passes out on the dance floor from too much champagne.
- After their front door is ripped off the hinges, Kathy argues with George about him wanting to buy a gun.
- As in the book, George is awakened by instruments playing downstairs (this was replaced by a single drum rolling).
- After being stricken blind, Delaney is harassed by flies as he sits outside at the monastic retreat.

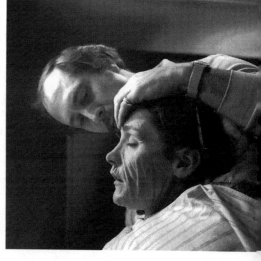

With filming complete on *The Amityville Horror* and the hype surrounding it at a fever pitch, the Cromartys followed the Lutzes' lead and vacated the house that December: not because of ghosts, but because they were sick of living in a tourist attraction and having to fend off a non-stop parade of trespassers. They put the now-famous home on the market for $100,000, and then turned around and sued the Lutzes, Anson, Prentice-Hall, Bantam, AIP and 45 newspapers for $1.1 million in damages (their claim was disallowed).

With a publicity campaign in excess of $3 million, *The Amityville Horror* opened on July 27, 1979, to a three-day gross of $8 million—the highest opening weekend of the summer. Its cumulative take of $86 million would be the highest in AIP's history—and the company's last solo outing before becoming part of the Filmways Corporation (AIP was renamed Filmways Pictures in March 1980).

Charles Champlin of the *Los Angeles Times* was impressed—'A damnably clever exercise in fright...the movie is boldly and shamelessly manipulative and as full of misdirection as a magic act'—as was *Variety* ('Has all the tingles and terrors of a classic haunted-house story, plus an address familiar to all the millions who bought the book'), but most critics were decidedly underwhelmed with the film version of the Lutzes' ordeal. Gary Arnold dismissed the movie as 'a feeble excuse for a haunted-house thriller, but given the source, who could ask for more? The woefully pedestrian bestseller, fabricated at the urging of an editor at Prentice-Hall and promoted as a "true" account, may have become the most profitable dog-ate-my-homework story ever told.' 'The real problem with *The Amityville Horror* is that, in a very real sense, there's nothing there,' reasoned Roger Ebert. 'We watch two hours of people being frightened and dismayed, and we ask ourselves...what for?' Janet Maslin felt that 'so many horror-movie clichés have been assembled under the roof of a single haunted house that the effect is sometimes mind-bogglingly messy. There is apparently very little to which...Stuart Rosenberg will not resort.' Gene Siskel's verdict was that '*The Amityville Horror* turns out to be just another haunted house picture and not a very good one. That's because it is more depressing than entertaining.'

Taking full advantage of the film's opening, Weber decided to go public with his allegations about the Lutzes to the Associated Press: 'We created this horror story over many bottles of wine that George was drinking. We were really playing with each other. We were creating something the public would want to hear about... If the public is gullible enough to believe the story, so be it.'

On September 10, Judge Jack Weinstein dismissed the rest of the Lutzes' suit and allowed the defendants' counterclaim to continue. He was moved to express his opinion: 'Based on what I have heard, it appears to me that to a large extent the book is a work of fiction, relying in a large part upon the suggestions of Mr Weber.' During the trial, Father Pecoraro swore under oath that he did in fact hear a disembodied voice in the house tell him to 'Get out!' But he would not confirm that the subsequent terrors portrayed in the book and the film actually happened. Judge Weinstein had as much a problem with Weber's conduct as with the alleged disingenuousness of the Lutzes—'There is a very serious ethical question when lawyers become literary agents'—and planned to refer the matter to the New York State Bar Association. Not surprisingly, the very next day the counterclaim was settled, and the entire case was dismissed.

Just one day later, *Newsday* published an article by reporter Jim Scovel that debunked the entire Lutz account: Father Pecoraro never went near the house or encountered demonic activity; supposed police witnesses never saw a thing (apparently

The night of February 5, 1976, George and Kathleen Lutz and their three children fled their home in Amityville, New York.

They got out alive!

Their living nightmare shocked audiences around the world in "The Amityville Horror."

But before them, another family lived in this house and were caught by the original evil.

They weren't so lucky...this is their story!

AMITYVILLE II: THE POSSESSION

DINO DE LAURENTIIS Presents AMITYVILLE II: THE POSSESSION
JAMES OLSON   BURT YOUNG   RUTANYA ALDA   ANDREW PRINE   JACK MAGNER
DIANE FRANKLIN and MOSES GUNN as "Burt" Music by LALO SCHIFRIN Film Editor SAM O'STEEN
Director of Photography FRANCO DIGIACOMO Production Designer PIERLUIGI BASILE Executive Producer BERNARD WILLIAMS
Screenplay by TOMMY LEE WALLACE From the Book "MURDER IN AMITYVILLE" by HANS HOLZER
Produced by IRA N. SMITH and STEVEN R. GREENWALD Directed by DAMIANO DAMIANI
Prints by DELUXE® A ORION PICTURES Release ©1982 DINO DE LAURENTIIS CORPORATION. ALL RIGHTS RESERVED

R RESTRICTED
UNDER 17 REQUIRES ACCOMPANYING
PARENT OR ADULT GUARDIAN

the Lutzes never called the police once during their 28 days of terror); and the curator of the Amityville Historical Society denied that the Shinnecock Indians corralled their sick, mad and dying on the site. Also, Scovel revealed for the first time that the Lutzes had a garage sale the day after they supposedly fled the house.

In November, Holzer's book about the DeFeo murders, titled *Murder in Amityville*, was published and almost immediately optioned by AIP. The next month, Professional Films snapped up the rights to Anson's yet-to-be-published follow-up novel *666* and announced a $10 million production for Orion Pictures. It was not to be, however, as Anson died of a heart attack in March 1980 at the age of 58 with the book still unfinished. Anson's editor at Simon and Schuster, Michael Korda, ended up playing ghost writer so that *666* could finally be published in April 1981.

That May, it was announced that Dino De Laurentiis would be producing *Death in Amityville* for Filmways. Based on Holzer's book, it was to be written by David Ambrose (*The Final Countdown*) and directed by John Hough (*The Legend of Hell House*). By November, the title had changed to *Amityville: The Possession*, with Ambrose and Hough replaced on the project by John Carpenter associate Tommy Lee Wallace and Italian director Damiano Damiani (*The Devil is a Woman*).

The Lutzes' own sequel, *The Amityville Horror II*, was written by John G Jones and published in January 1982. It recounted the supernatural happenings that continued to plague the family even after they fled the house in Amityville. While not the runaway smash that the first *Amityville Horror* had been, the Jones book was a bestseller in its own right and the Lutzes planned to turn it into a movie.[8] But since Filmways had right of first refusal on the project (left over from the original *Amityville Horror* agreement), the company was able to sit on it long enough to get their own *Amityville* property rolling once again in Toms River. Ten days of exteriors on *Amityville: The Possession* were shot there in March, with the bulk of the picture being filmed at the Churubusco Studios in Mexico City.

Orion Pictures, together with Home Box Office, had led an investor's group that bought a controlling interest in the financially troubled Filmways for $26 million in February. All of the company's non-film and television assets were subsequently sold off and Filmways was formally absorbed by Orion at the end of July. As a result, what became known as *Amityville II: The Possession* opened under the Orion banner in September, earning poor reviews and just $12.5 million at the box office. The film changed the name of the DeFeo family to Montelli and included a would-be exorcist and some incest between the Ronnie DeFeo stand-in and his sister.

The filmic decline of the house on 112 Ocean Avenue continued in November 1983 with the silly, PG-rated *Amityville 3D* (aka *Amityville: The Demon*), another De Laurentiis/Orion offering that made just $6 million at the box office. A six-year hiatus followed, broken in May 1989 with the TV movie *Amityville: The Evil Escapes*, written and directed by Stern and based on Jones's 1988 novel of the same name. The next in the series—*The Amityville Curse* (1990)—was based on Holzer's 1981 novel of the same name and went straight to video, as did the three unrelated follow-ups, *Amityville 1992: It's About Time* (1992), *Amityville:*

---

8 This was in fact their second attempt at a sequel, after a screenplay written in August 1980 by James Betts (aka Charles A Moses) called *Unwanted Company* had gone nowhere.

A New Generation (1993) and *Amityville Dollhouse* (1996). Other *Amityville* novels included Holzer's *The Secret of Amityville* (1985), as well as Jones' *Amityville: The Final Chapter* (1985) and *Amityville: The Horror Returns* (1989).

The Lutzes divorced in 1988 but the enterprise that was *The Amityville Horror* ensured that they would always be bound together. While the Amityville house was a cash cow, it was hardly a golden goose for the Lutzes, who received less than a half-million dollars from both book and film. While they were contractually obligated not to say anything that might jeopardise the original film's commercial success, George Lutz told Movieweb years later: 'It was someone else's interpretation of events. To say the...movie is inaccurate is an understatement.'

(2005)

We stick to the book religiously, which I think makes it even scarier. That's actually the reason I agreed to do the movie. It's just a hard-core psychological thriller. It really goes into the mind of George Lutz a little bit more.

–Ryan Reynolds, 'George Lutz'

Ryan Reynolds has...made a number of statements...with regard to promoting this movie. [He's said] things like, they had gone back and done additional research or they were more true to the original book. I don't blame the guy for taking the job, but if you're going to make statements about the truth of what you're doing then there should be some truth to that. You don't get to have a part-time commitment to truth.

–George Lutz

Having spent the better part of two decades in court over the book that made he and his ex-wife Kathleen household names, George Lutz in August 2000 petitioned the US government to make 'Amityville Horror' a federally-licensed trademark in his name. In January 2002, 'Amityville Horror' was officially registered as a 'Series of Non-Fiction Books in the Fields of Paranormal Studies and Demonology.' That September, Lutz took advantage of his newly-acquired brand name to negotiate a deal with Paul Mason's Barstu Productions for a trio of films about what happened after the events of the first *Amityville Horror*.

In June 2003, Barstu made a pact with Lutz's agent Steve Whitney, as well as producers Randall Emmett and George Furla, to make the first of these films, to be written by Daniel Farrands (*Halloween: The Curse of Michael Myers*), a friend of Lutz's who wrote and directed the documentaries *Amityville: Horror or Hoax* and *Amityville: The Haunting* for The History Channel in 2000. Shortly thereafter, Barstu sold the project to Avi Lerner's Nu Image film company.

A rival project reared its head that October, however, when Platinum Dunes announced that its follow-up project to *The Texas Chainsaw Massacre* would be a

FROM MICHAEL BAY, THE PRODUCER OF 'THE TEXAS CHAINSAW MASSACRE'

The Amityville Horror (2005)

THE AMITYVILLE HORROR
BASED ON THE TRUE STORY

METRO-GOLDWYN-MAYER PICTURES AND DIMENSION FILMS PRESENT IN ASSOCIATION WITH MICHAEL BAY A PLATINUM DUNES PRODUCTION IN ASSOCIATION WITH RADAR PICTURES "THE AMITYVILLE HORROR" RYAN REYNOLDS MELISSA GEORGE AND PHILIP BAKER HALL CO-EXECUTIVE PRODUCERS RANDALL EMMETT GEORGE FURLA PAUL MASON STEVEN WHITNEY MUSIC BY STEVE JABLONSKY EDITED BY CHRIS WAGNER ROGER BARTON PRODUCTION DESIGNER JENNIFER WILLIAMS DIRECTOR OF PHOTOGRAPHY PETER LYONS COLLISTER A.S.C. EXECUTIVE PRODUCERS TED FIELD DAVID CROCKETT PRODUCED BY MICHAEL BAY ANDREW FORM BRAD FULLER BASED UPON THE BOOK BY JAY ANSON BASED UPON A SCREENPLAY BY SANDOR STERN SCREENPLAY BY SCOTT KOSAR DIRECTED BY ANDREW DOUGLAS

www.mgm.com   www.amityvillehorrormovie.com

remake of the original *Amityville Horror*. Andrew Form told About.com how this choice was arrived at: 'We had a big meeting after *Chainsaw* and Michael Bay loves true crime, so we were thinking of what great true crime stories were out there and that led us right to *Amityville*. I grew up on Long Island, so I had seen the house as a kid. I went in and talked to Brad [Fuller] and Michael and I said, "You know, there's this great horror movie from the 70s that I bet you a lot of people haven't seen that might need a nice updating."'

'We don't want to do too many of these too quickly,' Bay told *Variety*, 'but studios have been circling and we've been poring through their libraries, looking for properties that fit.' The library in this case belonged to M-G-M, which, as owner of the rights to the first three *Amityville* movies, would serve as the sponsoring studio.[9]

While Bay and the boys were doing their deal with M-G-M, Nu Image turned around and sold the Lutz/Farrands project to the Weinstein brothers at Dimension Films. It was announced that Farrands' script would revisit the Amityville house 25 years after the Lutz family fled. 'The race is on,' Bob Weinstein exclaimed to *Variety*. 'We don't anticipate a lawsuit, because the story and the events surrounding the house are public domain. M-G-M owns the remake, and we will not touch that story; *Amityville* as an entity and a real story is another matter. We've come up with our own take on the story, and I'm sure that their remake can be a success. I know one thing: We're very good at coming out first.' The rivalry was short-lived: Dimension and M-G-M agreed that December to partner on a single *Amityville* film, which would be a remake of the 1979 original.

Feeling a distinct (and, by now, familiar) sense of being left out in the cold, Lutz sent three unanswered letters to M-G-M between October 2003 and April 2004, advising the studio of his objections to their proposed film, as he told Movieweb: 'We said straight out to them that, "We don't believe you have a right to be doing what you're doing. And we'd like to go over this." We were inquiring about their intent.' That June, Lutz finally got his response when M-G-M filed a federal lawsuit against him that sought judicial approval to proceed with its planned remake.

Far and away (for the moment) from the legal battles, *Chainsaw Massacre* writer Scott Kosar reprised his duties, penning a script that was initially called simply *Long Island* in an attempt to keep it from entering the public domain before production even began. 'When I was asked to do the remake,' he told Creature Corner, 'I read Jay Anson's book and thought, man, this is horribly dated, and little more than a hodge-podge of every tired haunted house convention in the book. Unlike my feelings about *Texas Chainsaw Massacre*, I thought it would be easy to outdo the original.'

'I felt that the remake should draw more on Ronnie [DeFeo]'s experience, and to draw parallels between that and George's experience. The tension lies in the realisation that George is heading down the same road as Ronnie, and that the Lutzes were facing the same fate as the DeFeos. I also felt that most horror fans aren't scared anymore by CGI images of ghosts [and] that the horror should come from the house's psychological effect on the family...I found it very challenging to try and make some sense of a senseless act, to try and re-imagine how the tragic

---

9 M-G-M had become the rights holder when it bought the bankrupt Orion Pictures for $573 million in July 1997.

events went down. It was the hardest part to write since I was dealing with the memories of innocent children who were ruthlessly slaughtered, and it was very difficult to portray it in a way that was sensitive to the subject while providing some "entertainment value."'

December, 1975. Newlyweds George and Kathy Lutz and her three children move into a Dutch colonial house in the Amityville district of Long Island, where just a year before a deranged Ronnie DeFeo murdered his entire family. While building an office in the basement, George begins to become possessed by evil influences: he becomes irritable, endlessly chops wood for the furnace, neglects his business and hears voices that repeat, 'Catch 'em and kill 'em.' Meanwhile, the

Lutzes' daughter Missy begins playing with an 'imaginary' friend—
Jodie—the ghost of Ronnie's little sister. A pot-smoking, sexpot
babysitter comes over and tells the kids about the DeFeo family
murders, then gets locked in Missy's closet with Jodie. When George
and Kathy come home, they find the girl a catatonic, bloody wreck.
As punishment, George forces the two boys—Danny and Chris—into
relentless, manual labour. George almost drowns in the bathtub,
being dragged under by cadavers. Arriving home from the hospital,
George and Kathy are shocked to see that Missy has followed Jodie
onto the roof and is preparing to jump. Kathy is able to grab her
daughter in the nick of time but the two begin to slide down the
roof; George manages to save both Kathy and Missy. Angered by
the experience, George begins to see demons in his family, which
culminates in him killing the family dog, mistaking it for a monster.
Desperate for help, Kathy goes to the local parish priest, Father
McNamara, who agrees to come and bless the house, even though he
knows its past. Upon arrival, he is assaulted by demonic forces and
a swarm of flies that drive him from the premises. Kathy goes to the
Amityville library to research both the DeFeo murders and the house
itself. She discovers to her horror that the place was used by the
insane Rev Jack Ketcham as a place to exorcise what he thought were
demon-possessed Indians; in reality, the man was a sadist and the
grounds were given over to torture and murder. At the same time,

George breaks through a wall in the basement to discover 'The Red Room'—Ketcham's torture chamber. It is here that George becomes fully possessed by Ketcham's evil spirit. Confronting George in the boat house that night, Kathy falls in and is almost killed by the boat's outboard motor, which George allows to torment his wife before reluctantly pulling her out. A distraught Kathy finds Missy in the basement, where Jodie has led them to find the four coffins that George has prepared for his family. George comes upon the girls and proceeds to chase them through the house with a shotgun, firing off volley after volley. Kathy and her children try to flee but the house, now bleeding and convulsing in a furious rainstorm, refuses to let them go. With Jodie's help, they make their way to the rooftop, with George in hot pursuit. After running out of shells, George is knocked out by Danny and sent sprawling off the roof to a mud pit below. Kathy and the children climb down an ivy-covered lattice to a nearby oak tree and make their way to terra firma. Suddenly George comes at them with an axe but the cries of his family miraculously cause George's spirit to return to his body; the ghosts of tortured Indians subsequently take their revenge on Ketcham's spirit. The entire Lutz clan make it to their boat, then speed down the river on a one-way trip away from their 28 days of horror.

After a script polish by Sheldon Turner, production on the new *Amityville Horror* began on August 2 with a $19 million budget; when the initial location northwest of Chicago was flooded out, a century-old Victorian mansion in Salem, Wisconsin, was used. 'Half of the house is real,' Fuller told Bloody Disgusting. 'Half of the inside architecture is real. We built half of the house out, like the iconic face. So half of the house is ours that we can rip down again, and then it would be a normal house.'

Just two weeks after shooting started, on August 17, Kathleen Lutz died of emphysema at the age of 57. 'It was disconcerting to find out that Kathy Lutz passed away,' said star Ryan Reynolds, 'and we took a moment to pause for her. They [also fished] a body out of the lake the first week we were there...That was definitely something a little bit strange for everyone...just a weird way to start a movie.'

'With Kathy Lutz, no one really knew her,' co-star Melissa George commented to Radio Free. 'So it wasn't necessary for me to try and mimic her or anything like that. I read a lot of her diaries and things that she went through to learn about who she was, but it was basically my interpretation of the role and what happened in this house, which is actually the number one credit in this movie. The house is the first character.'

Englishman Andrew Douglas would follow in Marcus Nispel's footsteps and become Platinum Dunes's second commercial/video director to get a crack at feature directing, although Douglas had also produced and directed the award-winning documentary *Searching for the Wrong-Eyed Jesus* in 2003. 'When I was invited to do this,' he reflected to Bloody Disgusting, 'it was sold to me as a psychological horror, more like *The Shining*...What we wanted to do with this is make it not a slasher movie but a psychological movie. A movie which is really as

much about a dysfunctional family as it is bleeding walls.'

'When I was trying to immerse myself in a lot of films to see where this film would go,' Douglas explained to *Film Monthly*, 'I found that I looked at...*The Shining*...not as a spectator anymore but as a storyteller, and I looked at a lot of Wes Craven's films, because he's such a master of the mechanics of suspense...and then I looked at a lot of Japanese, Chinese and Korean horror films, because...I was really interested in trying to find ways of making newer scares. Not least because there are so many horror films around, and I just didn't want to tap into the same imagery that all the horror films are tapping into, even though I'm probably guilty of doing that.'

Guilty as charged: the new *Amityville* was to shrug off the Anson chronicle of events and take creative license with evil ghost girls and malignant spirits reaching out through the bathtub, much like those of Hideo Nakata's *Ringu* (1998) and *Dark Water* (2002), as well as Takashi Shimizu's *Ju-on: The Grudge* (2003), all three of which were themselves remade in America between 2001 and 2004.

Brad Fuller went on to explain Platinum Dunes's approach to the material, but in little more detail: 'Hopefully fans will recognise some of the same scares but we kind of amped it up,' he told About.com. 'We've used technology to our advantage and hopefully made it scarier. Hopefully people will get to know the family so that when the family starts to descend into some horrible things, you feel for them and the horror resonates.'

For her part, Melissa George had taken it upon herself to make sure that things would resonate. 'When you read the diaries of the children that actually lived through it,' the actress told Bloody Disgusting, 'that's what they believe were in the house. The little girl did have an imaginary friend and I believe it was the little girl that had been shot by DeFeo. So those things maybe didn't make it into the book as such but a lot of new evidence in the past 30 years [has] actually come up that [was] never written in the book...the producers [and I] went and interviewed the coroners that were actually there and [found] new evidence and brought it all together.'

The million-dollar question was: did Douglas and his stars believe all this had actually happened? 'As an intellectual leap, I'll believe in ghosts in order to make the best possible horror film,' the director said matter-of-factly. 'I think it's legitimately a true story, but as storytellers, we elaborate on true because...if it can happen to you or next door to you or behind that curtain, it has a lot more potency and value. Releases more serotonin or whatever horror films do.'

Reynolds hedged his bets, telling Dark Horizons: 'I believe George Lutz went in there and had a psychological breakdown, but whether there was a supernatural element involved, I don't know. But the great thing about my job is [that] I don't have to worry about that...When you watch the movie you think, "Wow, this guy is becoming possessed," but I feel him going within and turning completely inward and psychotic.'

George was equally noncommittal, confiding to Bloody Disgusting: 'I'm not sure—personally, these things I don't really believe. But when you really read about what happened, you kind of think something did go on. As an actor doing a role in a true story, I'm not trying to imitate [Kathy] at all. I just got the facts and I wanted to keep my interpretation of the role, to play this tortured soul and actually feeling like I was the eyes for the audience in a way.'

GEORGE
Is Danny okay?

KATHY
He'll be fine. It's Missy I'm worried about.

GEORGE
It's always tough making new friends...

KATHY

Well, that's the thing. She did make them. Literally.
(off George)
She has all these…imaginary friends.

GEORGE

Ah, that's normal, Kath. Didn't you have an imaginary pal when you
were a kid?

KATHY

Yeah, we called him 'Dad'…

–Unfilmed exchange, from the original script

In the transition from script to screen, there was a tacit admission that this
Amityville was more fiction than fact by changing the children's names to Billy,
Michael and Chelsea—lest they be confused with the actual Lutz progeny. Likewise,
several scenes were eliminated or changed from the Kosar/Turner draft, including:

- Kathy persuading George to spend the day in bed after she is convinced he is coming down with a cold.
- Kathy finding George in Missy's bedroom after he has swum in the boathouse.
- Missy first talking to Jodie about seeing her deceased father before following the ghost out onto the roof.
- The exchange between Kathy and Father McNamara originally occurred in a cemetery and was much longer.
- George's partner Charlie calls to tell him the business is falling apart and George fires him.
- George takes a call from Kathy's mother, then tells her never to call again.
- Missy cries, 'Don't hurt him, Daddy!' as George goes after Danny. This overt acceptance of George as a father figure allows him to free himself from Ketcham's malign influence. However, as shot, George somehow effects his own exorcism.

Other scenes that were in fact shot but did not make the final cut included:

- At their first meal in the house, George (Reynolds) proposes a toast and Billy's (Jesse James) glass smashes so hard against his that it cuts George's hand.
- Charlie (Jason Padgett) pays a visit to his boss's house with his girlfriend, but she refuses to leave the car.
- After teasing Chelsea (Chloe Grace Moretz) about Jodie, Michael (Jimmy Bennett) is almost struck by a closing window (a reference back to the scene in the original where Greg Lutz's hand is slammed in the window).
- George and Kathy (Melissa George) come home from their date to find all the lights flashing off and on.
- George finds Lisa's (Rachel Nichols) bong in the bathroom; Kathy confronts him about how Chelsea found out about Jodie's murder.

Production wrapped on October 12, and Reynolds found himself pleasantly surprised by the experience, telling Dark Horizons: 'I never at any point in this movie felt like I was in a horror movie. It's not what I pictured; coming in, I was like, "Am I going to have those days when I leave feeling embarrassed for what we shot today?" I haven't done that once. I've done a complete 180 since I showed up here... [I figured] I'd come in and try something different...having very little expectations in what I'd find and I am just thrilled everyday because it blew my expectations out of the water. I'd love to do more horror if it's like this, but I don't think they are.

The shoot was not what Douglas had expected either—'You think you know what a studio movie is going in, but you really don't. I really had no idea how gruelling it was going to be,' he confessed to *Variety*—but he had a newfound respect for his mentor/producer: 'The lessons Michael taught me are so much more clear now. I wish I could do it again, because we certainly wouldn't have so many arguments!'

One scene in particular that caused serious friction between the producer and his director was the one in which Chelsea walks to the edge of the roof and prepares to jump at Jodie's behest. 'I was terrified,' Douglas admitted. 'I hadn't done a lot of stunts in my commercial work and my first instinct was to [use a] green screen. Michael was really committed to creating the reality of the scene, not just for the film but for Chloe herself—it was an industry lesson for me.'

George elaborated to Radio Free: 'No green screen. All that walking was for real. She had a crane with two pieces of skinny wire that was above her head, and she was balancing by herself. And then [in post-production] they just rubbed out the wire. They first took me up in a crane, and then they dropped me off on top of the roof...And then I'm leaning over, and then they just put a tiny wire around my waist, clipped to the side...And little Chloe had to have like a harness and hang over the edge. And then the crane would go around and shoot these great, gorgeous, romantic shots. And she was pretending like she was hung, as a joke...She was dangling off the edge eighty feet above the ground, not scared at all!'

Amityville Horror was released on April 15, 2005 to a $23.5 million opening weekend, which was good enough for first place. Its cumulative take was $65 million domestically, with another $43 million earned overseas. The film was particularly well received by Kevin Thomas ('A terrific scare show, fast and furious, made with a lot of style and energy, packing plenty of jolts yet never lingering morbidly over horrific images. It is anchored in strong characterisations, and its plot develops with chilling psychological suspense') and also earned a qualified endorsement from the *New York Times* ('Low-key creepy rather than out-right scary, the new *Amityville* marks a modest improvement over the original, partly because, from acting to bloody effects, it is better executed, and partly because the filmmakers have downgraded the role of the priest').

For most critics, however, the remake was a bust. '*The Amityville Horror* is the latest cannibalisation of a popular older horror film,' observed *The Boston Globe*. 'But the movie that this remake is dining on wasn't fresh to begin with, so the new version appears to be suffering a terrible case of botulism...it's an incompetent retread of the equally inane 1979 hit.' *Entertainment Weekly* was similarly dismissive: 'Nothing gets in the way of the rote staging, the ham-handed predictability, the feeling that you've been to this house, and yawned at these ghosts, once too often.' *USA Today* summed things up by saying, 'The performances are bad, the special effects ho-hum, and it's not even particularly scary,' while *The Village Voice* judged the film to be 'A Xerox so tattered and faded that it's impossible to determine who's to blame for the overproduced mediocrity before our eyes.' *The Washington Post* wasted little printer's ink in rendering its judgment: 'A mean, bloody and entirely unnecessary remake.'

That June, George Lutz filed his own suit for libel and breach of contract against Dimension, M-G-M, Platinum Dunes, Radar Pictures, and writers Kosar and Turner. He gave his reasoning to Horror.com: 'There's quite a bit of anger and contempt for the filmmakers...As a family, we have never had a problem with someone doing a true depiction. But when they do this kind of fantasy, an "Amityville Horror alternate universe", when someone dreams up things...Actually, when you look at this movie you'll see it pulls from about five other horror films.'

'They were constantly making little movie clips and announcements about how they had gone back to the original book,' Lutz continued, 'how they had done additional research that was going to make this film so much more accurate. Well, some issues were brought up to them and now they have admitted that they were looking for something that had a true story attached to it and they were looking to make a commercially profitable movie.'

Lutz, not surprisingly, had real issues with how he is portrayed in the film—attacking and killing the family dog, building coffins for his wife and children, attempting to kill his wife by drowning her, chasing his wife and children while brandishing a shotgun, attacking his son with an axe—none of which was true or in the original narrative. His lawsuit made the claim that Kosar and Turner's script 'exposes Lutz to hatred, contempt, ridicule and obloquy because it shows him committing various crimes... Kosar and Turner acted with malice in writing the screenplay in that they knew that the statements made about Lutz were false or else were made with reckless disregard for whether or not they were true.'

The libel claim was dismissed in Los Angeles in November, but the rest of the suit was still unresolved when Lutz died of heart disease in May 2006 at the age of 59. As far as Reynolds was concerned, doing right by the Lutzes was never the point anyway; he told the *Chicago Sun Times*, 'I really wanted to do a movie that was just a wild ride.'

At time of writing, two more competing Amityville projects have surfaced to vie for audience attention. The original Farrands draft is due to be filmed by Dimension as *The Amityville Horror: The Lost Tapes* and will be co-written, co-produced and co-directed by Farrands and Casey La Scala. Meanwhile, Hannibal Classics has announced that it will adapt John G Jones' book *Amityville: The Evil Escapes* (previously filmed in 1989) as *Amityville: The Legacy 3D*. Both films are scheduled for release in 2012/2013.

FRIDAY THE 13TH
(1980)

I showed I could make people throw up. My ambition with this film was to provide entertainment, not to make Art. The effectiveness of the film did not come from subtlety.

—Sean S Cunningham, producer and director

They were warned...They are doomed...
And on Friday the 13th, nothing will save them.

FRIDAY THE 13TH

A 24 hour nightmare of terror

PARAMOUNT PICTURES PRESENTS FRIDAY THE 13TH A SEAN S. CUNNINGHAM FILM STARRING BETSY PALMER ADRIENNE KING HARRY CROSBY LAURIE BARTRAM MARK NELSON JEANNINE TAYLOR ROBBI M
KEVIN BACON DIRECTOR OF PHOTOGRAPHY BARRY ABRAMS MUSIC BY HARRY MANFREDINI ASSOCIATE PRODUCER STEPHEN MINER EXECUTIVE PRODUCER ALVIN GEILER WRITTEN BY VICTOR MILLER
PRODUCED AND DIRECTED BY SEAN S. CUNNINGHAM A GEORGETOWN PRODUCTIONS INC. PRODUCTION

A PARAMOUNT RELEASE

I put the killer under the bed because any 9-year-old can tell you that's where killers hide. I put the axe in the face because I'm terrified of having my face messed up, and there's nothing quite as messy as a scout axe.

—Victor Miller, co-writer

On July 4, 1979, readers of the entertainment trade paper *Variety* opened to page 23 to find the following full-page ad: 'From the Producer of *Last House on the Left* Comes the Most Terrifying Movie Ever Made!' 'Friday the 13th', in huge block letters, came crashing through a windowpane. Potential buyers were advised that the film was 'Currently in Production—Available in November 1979'.

The ad was in fact bogus—there was no film, not even a script. It was simply a last-ditch effort by Sean Cunningham to salvage a movie career. 'Hollywood has this terrible tendency to pigeonhole you,' he lamented to *Fangoria*, 'and after *Last House*, I was hoping that would lead to more feature work, of a more serious nature. But because of that picture, people would only think of us when they had something really sick or disgusting or otherwise awful for us to do. I was trying to develop some projects that were *not* Son of *Last House*, and it wasn't easy.'

In 1973, Cunningham had co-produced and co-directed (with somebody named 'Brud Talbot') the X-rated comedy *Case of the Full Moon Murders*. The picture went through several title changes—*Case of the Smiling Stiffs, Night of the Full Moon Murders, Sex on the Groove Tube*—but despite featuring *Deep Throat*'s popular porno actor Harry Reems, it never found an audience. Cunningham subsequently graduated to the other end of the spectrum: two low-budget *Bad News Bears* rip-offs called *Here Come the Tigers* and *Manny's Orphans*. The former was released by AIP to lacklustre business in 1978 while the latter (also known as *Kick*) was passed between Warners, Disney and United Artists but never garnered theatrical exposure. Both were shot by Barry Abrams, scored by Harry Manfredini, written by Victor Miller (under the pseudonym of Arch McCoy for *Tigers*) and co-produced and cut by Steve Miner.

Cunningham rounded up this team one last time when he decided to return to what had brought him to the dance in the first place—a highly-exploitable horror film. 'All I was trying to do was to make a pot-boiler,' he confessed to the *New York Times*. 'To put it bluntly, I couldn't pay the rent. I asked myself, "What's the scariest phrase in the English language?" It's got to be 'Friday the 13th'.'

'The simple truth is that I need a hit film,' Cunningham admitted to *Fangoria*. 'So few people survive at all in this business, making *any* kind of film; it's all very nice to talk about 'cinema', but the truth of the matter is that *Friday the 13th* seems to me a strong commercial property, and I think now is the right time for it.'

While Hallmark Releasing was no longer in business, the men who had financed *Last House* were still running theatres in Boston. Philip Scuderi had seen the *Variety* ad and wanted in on the project—a slice at first, then the whole pie. He and Steve Minasian had established a new production company—Georgetown Productions—and had just released their first feature, the *Animal House* rip-off *King Frat*. In

October 1979, Georgetown announced that *Friday the 13th* ('The Perfect Day for Terror') would be their second feature and that it would be 'Available for Christmas 79'.

On July 4, 1958, two amorous young counsellors are brutally murdered at Camp Crystal Lake by an unseen assailant, who loses a little finger in the struggle. Twenty years later, the camp is being reopened for the fourth time since the murders (something has always happened in the past to sabotage things). On the morning of Friday, June 13, a young girl named Annie hitchhikes to her job as the camp cook. Picked up by a jeep for the last leg of the journey, she is assaulted and murdered by the driver. Later that day, Jack, his girlfriend Marcie and friend Ned arrive in a camper-van for their jobs as camp counsellors. They meet the director, Steve Christy, his assistant Alice and two other counsellors—Bill and Brenda—all of whom are hard at work renovating the campus. That afternoon, Alice is attacked by a snake in her cabin, placed there earlier by an anonymous pair of gloved hands. Fortunately, the snake is only able to bite Alice's bracelet before Bill arrives and cuts the reptile in half with a machete. That evening, when Bill and Jack go to start up the generator, Jack is electrocuted when he throws the switch while unwittingly standing in a strategically-placed puddle of water. Only Bill's quick thinking and brute strength save Jack's life. After faking a choking on chips and dip, Ned is banished to the boys' cabin, where he encounters a stranger. Later, Jack and Marcie make love in the same cabin, not seeing Ned's dead body in the bunk above them. After finishing, Marcie goes to the showers, where she is attacked by someone with a hatchet. Brenda later retires to the girls' cabin for the night but finds the bloody hatchet on her pillow. She runs outside to the softball field, where she is blinded by spotlights before making her way to the bushes and meeting a bad end. Bill and Alice hear Brenda's screams and go looking for her, finding only the hatchet on her pillow. Not finding any of the other counsellors around, Bill and Alice try to phone for help but the line has been cut. They then try to go for help in Jack's van, but it will not start. Meanwhile, Steve, who had gone into town for supplies and had to hitchhike back to camp when his jeep broke down, arrives back at Crystal Lake but is met by a stranger. While Alice sleeps, Bill goes to check the generator but does not return. Startled awake, Alice goes in search of her friend and finds him—hanging from a rope and shot full of arrows. Running back to the main cabin, Alice is stunned again when Brenda's corpse comes crashing through the front window. Flinging open the front door, Alice runs straight into Mrs Voorhees, a kindly, tall woman in her forties. She offers Alice her help and feigns shock when she sees Brenda's body. As she strokes Alice's hair and calms her down, she tells the girl that a young boy drowned in the lake the year before the

first two counsellors were murdered. It is only then that we notice that Mrs Voorhees is missing one of her little fingers. The woman's demeanour suddenly begins to change as she surreptitiously slips a hunting knife out of her jacket—she tells Alice that the drowned boy was her son Jason and that he died because the counsellors were busy making love and not paying attention. She then admits to killing Steve, which jolts Alice into action. She runs from the cabin, only to bump into two bodies—Steve and Jack—hanging from a tree. As she pursues Alice, Mrs Voorhees speaks in Jason's voice, egging his mother on her vengeful spree. After a long game of cat-and-mouse, Alice is able to knock Mrs Voorhees out with a skillet, then boards a canoe and heads for the middle of the lake. At dawn, a sleeping Alice, not noticing that the canoe has drifted to the edge of the lake, is suddenly awakened when Mrs Voorhees leaps upon the girl from one of the overhanging trees. They struggle and Alice is able to get the mad woman's machete away from her long enough to cut off Mrs Voorhees' head and send it to the bottom of Crystal Lake to join her dead son.

The seven-week shoot began on September 4 at Camp No-Be-Bo-Sco (which came to be known by the cast as 'Not-a-Very-Good-Boy-Scout-Camp'), near Blairstown, New Jersey, on a roughly $500,000 budget. Aside from Bing Crosby's son Harry and future star Kevin Bacon (who had just appeared in *Animal House*), the only name in the cast was Betsy Palmer, then 52 and a veteran of such films as *Mister Roberts* (1955) and TV showcases like *The Goodyear Playhouse* and *The US Steel Hour*, though her main claim to fame had been as the popular panellist/host of *I've Got a Secret* (1957-67). Palmer had replaced Oscar-winner Estelle Parsons (*Bonnie and Clyde*) at a cost of $1,000 per day for ten days' work.

In actual fact, perhaps the most famous person on the production was not in the cast at all, but make-up effects maestro Tom Savini, who was fresh from having his work showcased to great acclaim in *Dawn of the Dead*. 'Sean is a lot like [George] Romero on the set,' Savini told *Fangoria*. 'He always knows just what he's going to do next, what sort of set-up he wants to use. He's also like George in the way he listens when it comes time to shoot an effect and, like George, he likes everything to happen *right on camera*...all on screen, no cutaways, no cheating at all.'

EXT. LAKE - DAWN

ALICE lies, in MCU, in the canoe, sleeping. She has not changed her position since collapsing a few hours before. The water laps gently against the side of the canoe. Very slowly, she wakes. She opens her eyes.

The canoe has drifted into the shade of some enormous tree boughs that overhang the edge of the lake.

They shade ALICE from the bright rays of the sun. The canoe rocks

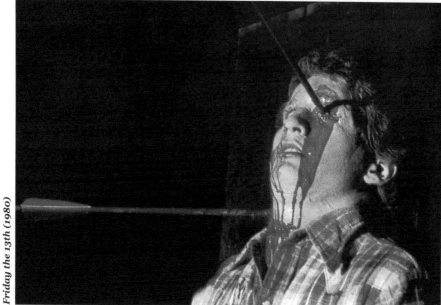

Friday the 13th (1980)

gently. ALICE is still, listening to the sound of the lapping water.

Suddenly there is a blood-curdling scream, a MUSICAL STINGER, and the screen is filled with the flying, whirling form of MRS VOORHEES, who leaps from the overhanging boughs into the canoe, barely missing ALICE's slumped form!

The canoe immediately overturns and both MRS VOORHEES and ALICE try to find their footing in the shallow water. MRS VOORHEES is covered in mud and blood. She sees ALICE struggling to get up and moves toward her, brandishing her blood-spattered machete. ALICE turns, sees MRS VOORHEES coming. ALICE grabs a paddle floating near her.

MRS VOORHEES pushes the canoe to one side, wading through the waist-high water as fast as she can. She screams with rage. Her face goes through a horrifying transformation. From her mouth comes the VOICE OF JASON.

JASON (LIP SYNC)

Mommy! Mommy! Mommy!

ALICE can't move fast enough to get away from MRS VOORHEES, who is slashing the air with her big knife trying to hit ALICE. ALICE slips, falls in the water, gets her footing back and has to turn and block the blow of the machete with the paddle, using it like a staff to ward off the blow. The machete cuts the paddle nearly in half. MRS VOORHEES raises the knife for another blow and ALICE lunges for her knees and succeeds in throwing MRS VOORHEES into the water. The machete flies out of her hand and lands in the water. The two women roll in the water. MRS VOORHEES is trying to strangle ALICE, her hands stretching to reach around her throat. They roll over and under the water. We cannot see who is winning.

Suddenly MRS VOORHEES finds her footing and stands up, looking for ALICE. She is screeching madly.

JASON (LIP SYNC)
(CONTINUING)

Kill her, mommy! Kill her, mommy!

ALICE shoots up out of the water holding the machete, and in one, wild swing, decapitates MRS VOORHEES, whose head flies off into the water.

The body stands for a minute, then falls heavily into the lake.
ALICE drops the machete into the water and starts to wade to shore.

CUT TO:

EXT. CAMP ROAD/SIGN - MORNING

ALICE walks slowly down the road away from the camp. We hear the sound of a car approaching. Now it comes into view. It is a state vehicle, black and white, with an emblem on the door that says 'State Department of Health and Safety'. There are two middle-aged bureaucrats inside.

ALICE waves down the car, which pulls up beside her.

1st INSPECTOR
Good morning, miss.

2nd INSPECTOR
(Leaning across the front seat)
Are you all right, ma'am?
                    ALICE

Help me.

The CAMERA PANS BACK while the two men get out of their vehicle and come around to help ALICE.

CUT TO:

EXT. CAMP - MORNING

LONG SHOT of the camp with the sun sparkling on the waters of Crystal Lake. The canoe lies half sunken in the shallows. One paddle drifts in the current. The lake has swallowed its secret.

ROLL CREDITS.

−Unfilmed ending, from the original script

Owing to the limited schedule and budget, a number of elements were cut from Miller's script—or were changed—including:

• A love triangle between 50s counsellors Claudette, Barry and Chloe before the first murders was eliminated.
• The first murders occur in the forest in the daytime; this was changed to night time in a loft.
• One of the murderer's little fingers is cut off in the struggle with Barry; this was eliminated.
• When Annie meets Crazy Ralph, he has two dead rats in his mouth; this was eliminated.
• Jack, Marcie and Ned are shown lighting up one last joint before arriving at Crystal Lake; this was eliminated.
• Jack and Marcie find a number of hunting knives in the equipment shed—later they are gone; this was eliminated.

- Scenes that establish a budding romance between Bill and Alice, including one where she tells him she is getting over an affair with a married man, were eliminated.
- A scene showing the murderer putting the snake in Alice's cabin, as well as the snake actually attacking Alice, was eliminated.
- Ned and Brenda showing each other their skills on the uneven bars was eliminated.
- Bill saving Jack from electrocution when they start the generator was eliminated.
- Ned fakes choking on chips and dip; this was replaced by a scene where Ned fakes drowning so he can get mouth-to-mouth with Brenda.
- Brenda finds a kitchen knife tied to a string dangling outside her cabin; this was changed to her hearing Jason's cries for help.
- Brenda finds a bloody axe on her pillow—the same one that killed Marcie. Then later, Alice and Bill find it. Only the latter was used.

At Scuderi's insistence, Ron Kurz (writer of *King Frat*) was brought on board to add new material to the script, including:

- Enos the truck driver giving the sordid history of Camp Crystal Lake to Annie.
- Officer Dorf, an overly serious motorcycle cop, showing up to warn the counsellors about Crazy Ralph.
- Ralph then showing up to warn the counsellors, 'You're all doomed!'
- Bill, Brenda and Alice playing 'Strip Monopoly' and getting high.

Other changes were made to showcase Savini's expertise. As written, Jack's killing was off-screen (we only see his dead body hanging with Steve's from a tree as Alice tries to make her escape), but this was changed to the film's most spectacular effect, as the young man has his throat punctured by an arrow that thrusts upward from under the bed. Likewise, as she tries to flee in Mrs Voorhees' jeep, Alice finds Annie's body in the front seat with her throat cut (this was not in the script). 'Tom Savini is so good at what he does,' praised Cunningham, 'and the effects that we had in this picture were so good, that you find yourself wanting to leave in more of an effects scene than you should to get a strong shock effect. It can go over the border of shock; gore itself isn't scary, it's disgusting. In the editing process you only see it as a special effect, and you get a little jaded. As it turned out, we shot an awful lot more of the effects than were used in the picture.'

Aside from its noteworthy effects, *Friday the 13th*'s main claim to fame was its 'Gotcha!' climax, in which a waterlogged, mongoloid Jason comes up from the depths of Crystal Lake to attack Alice just as the police arrive on shore. Alice then awakes screaming in the hospital, where the police deny having found any trace of Jason. This was, of course, a complete rip-off of *Carrie*'s shock, 'Is it a dream or not?' ending. Because it was a total departure from the original script, it is perhaps not surprising that three different people take credit for the idea: Miller, Kurz and Savini. In *Crystal Lake Memories*, Peter M Bracke's 2005 oral history of the *Friday the 13th* series, all three make their case for a denouement that rather inadvertently set the stage for one of the most successful horror film franchises in history:

MILLER:

Sean called me up and said we need a chair jumper after the climax. So I wrote the sequence where Alice is in the little canoe, she sets off, the sun rises, we think she's safe and Jason comes out of the water. Then she wakes up in the hospital bed. Which was as close as I could steal from Carrie without being arrested.

KURZ:

Let me make one thing crystal clear...the scene of [Jason] leaping out of the lake at the end was mine. The ending was mine. I conceived it, I wrote it. Phil [Scuderi], having the power over Sean, carried it through onto film.

SAVINI:

I had just seen Carrie, and its ending was terrific...[it] scared the piss out of everybody. So great, let's do the same thing. But how are we going to do that here when everyone's dead? So I said, 'It might be psychologically disturbing if Jason suddenly pops out of the water and grabs her.' Because Jason is already registered in your head. You've kind of dismissed him, he's gone, and that's why Betsy Palmer is killing everybody. Then just have Alice wake up out of a dream. Which worked, because if it's a dream, you can show anything and get away with it, no matter how preposterous it is.

Likewise, Kurz and Savini both lay claim to the concept of turning Jason into a mongoloid, a notion that also was not in the original script:

KURZ:

In rewriting, I came up with the idea of making Jason 'different'—a mongoloid—and having him appear out of the lake in the shocker scene at the end, still in the form in which he drowned.

SAVINI:

When I designed the look of Jason, I just kept thinking of this guy that I saw in my neighbourhood when I was a kid...he was misshapen. He had one ear that was lower than the other one, and one eye was kind of lower, like Quasimodo. Originally we were thinking Jason was gonna have hair, but it just didn't look quite right. So we just left him bald as if he was like a hydrocephalic, mongoloid pinhead or something...And that's been the look of Jason ever since.

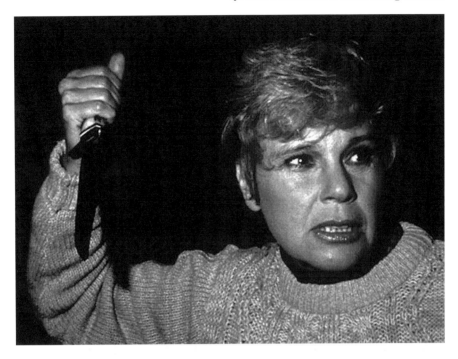

In February 1980, *Friday the 13th* was screened for executives from M-G-M, Paramount, United Artists and Warner Bros. Paramount and Warners ended up splitting the rights down the middle—Paramount would release the film domestically while Warners handled it overseas—for which each company paid Georgetown $1.5 million.

With just 10 seconds of gore effects cut out for the sake of an R rating, *Friday the 13th* opened on May 9. This was to get into theatres before such heavy hitters as *The Empire Strikes Back* and *The Shining* arrived on the scene, but had Paramount waited until June 13, the film would have opened on an actual Friday the 13th as well as the very day the picture itself takes place. No matter: the company spent $4 million to launch the picture and the payoff was immense—a first place opening weekend gross of $5.8 million, as the film went on to become the second biggest hit of the summer, grossing nearly $40 million (it would earn an additional $30 million overseas for Warners). As Frank Mancuso, then Paramount's head of distribution, told the *New York Times*, 'The minute we saw *Friday the 13th* we knew we had a hit. A lot of these pictures don't live up to their ads so the movies die because of bad word of mouth. Once audiences saw that *Friday the 13th* delivered all the shocks it promised, however, they told their friends about it. After the first week, their word of mouth did the advertising for us.' Almost to a man, critics absolutely hated *Friday the 13th*—so much so, in fact, that Victor Miller began to take their vitriolic rants personally. 'It really does hurt to have to deal with the incredible vitriol that has come my way since we opened,' the writer penned in *The Washington Post*. 'Hundreds of reviews of *Friday the 13th* have appeared in print, and I have seen only one that was positive...*Friday the 13th* seems to have pushed a button in the critical solar plexus producing not just negative reviews, but *rage*.'

Perhaps no critic exemplified Miller's point more than Gene Siskel. His 'no stars' review of *Friday the 13th*, which appeared in the May 12 edition of the *Chicago Tribune*, came to be almost as infamous as the movie itself:

It has been suggested to me that a great way to keep people from seeing a truly awful movie is to tell them the ending. I like that idea a lot, and I know it is a powerful (and controversial) weapon. So you're going to have to trust me to use it wisely...and sparingly. In the meat-cleaver-in-the-forehead movie Friday the 13th, which also features a bloody, slow-motion decapitation, the killer turns out to be a bitter old lady played by Betsy (I've Got a Secret) Palmer. It seems that 23 years ago her son drowned at a summer camp while a couple of counsellors were off having sex in a hayloft. Since the boy's drowning, there have been a rash of unsolved murders at the camp, and after about 85 minutes of Friday the 13th we learn that, sure enough, it's Palmer's fault. She's got this thing for counsellors at Camp Crystal Lake. And if you wait another 10 minutes, you can see one of the teenage girl counsellors cut Palmer's head off. Now, there—I hoped [sic] I've ruined Friday the 13th, which is the latest film by one of the most despicable creatures ever to infest the movie business, Sean S Cunningham. You may have heard of

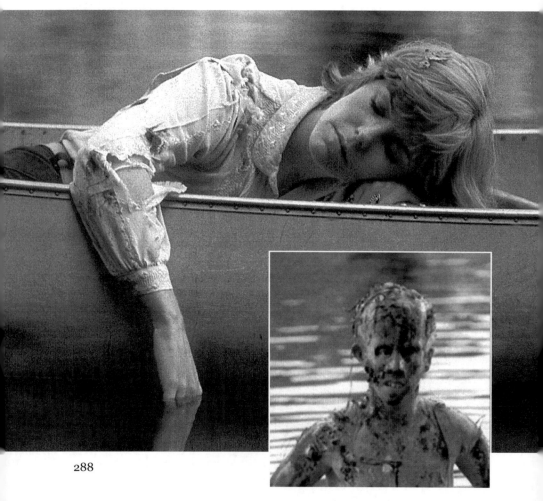

one of his other films, The Last House on the Left, a film in which a teenage girl is forced at gunpoint to urinate on herself and then is shot in the head. Cunningham's speciality is that old, sick standby, teenage-girls-in-peril. In scene after scene in Friday the 13th, we see girl counsellors strip down to their underclothes, only to be stalked by the unseen killer, who we now know is Palmer, looking very much like a lumberjack. One girl gets the meat cleaver slammed into her forehead, another's throat is slashed, and we see the fake blood spurt toward the camera. Cunningham takes it a little easier on the boys; one is merely stabbed in the stomach, another's throat is pierced from the back of his neck by a knife. In more than one scene, Cunningham rips off sequences from the hit shocker Halloween, which was much less bloody, much less explicit about its attacks, and much better directed by John Carpenter. The point is this: There is nothing in Friday the 13th other than its sickening attack scenes; remove them and you're left with an empty movie. Friday the 13th is being distributed by Paramount Pictures, and it is very surprising to see a major, publicly held film company handle a movie as bloody as this. Previously, Cunningham has had to work with small-time, independent releasing companies. Paramount is a division of Gulf & Western Industries. If you want to complain about the film, you can write to Charles G Bluhdorn, the chairman of the board of Gulf & Western...(Betsy Palmer lives in the little town of Rowayton, Conn. I'm sure a letter sent to General Delivery there will get to her.) Friday the 13th has been given an R rating by the Motion Picture Association of America (MPAA). If any film should be X-rated on the basis of violence, this is it. But Paramount pays part of the salary of the MPAA people who determine the ratings, and this is clearly a case where a big studio gets a less-restrictive rating than is proper.

While Siskel was not the only critic to divulge the killer's identity (Tom Allen, Janet Maslin and *The Washington Post*'s Joseph McLellan did so as well), he was the only one to encourage a letter-writing campaign to protest the film. And he may also have been the only critic in history to publish a star's home address (incorrect, as it turned out) for the express purpose of hate mail.[10]

But Siskel was not through expressing his displeasure about the film. In the September 18 broadcast of his PBS TV show *Sneak Previews*, Siskel and his partner Roger Ebert decried the rise of so-called 'Women in Danger' films. While praising *Halloween*, they simultaneously denounced *Friday the 13th* and similar films as 'movies that systematically demean half the human race...movies that are gruesome and despicable...[movies that are] a freak show.' Three days later, Siskel renewed his crusade in print, proclaiming that 'There is a plague upon the land, and if that sounds like a preamble to a fire-and-brimstone lecture, so be it. Because the plague in question is the most nauseating trend in films today—films that feature brutal attacks on young women.'

While few critics joined in Siskel's anti-stalker crusade, the chorus of disapproval when it came to *Friday the 13th* was truly deafening. Tom Allen called the film 'an obvious attempt to cash in with a junk-food *Halloween*...Cunningham is a methodical, imitative, pedantic artisan.' *The Boston Globe* advised its readers:

---

10 With his typical cluelessness, Siskel somehow thought that Palmer lived in Connecticut when in fact she lived in his back yard—East Chicago, Indiana.

'Unless your idea of a good time is to watch a woman have her head split down the middle by an axe or a man stuck to a door with arrows, you should stay away from *Friday the 13th*. It's bad luck.' The *Los Angeles Times* dismissed the film as 'a silly, boring youth-geared horror movie...Cunningham's pace is downright pokey: the action is as anticlimactic as it is unmotivated.' *Variety* warned that 'Paramount will have to do a yeoman's selling job to squeeze major cash from the sprockets of this sporadically gory but utterly suspenseless pickup. Low budget in the worst sense— with no apparent talent or intelligence to offset its technical inadequacies—*Friday the 13th* has nothing to exploit but its title and what oomph Paramount puts into the campaign. Quick, in-and-out playoff is in order.' *The Washington Post* lamented, 'When the names of the players flash on the screen in *Friday the 13th*, it is not so much a list of the cast as a body count. Practically everyone who spends more than five minutes on camera dies horribly...Considering the quality of the acting, most of them deserve no better.'

The only major critic to give *Friday the 13th* a halfway decent review was Janet Maslin, who managed to find some redeeming qualities in the midst of the mayhem: 'Mr Cunningham's brand of horror is reasonably suspenseful, though none too new... More interesting than the bloodshed, somehow, is the middle-class ordinariness with which Mr Cunningham invests the characters' conversations...The counsellors are played by a cast of pleasant newcomers, and what happens to them really is a shame.'

'It's all very nice to talk about the 'art of cinema,' but in this business you need a hit to survive,' Cunningham remarked to the *New York Times*. 'Before *Friday the 13th* nobody would even listen to me. Now I've made buckets of money and everyone is coming to me with offers. A lot of critics were bothered by the amount of blood and violence in the movie, but *Friday the 13th* isn't half as horrifying as *Last House on the Left*. Things have changed since then. We've got stronger stomachs now. Audiences today are simply looking for quick thrills. Thanks to television we have a real short attention span, so the filmmakers have to dish out the shocks before everyone gets restless. Believe me, even Hitchcock would be making different movies today.'

Cunningham found himself courted by producer Sidney Beckerman (*Cabaret, Marathon Man*) to shoot an adaptation of Mary Higgins Clark's 1977 bestseller *A Stranger is Watching*, as well as by Filmways Pictures for two thrillers (*Ridge Run, The Witness*) and by Columbia for the romance *Parlor Games*. In February 1981, he began directing the $3.5 million *Stranger* for Beckerman and M-G-M, starring Rip Torn and Kate Mulgrew. 'I was offered everything to do the *Friday the 13th* sequel,' the director told *Variety*, 'but I've already made that film. With *Stranger*, I'm getting out of the low-budget horror genre to make a straight suspense picture. If it successfully captures the tense, nightmarish quality of the novel we're adapting, we can have a hit in today's market. You can't do that with last year's movie.'

Georgetown and Paramount were out to prove that you could. With an increased budget of $1.2 million and Steve Miner taking over from Cunningham, *Friday the 13th Part 2* went into production in September 1980. 'Because Georgetown wanted to shoot the sequel so quickly, Sean wasn't going to be able to do it,' Miner explained to *Fangoria*. 'I was originally approached to only *produce* the sequel, but it soon became clear to me that I would do as good a job at directing *Part II* as anybody else could.'

The sequel actually went into production under the title *Jason,* which marked the official debut of a new horror icon—the hooded, indestructible killer Jason Voorhees. *Part 2* was released in April 1981 to a first-place opening weekend gross of $6.4 million, on its way to a final take of $21.7 million. In contrast, Cunningham's *Stranger,* released in January 1982, was a complete flop, earning a paltry $2.5 million on its entire run.

Jason's trademark hockey mask came the next year with the August 1982 release of Miner's *Friday the 13th Part 3,* which was shot in 3D. Arriving at the height of the early '80s 3D craze, the $4 million film earned $36.6 million. Over the next seven years, Paramount would release five more *Friday the 13th* films, each with an average cost of $3 million and an average return of $21.5 million.[11]

During his time away from Crystal Lake, Cunningham directed the teen comedy *Spring Break* (1983), the teen thriller *The New Kids* (1985) and the underwater horror film *DeepStar Six* (1989). In addition, he produced the successful horror-comedy series *House* (1986), *House II: The Second Story* (1987), *House III: The Horror Show* (1989) and *House IV* (1992).

In 1992, Paramount sold the rights to the *Friday the 13th* series back to Sean Cunningham, who then went to New Line Cinema with the intention of making the long-rumoured *Freddy vs Jason.* When that project failed to materialise, the $3 million *Jason Goes to Hell: The Final Friday* was substituted. Produced by Cunningham and directed by newcomer Adam Marcus, the film was released in August 1993 and earned $16 million. Crystal Lake's favourite son then went dormant for the rest of the decade, finally returning in the much-delayed, much-troubled $11 million Cunningham production of *Jason X,* which was released in April 2002 to an underwhelming $13 million at the box office. With some help from his partner-in-crime Freddy Krueger, however, Jason got his mojo back in August 2003, when the $30 million *Freddy vs Jason* earned $82.6 million, the highest-ever for either a *Friday the 13th* or *Nightmare on Elm Street* movie.

'I think there are three main elements in the success of the *Friday the 13th* movies,' Cunningham reflected in an interview with Roger Ebert. 'The first one I call the Shark Factor. Some of our greatest fears centre on the possibility that we will have terrible things happen to us, even if we don't deserve them. If you're a bad person and you get killed, well, these things happen. Maybe you deserve it. But if you're a good person, and a shark comes along and bites your leg off, that's horrible. Jason's first victims sometimes deserve to be punished. They're the bad kids. But then the good kids get whacked, too. At some sort of deep, basic level, maybe the movie is acting out our fears and making them tolerable. The second element is the completely artificial setting of the films. They're off there in the woods, and Jason is attacking, and the dead bodies are piling up. Why doesn't somebody call the cops? Maybe because that would allow too much reality in, and the stories are like nightmares. The third big element is the audience itself. It always talks back to

---

11 *Friday the 13th: The Final Chapter* (1984), *Friday the 13th Part V: A New Beginning* (1985), *Friday the 13th Part VI: Jason Lives* (1986), *Friday the 13th Part VII: The New Blood* (1988), *Friday the 13th Part VIII: Jason Takes Manhattan* (1989).

the screen. "No, dummy, don't do it!" Talking to the characters becomes part of the social interaction of those kids on dates.'

(2009)

I shot at this house, this party house, and we would do all these gruesome kills. There are kills you didn't even see where guys are bopping around in the Jacuzzi with their tongues cut out, horrible things, right? My family would come and visit me on the weekends... so I said to my wife, 'Bring the kids, we'll hang out at the house. There's a great lake, you know.'

—Marcus Nispel, director

In my head, this Jason is a mixture of John Rambo...a little bit of Tarzan and the Abominable Snowman from Looney Tunes. You really see Jason thinking and planning in this one, setting people up; in my opinion it's very similar to *First Blood* where he's been wronged, people invade his space and he fights back and it's just brutal, but you also understand why he's doing it. You have sympathy for the character. You realise that this Jason is much more intelligent...I'm really, really excited because he's a much smarter Jason.

—Derek Mears, 'Jason Voorhees'

In the wake of *Freddy vs Jason*'s huge success, there were several treatments and scripts for the next *Friday the 13th* film: *Friday the 13th: The Beginning* (showing the events of Jason's life from his childhood until the very beginning of *Friday the 13th Part 2*), *Friday the 13th: The Homecoming* (Jason slices his way through a homecoming dance at Crystal Lake), *Freddy vs Jason vs Ash* (pitting the two titans of terror against the hero of *The Evil Dead* films; this was actually turned into a comic book series by WildStorm in 2007), and the self-descriptive *Jason vs Leatherface*. None of these came to fruition.

In February 2006, it was announced that New Line had contracted with Platinum Dunes to produce the newest outing in the *Friday the 13th* franchise, with an eye to releasing the picture on Friday, October 13. 'For us, to work with an iconic villain like Jason Voorhees is a dream come true,' Brad Fuller enthused to Dread Central. 'It wasn't a discussion. Michael, Drew and I all wanted to do it.'

'If you look at all the horror movies over the past 5-6 years, you really can't count on your hands how many have been that type of a fun, slasher-type horror film with, you know, sex and drugs and rock 'n' roll and kids having the time of their life and paying the price for it,' Andrew Form explained.

Horror film journalist Mark Wheaton was hired to write a script, based on the buzz surrounding his debut screenplays *Feral* and *Son of the Morning Star* (an adaptation of Evan Connell's novel). Regarding what direction the new *Friday the*

Friday the 13th (2009)

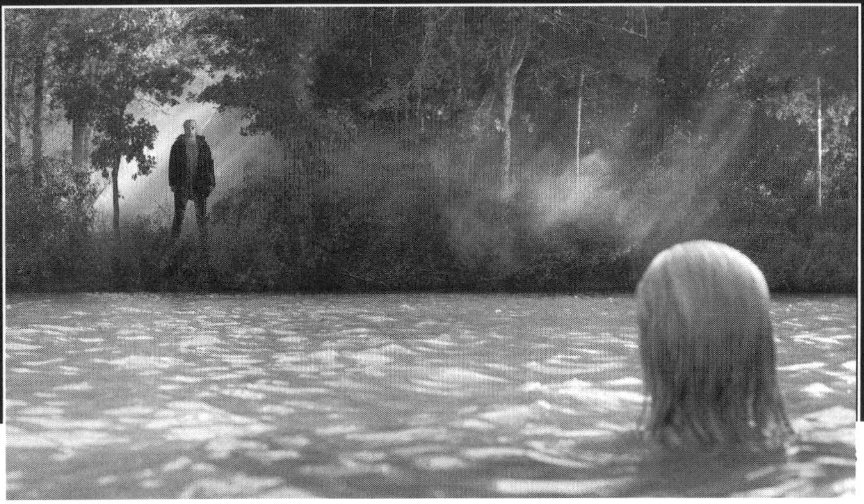

13th movie would take, Fuller told *Fangoria*, 'We don't know exactly what it's going to be yet; it's definitely not going to be set after *Freddy vs Jason* or *Jason X*. This was such a juicy title, we couldn't pass it up. So we've been talking to Wheaton, and we're figuring it out. Jason didn't really start killing until *Friday the 13th Part 2*, so this isn't a remake of the first one—Jason's definitely going to be killing people in our movie. He didn't wear the hockey mask until the third film, and our Jason is definitely going to wear the mask—so this is how we're going about it right now.' It was subsequently announced that Jonathan Liebesman, who had just finished shooting *Texas Chainsaw Massacre: The Beginning* for Platinum Dunes, would be serving as director for Jason's latest adventure.

Things came to a screeching halt that May, however, when Wheaton and producers Fuller and Form reached an impasse about what they could legally use in the film and what they could not. Form explained to *Fangoria*: 'It was a rights issue. Paramount owned certain rights and New Line certain rights; New Line owns the sequels and Paramount has the original. When Mark Wheaton did the script, we were all trying to figure out what that movie should be. Is it a prequel? Is it a remake? Is it a combination of *Part 2* and *Part 3* put together, because we know Jason doesn't put the mask on until the third film? But we didn't want to make another movie about Jason's mother killing kids again, so we had to figure out what rights we could use and which movie to make.'

'We were put in a box,' Form told CHUD.com, 'we couldn't use anything from the first one. So we started going down the road of making a *Friday the 13th* movie that didn't include anything from part one.' Added Fuller: 'We had to create our own back story.' Having just explored the origins of horror icon Leatherface, the Platinum Dunes boys were eager to do the same with Jason Voorhees, but the rights situation made that extremely difficult.

Making things even muddier was the presence of Sean Cunningham, who was legally obliged to be involved in any *Friday the 13th* remake. 'The situation was that

I control the rights, but the subject of the rights is owned by the distributors,' he outlined to *Fangoria*. 'So New Line had the rights to do the sequels and I made a deal with them, but the rights for the original *Friday the 13th* were with Paramount. So they said, "We have to do something different; we can't make Freddy vs Jason or vs Pinhead, Ash or whatever; we should go back and make the remake of the original one"...at that point, we had to figure out how to get the rights from Paramount and doing the movie without problems; everything became very complicated. But one day, someone woke up and said, "Excuse me, do you know that Jason is [barely] in the first *Friday the 13th*?" And so, suddenly, the project became not a remake of the original but a sort of recombination, something new. So the difficult job was to create a movie that seems to be the remake of the first film, but it's a kind of synthesis between parts one, two and three. But it has to be a good work of synthesis in order to be accepted by the fan base.'

The dilemma was solved in January 2007 when Paramount officially came on board as a partner. However, gaining Paramount meant taking a whole new approach to the material, which would require a new writer. When Wheaton wrote it, he wasn't given the right direction,' Form admitted. 'It was before all these rights were put together, so we were boxed into a corner where we couldn't use certain things. Now...we can use everything, so that really opens things up for us. We're going to bring in a writer and say, "We can use this, this and this. Put Jason in here and go to Crystal Lake." We just want to have fun with it."

In September, Form and Fuller finally settled on having the team of Damian Shannon and Mark Swift, who had been the ones to finally pull off a script of *Freddy vs Jason* that worked (after 18 other scripts were turned down)[12], to give Jason his 'reboot'. Fuller explained the choice to Dread Central: 'We felt that a lot of the horror movies, and some of our own, were so dreary that we wanted to kind of take a step away from that and kind of bring in the horror, which you have to have there, and bring in some great characters and funny, amusing situations. Out of all the writers we met with they were the only ones who really had a handle on that portion of the movie. We knew they could do the scares because they've been doing that for a long time, but the characters that they've created, the kids you go on this journey with are so fun—and a blast to be around. So that was really what clinched it for them.'

Two months later, it was announced that Marcus Nispel, who had directed *Texas Chainsaw Massacre* for Platinum Dunes, would be replacing Liebesman as the man in charge of Crystal Lake. 'We don't want *Friday the 13th* to be campy,' said Fuller, 'but there will be laughs in it. There'll be girls in it running around scantily clad, I hope. There's going to be fun and chases...We don't want to continue making movies that are dreary. *Saw* and *Hostel* are excellent at that, and those aren't places we want to be competing.' Nispel expanded on this philosophy to Movies Online: 'The mandate of the studio...was, "We don't want to make torture porn." Really, that's never what *Friday the 13th* was. *Chainsaw* was dreadful. I mean, it was dread-full. *Friday the 13th* always had some levity in it, but it was levity that was found in the behaviour of kids. They go camping...It's the 80s, we're having fun. This is not real.'

---

12 By over a dozen screenwriters, including Lewis Abernathy, Jonathan Aibel & Glenn Berger, Brannon Braga & Ronald D Moore, Peter Briggs, and Mark Protosevich.

On June 13, 1980, Pamela Voorhees chases down the lone surviving counsellor at Camp Crystal Lake. Blaming the girl for the drowning of her deformed son Jason, Voorhees means to finish her murder spree but is beheaded by a machete instead. After the counsellor escapes, young Jason emerges from the shadows, gathers his mother's head and the machete and wanders off. Thirty years later, a group of young campers—Amanda, Mike, Richie, Wade and Whitney—are looking for a pot farm near Crystal Lake. What they find that night is a full-grown, hooded Jason, who impales Wade on a tree, burns Amanda alive in her sleeping bag, cleaves Richie's head with a machete, rips Mike apart and holds Whitney captive in the catacombs beneath the ruins of the camp. Six weeks later, Whitney's brother Clay comes looking for her just as another group of college kids—Bree, Chelsea, Chumbler, Jenna, Lawrence, Nolan and Trent—arrive at the lake for a weekend of drinking, drugs and sex in Trent's family vacation home. Jason, while stealing kerosene from a nearby barn, encounters redneck farmhand Donnie, who just happens to have found an old hockey mask. Decapitating Donnie, Jason trades his hood for the mask. While out boating, Nolan is shot through the head with an arrow; without a driver, the boat runs over Chelsea, who has been waterskiing. Fatally injured, Chelsea makes her way to the shore, but Jason prevents her from getting help, watching passively as she drowns. That night, Chumbler is killed in the tool shed with a long screwdriver to the neck. Whitney has managed to escape from the labyrinth and makes her way to the house, but Jason captures her again before returning to impale Lawrence on an axe. Jenna, who has joined Clay in his fruitless search for Whitney, returns to the house with her new friend just as Trent phones the police. Suddenly, the power goes out, allowing Jason the cover of darkness to gain entry to the house. He then corners Bree in the bathroom and impales her on a pair of antlers. A policeman arrives at the scene, but is nailed to the front door by a fireplace poker in the eye. While making their escape, Clay discovers Whitney's locket and knows that she has been to the house. He convinces Jenna to come with him to look for his sister, but Trent runs off on his own. Jason catches up with Trent when the young man tries to flag down a passing tow truck. Gutting him with a machete, Jason then impales Trent on the truck's hay bailer. Clay and Jenna make it back to the camp ruins and discover Whitney in Jason's underground lair. They manage to free her, but Jenna is killed by Jason in the ensuing escape through the tunnels. Clay and Whitney make their way to the barn where Donnie was killed earlier with Jason hot on their heels. After Jason and Clay do battle, Whitney distracts Jason long enough for Clay to get a chain around him and put it in the spinning wood chipper. Helpless with the chain tightening around him, Jason's neck is broken and he is seemingly

killed. The next morning, Clay and Whitney dump Jason and his mask in the lake. Just as they turn to leave, the hockey-masked killer bursts through the dock to claim two more victims.

Filming began on April 21, 2008 in Bastrop, Texas, on a $19 million budget and a seven-week schedule, finishing on—appropriately—Friday, June 13. In this latest outing to Crystal Lake, seemingly everyone—from actor/stuntman Derek Mears (who was playing Jason) to Nispel, Shannon and Swift—wanted Jason to be seen as a sympathetic figure. 'He's a victim,' Mears told Dread Central. 'He represents those people in high school who were different, the ones with the lisps or the hair loss, the outsiders and the misfits. Being rejected by society and the beautiful people. We're not allowed, socially, to lash out and get our revenge, but Jason does, albeit in a poor way. He just wants to be left alone but people keep crossing into his territory.'

'When I worked with the writers, I noticed a very interesting thing,' Nispel revealed to Movies Online. 'They never referred to [Jason] as the monster or as the bogeyman or anything. They always called him our anti-hero. He was our anti-hero and the villain really was the jerk kid [Trent], the pretty boy, which tells you a lot about the writers and the people who make these movies. We're really the guys who weren't so popular on prom night.'

The two line producers had a somewhat different opinion about their 'anti-hero', however. 'We want it to feel real, and he is a brutal killer,' Form stated to CHUD. Fuller agreed, telling Crave Online: 'We were always adamant that we wanted to make a movie where Jason Voorhees is a brutal killer. Where he runs and it's real and it's really horrifying.' 'Every discussion about this movie,' Fuller elaborated to CHUD, 'you talk about the kills, you talk about the hot chicks, you talk about the nudity, you talk about Crystal Lake—but at the end of the day, the question is, "Is there a supernatural element to this movie?" Is Jason a demon? I think you can't figure out any of the other things until you figure that out.'

Nispel's answer was to keep things based in reality, telling Movies Online: 'I said to them, "Whatever you do, bring the fun back and find a way to incorporate an underground system for Jason to operate from." I liked that idea because I don't think summer camps in general are particularly scary in this day and age—you needed something more...I really believe the movie tells you what's going on. You're underground, you're in the forest, you have a guy who's dressed in black and you have a black background you put behind him. Out of that, a style sort of evolves. I'm fairly puristic...I don't like to go in and get overly fancy. And really...my job is to sometimes just blend into the wallpaper, almost like you're doing reality TV, and let the cameras rattle and make sense out of it later in editing, so it still seems somewhat authentic and not contrived.'

EXT. CABIN—FRONT DOOR--NIGHT

Clay and Jenna hurry onto the front porch. Jenna cringes as Clay quickly frisks the cop impaled to the door—
Trent comes out wild-eyed, gun still at the ready.

Retro Screams

                              TRENT
What are you doing?! Let's go!

                              CLAY
No gun. No keys.

                              JENNA
He took 'em.

Clay hurries over to the police car—

Clay pulls the police car open—sees the RADIO PULLED OUT, exposed wires everywhere—

                              CLAY
Shit. Radio's dead too.

JENNA backs up, eyes on the second story windows of the cabin. Is he still in there?! She steps on something: A SMALL LOCKET ON A CHAIN. Music now plays from it...

ON CLAY AND TRENT
                              TRENT
Fuck the radio, let's make a run for the road,
flag someone down.

Clay holds a hand to Trent stopping him from talking. They hear faint music, like from a tiny music box...

Something comes over Clay: RECOGNITION.

                       TRENT (CONT'D)
What?!

Clay looks over slowly, knows what he's gonna see—

Jenna holds the locket. Clay moves to her, takes it from her. He opens the locket wider. A picture of an older woman inside...

                       TRENT (CONT'D)
The fuck are you doing?! LET'S GO!

                              CLAY
My mother.
(beat)

298

This is Whitney's. She was here.
(beat)
She's alive. She could be close.

TRENT
You don't know that.

Jenna shares an emotional look with Clay. Clay turns to Trent, new determination on his face—

CLAY
We gotta look for her.

TRENT
Are you insane?

CLAY
I'm going after her.

TRENT
Then you're going after her alone.
(beat. They stand off, neither giving an inch.)

CLAY
I need that gun. Please.

TRENT
No chance. She's dead. C'mon, Jenna...

Clay gives Trent a hard look now— like he's not willing to take no for an answer—

Clay moves at Trent ever so slightly— and Trent trains the gun on him.

Trent takes a step, but Jenna isn't moving.

TRENT (CONT'D)
Jenna? You stay with this guy... you're gonna die.
You know that, right?

Jenna looks at both of them, makes her decision—

JENNA
Right now...I feel a lot safer with him than you.

Trent nods.

TRENT
You just dug your own grave, bitch.

Trent runs off down the dirt path, disappearing into the darkness.

—Unfilmed scene, from the original script

With much of the dialogue changed from the script (apparently Nispel encouraged his young cast to frequently ad-lib), there were also several other notable differences between the page and the screen, including:

- In the script, Whitney wears a musical locket that has a picture of her mother. This was changed to her finding Pamela Voorhees' locket in Jason's lair and using it to calm Jason's homicidal tendencies (presumably this is the reason he kills all her friends but captures her alive).
- The script includes a scene at the gas station where Bree and Chelsea talk about which guy they plan to hook up with over the weekend. This was not shot.
- After Jenna joins Clay in his search for his sister, the script has a scene where Bree seizes the opportunity and approaches Trent about going into town together. This also was not shot.
- In the script, Lawrence runs a trucking business; this was changed to him running his own rap music label.
- In the script, Clay tries to convince Trent and Jenna to go with him to find his sister after he discovers her locket outside the house. Jenna agrees, but Trent goes off by himself. This was changed to Trent (Travis Van Winkle) getting in the police car to radio for help, only to have Bree's (Julianna Guill) dead body dumped through the windshield. In a panic, he runs off through the woods, leaving Clay (Jared Padalecki) and Jenna (Danielle Panabaker) on their own.

Two scenes ended up being reshot during postproduction: Donnie's (Kyle Davis) murder and the climax. With regard to the former, the scene was originally shot to the script, but was then changed to Donnie (*sans* hockey mask) encountering Jason upstairs in the barn, pulling off Jason's hood and having his throat cut. While searching for his hood, Jason then finds a hockey mask in the rubbish pile and puts it on. This change was made because the producers felt that no one besides Jason should be seen wearing a hockey mask.

The climax likewise was originally shot to the script, but Jason's death—simply having his neck snapped—seemed rather anticlimactic. The scene was subsequently changed to have Jason strung up, pulled into the chipper and finally stabbed with

his machete by Whitney ('Say hi to mommy...in hell!' she tells him) so that his death is much more dramatic and convincing.

Nispel's original cut ran 106 minutes, and he was forced to remove nine minutes from the film, both for ratings purposes and to tighten up the narrative. As a result, a number of things were either shortened or eliminated altogether:

- In the prologue, Jason was originally shown watching his mother confront the last counsellor. These shots were excised and no shots of Jason's face were used when he retrieves his mother's head and machete.
- There is less nudity when Amanda (America Olivo) seduces Richie (Ben Feldman) and less explicit sex between the two in their tent.
- Mike (Nick Mennell) is subjected to fewer cuts from Jason's machete when he is attacked in the cabin.
- There are no scenes of Clay and Jenna entering the camp grounds after she joins him in his search for Whitney (Amanda Righetti).
- There is no scene of Jason sharpening his machete and having a flashback to the prologue that causes him to fly into a rage.

- Whitney's entire escape and recapture has been eliminated.
- The sex scenes between Bree and Trent are less explicit.
- Trent's death is much less graphic, showing him being impaled on a hay bailer but not gutted with the machete beforehand.
- There is no scene of Jenna and Clay finding Chelsea's (Willa Ford) body.
- The montage at the end, of scenes of Jason's crimes, was eliminated.

The latest excursion to Camp Crystal Lake opened on Friday, February 13, 2009. Taking advantage of the four-day President's Day weekend, *Friday the 13th* scored a first-place showing with a huge $43.5 million gross. Things took a nose dive from there, however, as the picture lost 80% of its audience the second weekend and ended up earning a total of $65 million (plus an additional $26 million overseas).

Not surprisingly, the film was met with near-total critical hostility. 'All Nispel does is repackage what's been hot recently in horror,' declared *The Boston Globe*. 'The slayings here are indistinguishable from the atrocities of *Saw* and *Hostel*. His psychological scars lasered away, Jason now kills for sport. Like the filmmakers, our bogeyman is merely a copycat hack. And for those of you watching the box office, he continues to serve a far grimmer end: He's still just an ATM.' The *Los Angeles Times* likewise took Nispel to task: 'The film is certainly not torture porn, but it is unnecessarily grim. Nispel grasped the slaughterhouse despair that was at the core of *The Texas Chainsaw Massacre*, but he entirely misses the goofball giddiness that has always gilded the edges of the best stalker/slasher films.' 'Perhaps there's not much that can be done, beyond the expected, with the *Friday the 13th* franchise,' reasoned *USA Today*. 'But it would have been fun to see someone try...While it's billed as a 'reimagining' of the horror franchise, this *Friday* is more like a rehash,

delivering just what you expect and nothing more.' *The Washington Post* decided to go straight for Platinum Dunes's head honcho: 'Michael Bay is destroying horror films by exhuming the genre's standard-bearers, stripping them of genuine terror, refusing to either recreate faithfully or reimagine boldly, and upping the irony until the original concept stands rigid like a taxidermied grizzly, its teeth bared but its presence, most of all, sad.'

What *was* surprising was the relatively strong endorsement *Friday the 13th* got from the *New York Times*: 'This movie attempts to reboot the concept, if that's the word, of this undying series. The surprise is that it does so with vicious aplomb, massacring its generic clutch of topless young girls and their inebriated boyfriends... with a gleeful sense of fun...Granted, most people's notion of entertainment doesn't involve watching sexed-up, beer-guzzling morons impaled, decapitated or burnt alive. But there's an itch for this kind of material, and here it is scratched—to the bone.'

In October, New Line announced that they planned to release yet another *Friday the 13th* film—the fabled thirteenth entry—on August 13, 2010. Two months later, the studio changed its mind and put the sequel on the back burner, despite a script having been completed by Shannon and Swift. As of the time of writing, *Friday the 13th Part 2* is still in limbo, being mentioned as a possible 3D project for Platinum Dunes sometime in the future, should New Line decide to go ahead with it.

'When we make one of these films, we go in hoping we can elevate it,' Fuller declared to the *New York Times*. 'There's a tremendous benefit to staying in the same genre and producing movies for the same amount of money over and over, because you really learn who your key players are and how best to work with them.' Apparently so, as Platinum Dunes continues on the remake route, despite the failure of their most recent 'reboot', *A Nightmare on Elm Street* (q.v.). Bay, Form and Fuller have announced their intention to revisit everything from Hitchcock's 1963 classic *The Birds* to the 1987 cult film *The Monster Squad*, as well as yet another entry in the *Teenage Mutant Ninja Turtles* series (this despite the fact that a $34 million animated *Turtles* movie failed to make its cost back in 2007). The company also plans to bring the popular board game *Ouija* and the comic book *Zombies vs Robots* to the big screen.

BLACK X-MAS

BLACK X-MAS

THE
MAN
UPSTAIRS

BLACK
CHRISTMAS

(1974)

When I first read the Roy Moore script I thought to myself, 'Now, here's an opportunity to use the camera as a character.' I didn't think it had been done. I'd never seen it. And I thought that would be novel and more frightening.

—Bob Clark, co-producer, co-writer and director

Warners are going in for some unusual forms of exploitation on this. There have been some Santa Clauses walking around in black suits, some provocative sky-writing and a number you can dial to listen in on some rather obscene telephone calls from the film soundtrack.

—John Saxon, 'Lieutenant Fuller'

A fter publishing his *The Vanishing Hitchhiker: American Urban Legends & Their Meanings* in 1981, Jan Harold Brunvand, professor of English at the University of Utah, was credited with both chronicling said legends and actually introducing the term 'urban legend' into the popular lexicon. One such tale from the 1960s became known as 'The Babysitter and the Man Upstairs': a young girl receives threatening phone calls while minding a neighbour's children; the twist has the local police tracing the calls to an upstairs room of the very house in which the young woman is sitting.

This urban legend formed the basis for *The Babysitter*, a spec script written by Canadian Broadcasting Corporation staffers Timothy Bond and Roy Moore as a follow-up to their 1973 TV movie *She Cried Murder*, which was shot in Toronto and featured Telly Savalas and Lynda Day George. *The Babysitter*'s concept caught the attention of producers Richard Schouten and Harvey Sherman (who had been unit manager on *She Cried Murder*), who had Moore rewrite the script for a university setting.

At the University of Toronto, Kappa Gamma sorority sisters Jessica (Jess) Bradford, Clare Harrison, Barbara (Barb) Pollock, Phyllis (Phil) Thompson and housemother Mrs MacHenry (Mrs Mac) are busily preparing for the Christmas break, unaware that a stranger is living in the attic. When they begin receiving obscene phone calls, the girls first ascribe them to a fraternity prank. While in her room packing to leave, Clare is attacked and suffocated with a plastic bag; her dead body is then taken up to the attic. The next day, Jess informs her boyfriend Peter Smythe, a troubled graduate music student, that she is pregnant and wants to abort the baby, something to which he does not take kindly. Returning home, Jess picks up the phone and hears a woman's voice scolding someone named Billy. That night, Jess and Phil join Lieutenant Ken Fuller, Clare's father, her boyfriend and several others in a search party to try and find both Clare and a missing teenager who never came home from band practice. The latter's mutilated body is eventually discovered by some youngsters. Mrs Mac prepares to leave for her sister's house, but when she goes up to the attic to find her cat, a noose tightens around her neck and she is hanged from a rope. The caller rings again; when Jess picks up, she hears a little girl's sobbing which changes to a man pleading with her to 'Help me! Stop me!' Having failed his senior recital, Peter comes over and announces his intention to leave the conservatory and marry Jess. She refuses his proposal. Peter at first begs Jess not to abort the baby, then threatens to go to the police if she tries. As he storms out, Lt Fuller and Phil come in with a technician who puts a tap on the house phone. Fuller also assigns patrolman Jennings to watch the house. Later on, as children sing Christmas carols outside, Barb is murdered in her sleep by the stranger, who admonishes, 'Don't you tell, Agnes.' The phone rings again, a woman's voice scolding, 'Nasty Billy! What an evil child!' but the call is not long enough to get a trace. We also see that, outside in his car, Jennings has had his throat cut. Peter calls sobbing and begs Jess not to abort the baby before abruptly hanging up. Phil goes up to check on Barb and is murdered. The call comes one last time and is the mother scolding Billy for molesting his sister Agnes before changing back into a man once again pleading, 'Stop me!' The mother's voice comes back on and accuses Billy of killing Agnes. This time the trace comes through—the call is coming from inside the sorority house. The police call Jess and tell her to get out of the house; before she can, Billy strikes. While hiding from Billy, Jess mistakes Peter—who has been lurking outside the house—for the murderer and kills him. Now catatonic, Jess is sedated and left under police surveillance at the house until her parents can come and pick her up. After Lt Fuller and the coroner leave with the bodies of Barb and Phil, we hear the offscreen voice of Billy's mother telling him what a good boy he is. Then the phone starts to ring...

After retitling the script *Stop Me!* (a reference to Billy's pleas), the producers showed it to a horror film director who only recently had become an expatriate: Robert Benjamin Clark. Born in August 1939 in New Orleans, he and his family relocated to Florida in 1946. Clark had always wanted to be a writer, but while attending the University of Miami in the mid-1960s, he became interested in film. His path eventually intersected with one Charles Brune, a cross-dressing funeral parlour owner who also happened to operate a movie studio on the edge of the Everglades. Clark wrote and directed two films for Brune—*The Emperor's New Clothes* (1966) with John Carradine, which was never released, and *She-Man* (1967) which, unfortunately, was.

Four years later, Clark linked up with his former college roommate Alan Ormsby and the two decided to make a low-budget horror film as a way of breaking into the industry. They co-wrote *Children Shouldn't Play with Dead Things,* a comedic riff on *Night of the Living Dead.* With a total of $40,000 raised from Clark's brothers and Gary and Ken Goch, along with their uncles, the film was shot over eleven nights at Miami's Coconut Grove in late 1971. Clark co-produced and directed the film, while Ormsby starred, along with his wife Anya, and did the make-up. *Dead Things* was subsequently bought and released by Grade Z exploitation king Ted V Mikels (*The Astro Zombies, The Corpse Grinders*) in June 1972.

Dead Things made enough of an impression that Clark was able to secure a decent budget ($250,000) for his next film *Dead of Night* (aka *Deathdream*), courtesy of Canada's Quadrant Films. A modern version of WW Jacobs' classic 1902 short story *The Monkey's Paw* with a Vietnam War background, Clark produced and directed the film in Florida at the end of 1972 but did the editing and sound mixing in Canada. Falling in love with the country, Clark decided to relocate to the Great White North, where he would live and work for the next 12 years. His first project in his newly-adopted homeland was to act as co-producer for Ormsby's unofficial Ed Gein biography, *Deranged*, a $200,000 wonder financed by concert promoter Tom Karr and shot in Toronto in the winter of 1973.

While waiting for both *Dead of Night* and *Deranged* to play theatres (which neither would do until 1974), Clark was presented with the script for *Stop Me!* and decided that it was in need of some serious adjustment. 'I often rewrite and work on scripts,' he told Icons of Fright, 'and I did a tremendous amount of work on [*Stop Me!*].'

INTERIOR—UPPER HALL—NIGHT

We hear the rest of Jess and Barb's conversation over a subjective shot of the door to Barb's room. There is breathing over the shot.

JESS
(VOICE ONLY)

Peter was here. We had a fight.

BARB

What about?

JESS

Oh, it's not worth going into. He was screaming by the time he left. His behaviour is really getting to be psychotic.

BARB

Do you think he might be dangerous?

JESS
(STOPS AND THINKS A MOMENT)

No. Why would you ask a thing like that? Well, I don't think so. No. I'm sure he isn't.

Barb is falling back to sleep.

BARB
(DROWSILY)

Well, maybe you should call him just so things aren't left in such an unfriendly state. Remember it's Christmas...

Her voice trails off as she falls asleep.

—Deleted exchange, from the original script

It is true that Clark rewrote much of the script's dialogue, but the fact remains that he was *not* responsible for virtually all of the things he came to take credit for over the years, starting with the first-person camera that gave an audience the killer's eyes. 'When they gave me the original script,' Clark claimed to Bloody Disgusting, 'it didn't have that subjective camera approach.' Yet this is how the Moore's script opens...

A hand-held, subjective shot establishing that this is the point of view of the person who is walking outside. We see from the camera's POV as it walks around the side of the house, glancing quickly into the windows. We see the camera's breath on the cold night air and hear the crunching footsteps in the snow. It reaches a trellis running up the side of the house, looks around carefully and begins to climb. As it reaches the second floor, it looks through a large window down a long empty hallway. The sounds of the party are heard downstairs. The camera continues to climb.

Clark also proclaimed to Icons of Fright that 'I had this idea from the beginning that I would obscure the killer and make him all the more frightening and ominous.' But this is how the script describes the killer as he observes Clare from her closet:

As the clothes are swept past, we see a clear plastic bag and through the bag we think we see the distorted face of a man, staring wide-eyed at the girl. At least we think we see the face. It is so distorted and vague we are not sure.

Clark made the claim to Bloody Disgusting that 'there was no humour in the [script]...I added all the humour from [Barb], [Phil] and Mrs Mac.' However, Mrs Mac's lush personality was already in the script and Clark actually eliminated a scene in which the housemother does a comical vaudeville routine for the girls. Similarly, Barb's joke on Sgt Nash about the 'Fellatio' telephone exchange was already in the script, as well as the comic interlude with the two dopes from the search party popping up outside the sorority house.

In the documentary *Black Christmas Revisited*, Clark asserted that 'The original script was more graphic but Roy was very pleased to see it moved towards...more subtle, more subliminal ideas; suggestive rather than graphic.' As a prime example, Clark cited how the murder of Barb was shot: 'You see almost nothing; it's just all illusions and sound is a tremendous part of [it].' Once again, this is how the scene was described by Moore...

> The children's singing can be heard in the distance. Light begins to come onto the screen and we see Barb's face sleeping against the pillow. Someone moves across the room. A shadow crosses Barb's face...Barb's eyes slowly open. A shot of just the eyes of the caller. They are very fierce and animal-like. Terror comes onto Barb's face. A knife blade flashes in the air. Barb's hands reach out to ward off the blow. Small glass animals on the headboard rattle and topple off the shelf. Barb gasps. The knife flashes again. She gags. The camera ZOOMS all over the room from Barb's POV. The caller makes ferocious growling sounds. Barb's hand grips the blood-spattered sheet. There are more 'thunk' sounds. Her hand jumps and then relaxes. The little glass animals lie broken and bloody on the floor. The ferocious sounds continue.

Change to a glass unicorn instead of a knife and intercut with the carollers, and you have the exact same scene as the one in the film.

Strangely, given his subsequent claim that 'Barb is essentially my character,' Clark rather carelessly eliminated Moore's attempts at sympathy for her, including Mrs Mac speaking reassuringly to her as she changes the drunken girl for bed and Barb later confessing to Jess, 'The girls here are the only family I've ever really had and all I do is drive them away.' Clark also deleted scenes that built suspicion around Peter, including the one above as well as another one between Jess and Phil, where Jess tells her friend, 'He had a terrible childhood. He doesn't really talk about it too much though. He's seeing a psychiatrist, but I don't know why. Ever since he started going he's felt terrible.'

Production began on March 25, 1974, on a $700,000 budget, with 40 days of filming at the University of Toronto and the surrounding area. The lead role of Jess went to *Romeo and Juliet*'s Olivia Hussey, while Barb and Phil were to be played by Canadian ingénue Margot Kidder and comedienne Gilda Radner. A long-haired Keir Dullea (*2001*) came from London for a few days to play Peter, and more pedigree in the form of Oscar-winner Edmond O'Brien (*The Barefoot Contessa*) was also on board as police Lt Fuller. Radner, however, would answer the summons from the producers of a new TV show called *Saturday Night Live*, which necessitated that she

be replaced by Andrea Martin, who had just appeared in Ivan Reitman's horror comedy *Cannibal Girls* (1973).

Unfortunately, the production was not finished playing musical chairs with its cast, as it was about to find out that its star policeman was suffering from Alzheimer's disease. 'I went and met [Edmond O'Brien] at the airport,' co-producer Gerry Arbeid remembered in *Black Christmas Revisited*, 'and when he landed...he didn't know where he was. He didn't know whether he was in Toronto or Chicago or New York. He was very confused. But I didn't say anything. I thought, "Well, maybe he's tired and maybe he's confused and once he's had a bit of a rest and had some dinner he'll have all of his marbles together." [When] we knew that Mr O'Brien was not capable of playing the part, I immediately phoned Bob and went over to his house and told Bob the news that we were shooting on the detective the next morning [but] we don't have any detective. I had some very, very short and very tough words to say to [O'Brien's] agent, who should never have sent him out in such a condition. He must've known that Mr O'Brien was not capable of playing that part. That was a big glitch.'"

Thankfully, the film's composer Carl Zittrer was acquainted with actor John Saxon, who had just co-starred with the late Bruce Lee in the latter's final film, *Enter the Dragon* (1973). Saxon responded favourably to Clark's personal entreaties and flew to Toronto on the spur of the moment to take over from O'Brien.

In fact, necessity was the mother of invention during the whole shoot, from the improvised casting (including having Arbeid cameo as a taxi driver) to using lots of fake snow to jerry-rigging a pre-Steadicam harness for the subjective shots. 'Basically Bert Dunk, the camera operator, designed a camera rig that attached to his head!' Clark revealed to Icons of Fright. 'No one had ever done that before... those are his hands climbing with the small camera. The moving shots when we were on the ground were just standard handheld shots. But the climbing ones were the unique style camera; when he looked up, the camera looked up.'

'One of the most serious aspects of a horror film that you have to apply yourself to is credibility,' Clark reflected to Bloody Disgusting. 'That is why I treated the girls like they were real girls and not beach blanket bimbos...All those subliminal ideas create the reality of the *Black Christmas* world so [the killer] can invade it and something is at stake. I think you care that the girls are being terrorised in this way. Classically, the bad girl is the first one to go...[but] I killed the sweetest girl of all first.'

Premiering in Canada in November via Ambassador Films, *Black Christmas* quickly became English-speaking Canada's #2 all-time grosser after the same year's *Apprenticeship of Duddy Kravitz*, earning $1.2 million. Its critical reception was hardly a warm one—'Silly and tasteless...notable primarily for its foul language and its assumption that sexual psychosis makes for good entertainment' (*Calgary Herald*); 'This Canadian-made Gothic is enough to curdle your turkey dinner and squeeze most of the enthusiasm out of the Canadian film industry' (*Montreal Gazette*); 'There's some Canadian content, but not enough to notice, in this conventional spine-chiller dressed up with obscene phone calls and shadows on the wall' (*Ottawa Citizen*)—but its commercial success did not go unnoticed, and *Black Christmas* was rewarded with two Canadian Film Awards, for Best Actress (Kidder) and Best Sound Editing (Kenneth Heeley-Ray).

Warner Bros was suitably impressed and in February 1975, the studio contracted for the film's US distribution. Warners' executives, however, were bothered by the open ending and asked Clark to reshoot it. They proposed leaving Jess alone with Chris Hayden, Clare's boyfriend, who turns out to be the killer. Clark refused this idea and the ending remained as he originally intended it, though he would come to regret this decision. Years later, he told *Cinefantastique*, 'Black Christmas has always been accused of being a cheat, but it was a bloody honest ending, saying, "Look, we don't know who the killer is." He was not anybody in the film to my mind but his identity invoked an enormous response...He was an unseen, unknown, of this earth, homicidal maniac. It was always to be an unknown presence. In retrospect that was a mistake. The audience wanted the gratification of a pleasant ending. That really isn't important, but what I hadn't counted on was that [Jess] had deserved and earned the right to live. Left alone in the house with the maniac was a bit hard to take.'

With some justification, Warners felt that *Black Christmas* would be mistaken by American cinemagoers for a race-focussed film and changed the title to *Silent Night, Evil Night*. The studio then had the brilliant idea to release a Christmas-themed movie in May and June ('Christmas is coming early this year. And it's murder,' the ads said). Not surprisingly, it flopped, earning just $2 million.

With Arbeid and Findlay Quinn of August Films, *Black Christmas*'s production company, picking up the tab, Warners agreed to test market the film under its original title and Canadian ad campaign in Los Angeles that August. The result was over $150,000 in two weeks, which was enough to convince the studio to re-release the movie as *Black Christmas* that October, giving the picture an additional $2 million in revenue.

Regardless of which title they saw it under, American critics were almost evenly divided in their reaction to the film. 'A taut exercise in terror which, after its hour-and-45 minute onslaught, is certain to rattle what's left of your sensibilities,' praised *The Boston Globe*, while the *Los Angeles Examiner* described *Black Christmas* as simply 'a good old fashioned scary movie.' TV personality Regis Philbin was one of the movie's admirers, as he enthused: 'The purpose of this film is to frighten the audience—and I mean it really scares them. Just the shrill ringing of *Black Christmas* is enough to raise the hackles on your neck.' And Kevin Thomas rounded out the chorus of praise by writing, '*Black Christmas* is a smart, stylish Canadian-made little horror picture that is completely diverting.'

Others were not so impressed, however. The *New York Times* dismissed *Black Christmas* as 'a whodunit that begs the question of why it was made. The answer is hard to come by.' Predictably, Gene Siskel could not see past the violence in the piece: '*Black Christmas* is notable only for indicating the kind of junk roles that talented actresses are forced to play in the movies. Olivia Hussey and Margot Kidder are reduced to playing manikinlike coeds waiting to be stabbed.' The *Syracuse Herald Journal* managed to catch the film in its initial release and was unequivocal in its scorn: 'It's a tossup whether the pre-Christmas or pre-Memorial Day films mark the nadir of the motion picture year. But the decision goes to *Silent Night, Evil Night* as the tackiest spring movie...the thriller is more horrible than horror and

more familiar than freaky.' *Variety* was in full agreement: 'A foul-mouthed, bloody, senseless kill-for-kicks feature [that] exploits unnecessary violence in a university sorority house operated by an implausibly alcoholic ex-hoofer. If it was made to play less discriminating situations, *Black Christmas* will succeed, but if its aim is to run anywhere else the venture can be marked as a failure.'

Retitled yet again to *Stranger in the House,* the film premiered on the pay-TV network Home Box Office in June 1977. Under its new name, it was subsequently scheduled to be shown in late January 1978 on NBC-TV as a prime-time, Saturday night movie, but was pre-empted at the last minute with a showing of *Doc Savage, Man of Bronze* (1975). This was due to a personal petition from Florida governor Reubin Askew, who asked NBC president Robert Mulholland not to show the film, fearing its plot was too similar to what had actually happened just two weeks earlier at Florida State University. In the pre-dawn hours of January 15, four young women were attacked at the Chi Omega sorority house; two were killed, the others badly injured. At first, Mulholland agreed to 'black out' just Florida, but soon decided not to show *Stranger* at all. NBC finally aired the film the following May as a late night Sunday movie.

Just five months later, a film that seemed to take a lot of creative inspiration—notably the first-person stalker camera—from *Black Christmas* was released: John Carpenter's *Halloween* (q.v.). As it turned out, the connection between Carpenter and Bob Clark was not just similar styles, but an aborted professional collaboration that may well have resulted in the former's breakthrough film. As Clark remembered years later to the *Toronto Star,* 'John was a big fan of *Black Christmas*. He got me hired by Warner Brothers to do this slasher film [*Prey*] he'd set in Tennessee. We got into preproduction in the movie but it wound up not going. But John asked me one day, "You going to do a sequel to *Black Christmas*?" And I said, "John, your film will be the last horror film I will do. At least for a lot of years. After yours I want to move into a more eclectic part of my career." He said, "Well, okay, if you were going to make a sequel what would it be?" I said, "It would be later in that year and the killer has been caught. At the beginning of the movie he's escaped from the asylum. And he comes back to the girls to haunt them once again, only it's Halloween. And [I'd] call it *Halloween*."' Though he never made a sequel to *Black Christmas*, Clark did indeed become known for his eclectic choice of material, from the Sherlock Holmes vs Jack the Ripper thriller *Murder by Decree* (for which he won a Canadian Genie award, 1979) to the popular coming-of-age sex comedy *Porky's* (1982) and that much-beloved valentine to the holiday season adapted from the writings of Jean Shepherd, *A Christmas Story* (for which he won Genies for both writing and directing; 1983).

After returning to the States in 1984, Clark unfortunately seemed to have left his career judgment north of the border. He became a hired gun on a series of flop comedies—*Rhinestone* (1984), *Turk 182!* (1985), *From the Hip* (1987), *Loose Cannons* (1990)—and even his eagerly-awaited follow-up to *A Christmas Story*, entitled *It Runs in the Family*, barely received a theatrical release in 1994 under the moniker *My Summer Story*. Clark enjoyed a minor hit with the disposable comedy *Baby Geniuses* (1999), but its sequel *Superbabies: Baby Geniuses 2* was so awful that Columbia Pictures dug up an old subsidiary (Triumph Films) for an abortive 2004 release. Clark's downward spiral continued the same year with the made-for-TV abomination *The Karate Dog,* featuring the voice of hard-up comedian Chevy Chase.

(2006)

This film came along and I met Bob [Clark] and I wanted to be sure that it would be respectful, but not a shot-for-shot remake. He came [to the set] for a week, checked in, read the script, and he's been staying out of the way.

—Glen Morgan, co-producer, writer and director

We have the advantage of having a totally undeveloped story...Who is Billy? What is Billy? That is what Glen has been so clever in doing, using that and developing it. The audience will love finding out about him. We get the history before we go, to see how and why Billy [is who he is] so you know something about him. All we knew about Billy [in the original] was what he revealed to us in his madness over the phone.

—Bob Clark, co-executive producer

In September 2000, a $5 million Canadian film called *Ginger Snaps,* directed by John Fawcett, won a special jury prize at the Toronto International Film Festival. The story of two sisters—one bitten by a werewolf and the other trying desperately to find a cure for her sibling—it received critical acclaim and became a cult hit. Its success prompted the shooting of both a sequel (*Ginger Snaps: Unleashed*) and a prequel (*Ginger Snaps Back: The Beginning*) back-to-back in 2003 and the release

Black Christmas (2006)

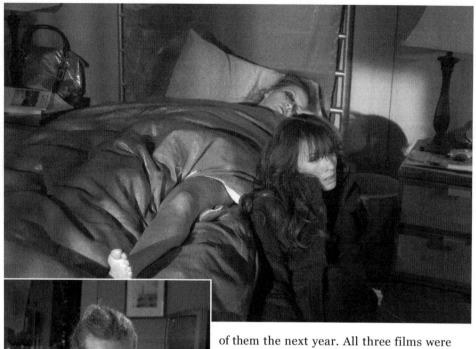

of them the next year. All three films were produced by Steven Hoban's Copperheart Entertainment, which announced in May 2004 that its next project was a remake of *Black Christmas*, with Bob Clark as executive producer.

At the end of April 2005, 2929 Productions (producers of the revived *Star Search* TV series and the Robert De Niro horror film *Godsend*) acquired the remake rights to *Black Christmas* from Copperheart and hired Hard Eight Pictures, the production company of Glen Morgan and James Wong, to produce the film, with Morgan writing and directing.

The Morgan-Wong combine began when they co-wrote *The Boys Next Door* (1985) and *Trick or Treat* (1986) and continued in the 1990s as writers/producers on such TV shows as *21 Jump Street*, *The Commish*, *Space: Above and Beyond*, *The X Files*, and *Millennium*. Their first feature together was New Line's *Final Destination* (2000), which they co-wrote and Wong directed. Its success led to others that they would write and produce together, including the Jet Li martial arts film *The One* (2001), a remake of the 1971 rat thriller *Willard* (Morgan's directorial debut; 2003) and *Final Destination 3*, which was in production at the time of the *Black Christmas* announcement and would be released in February 2006.

'We didn't want to do it if [Clark] didn't give us his blessing,' Wong told Dread

Central, 'so we met with him and his partners before there was a script or anything and he knew of our work. Glen basically did all of the talking but we told him what we wanted to do and how we thought we could update it a little bit. Then Bob says, "Well, I have an idea about Agnes." It was a really good conversation. His thing was that he didn't want to be too involved, he just wanted to leave you alone and [let you] do your thing. He really hated it when people put their fingers all over his projects and he didn't want to be that person. So he was very gracious and open.'

'One of the advantages of *Black Christmas* is that there is this Billy/Agnes demonic untold story,' Clark related to Bloody Disgusting. 'I know Glen [is] going to explore it and I think it's a good idea. That phone call is really the villain, the demon of that movie in a way. So he [is] going to explore that and give a history to the stalker. He [has] a remake but with a twist...I think finding out more about that strange individual [will] be intriguing.'

A September production start was planned, and then later changed to January 2006. Clark was to serve as one of six executive producers, while Hoban would get a producer's credit along with Clark's partner Victor Solnicki (*Scanners, Videodrome*) and some eight others. 'It's going to be a classic horror film, but it won't be a gorefest,' Hoban told *Variety*. 'This is an era of paranoia, so I think the timing could be really good, because this is a film all about paranoia.' In October, Dimension Films contracted for the distribution rights to the picture and announced it for a Christmas 2006 release.

'We did a first draft with a Canadian set of writers,' Clark told *Fangoria*. 'Glen felt that they strayed too far from the original. He wanted to pull it back to the house more.' Wong elaborated: 'That script was very different from the original *Black Christmas*. We read it and said, "This is not what we want to do." But *Black Christmas* is a great movie, and Glen had a take on it. He really thought that we had to go back to the sorority; that that was the way to do it.'

Christmas 1970. Billy Lenz is born with chronic jaundice to a Vietnam veteran father and alcoholic mother. Five years later, Billy's mother and her lover murder the boy's father before his eyes, then lock the youngster in the attic. In 1982, Billy's mother rapes her own son—nine months later, Agnes Lenz is born. At Christmas 1991, Billy escapes from the attic and goes on a rampage, gouging out his daughter's eyeball, impaling his stepfather on an ornament and pummelling his mother with a rolling pin before using a cookie cutter on her face. The police arrive to find Billy calmly eating his mother's flesh; Agnes is sent to an orphanage and Billy is committed to an asylum. Fifteen years later, the Lenz house has been converted into the Phi Kappa Sigma sorority, home to Clair Crosby, Eve Guaraldi, Lauren Hannon, Megan Helms, Melissa Kitt, Heather Lee, Dana Mathis and Kelli Presely, along with their housemother Mrs MacHenry. As they prepare to leave for Christmas break, the sorority sisters receive disturbing phone calls before meeting their deaths one by one at the hands of an unknown assailant: Clair is smothered and

**has her eyes poked out with a fountain pen; Megan's eyes are gouged
out before the killer bashes her brains in with a hammer; Dana is
attacked with a lead pipe and has her head cleaved with a cultivator;
Eve is found stabbed to death in her car with her eyeballs missing;
Heather is slashed across the windshield of Mrs Mac's car; Mrs Mac
is impaled on a falling icicle; Melissa is smothered; Lauren is stabbed
to death with a glass unicorn (as is Kelli's cheating boyfriend Kyle).
Only Kelli and Clair's visiting big sister Leigh survive to confront the
perpetrators—Agnes and Billy (who was thought to have perished in
a fire a year earlier)—before another fire seemingly takes the lives of
the jaundiced father and his androgynous daughter.**

'You can't just do the same thing because it has been ripped off by other movies,'
Wong said to Dread Central, 'so while you don't have to put an entirely new spin on
it, you have to have something about it not only for the audience of *Black Christmas*
to see and enjoy but others as well...I think this is a good compromise between the
old one and a new take on it. It's not a complete new take but there is new stuff that
is interesting.'

'I wanted to deal with some of the family thematics,' Morgan would comment
in the documentary *What Have You Done? The Remaking of Black Christmas*.
'Edmund Kemper was a serial killer whose mother locked him in the basement
because she was afraid that he was going to attack and rape her. Now he had these
feelings of guilt for feelings that he didn't really have but then he had them so he had
hate and arousal and everything just mixed together down in the basement. So they
just kind of cooked a serial killer. Ultimately, he attacked his mother and ripped
out her larynx...and put her head on a mantle and threw darts at it for three days.
Believe it or not, that's where the Billy thing started.'[1]

Filming on the new *Black Christmas* began at the end of January 2006 in
Vancouver on a $9 million budget. 'It's interesting, because it's sort of both a prequel
and a sequel,' co-star Mary Elizabeth Winstead told Canada.com. 'The first chunk
of the film follows the childhood and back-story of Billy, who's the crazed killer.
And then it picks up with the girls in the sorority house in the present day, and Billy
comes back for a visit. Then there are a lot of twists and disturbing turns, and things
that you wouldn't expect.'

The only returning cast member from the original was Andrea Martin, who now
played the housemother Mrs Mac. 'The premise is all the same,' Martin asserted to
Bloody Disgusting. 'I would say that the special effects probably are much more gory.
And I would say that the attitude of the girls is more sophisticated. I was intrigued to
find out what sorority life would be like 33 years later. I did not know that housemothers
still were a part of the sorority system...Glen has very cleverly given a back story...how

---

1 Known as 'Big Ed' because of his size (6'9", 300 lbs), 24-year-old Edmund Kemper III
garnered a new nickname—'The Co-ed Killer'—when he killed and dismembered six female
hitchhikers in Santa Cruz, California, between May 1972 and February 1973. He then
murdered his mother and one of her friends before turning himself in to the authorities days
later. That November, he was sentenced to life in prison.

[Billy] grew up as a very troubled and abused young boy and how he went to a mental institution...In the original movie you knew nothing except hearsay about the killer.'

EXT. INSANE ASYLUM—NIGHT—(2005)

CAMERA MOVES ALONG a Hellish prison-like institution; high walls encased by rusty razor wire, while snow falls outside.

CAMERA CONTINUES until finding a room, set apart from the others, outlined by a string of coloured Christmas lights.

Inside, a figure, Billy's silhouette, stands in the window.

> **KYLE (CONT'D, O.S.)**
> Last Christmas Eve, Billy used cleaning fluid and a string of Christmas lights decorating his cell...to set himself on fire.

Suddenly, the lights turn off. Inside, the room erupts with violent orange flame. The figure vanishes within the fire...

> **KYLE (CONT'D, O.S.)**
> The fire was so hot, the attendants couldn't open the cell. All that was found of Billy were ashes.

EXT. ASYLUM CEMETERY—NIGHT (2005)

CAMERA TRACKS ACROSS several unmarked gravestones until STOPPING on one.

> **KYLE (CONT'D, O.S.)**
> And, now, that's his home. Where he'll be spending the rest of his Christmases. Alone, in an unmarked grave in the asylum cemetery.

Snow falls gently on Billy's lonely tombstone. After a beat...a form ENTERS and holds over the grave.

—Unfilmed flashback, from the original script

The above passage shows the extent of Billy's present whereabouts in the script. This, however, was drastically changed during shooting to add three new scenes showing him to be alive: outside Billy's cell, an orderly and a guard tell a visitor playing Santa about Billy's tortured past and myriad escape attempts; later on, the guard enters Billy's cell and is impaled with a candy cane; finally, Billy kills Santa and dons his costume to escape.

A number of other changes were made as well, including several scenes that wound up on the cutting room floor:

- In the opening shot, a roving camera looks through the windows of the different sorority sisters.
- The killer sets up a rocking chair at the window in the attic, awaiting the first victim.
- Kelli (Katie Cassidy), Melissa (Michelle Trachtenberg) and Dana (Lacey Chabert) discuss the nuances of cell phone ring tones.
- The girls speculate that Kyle (Oliver Hudson) is the one making the phone calls.
- Later, the girls speculate that Eve (Kathleen Kole) may be the one involved.

Three other scenes ended up being reshot:

- Melissa is suffocated and has her eyes plucked out and eaten by Agnes (Dean Friss); this was changed to a chase that ends with a skate being thrown at her head.
- Agnes enters Lauren's (Crystal Lowe) room, sets down a snow globe that plays 'Dance of the Sugar Plum Fairy', and proceeds to stab Lauren with a glass unicorn. This was changed to Lauren waking after being molested in bed, stabbing the adjacent pillow with the glass unicorn, then being strangled and stabbed by Agnes. (This change proved to be a waste of effort—the entire scene was cut at the last minute to tighten the film's running time.)
- Originally, after Agnes tells Kelli and Leigh (Kristen Cloke) that her daddy is in the house, Kelli's cell phone rings and Billy's (Robert Mann) voice is on the other end. This was changed to having Billy pop up and attack the two women.

Given his predilection for monkeying around with various scenes, it is perhaps not surprising that Morgan could not decide how exactly to end his film. Because of this, he ended up shooting no less than *four* different conclusions:

- The first ending is the same as that in the script, with Leigh at Kelli's bedside in the hospital, opening Clair's Christmas present to her big sister. Kelli's cell phone rings—thinking it to be her parents, she and Leigh are startled when the caller ID reads 'Kyle Autry's cell'. The camera tracks out the window into the snowy night as the phone continues to ring unanswered.
- The second ending has doctors try to save a badly burned Billy but he flatlines in the operating room. Leigh is asked to identify Agnes' body, but when she arrives, she finds Clair's body instead. She rushes back to Kelli's hospital room, where Agnes is waiting and murders Leigh. Kelli returns to her room and is attacked by Agnes. Using a defibrillator, Kelli kills Agnes. The film ends with Kelli's parents taking her home from the hospital.
- The third ending is the same as above, only with Kelli wheeled in to see Billy's dead body. After her parents take Kelli home, a morgue attendant comes for Billy's body but it has disappeared—the camera pans to the smoke detector on the wall, where Billy's eyes peer out.
- The fourth ending sees Billy revive in the morgue and kill the attendant. The action then follows the previous two endings, only now Billy attacks Kelli after she kills Agnes. A chase between the two ensues through the hospital corridors until Billy falls down a staircase and is impaled on a Christmas tree in the hospital atrium. It was this ending that was ultimately chosen for the theatrical release.

Released by M-G-M on Christmas Day as counter-programming to family films like *Charlotte's Web* and *Night at the Museum*, *Black Christmas* was a complete flop; with a cumulative take of just $16 million, the film did not even pay for itself. To make matters worse, *Black Christmas* had virtually zero appeal overseas, where it earned a paltry $5 million.

While its predecessor received a split critical decision, this *Black Christmas* got a unanimous thumbs-down. 'Silly, obvious, clumsy, and just gruesome enough to keep jaded genre fans from angrily throwing popcorn at the screen,' derided *The Boston Globe*. 'It's old-school stupid...a return to horror roots that plays like ineptly filmed nostalgia,' dismissed *Entertainment Weekly*. The *Los Angeles Times* predicted, 'Like an ugly tie or a pair of slipper socks, *Black Christmas* is destined to be forgotten the instant it's unwrapped, gathering dust until the season rolls around again.' The *New York Times* suddenly found the original film inspired by comparison: 'Glen Morgan's disastrous remake not only sidelines the original's hilariously obscene phone calls but also drags its unseen killer, and his psychoses, into the light.' *Variety* wrote the picture off as a 'slapdash, soporifically routine remake, suitable only for the least discriminating of gorehounds,' while *The Washington Post* followed suit: 'A drab, unimaginative remake...[that] neither pays perceptive tribute to the original nor updates it in anything but hackneyed form.'

At 2:30am on the morning of April 4, 2007, Bob Clark and his 22-year-old son were killed when the car they were driving was struck head on by a drunk driver in Pacific Palisades, California. Clark was 67. At the time, he was working on a remake of *Children Shouldn't Play with Dead Things*, having written a new script based on the one he co-wrote with Ormsby over 30 years earlier. He planned to co-produce the picture with Solnicki on a $12 million budget (300 times that of the original) and direct it in British Columbia.

For their part, the Morgan-Wong duo went their separate ways after the *Black Christmas* debacle, with Morgan producing the short-lived 2007 *Bionic Woman* reboot and writing/producing the Cartoon Network series *Tower Prep* in 2010. Wong directed *Dragonball: Evolution* (2009) as well as writing, producing and directing for the TV series *The Event* in 2010-11.

WHEN A STRANGER CALLS

(1979)

I really dislike the cinema of the grotesque where bloody effects and gruesome things are shown to the audience. But I knew I had one shot to make a movie and to try to impress people in this town. My partner and I chose this genre because it's obviously commercial.

—*Fred Walton, co-writer and director*

Once I'd read the script I just wanted to play it very, very badly. I thought, as I read it, it was probably the most frightening, scary thriller of its kind.

—*Tony Beckley, 'Curt Duncan'*

One night in December 1977, Douglas Chapin and Barry Krost, managers of an up-and-coming young star named Richard Gere, decided to go to the Village Theatre in Westwood, California to check out audience response to their client's performance in *Looking for Mr Goodbar*. But no one in attendance was talking about Gere or *Goodbar*—they were all abuzz over the 20-minute short that had preceded the main attraction, which was in a single-week showing in order to qualify for an Oscar in the short subject category. The name of the short was *The Sitter*, starring Lucia Stralser, in a literal adaptation of the same urban legend that had inspired *Black Christmas* three years earlier. Shot in just three days the previous May at a cost of only $25,000, *The Sitter* did not receive Academy recognition, but it definitely got the attention of Chapin and Krost.

The Sitter was the work of 28-year-old writer/director Fred Walton and 30-year-old writer/producer Stephen Feke, who had forged a friendship while attending

Ohio's Denison University. Both young men had come to Hollywood with dreams of hitting the big time but found reality rather more mundane—Walton was answering phones for producer Allan Carr and Feke worked for game show maven Monty Hall on *Let's Make a Deal*.

'We sat around one night trying to put a story together to sell to a television show,' Walton told the *New York Times*. 'We degenerated into telling each other horror stories. Steve told this true story about a babysitter who is getting menacing telephone calls from a man who was actually inside the house. It sent chills up and down my spine. I told Steve, "Let's do it as a short. At least we'll have a showcase for our talent!"'

'I knew that if the short looked like a student film, we were dead,' Walton continued. 'That's why we didn't make it in 16-millimeter [shooting it in 35mm instead]. To raise the money, I sold my grandmother's Tiffany engagement ring [to his parents] for $4,500. Steve's wife was pregnant, but he used his savings and quit his job. His relatives thought I was a bum, a disreputable salesman who had filled him with awful notions of glory and success.'

The $12,000 the two men raised was enough for the film stock, cameraman and actors. But the additional cost of processing the completed film at M-G-M would cost another $13,000. 'I got on the phone and called all our friends,' said Walton. 'I told them they would be investing in our future and that, somehow, sometime, we'd pay them back.' The duo was able to raise an additional $11,000, and Walton was allowed to carry the processed film off the M-G-M lot despite still owing $2,000.

Judging by the audience's reaction in Westwood, it was money well spent: 'After the first 15 minutes, they began getting tense,' Walton told the Associated Press. 'Some relieved their tension by talking back to the screen...The climax brought a big scream. I floated out of the theatre.'

Once Walton came back down to earth, he found Chapin and Krost waiting for him. 'We all got together later on,' Chapin told the *Los Angeles Times*. 'Fred told us the rest of the story, and he and Steve started working on the script of *When a Stranger Calls*. Barry already had a relationship with Melvin Simon...Mel's great—he simply said, "OK, go ahead and do it." There was never any question that Fred wouldn't direct it.'

324

Melvin Simon was the 52-year-old Indiana shopping centre tycoon who had unsuccessfully launched into moviemaking in 1977-78 by putting up the money for a trio of flops—*The Manitou*, *Matilda* and *Somebody Killed Her Husband*. However, he was not dissuaded and had solicited the services of Krost to form The Movie Company, to develop projects specifically for Melvin Simon Productions. *Stranger Calls* would be the first film to come of that arrangement.

March 1971. Seventeen-year-old Jill Johnson arrives at the Mandrakis home to babysit the couple's son and daughter, both getting over colds and asleep upstairs. Shortly after the Mandrakises leave for the evening, Jill begins receiving phone calls from a stranger who asks only, 'Have you checked the children?' As the night wears on, Jill's nerves begin to wear thin. She calls the police, who are of little help until they are able to trace the calls, which are actually coming from inside the house. Jill manages to escape in time, but the police make the grisly discovery that the children have been brutally murdered by a deranged English sailor named Curt Duncan, who was using an old phone in the children's bedroom to make the calls. Duncan is apprehended and tried for murder, but is found to be insane and confined to an asylum. Seven years later, Duncan escapes and John Clifford, formerly a detective on the case but now a private investigator, is hired by Dr Mandrakis to kill the runaway lunatic. Duncan makes his way back to the city, where he tries to form a relationship with an ageing barfly named Tracy Fuller, but she rebuffs his advances. Hot on Duncan's trail, Clifford uses Tracy to trap the errant sailor, but Duncan manages to escape Clifford once again. Unfortunately, Clifford's pursuit has pushed Duncan back into his psychosis and when he chances upon a newspaper article about the charity work of Jill Johnson—now Jill Lockhart—he decides to pick up where he left off seven years ago. Jill and her husband John are out for dinner, having left their two children at home with a babysitter, when Jill gets a call at the restaurant, asking her in a familiar voice, 'Have you checked the children?' In hysterics, Jill calls home and finds that the children are fine and nothing abnormal has happened. Later that night, after checking on her children, Jill returns to bed to find that Duncan has assaulted her husband and is after her. Just as he is about to choke Jill to death, two shots ring out, finally putting an end to Curt Duncan's madness—Clifford has got his man.

Appropriately, the first two roles cast were of Jill Johnson and Curt Duncan and they would be played by Krost clients. Carol Kane, then 26, had made her mark in *Carnal Knowledge* (1971), *Dog Day Afternoon* (1975) and *Annie Hall* (1977) and been nominated for an Oscar for her performance in Joan Micklin Silver's *Hester Street* (1975). 'We've been hearing over and over again how this story reminds someone of something which really happened,' the actress told the *Chicago Daily*

Herald. 'There could be a man like that. The movie is a straight-out thriller. But I think it's also a study almost of a personality which is capable of committing a terrible crime.'

The personality in question would be played by Tony Beckley, 49, known mainly for his work on British TV, although he had co-starred with Michael Caine in *The Italian Job* (1969) and *Get Carter* (1971) and had just enjoyed a high-profile role in the hit comedy *Revenge of the Pink Panther* (1978). 'I thought that there ought to be a lot of sympathy going for [Duncan] in spite of the terrible things that he'd done,' Beckley remarked to the *New York Times*. 'I felt there were opportunities for one or two kinds of bravura work in it.'[2]

Veteran character actor Charles Durning (*The Choirboys, The Sting*) was cast as John Clifford and he in turn recommended his friend, stage siren Colleen Dewhurst, for the role of Tracy Fuller. Shooting began in Los Angeles on October 9, 1978, lasting just 18 days.

INT. ANOTHER ROOM - NIGHT

Dark. A little BOY is lying in bed, apparently asleep. This is Curt Duncan as a child.

Some voices approach in the hallway outside the bedroom. They are gruff, with heavy English accents, but subdued; a MAN and a WOMAN, well into middle-age.

The boy's eyes open as he listens:

MAN (O.S.)
What's the matter?

WOMAN (O.S.)
Save it for later. Let's go out and get some food.

MAN (O.S.)
What about the lad? You can't leave him.

---

2 Tony Beckley was, in fact, terminally ill during the shoot and died of cancer at the age of 52 in April 1980.

WOMAN (O.S.)
Curt's asleep. He'll never know we're gone.

From outside, a key enters the lock of the bedroom door and turns. The bolt slips and the door is securely shut.

The boy sits up in bed, apprehensive. In TIGHT SHOTS of the floor we see a rat come out from under the bed, then another. They make 'chit-chit' noises as they begin to explore. One of them maybe goes up on its hind legs and nibbles on the bedpost. Then we see two more rats appear.

We go for a TIGHT SHOT of the boy on top of the bed. The 'chit-chit' noises grow steadily louder as the boy's apprehension turns to fear, then to terror. The boy starts to whimper.

Suddenly, we cut back to a WIDE SHOT of the room. The floor is crawling with rats, hundreds of them. The 'chit-chit' rises to practically a roar as the boy, alone on top of the bed, begins to wail.

The room seems to darken, and the boy becomes just a little white speck in it. The focus is turned. The picture becomes a black and white blur.

—Unfilmed flashback, from the original script

With such a quick schedule, several of the scripted scenes had to be shortened or eliminated:

- There was originally a much longer exchange between Jill and her friend Nancy on the phone about their mutual crush, Billy.
- In Clifford's meeting with Dr Mandrakis, the mourning father was meant to tell the detective that his wife is unable to have any more children. After Clifford leaves, we were meant to see Mrs Mandrakis, now 'a brooding, barren woman.'
- There was originally a much longer exchange between Clifford and Dr Monk (a man in the script, changed to a woman in the film) at the asylum regarding Duncan's condition, particularly his Tourette's syndrome (incorrectly labelled after Guy du Marraux in the script, it was actually named after French physician Georges Gilles de la Tourette).
- A flashback to Duncan's arrival in California on a merchant ship was dropped.
- Clifford's pursuit of Duncan at the rescue mission was originally to have played out through the adjoining church and all the way to the top of a bell tower, where Duncan escapes by sliding down a rope (ringing the bells in the process) and then jumping to the stone floor below. This was replaced by a simple chase through the mission and into the alleyway out back.

- Clifford and Tracy were meant to have a final exchange where he promises to take her out for ice cream some time.
- After losing Duncan, Clifford was to go to the Mandrakis house to warn them that Duncan may come after them. They are on vacation and only the houseboy is in residence.
- Relaxing in bed, John Lockhart was to have speculated that Jill might have suffered 'hysterical recall' and imagined the phone call in the restaurant.

'We brought it in for $1.5 million,' Walton claimed to the *Los Angeles Times*. 'Without as professional a cast and crew as we had for our first time we could never had done it. And when the audience screams when it's supposed to, nobody can ever take that away from you.'

The film was picked up for distribution by Columbia Pictures, whose head of advertising and publicity, Irving Ivers, told the *New York Times*, 'When we first saw *When a Stranger Calls*, we knew that there were at least two moments in it that were among the most terrifying ever experienced—and director Fred Walton was able to achieve them without resorting to gore and violence. We quickly came to realise that it was in the genre of *Psycho* rather than an exploitation-type movie.'

'The telephone is the instrument of terror,' Ivers continued, 'so we tried to think of a campaign that would play to that. We felt it was sufficiently suggestive to get people into the theatre. I'd bet that you could now run the visual without the title and most people would recognise the name of the movie or, at least, what it's about. We found the common denominator, the one element that's synonymous with the film. We've established its identity.'

After being test-marketed in four cities (Albuquerque, Indianapolis, Providence and San Antonio) in early September 1979, when it earned nearly $250,000, *Stranger Calls* went into general release a month later and grossed over $21 million.

Walton's film was equally popular with the critics. Tom Allen declared *Stranger Calls* 'The big one of the year for scare buffs...Walton is a rare craftsman who can evoke the best genre moments without playing the film school game of quoting passages from favourite cult movies. He is neither classicist nor virtuoso. He adds only twists to sure-fire shock techniques, and he lets dominating actors find an emotional hook for each scene.' Gary Arnold observed that 'Walton...seems more skilful at orchestrating creepy atmosphere than John Carpenter was in *Halloween*.' Janet Maslin lauded *Stranger* as 'an energetic first film; if Mr Walton hasn't yet learned his lessons well, he's certainly chosen the right teachers,' while Kevin Thomas praised the picture as 'a thoroughly scary thriller in the classic mould...Not since *Carrie* has there been such a shriek-inducing climax; this modest but high-style Columbia release could very well turn out to be the sleeper of the year.' *Variety* singled out the film for 'a fine cast, a rich and atmospheric score by Dana Kaproff, and astute direction.'

Despite such a blockbuster debut, Walton did not direct again until 1985, when he helmed the pilot for the revived *Alfred Hitchcock Presents* series. He then returned to theatrical features with *April Fool's Day* (1986) and *The Rosary Murders* (1987) before spending the next ten years exclusively directing movies for TV, including *I Saw What You Did* (1988), *The Price She Paid* (1992) and his last credit, *The Stepford Husbands* (1996). Feke went on to write and direct two features—*Papa Was a Preacher* (1985) and *Keys to Freedom* (1988)—before becoming a writer/producer for TV shows like the 1990 revival of *Dark Shadows*, along with *Beastmaster, Missing Persons, Profiler, Sins of the City* and the 2005 reboot of *Kojak* with Ving Rhames.

In October 1992, Durning, Kane and Walton reunited for the made-for-cable sequel *When a Stranger Calls Back*, shot in Vancouver and aired on Showtime in April 1993. Jill Johnson (*sans* family) is now the director of a women's crisis centre at a Pacific Northwestern university. She comes to the aid of a young coed named Julia Jenz (Jill Schoelen), who is being stalked by the same maniac who kidnapped the two children she was babysitting five years before. Jill calls Clifford in on the case and the two try in vain to protect Julia, who winds up in the hospital after an attack from the deranged performance artist William Landis (Gene Lythgow). With Julia in critical condition, Landis shifts his designs to would-be protector Jill.

(2006)

The type of films of this nature that appeal to me the most are the ones that have the most suspense in them. To me, it's always about walking down the corridor and what is going to jump out. As soon as it jumps out, to me, it's less scary. Once you know what you're dealing with it's only a question of are you going to survive once the monster jumps out? The bit I enjoy, and I enjoy watching the audience cringing and holding onto the side of their seats, is the bit before the monster jumps out. I'm more interested in the suspense than the payoff.

—Simon West, director

They were telling me about this script...and I was kind of sceptical about doing it...I was like, 'That sounds like a horror movie, I don't think I want to do it.' Until I sat down with Simon and he told me, 'This is the type of film I want to make. I want to make it like *Wait Until Dark*, really classy, not blood and guts everywhere. It's going to be just a really psychological thriller.'

—Camilla Belle, 'Jill Johnson'

In December 2003, before he vacated his post at Sony Pictures in Hollywood, retiring company co-president Ken Lemberger stopped by the office of newly-appointed chairman Amy Pascal. 'I asked...if she would mind my going through the library of features as well as the abandoned properties file to look for material to re-adapt. I was looking for films which weren't overwhelmingly successful commercially and

WHEN A STRANGER CALLS

literally, the first picture that attracted my attention was *When a Stranger Calls*. I remembered...that it was probably the scariest twenty-minute beginning of a film I had ever seen.'

Lemberger took the idea to Clint Culpepper, president of Screen Gems. Once Columbia Pictures' television division (responsible for such shows as *Bewitched, I Dream of Jeannie* and *The Partridge Family*), it had been revived in 1999 to serve as Sony's B-movie subsidiary, producing such films as the successful *Resident Evil* and *Underworld* series. Culpepper and Lemberger agreed that any new version of *Stranger Calls* should concentrate on the original's opening sequence, expanding it to feature length.

To accomplish this, they hired screenwriter Jake Wade Wall, an NYU grad who had created a stir when his spec serial-killer script *Next Door* was picked up by Lionsgate. This in turn had led to him being commissioned to write *Halloween: The Missing Years* for Moustapha Akkad. Both projects ended up in turnaround, but a fortuitous housesitting appointment would land Wall his first screen credit, as he told Bloody Disgusting: 'I was on my way to housesit for my sister in Nevada when I got the call for the *Stranger* script and the timing couldn't have been more perfect. There I was, in this big, empty four-story house where even the most mundane noise, like the refrigerator turning on and off could startle you, and I started playing with that idea, of being in unfamiliar territory and the fear that invokes, which wasn't fully explored in the original film.'

In August 2004, it was formally announced that Screen Gems was going to remake *When a Stranger Calls*. Lemberger would produce alongside John Davis, who had served in the same capacity on the *Predator* films as well as such diverse titles as *Doctor Dolittle, The Firm, Garfield* and *Waterworld*. 'We agreed to make the film more of a psychological thriller than the original,' Davis remarked. 'Terror lies with what you don't see versus what you do. Having a young girl trapped in a

house being stalked is a really relatable, scary notion. We all know babysitters or we've all baby-sat, and what makes this movie scary is that it could happen to any of us. One of our worst nightmares is having a family member being put into jeopardy like this.'

In April 2005, it was announced that Simon West (*Con Air, The General's Daughter*) had agreed to direct the film. 'I didn't know if I could make it work,' he admitted to *Fears* magazine, 'and it certainly isn't like the other films I'd done. It is so contained, taking place all in one house, and with almost only one actor. That appealed to me...The idea of trying to think up different ways the house could be scary also appealed to me.'

The one actor turned out to be 19-year-old Camilla Belle, first seen in *The Lost World* (1997) and *The Patriot* (1998), who had just won raves for her starring role in *The Ballad of Jack and Rose* (2005). 'There's really no script that a female character so young is able to play and to carry a film,' she told Horror.com. 'There's really no roles like that around; it's very rare. So I wanted to take on that opportunity and see if I could pull it off.'

Fernhill, Colorado. High schooler Jill Johnson is breaking up with her cheating boyfriend and has gone over her cell phone limit by 800 minutes. Her parents demand that she pay it back, so she accepts a job babysitting rather than attend her school's pep rally. Her father takes her to the beautiful lakeside home of Dr and Mrs Mandrakis, which is almost totally isolated in the woods. Not long after the couple leave, Jill begins receiving mysterious phone calls from a man who seems to be observing her every move, especially when she heeds his advice to 'check the children.' The stranger at first toys with

Jill—leading her through the darkened house, forcing her outside to check the guest house—but things get deadly serious when she finds the housekeeper's dead body in the bathroom and the police, who have traced the calls, inform the teenager that they are coming from inside the house. Jill races to awaken the sleeping children, only to find that they have been locked in the house's atrium, which is actually an arboretum and koi pond. Once inside the atrium, Jill and the children are trapped by the stalker, who allows the children to escape but focuses his murderous intentions on Jill. The young lady gamely battles back and manages to flee the house into the waiting arms of the police. They apprehend the madman, but Jill's nightmares in the hospital prove that the long night of terror will not soon be forgotten.

Filming began on July 25 in Running Springs and Signal Hill, California, on a $15 million budget, much of which went towards the construction of the Mandrakises' ultra-modern lakeside home. 'From the very beginning I decided I wanted to build the house,' West remembered. 'I wanted to get away from the traditional gothic, scary, old creaky wooden house that you've seen a million times over. But I wanted to keep it dark so I had to go with an architectural style that had a lot of dark woods, and I wanted a lot of glass because I wanted it to be like she was in a fish bowl, which is even more uncomfortable. Then a modern house gives you the chance to have some unusual things in there. Like you can have an atrium, with a fishpond, that is in the middle of the house. You don't usually see that in traditional houses. It gives me a chance for another type of room that is very unusual. If you're stuck in a house for an entire film you want to have things as varied as possible in the rooms. So

we have an atrium and we decided to put birds in it to make it alive, and I guess it was my Hitchcock reference, because they are kind of disturbing and make you uneasy, especially the sound they make.'

'I wanted to have an intelligent lead who was constantly trying to persuade herself that this stuff wasn't happening,' West continued, 'that there is going to be a rational explanation for this. But, when it is bad, she just doesn't go to pieces. She pulls herself together to think and fight her way out of it. It is a strong female role model, and if you're up against it, you fight like mad. I didn't want to make a film where in the first five minutes something scares her and she screams, and then she just keeps screaming until the very end of the film, and it's all on one level.'

'Every day I went home emotionally and physically drained,' Belle admitted. 'I looked forward to every weekend just to sleep and kind of relax my mind and my body a little bit. It was exhausting...but it was a good experience.' Not only was the film essentially a one-woman show for much of the time, but Belle served as her own stuntwoman as well. 'I did all that myself, which was so much fun. And I've never gotten so many welts and bruises in my life. It hurt a lot and I definitely got more bruises than Tommy [Flanagan, who plays the Stranger] because he was kinda slow in pushing me around but we had a really good time. I wore the bruises with pride.'

By Wall's admission, West went ahead and made several changes to his script, of which the writer generally approved:

- The title sequence, in which the Stranger stalks a babysitter, did not originally take place during a carnival.

334

- Wall wrote the house to have the fancy atrium/arboretum but not the California modern, Frank Lloyd Wright-style it ended up having.
- There were no cutaways to Jill's friends at the school.
- Jill was to find Rosa's body in the bathroom upstairs, not that of her friend Tiffany, who had earlier come to visit her.
- Jill was to find the kids locked in the atrium, not hiding in the toy chest in their room.
- There was not the run of false scares involving the Mandrakises' black cat.
- Jill does not find Rosa's dead body in the koi pond.
- The final pursuit of Jill by the Stranger was written to be much longer and more involved.

Tiffany's (Katie Cassidy) outdoor death scene was added in post-production, while two scenes were deleted, one showing Officer Burroughs (David Denman) at the police station overhearing about the murders that were shown in the title sequence and the other a montage of Jill's classmates dancing at the bonfire while she receives phone calls.

Much work was done in post-production to heighten the tension, as West himself outlined: 'We ended up changing the music to make it much more suspenseful, even though [Jill] isn't scared in the slightest. We're actually playing the score for the audience, because they know that something horrible is going to happen. The audience has seen the first five-minutes of the film that she didn't. That happened quite a few times in the film where we...reworked the music to really squeeze every drop of suspense and fear out of a scene. Basically it's the same with the sound effects. All the sound effects were done two or three different ways because if something was too loud it wasn't ambiguous. You need some of the sounds to be ambiguous because that's what most frightening about these houses. Was that a branch scratching at a window or someone opening it?'

The decision was taken to make this a PG-13 thriller and not a gory horror film, which suited Belle just fine: 'Simon and I always go, "It's a psychological thriller." We don't call it a horror film...It's not in-your-face scary, [you] use your mind... [which] can make it a lot scarier than what we presented to you on film, so that's what's fun about it.' West concurred: 'In some ways I took it as an advantage. Nobody could rely on blood and gore, and it kept it psychological...Morally, it felt better because it's good old-fashioned scares instead of trying to be more and more gory. That eventually becomes a dead-end, sooner or later you're making something that is so offensive that it's no longer fun to work on, let alone watch.'

'The thing is that it's a situation that everyone has been in,' said West. 'Everyone has experienced being in a house at night and been spooked by weird noises and shadows. You could tap into people's real experiences. So there was a strict set of rules for us because it's all real world, no hocus pocus, no supernatural element.'

Released on February 3, 2006, *When a Stranger Calls* enjoyed a $21.6 million opening, ranking #1 for the weekend. Its total US gross was $47.8 million, with an additional overseas gross of $19.1 million. Critics, however, collectively hung up on this *Stranger*. 'Even by the lowest standards, this is a frightless, cynically made movie,' derided *The Boston Globe*. 'Pulpy director Simon West appears much more excited about the Zen-ish architecture of the house...than about creating a useful sense of anxiety,' observed *Entertainment Weekly*. 'This leaves young Belle to wander rooms aimlessly, and for the musicians and Foley artists to work feverishly pretending there's reason for suspense.' Commenting on the film's setting, the *Los Angeles Times* noted, 'Nothing in this droopy remake...could possibly be as frightening as the Windex bill for those two-story, picture windows, not to mention the ones that surround the indoor arboretum and fish pond.' The *New York Times* found the film to be 'not quite suspense-free, but almost. When finding a dead body underwater isn't scary, something is very wrong.' And *The Washington Post* branded Simon West 'a reliable purveyor of Hollywood's dreckiest dreck.'

That June, Fred Walton and Stephen Feke filed a multi-million dollar lawsuit against Sony over allegedly being cut out of the development and profit participation in the studio's remake of their film. This did not prevent yet another Sony subsidiary, Stage 6 Films, from picking up the distribution rights to the 2007 remake of Walton's *April Fool's Day*—another project on which he was not involved.

PROM NIGHT

A NIGHT TO DIE FOR

IN THEATERS THIS SPRING

TAX SHELTER TERRORS

PROM NIGHT

(1980)

It's an axe-in-the-face picture. I did *Prom Night* because I was washed up in the industry...One does *Prom Night* to survive.

—Paul Lynch, director

I had only made two movies up to that time, they offered me three times the money I was paid on *The Fog*, and it was the first role that was actually offered to me; I didn't even have to read for it.

—Jamie Lee Curtis, 'Kim Hammond'

In 1968, the Canadian government implemented the Canadian Film Development Corporation (CFDC) to create a legitimate feature film industry. However, within three years, the CFDC had exhausted its initial budget of $10 million. Given another $10 million in 1971, the CFDC changed its primary focus to assist films it thought could generate revenue and put money back into the system. Added incentive came in 1974 with the Capital Cost Allowance (CCA), which created a tax shelter for film investors, enabling them to deduct 100% of their investment from their taxable income in features certified as Canadian, and thus defer taxes until profits were earned.[1]

Between 1975 and 1982, some 345 features, known as 'tax shelter films', were made. One of the most popular genres under the tax shelter laws was horror films, particularly those of David Cronenberg: *They Came from Within* (aka *Shivers*, 1975), *Rabid* (1977), *The Brood* (1979), *Scanners* (1981) and *Videodrome* (1982). Others hopped aboard, producing such titles as *The Haunting of Julia, The Uncanny* (both 1977), *The Changeling, Death Ship, Funeral Home, Terror Train* (all 1980), *Happy Birthday to Me* (1981) and *Visiting Hours* (1982).

Unfortunately, the legislation which gave birth to the film boom was ripe for

---

1 To be eligible, films had to be at least 75 minutes long, have a producer and two-thirds of the creative personnel who were Canadian, and have at least 75% of the technical services performed in Canada.

abuse. Some investors contributed large amounts of money for film budgets only on paper, allowing just a small portion to be used for actual production. Others wrote off large sums of money for movies which they had no intention of ever releasing. Badly skewed and bloated on expensive, star-heavy flops like *City on Fire* (1979) and *Bear Island* (1980), the party came to an end in 1982 when, persuaded by the discovery that many of the feature films produced in Canada were never actually released, the tax allowance was cut in half.

The year 1979-1980 would prove to be the peak of the boom, with 66 feature films produced at a combined investment of $172 million. Two of the biggest successes were the Bill Murray comedy *Meatballs*, which grossed over $40 million, and what would be Canada's most profitable non-Cronenberg horror movie, *Prom Night*.

It started simply enough: Peter Simpson, the head of Canadian distributor Simcom, was approached by director Paul Lynch with a rather straightforward

Prom Night (1980)

pitch: 'Paul brought me a piece of art,' he told the website The Terror Trap, 'it was a knife in a heart with blood dripping out...And it said *Prom Night*. For Paul, that was thinking it through!' Lynch was a 33-year-old Englishman who had moved to Canada in 1960. After serving as a cartoonist for the *Toronto Star* and then a

340

photographer for a number of small-town newspapers, he began working in film, including a 90-minute documentary on *Penthouse* magazine commissioned by its publisher Bob Guccione.

The editor on Lynch's first feature, *The Hard Part Begins* (1973), was William Gray, the *Toronto Sun*'s first rock music critic. He would later serve as one of three writers on Lynch's *Blood and Guts* (1978). He then wrote a script that never got made but did get him an agent and a commission to co-write the George C Scott ghost story *The Changeling* (shot in late 1978-early 1979 but not released until 1980), with actress Diana Maddox, who was co-producer Joel Michaels' wife. The two ended up sharing a Genie award for Best Screenplay. *Prom Night* and a reunion with Lynch came next, following a story outline provided by Simpson's jogging partner Robert Guza, Jr. 'To do horror you have to be a craftsman, not an artist,' Gray told the *Montreal Gazette*. 'I'm not an artist. I'm the kind of guy who writes what people suggest. I'm a hired writer. I have my own scripts, but they haven't been made yet. There's no place out there for a nice little movie.'

April 1973. A group of grade-schoolers are playing a macabre game called 'Murder' in an under-construction apartment building when one of the kids, Robin Hammond, is accidentally decapitated by a sheet of glass. The other children—Nick, Wendy, Jude and Kelly— leave the scene and vow never to tell anyone about what really happened. Seven years later, Robin's older sister Kim is preparing for the Junior-Senior Prom, where she and Nick—now her boyfriend— have been voted King and Queen. Meanwhile, Wendy, Kelly and Jude receive threatening phone calls, vowing revenge for Robin's death. That night, all three girls are brutally murdered by a killer in a black ski mask. But when the killer makes his play for Nick during the coronation, he gets tripped up by a live electrical wire and an axe wielded by Kim. Trying to make an escape, the killer runs right into a police dragnet; before the police can shoot, Kim—having recognised the eyes behind the mask—rushes to his side. He is revealed to be Alex Hammond—Kim and Robin's brother—who secretly witnessed what really happened seven years ago. Adopting his dead sister's stutter, hairstyle and even make-up, Alex has crossed the line into total madness, while Kim and her parents (the high school principal and his traumatised wife) can only look on in shock and disbelief.

On a budget of roughly $1.5 million, filming began in Toronto on August 7, 1979, and lasted five weeks. In a role originally intended for Eve Plumb (Jan in TV's *The Brady Bunch*), Jamie Lee Curtis was cast as Kim Hammond. 'I never thought that Jamie Lee was quite right for that part,' Simpson confessed, 'because when you meet her, she's anything but innocent. We were looking for the ultimate virgin...the ultimate victim. Jamie Lee comes into the office and puts her feet on your desk. It's hard to think of her as this little innocent.'

Simpson did come to appreciate Curtis's work ethic, however: 'Jamie Lee was a team player and still very enthusiastic about the business. She came to the set on her days off. That spoke more to her social life than it did to her enthusiasm for the film but she was certainly a team player.' Just two months after shooting *Prom Night*, Curtis would star in her second Canadian horror picture, *Train to Terror* (released as *Terror Train*).

INT. CORRIDOR--DAY

Hammond leans against the wall outside Fairchild's office. He glances at his watch. The door opens and Fairchild steps out, holding a container. Hammond walks with him down the corridor towards the water fountain.

                    HAMMOND
She's at it again.

                    FAIRCHILD
                     (NODS)
Today's the date?

                    HAMMOND
Seven years ago today Robin was killed.

Fairchild looks up from filling his container with water.

                    HAMMOND
               (CONTINUING; MUSING)
This would have been her first prom.

                    FAIRCHILD
Pardon?

                    HAMMOND
Tonight's the Junior-Senior Prom at our high school. Robin would have been sixteen. She and Alex.

                    FAIRCHILD
The twins...How is Alex?

                    HAMMOND
Fine. I just thank God he was too young to really understand what happened to his sister.

                    FAIRCHILD
And your older daughter?

HAMMOND
(SMILES)
Kimmy's my princess. Sometimes she'll get depressed for a while...
but it never lasts long. Young people seem so much more...resilient.

They walk back to the office.

FAIRCHILD
(LOOKING UP AT HAMMOND)
And yourself? No scars?

HAMMOND
(AFTER A PAUSE)
I've learned to live with them...Vivian seems worse this time.

FAIRCHILD
(NODS)
The persistence of Vivian's trauma...I wonder if there isn't something more serious at work here?

HAMMOND
Something more serious than her daughter's death?

—Scripted exchange, shot but deleted from the final cut

'If you directed a film for Pete Simpson, you had a very good chance of getting fired before the film was finished,' *Prom Night*'s composer Paul Zaza told The Terror Trap. 'He almost *never* got along with any director he hired.' According to Simpson, this film was no different: 'We recognised that the story didn't have enough red herrings and it didn't have a subplot. So we had to manufacture one. Lynch was involved in the first re-shoot but by the second, he had used up his patience in the project.'

To say that *Prom Night* was drastically altered in post-production would be an understatement. The subplot that Simpson added was to have an escaped lunatic named Leonard Murch (played by stuntman Terry Martin) be the prime suspect for

the murders. Murch was a known sex offender and a suspect in Robin Hammond's murder, but when fleeing the police, he got into a car crash and was severely burned. In the years since Robin's murder, Murch has been in an institution, but Lieutenant McBride (George Touliatos) is informed of his escape. What follows is a number of interludes with McBride first meeting with Murch's former psychiatrist Dr Fairchild (David Gardner), the two men finding the dead body of Murch's nurse at the scene of Robin's death, and then McBride canvassing the high school with his deputies waiting for Murch to show up.

Curtis, for one, thought this all sounded rather familiar and was not best pleased, as she told *Fangoria*: 'All that psychopathic killer stuff was not in the original script, not in the script I agreed to do. They added that after they cut the movie. I'm very angry about that, and I'll always be angry about that because I feel I wouldn't have made the movie had it been a remake of *Halloween*—which is exactly what they were trying to do.'

Two others who were less than happy with the changes were top-billed Leslie Nielsen (before *Airplane* gave him a whole new career in comedy) and Antoinette Bower, who found themselves relegated to little more than cameos as Raymond and Vivian Hammond. Gray and Lynch had in fact taken care to include several scenes showing how Robin's death greatly affected her parents and their marriage...

345

- At breakfast on the morning of the prom, Raymond tells Vivian that he's made an appointment with their psychiatrist, Dr Fairchild, since it's the seven-year anniversary of Robin's death.
- She protests that the visits are of no use.
- On the way up to see Fairchild, Vivian is taking Valium. The cleaning lady asks if she can have one.
- Kim comes home from school to find her father chopping wood. Raymond asks her to talk to Vivian about going with him to the prom. When she does, Vivian mistakes Kim for Robin.
- Vivian is mortified when Raymond jokes that her pantsuit is like his tuxedo. What follows is a heated exchange about him treating her like a child.

Because of the newly-added Murch subplot, however, these and several other scenes were scrapped:

- Elizabeth Mason (under the pseudonym Liz Stalker-Mason), as Raymond's new secretary Adele Cooper, originally had five scenes—one with Raymond, two with Kim and two as McBride's date at the prom. In the final cut, she is barely seen at all.
- There was originally much more interaction between Slick (Sheldon Rybowski) and Jude (Joy Thompson) before their prom date. After he introduces himself, Jude was supposed to check out Slick's van—complete with stereo cassette deck, waterbed, and a history book full of joints. Slick confesses that he's just 16 but his date for the prom is sick, so he and Jude agree to go together. Later, in the biology lab, Kim, Jude and Vicki (Pita Oliver) are entertained by Slick's impersonation of their boring instructor, Mr Weller (David Bolt). Kim then gets caught passing a note and is made to read it in front of the class. All three girls are given detention.
- Most of the scene of the girls at the tennis courts was deleted, including a stoned Jude erratically hitting the ball to Vicki and the girls telling their PE instructor Miss Benton (Melanie Morse MacQuarrie)—who has it in for Mr Weller—that he has a crush on Kim. Since Benton is in charge of prom preparations, she decides to forcibly enlist Weller's help.
- Nick (Casey Stevens) and Kim were originally seen looking for her parents but finding Slick's rocking van instead.
- After abandoning Kelly (Mary Beth Rubens) because she refuses to have sex with him, Drew (Jeff Wincott) was originally seen searching for her later on, hoping to make amends.
- When Kim takes off Alex's (Michael Tough) mask, their parents were supposed to react with shock before Vivian lunges forward, thinking her son to be her dead daughter. Raymond then has to restrain his hysterical wife. In the final cut, the parents are not seen again after Raymond dances with Kim.

Mixing the plots of *Halloween* and *Carrie* (vindictive, lustful teens plan to publicly humiliate the virgin Prom Queen at the dance) was not enough for Simpson—he decided to throw *Saturday Night Fever* into the mix as well. Not just by having Curtis and Stevens recreate John Travolta's show-stopping dance solo, but also in generating a soundtrack that was all Top-40 disco hits. That is, until he saw the bill. '[Simpson] had one of his minions go to the store,' recalled Zaza. 'And he bought a dozen of the biggest disco hits at the time...and he puts these songs right in the movie itself. Paul Lynch actually shot those sequences to those hit records...And in Peter's unique style, he said, "Well, we've got these songs and this will be great, because these are big hits and will make the movie more successful." So he had his legal people go buy the rights, and as soon as they got on the phone with the record labels...the usage people wanted something like $300,000, which was a third of the movie's budget. And then of course, the more calls they made, the more the cash register was ringing up a higher number. When he realised how much money it was going to cost to buy these tunes, he freaked and said, "This is insane!"'

'Peter turned to me and says, "Well? Whatta you got? You've got to fix this." I asked him what he meant and he said, "We can't afford these songs. You've got to come up with knock-offs. Come up with stuff that sounds exactly like them." I told him we were mixing the film the following week and he says, "That's right." I said he had at least a half a dozen songs in there and he goes, "That's right." I told him, "So you're giving me five days to come up with six original tunes that sound exactly like these...and fit the same tempo?" He said, "That's right...what are you still doing here?"'

'I went home and I examined closely all these tunes and I thought, these songs have some very distinct sounds. I requested another meeting with [Simpson], and I went in and said, "How close do you want me to come to these things?" He said, "I want you to come close enough that we get sued—but not close enough that they'll win."'

Released on July 18, 1980, *Prom Night* found a surprising number of admittedly qualified endorsements: 'Sloppily edited and paved with plot holes, it's junk alright, but it is also *fun*, in much the same way that stupid movies like *I Was a Teenage Werewolf* were fun for moviegoers' (*Cinefantastique*); 'An efficient rather than stylish Canadian-made horror picture that mercifully lets you complete its grislier moments in your imagination. Even so, its various jolts should be sufficient to satisfy scare-show fans' (Kevin Thomas); 'Borrowing shamelessly from *Carrie* and any number of gruesome exploitationers in past history, pic manages to score a few horrific points amid a number of sagging moments. It also produces some deliciously ridiculous situations that will entice fans of this genre and consequently ensure some nice initial box office action' (*Variety*); '*Prom Night* also brings a new dimension to the 'kill the teenagers' theme...because William Gray has given *Prom*'s script something resembling a plot and director Paul Lynch has infiltrated his cast with people who can act' (*Washington Post*).

There were, however, just as many critics who were unwilling to cut Lynch's effort any slack, including Tom Allen ('*Prom Night* has got to be the sorriest rip-off of the year'), *The Boston Globe* ('When the situations are as ridiculous as those presented in this slice and dice exploiter, people begin to laugh. And *Prom Night* is laughable'), Vincent Canby ('More often than not the camera cuts away, or the screen goes discreetly gray, before the audience is drenched in gore. This may or may not be the reason that the audience with which I saw the film yesterday booed

Prom Night (2008)

at the end') and Gene Siskel ('Curtis, who appears to be about 30 years old, has been cast as a high school student in the film, and that's ridiculous. The picture would have been just as ineffective and a lot more credible if it had been set in a college rather than a high school').

The film grossed nearly $15 million and was nominated for two Genie Awards, including Best Performance by a Foreign Actress (Curtis) and Best Film Editing (Brian Ravok). *Prom Night* was quickly sold for $1.5 million to network television, bypassing cable TV and premiering on NBC-TV in February 1981, barely six months after its theatrical engagements. Simpson decided a franchise was in order, and produced three unrelated sequels--*Hello Mary Lou: Prom Night II* (1987), *Prom Night III: The Last Kiss* (which he also directed, 1990), and *Prom Night IV: Deliver Us from Evil* (1992)—before dying of lung cancer in June 2007 at the age of 63.

Gray and Lynch continued their collaboration on *Humongous* (1982) and *Cross Country* (1983), as well as the revived *Dark Shadows* and *RoboCop* TV series in the 90s, both of which had Gray as a story editor. Lynch has in fact directed extensively for horror/sci-fi television over the past 30 years, including such shows as *Darkroom, F/X, Poltergeist: The Legacy, Star Trek: Deep Space Nine, Star Trek: The Next Generation* and the '80s version of *The Twilight Zone*.

(2008)

This is a coming-of-age, right-of-passage study of teen lives. There is something thematically correct about this night in the youth of America. For a lot of people prom night is a very bittersweet time because it is the last chance you have to be a kid. Right around the corner you are going to enter the work force or join the army or go off to college. So associated with that night is a sense of the unknown and a lot of fear—it is the final night of living in a safe world and a lot of people will never see each other again after the last dance.

—Nelson McCormick, director

One of the first things they asked me when I went out for this part was, 'How was your prom?' I told them I never went to prom, because I was working on [the TV series] *American Dreams* at the time and was working the day of my prom. But I went to prom on *American Dreams* and worked on *Prom Night* for three months, so I pretty much fulfilled my prom wishes by being in a prom dress for three months.

—Brittany Snow, 'Donna Keppel'

In October 2004, it was announced that Neal Moritz's Original Film (*The Fast and the Furious, xXx*) was developing a remake of *Prom Night* for Screen Gems. The project had actually been brought to Original by Marc Forby, the head of Trailblazer Films, and producer of such titles as *Devil in the Flesh* (1998) and *29 Palms* (2002). The film was to be a co-production with Newmarket Films (*Donnie Darko, Monster*) with shooting slated to begin early in 2005. It was also announced that *The Grudge* scribe Stephen Susco had been engaged to write the script.

Nothing more was heard about the project until over two years later, when Screen Gems announced a tentative February 2008 release date for the remake, which had now gone through two scripts (one by Susco and another by *Better Luck Tomorrow*'s Ernesto Foronda) and was currently being completely rewritten by J S (Joseph Stephen) Cardone, best known as the one-man band behind the cult 1982 slasher film *The Slayer*. 'The studio really wanted it updated,' Cardone told Horror.com. 'They wanted something that...had a bit more adult twist to it while keeping as close to the original concepts.'

'The first film works within its context,' the writer continued, 'but it was kind of a truncated story and we tried to go in a totally different direction with that. They had two converging storylines. One was the prom where Jamie Lee Curtis was not the most beautiful girl at the prom...and then you have the killer. Our movie, as we came at it, was from the standpoint of having a dual storyline converging because that always really works well. But ours was the murders and then the police investigation, which slasher films have not used in the past. That's the reason I feel that we are kind of going in more of a *Klute* kind of approach.'

> **In the prosperous suburb of Bridgeport, Oregon, 14-year-old Donna Keppel comes home from the movies to find her brother and father brutally murdered. Hiding under her brother's bed, she witnesses her mother being assaulted by a madman who insists on knowing Donna's whereabouts. When the mother refuses to give her daughter up, she is killed in front of Donna's eyes. Three years later, Donna is living with her aunt and uncle and preparing to go to the high school prom with her boyfriend Bobby, as well as two other couples—Lisa and Ronnie, Claire and Michael—who have all pitched in for a limousine and a suite at the hotel where the prom is being held. Meanwhile, Bridgeport Detective Winn receives word that the Keppels' killer has escaped from a mental institution. Winn tells his partner Detective Ruvolo the story—Richard Fenton was one of Donna's teachers who became dangerously obsessed with her and went over the edge when a restraining order was issued. After the Keppel murders, the police arrested Fenton at his apartment, which was full of Donna's pictures and journals of her former teacher's sick fantasies. Despite a plethora of forensic evidence and Donna's testimony, Fenton nevertheless avoided the death penalty and was committed to an asylum. After escaping, Fenton murders a businessman and adopts his identity, with which he is able to secure a suite right next to Donna and her friends. Wasting no time, he murders one of the housekeepers to obtain a master key. As the night wears on, he also murders Claire, Michael and a bellhop. On her way up to the suite with Ronnie, Lisa bumps into Fenton and later on realises who he is, just as the police find a stolen car in the hotel parking lot. As Lisa rushes to warn Donna, she is cut off by Fenton in the hotel mezzanine and butchered. When the police discover the trail of bodies, they order the hotel to be evacuated. Donna goes looking for Lisa, only to find her old stalker instead. She manages to escape Fenton's knife and rushes to Winn, but Fenton dons the dead bellhop's uniform and makes his way out of the hotel. Taken home, Donna relaxes with Bobby not knowing that Fenton is still loose. As Winn rushes to Donna's aid, Fenton cuts the phone lines and slits the throat of the policeman watching the house. After going to the bathroom, Donna returns to smooch with Bobby, only to find her boyfriend dead and Fenton in her bed instead. Just as he is about to stab Donna to death, Winn arrives and fires several shots that end Fenton's reign of terror for good.**

'In the original one, it was revenge, and we didn't want to go that route,' Cardone explained. '[Richard] just wants success in getting to [Donna] and [the murders are] by circumstance...It's one of the reasons that I finally took the project on...because it was more Hitchcock in that respect. Someone just was in the wrong place at the wrong time. He doesn't really kill in anger...He's just eliminating an obstacle.'

In total agreement with this approach was director Nelson McCormick, here making his feature-directing debut after calling the shots on such TV shows as *ER, Nip/Tuck, Third Watch* and *VIP*. 'The interesting thing about this film is that Fenton is not like the shark in *Jaws* or the creatures in *Aliens*,' McCormick told Total Sci-Fi Online. 'He is not driven by bloodlust, he just wants this girl. He is a bit like John Hinckley, Jr—the guy who had an obsession with Jodie Foster. That man was convinced that he had a relationship with her but it only existed in his mind. However, that idea drove him to rage. If you have ever wanted something so bad in your life that you started to act irrationally when you didn't get it then you can probably relate to this guy...His goal is not to rack up a body count and people only die if they are unfortunate enough to run into him.'

20-year-old Brittany Snow, best known for her work on the soap opera *Guiding Light* and the prime-time retro series *American Dreams*, won the leading role of 17-year-old Donna Keppel, the object of Fenton's obsession. 'I was very hesitant on doing this film,' the actress told FearNet, 'because I wanted it to be a good choice for me and my career. When I found out it wasn't a remake that was nice, because I feel like there are too many remakes right now. I also really loved the director...and this is the first project where I've been able to have a big hands-on approach to the movie in general. I got to kind of create the script with Nelson and [Cardone], and worked as kind of a producer on it and got to share my ideas. The script turned out to be something really good for the age range, and isn't over-the-top bloody-gory. It's more about the psychological aspects of it.'

Three months of filming began in March 2007 on a $20 million budget, with opening shots in Newport, Oregon, with the rest filmed either at the famous Biltmore Hotel in downtown Los Angeles or the nearby Sony Pictures Studios. 'I never really realised how hard a horror movie could be,' said Snow. 'You want to be fun and funny on set...so having to go from laughing to hysterically crying because you're being chased by a madman...It's really hard to go in and out of those places and still maintain a life...I sort of developed a system to have fun and then know when it was time to get myself together. I definitely respect anyone that does horror movies, because it's not an emotion that you deal with everyday—getting almost killed.'

INT. TURNER HOUSE—EVENING

Donna's AUNT and UNCLE, KAREN and JACK TURNER, sit at the kitchen table, in the middle of dinner...
A THIRD PLATE is also set, the FOOD completely untouched...

KAREN
Donna, your food's getting cold!

From another part of the house, Donna yells back...

351

DONNA (O.S.)
It's Prom, Aunt Karen! Dinner, then dance, remember?
Her aunt and uncle gaze across the table at one another for a thoughtful moment, and then Karen smiles...

KAREN
She's come so far. Going to her senior prom. With a boyfriend.

JACK
The boyfriend, I'm not so happy about.

KAREN
Will you stop it! He's a good kid. And he's stuck by her through some really bad times. I trust Bobby.

Jack hits her with a teasing grin...

JACK
Your dad probably trusted me, and look what happened on our prom night.

And Karen grins back...

KAREN
That was purely out of pity. I was tired of listening to you beg...

—Unfilmed exchange, from the original script

With Cardone working closely with McCormick and serving as one of *Prom Night*'s executive producers, very few changes were made to his script. The biggest difference came in identifying the killer as Richard Fenton; in Cardone's original draft, he is unnamed. Similarly, flash-cuts of Fenton murdering Donna's father and brother were eliminated, as was a reference back to the original *Prom Night* with reluctant chaperone partners Miss Waters, the PE teacher, and Mr Harris, the nerdish math teacher—the latter part was cut. Cardone also originally had Lisa sharing the Prom

Queen and King honours with Rick, the boyfriend of her bitchy rival Crissy. This was changed so that the winners were Lisa and her own boyfriend Ronnie.

Additionally, four scenes were shot, but ended up on the cutting room floor:

- After escaping, Fenton (Johnathon Schaech) pulls up at Donna's old house and then at the high school.
- Crissy (Brianne Davis) promises to kill Rick (Kellan Lutz) if he ruins her chances at Prom Queen by getting caught bringing a keg of beer into their hotel suite, then lists her qualifications to her friends.
- Detective Winn (Idris Elba) explains to Jack Turner (Linden Ashby) how Fenton escaped, triggering a flashback montage.
- Donna confesses to Lisa (Dana Davis) that she once kissed Rick.

As per Screen Gems's *When a Stranger Calls, Prom Night* was pre-ordained to have its horror muted to achieve a more broad-based PG-13 rating. Cardone took this as part of a larger approach: 'We have found out that there are two basic audiences to horror: one is basically a cynical, jaded, psychotic audience who loves *Hostel*, and then there is a female audience that was never there before...what they want...is something intelligent as opposed to just something blindly archaic and violent. That is where we kind of took our cues for this particular picture.'

McCormick also saw it as beneficial to the picture's overall tone: 'It forced me to think of designing the scares and the kills in such a way that you have to imagine a lot more. We were thinking about how to tell the story visually and what came to my mind were movies like *Psycho, Deliverance* and *Dead Calm*, where the violence is real but you feel it more internally and it is less in your face.' With that in mind, three changes were made before the film's release: Claire's death scene was shortened; Fenton's pursuit of Lisa was shortened and a close-up of her slit throat was eliminated; and Fenton's struggle with Donna was shortened.

Released on April 11, 2008, *Prom Night* enjoyed a first-place opening weekend gross of $20.8 million, on its way to an eventual domestic total of $43.8 million, with an additional $13.3 million earned overseas. However, despite that fact that the film's press notes said that this particular *Prom Night* had been 'reimagined for a more sophisticated audience,' critics failed to see anything sophisticated at all: 'There's no suspense or perversity. You don't care who lives or who dies—just please make it soon' (*Boston Globe*); 'There's no need to wear a corsage to *Prom Night*. And leaving your higher brain functions at home might be a good idea, too' (*Entertainment Weekly*); 'This is as listless, mindless and utterly useless a piece of corporate brain-clog as one is likely to come across for quite some time' (*Los Angeles Times*); 'The movie offers less gore than the average Band-Aid commercial and fewer scares than the elimination episodes of *Dancing with the Stars*' (*New York Times*); 'By far the worst slasher movie remake to date, replaying all the clichés, but delivering none of the guilty pleasures' (*Time Out*).

Despite the brickbats, Cardone and McCormick segued immediately into Screen Gems's next PG-13 remake, that of the 1987 thriller *The Stepfather*. Released in October 2009, the $20 million film was far less successful than *Prom Night*, grossing just $31 million worldwide. After this, Cardone went dormant and McCormick went back to TV land, directing for such shows as *The Closer, Southland* and Steven Spielberg's *Terra Nova*.

MY BLOODY VALENTINE

(1981)

It's pretty terrible when you've sweated and toiled for months and sometimes years to get something in your movie just right and then find out that some misinformed guardian of public morals has decided to clip out the whole point of your film.

—George Mihalka, director

My belief is that Paramount didn't want any more heat after *Friday the 13th*, because the MPAA were giving them hell and saying they shouldn't be in the business of making these kinds of movies. So, when they came down and they saw ours, they said, 'Oh my God— YOU get it through because we can't take the heat.'

—John Dunning, co-producer

In 1962, John Dunning and André Link co-founded the Montreal-based distribution company Cinépix. They started with European horror pictures (*The Horrible Dr Hitchcock, The Whip and the Body*) and Russ Meyer skin flicks before writing and producing their first in-house production, the sex comedy *Valérie*, in 1969 with $100,000 borrowed from the CFDC. The film was a huge success, earning over $1 million at the Canadian box office and was followed the next year by *Initiation* and *Love in a 4 Letter World*. Cinépix's main focus for most of the 1970s was on the distribution of soft-core porn films (*Can I Keep It Up For a Week?, Inside Jennifer Welles, Little Girl Big Tease, Massage Parlour Wife, Memories Within Miss Aggie*, etc.) but the company also released both British (*Blood on Satan's Claw, Vampyres*) and Spanish (*Tombs of the Blind Dead, The Vampires' Night Orgy*) horror films. Cinépix began releasing homegrown horrors with their own *Satan's Sabbath* (aka *The Possession of Virginia*, 1972), as well as *Cannibal Girls* and *The Pyx* (both 1973), before hitting the jackpot with David Cronenberg's *They Came from Within* and *Rabid*. In 1979, Dunning and Link enjoyed their greatest success with Ivan Reitman's *Meatballs*.

Looking for a way to make lightning strike twice, the duo hired 27-year-old director George Mihalka, whose debut feature *Pinball Summer* had yet to be released, and set him to work with *National Lampoon* editor Michel Choquette on a medical farce called *Stitches* in the summer of 1980. When Choquette's *Lampoon* duties delayed the project past the tax shelter financing window, *Stitches* was put on the back burner but Dunning had something else in mind for Mihalka: an outline by Stephen Miller for a slasher film set in a mine, called *My Bloody Valentine.*[2]

'I looked at the outline and it seemed pretty interesting compared to a lot of the other slashers that were going on at the time,' Mihalka remembered to The Terror Trap. 'Dunning told me he had a writer in mind named John Beaird. Beaird was willing to come up from Los Angeles and work with me on it. The only thing we had to do was be ready to shoot in a couple of months. We went up to Nova Scotia at that time. Basically, we had five or six weeks to write the script. We had to go through scene by scene so people could start prepping before we actually even had a full script out.'

'The major driving force was the fact that Paramount and Frank Mancuso were willing to do a pick up and a national distribution as long as we could get it out for Valentine's Day. With the kind of technology we had to use in those days, it was an incredible challenge. One of the reasons that we were able to do it is that we didn't know any better. We just figured we were good and smart enough technicians and we were good enough organisers and filmmakers. Just because everybody else thought it was really tight and almost impossible, that just put more fire underneath us.'

Valentine Bluffs, Nova Scotia, 1960. While the mining town celebrates its annual Valentine's Day dance, five coal miners are trapped after a methane explosion. Rescue workers spend six weeks digging them out, but only one miner—Harry Warden—is found alive, now insane from isolation and cannibalism. He is confined to an asylum but escapes a year later and, wearing his mining gear and gas mask, murders the two supervisors who left their posts early to go to the dance the year before. Warden then warns the town never to hold the dance again and disappears. Twenty years later, the locals are preparing to hold the first Valentine's dance in two decades when Harry seemingly returns to the scene, killing first the lady sponsor of the dance and then the local bartender who keeps trying to warn everyone of impending doom. After receiving their hearts in candy boxes, the mayor and chief constable call off the dance, but the miners and their girlfriends simply move the party to the mine's recreation hall. Three couples decide to take the party into the mine itself, unaware that two of their friends have just been murdered. The owner's son TJ and his onetime friend, now rival, Axel descend into the mine to rescue their friends who are being picked off one by one. Ultimately, only TJ and his former girlfriend Sarah are left to confront Harry, but after they tear off his mask, he is revealed to

---

2 *Stitches* was eventually made in 1985 by another company. Starring Parker Stevenson and Eddie Albert, it was so bad that director Rod Holcomb used the 'Alan Smithee' industry seudonym for his directorial credit.

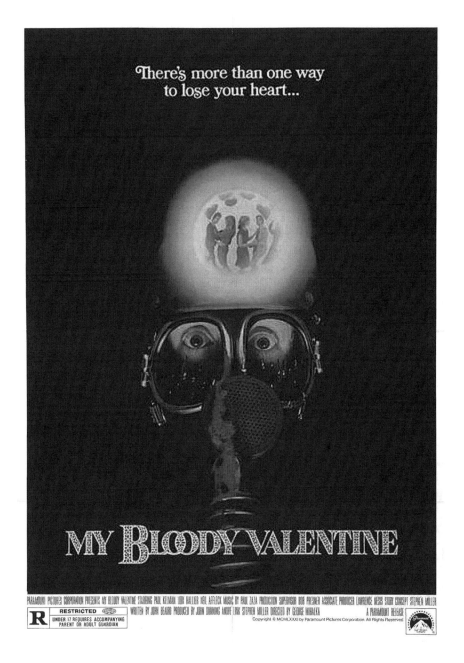

There's more than one way
to lose your heart...

MY BLOODY VALENTINE

PARAMOUNT PICTURES CORPORATION PRESENTS MY BLOODY VALENTINE STARRING PAUL KELMAN LORI HALLIER NEIL AFFLECK MUSIC BY PAUL ZAZA PRODUCTION SUPERVISOR BOB PRESNER ASSOCIATE PRODUCER LAWRENCE NESIS STORY CONCEPT STEPHEN MILLER
WRITTEN BY JOHN BEAIRD PRODUCED BY JOHN DUNNING ANDRÉ LINK STEPHEN MILLER DIRECTED BY GEORGE MIHALKA   A PARAMOUNT RELEASE

R — RESTRICTED — UNDER 17 REQUIRES ACCOMPANYING PARENT OR ADULT GUARDIAN

Copyright © MCMLXXXI by Paramount Pictures Corporation. All Rights Reserved.

be none other than Axel, the son of one of the murdered supervisors who witnessed his father's death 20 years earlier.

With a $2 million budget, seven weeks of filming began on September 22 at the Princess Colliery mine located in Sydney Mines, Nova Scotia, which had closed down

its active operation in 1976. To avoid the competition stealing the Valentine's Day theme, the film went into production as *The Secret* and the press was duly informed that everyone involved would be keeping things to themselves. 'Even our actors do not know how the film ends,' line producer Robert Presner told the Canadian Press. 'And in no way shape or form are we going to let out who the culprit is at the end of the film and people on our crews have signed affidavits to the effect saying if they do know the ending, they will not tell what it is...the resolution of the film happens four minutes before the end when we find out who this strange gentleman happens to be. If I am being devious, it's because I can't tell you what the secret is.'

For Beaird and Mihalka, however, there was no secret as to how they wanted their film to separate itself from the pack: 'The *people* are the main storyline and the strange, inexplicable murders that keep on occurring are happening *around* them,' the director told *Fangoria*. 'Most of the time, our main characters really don't know what's going on. We didn't start off with the idea of making a film that was terror or suspense from beginning to end. I think that we spent more time on story development than some of the other horror movies. We tried to deal with the characters' backgrounds: their loves, lives, and small town mentality. The more likable and human your characters are, the more the audience will be able to empathise with them and react when they get killed. The people in some of the recent terror pictures are just like grass swaying in the wind waiting for the scythe to come to cut them. You never find out much about them. You just watch them get killed. Hopefully, *My Bloody Valentine* operates on many levels.'

Filming in an actual coal mine took things to a whole new level—2,700 feet underground, to be exact. While this certainly added to the film's verisimilitude and atmosphere, it nevertheless caused numerous logistical headaches. 'It took about

fifteen minutes to get down to the bottom,' Mihalka related to The Terror Trap. 'There were two [elevators] and you could only put about twelve people in them... even if you didn't have claustrophobia when you started, you certainly started getting it eventually. So basically what would happen is it would take almost an hour to get everybody down into the mine. If your daytime call is at 7:00 in the morning, by the time you actually assembled your crew ready to work, it was already 8:00... we had to send people up an hour before lunch arrived so that they could make their lunch hours without going into overtime. An hour lunch would take three hours. So

basically, we had to shoot a regular day of shooting but we ended up with only 3-4 hours left because of all the ups and downs with the elevators.'

'Another problem is that methane gas is a by-product of coal,' Mihalka continued. 'Now, when methane gas builds up, it becomes very explosive...We'd go down into the mine and then we'd have a 'methane morning', which meant everybody out. And the mine would be closed until the methane gas would clear. Because the minute it got very cloudy, the low-pressure systems would then put pressure onto the airshafts that the mine breathes with. So normally the mine should have this constant draft going out...That's what would get rid of the methane. On the other hand...if you have a cloudy day with a lot of moisture and humidity pressing down on the atmosphere, that would stop the methane gas from escaping and you'd have a methane build-up. It was quite scary working like that because at a certain point, it becomes extremely dangerous.'

While the film would become known for the moodiness of its low-key lighting, Mihalka admitted that this was less an aesthetic choice than a safety necessity: 'The only lighting equipment we were allowed to use was safety lighting equipment because there were no sparks. The brightest bulbs you could use with no-spark equipment [were] 50 watts. That's smaller than most people have in their kitchen.'

Friday the 13th had instituted the 'body count' gimmick and raised the bar on graphic violence in the slasher film, and Mihalka resigned himself to the fact that *Valentine* would have to follow suit, telling *Fangoria*: 'Gore has only become necessary because it's been used so often that if you don't have it, people would say that your picture wasn't a horror film. Today's audience has been spoiled by extremely good makeup and special effects. It really depends on the picture you're trying to make. In *My Bloody Valentine*, we tread a fine line. Instead of making the killings cold-blooded, we attempted to put some emotion into them. We tried to make our violence extremely believable, but not exorbitantly graphic.'

'One of the goals that we set out to do and what [make-up effects supervisor] Tom Burman created for us was to be able to create these special effects in one shot,' the director later elaborated to The Terror Trap. 'So often, what you had in those days is you'd see the arrow going towards the back of somebody, then it would cut to the front, then it would cut to the top, then it would cut to the side. It would take three or four shots to actually achieve the effect. Once you got finished with that type of multi cut scare, we felt it took away from the creepy realism we wanted to get with *Valentine*.

One of the most celebrated effects in *Valentine* is actress Helene Udy's impalement on a water pipe, which effectively turns her character into a human showerhead, with bloody water spurting out of her mouth. Not surprisingly, according to Mihalka, this was the most difficult effect to achieve, though not necessarily for the reasons one might think: 'We actually re-shot a part of that because she was wearing an angora sweater...[and] moisture beads on angora. It doesn't flow. So basically what happened was that when the blood came out of her mouth, it sort of just beaded. It rolled off as opposed to staying on. It wasn't bloody enough...I remember I had a very bad cold at the time and we were sitting in this horrible, freezing place with water running everywhere. And I'm thinking, "I'm gonna catch pneumonia here just for a couple more drops of blood!"'

At around 10:50 pm on December 8, 1980, as ex-Beatle John Lennon and his wife Yoko Ono returned to their New York apartment, the rock star-cum-peace activist was shot four times in the back by deranged fan Mark David Chapman. Lennon was taken to nearby Roosevelt Hospital where he was pronounced dead on arrival; Chapman would plead guilty to second-degree murder and was sentenced to 20 years to life in prison.

The world was shocked at the violent death of the man who preached a mantra of giving peace a chance. Cutting *Valentine* in Montreal, Mihalka was no different: 'I remember I was driving up to the editing room and it was an ugly, ugly horrible day in Montreal. I walked into the editing room and all of us just said, "Fuck it, let's just all go home and get drunk." This was the most meaningless crime as far as we were concerned, the most meaningless form of violence we'd ever seen.'

In the predictable soul-searching that followed Lennon's death, many people pointed the finger at the usual suspect—televised and filmic violence—as the root cause of Chapman's crime (actually, Chapman's confessed inspiration was J D Salinger's 1951 bestselling novel *The Catcher in the Rye*). The MPAA, already stinging from the barbs it had received over its lenient treatment of *Friday the 13th*, was not going to give its critics any more ammunition in the wake of the Lennon assassination. I honestly do believe that there was a major backlash against gratuitous violence because of [Lennon's death],' said Mihalka. 'And it was an

immediate reaction...Everyone, even people whose economic interest was to allow *Valentine* to be what it was, jumped on that bandwagon. I think the MPAA's reaction at the time mirrored the average person's reaction. Nobody in the film business was going to allow themselves to be the ones to have a finger pointed at them saying, "Look...they're still doing it." And of course, we were locked into this release date and the Valentine's Day phenomenon. All the marketing, all the promotion. If it had another title and release date, things might have been different...I believe that letting *Valentine* go uncut was gonna look like a major slap in the face to that solemn, chest-beating, "we're all responsible for the senseless violence" feeling.'[3]

In January 1981, *My Bloody Valentine* was duly submitted to the MPAA for classification and immediately received an X rating. Because of Cinépix's negative pickup deal with Paramount, Mihalka and company were contractually obligated to deliver an R-rated picture. What followed, according to its director, was a frantic attempt to soften the picture ahead of its February 13 release date: 'At the time we were working twenty-four hours a day, seven days a week...to do the final mix of the film because we have to deliver this picture by...February 5 so that they could

3 This was compounded by the March 30, 1981, assassination attempt on President Ronald Reagan by John Hinckley Jr, who sought to impress Hollywood actress Jodie Foster.

make the 1,200 copies.... Anyway, the process was going like this: the editor in Los Angeles takes out 3 or 4 frames of one shot, we're taking out 3 or 4 frames of our working copy that we're doing the mix to. Meanwhile, we're taking 3 or 4 frames out of our master sound copies that have already been mixed and at the same time, somebody is taking 3 or 4 frames out of a negative that's already been cut. We'd take out the eight frames that the MPAA asked to take out and we'd send the film back to them because they'd have to see it. Unfortunately, what happened was that the sound effects were so damned good. Even if you didn't see anything, you heard it and that made them cringe again so here another round would take place with the MPAA because of that. Take out another four frames. To the point where it was getting kind of anaemic. Because of the sound, they still thought they saw what was no longer there.'

By the time it was over, *Valentine* had lost over three minutes of graphic footage, to include the following:

- In the credits sequence, a young lady (Pat Hemingway) with a heart tattoo above her breast is impaled on a pickaxe. A 5-second close-up of her impalement through the tattoo was cut.
- Mabel Osborne (Patricia Hamilton) is stuffed in a dryer in her Laundromat. 17 seconds were cut showing her corpse spinning in the dryer after being found by Chief Newby (Don Francks).
- Happy the bartender (Jack Van Evera) is impaled on a pickaxe outside the mine's recreation hall. 12 seconds were cut showing Happy's eye being gouged out by the axe.
- Dave (Carl Marotte) is drowned in scalding water and stuffed in a refrigerator. 11 seconds of his drowning was cut.
- A close-up of Happy's mangled face after his body drops from the miners' uniform racks was cut.
- Sylvia's head is impaled on a shower pipe. 25 seconds were cut which showed her impalement and blood spurting from her mouth; 8 more seconds were cut of her boyfriend John (Rob Stein) discovering the body.
- Lovers Mike (Tom Kovacs) and Harriet (Terry Waterland) are impaled on a drill bit (offscreen). 27 seconds were cut from the aftermath when Hollis (Keith Knight) finds them.
- Hollis is subsequently shot twice with a nail gun. 32 seconds were cut from this scene, including the second shot to his forehead.
- A close-up of Howard's (Alf Humphreys) decapitation was cut.
- Patty (Cynthia Dale) is gutted with a pickaxe. 20 seconds of her writhing in agony was cut.
- In the flashback showing the murder of Axel's (Neil Affleck) father by Harry Warden (Peter Cowper), a shot of the killer ripping out the man's heart was cut.
- After being trapped in a cave-in, Axel cuts off his arm to escape the authorities. A 30-second sequence of him grabbing Sarah (Lori Hallier) and then sawing at his arm—which comes loose still clinging to Sarah—was cut, leaving the ending abrupt and confusing.

'The whole thing was very disappointing and actually kind of depressing,' Mihalka remembered. 'My feeling about making any film has been that you make the best you possibly can. If you're making a slasher horror film, you've got to make it a slasher. Horrible and ugly. One of the things we always wanted to do philosophically was not to make it pretty. I mean, this shit was supposed to hurt.'

'Unfortunately, no one [saw] what *Valentine* was meant to be like in terms of a horror film,' he continued. 'Because of the cuts, it was asked to stand on its own as a drama...*Valentine* got to be judged more on that than it did on its impact on an audience for what it was supposed to have been. That's like asking somebody to create the best chicken soup possible and by the time you're serving it, there's no chicken meat in the soup. Then have it judged along with all the others that still have chicken in them.'

Dunning was convinced that *Valentine* was singled out by MPAA president Jack Valenti as part of a larger crusade against the horror genre: 'He was determined to give us a hard time...I think he wanted to suppress the horror movies that were slipping through into the major studios. He didn't want to see the majors in it...he wanted to repress it. It was vindictive and that's the way it went down.'

Mihalka could take solace in the fact that he had accomplished something other than a straight-out gorefest, however: 'One of the things that both John Beaird and I wanted to do...was that we wanted to take [the slasher film] out of the suburban bungalow context. We wanted to set this in some place where there is a slight hint of social consciousness. This was really the first film in that era where teenagers are actually talking about the fact that there's no future left. There's no jobs...Not a lot of hope. It was, in a strange way, the first of a Generation X mentality.'

My Bloody Valentine premiered in New York on February 11, then was released nationwide two days later, on Friday the 13th. Not that this opportune timing made much difference: the film ended up grossing just $5.6 million. 'I guess if we didn't have the problems of censorship and ratings it would probably have been one of the all-time grossing films in the genre,' Mihalka reflected. 'Unfortunately, with the cuts *Valentine* had to endure, there wasn't much blood left.'

The critical reaction, predictable as ever, also did nothing to bolster the film's cachet: 'The shocks are strictly mechanical and redundant, the script uncomplicated by incidental horror or character byplay. It comes as no great surprise when the killer is revealed to be a *Halloween* clone and then allowed to vanish, aggravating the pathetic resemblance. The reviewers who made a fuss over *Halloween* have a lot to answer for' (Gary Arnold); '*My Bloody Valentine*...should be wrapped in red crepe paper, tied with a big red bow and marked return to sender. It's a gruesome greeting card for which the sentiment might read: Roses are Red, Violets are Blue, In movies like this, there's nothing new' (*Boston Globe*); 'The screenplay...is too convoluted, derivative and, oddly, too ambitious to properly coagulate into the kind of exploitation movie that it tries to be' (*Los Angeles Times*); '*My Bloody Valentine* probably won't make you shiver with fright, but it's almost certain to make you squirm, first with irritation and then with revulsion. Just when it seemed that quickie horror movies had touched bottom, this Canadian production...drops the level of shoddy exploitation another 2,000 feet or so' (*New York Times*); 'I wonder if the citizens of Canada know that their tax money is in effect paying for such dismal and depressing horror films as *My Bloody Valentine*' (Gene Siskel); 'Wildly implausible, totally derivative and thoroughly lacking in characterisations' (*Variety*).

At the same time that they were producing *Valentine*, Dunning and Link were bankrolling yet another slasher film, *Happy Birthday to Me*, only this one had a higher budget ($3 million), a couple of American stars (Melissa Sue Anderson and Glenn Ford) and a veteran director (J Lee Thompson of *The Guns of Navarone* and *Cape Fear*). None of this helped it avoid the same fate as its stablemate: acquired by Columbia, *Birthday* also ended up losing much of its gore in order to accommodate the demands of the MPAA. Released in May 1981, *Birthday* received no well wishes from critics but its box office take was roughly double that of *Valentine*.

Mihalka would direct two more films after *My Bloody Valentine*—*Scandale* (1982) and *The Blue Man* (1985)—before settling rather comfortably into Canadian television, where he has spent the past 30 years directing for such shows as *Charlie Jade, Crossbow, Da Vinci's Inquest, The Hitchhiker, The Hunger, Lonesome Dove: The Outlaw Years* and *Race to Mars*. Dunning and Link continued releasing exploitation in the '80s and '90s through Cinépix, including such films as *Carnosaur, Death Wish V, Henry: Portrait of a Serial Killer, The Surrogate, The Toxic Avenger*, and the in-house *Snake Eater* series, starring Lorenzo Lamas. In 1997, they sold Cinépix to Vancouver investment banker Frank Giustra, who renamed the company Lionsgate Films, the precursor to today's independent powerhouse Lionsgate Entertainment. The last Cinépix release was *Les Boys II* in 1998.

(2009)

I think one of the things we may have missed in horror the last few years is how much fun those movies are to watch. They're a good time...Our intention here was to make a movie that was fun. A movie where you could participate, not just through the 3D, but via the mystery and the characters and have a good time with it.

—Patrick Lussier, editor and director

The new 3D is different. The 3D of the past, where everything was flat, flat, flat and then something flies at your face, those days are over. Now it's a completely immersive experience, so that could change the way 3D movies are written. Certain things will become more prominent in the 3D experience.

—Todd Farmer, co-writer

While *My Bloody Valentine* was no great shakes at the box office, it slowly found an audience over the years via cable television and home video. In fact, by the year 2004, its cult appeal had grown to the point that John Dunning attempted to interest Paramount in a sequel he had written called *The Return of the Miner*. The

My Bloody Valentine 3D (2009)

idea was to use all the gore footage cut from the original film in flashback sequences, while the story proper would focus once again on TJ and Sarah—now married and with teenage sons—who are forced to confront a returning and psychotic Axel Palmer when Valentine Bluffs decides to turn their now-inactive coal mine into a theme park.

Paramount took an option on the script, only to shelve it, but Dunning had given himself a consolation prize: in taking the option, Paramount had agreed that, if it decided against making the sequel, the rights to the excised footage from the original *Valentine* would revert to its co-producer. Armed with this now-legendary celluloid, Dunning approached Mike Pasternak, the head of production at Lionsgate. Dunning found the successor to his old company highly receptive to the idea of remaking *Valentine* but not much more interested than Paramount in the notion of a sequel. '[Pasternak] decided the remake should be a "date movie",' Dunning told The Terror Trap. 'Now, we didn't even understand what a date movie is. So they canned my script. They bought me out. We had thought they were gonna make it, but to our surprise, they shelved it.'

In June 2007, it was announced that Lionsgate was indeed developing a *Valentine* remake and was looking for writers. They settled on Zane Smith, author of the novel *Romance of a Hitman* and a screenwriting novice, and pencilled in a tentative release date of February 13, 2009. Six months later, Lionsgate announced it had tapped Patrick Lussier, editor of numerous Wes Craven films and director of *Dracula 2000* and *White Noise 2*, to helm the *Valentine* remake. 'I worked in a video store in the '80s so I'd seen the original, remembered the trailers and the reputation it had,' Lussier told Bloody Disgusting. It's a Canadian cinematic tax shelter classic—a stand out because it's about...working-class adults and not John Hughesian teenagers. The industrial setting and that iconic Miner, a truly inventive killer. That's what resonates.'

Shooting was scheduled for late March/early April 2008 in Pittsburgh and the film would be shot in 3D. At Lussier's behest, Smith's script was rewritten by Todd Farmer, an associate of Sean Cunningham who had written the latter's *Jason X* as well as the original script for the Sam Raimi production *The Messengers*, which was largely overhauled before being shot in 2006. 'The original [*Valentine*] terrified me when I was young,' Farmer admitted to *Cinefantastique*. 'It screwed me up so bad that I never saw the movie again until we started doing this. I subconsciously just stayed away from it. It was great to watch it again while working on this because I had forgotten how great a movie it really was.'

Harmony, Pennsylvania: Valentine's Day, 1997. An accident in the town's mine (caused by the negligence of the owner's teenage son, Tom Hanniger) traps miner Harry Warden and his crew for six days below ground. When a rescue team reaches them, only Warden is left alive, having killed the other five miners to conserve oxygen. Warden spends the next year in a coma, only to awaken on Valentine's Day and kill nearly everyone in the hospital. The local teens are having a party at the mine but Warden shows up in full mining gear to put a stop to things with his pickaxe—nearly killing Tom's girlfriend

Sarah, best friend Axel and Axel's girlfriend Irene in the process. Then, the official story goes, Warden was cornered in his home by the local police and he burned himself alive rather than be caught. After disappearing for ten years, Tom returns to the town after the death of his father to take over the mine. He gets a cold reception from mayor Ben Foley, who just wants Tom to sell the mine to a Detroit conglomerate and get out of Harmony. Axel is now the town sheriff and unhappily married to Sarah, who still pines for Tom. To compensate, Axel is having an affair with Megan, Sarah's co-worker at the local grocery store. The relative tranquillity of the last decade is violently shattered when someone in a miner's outfit attacks the motel where Tom is staying, murdering Irene, her trucker lover and the manager. The next day, Irene's heart is delivered in a candy box to Axel's office: apparently Harry Warden has also returned to Harmony. That night, Tom's acquaintance Jessie—who tried to coax him into bed—is murdered by Warden. Axel begins to suspect his old friend in the murders, and his anger is piqued when Tom furtively renews his relationship with Sarah. The picture is clouded even further when Tom goes down into the mine with burly Red Burton and the two encounter Warden, who decapitates Burton. To disprove the hysteria about Harry Warden, Axel forces Ben Foley to tell the truth about the mad miner's demise: Foley, along with Tom and Axel's fathers, hunted down and killed Warden, then buried him in an unmarked grave near the mine. Along with Tom and Sarah, Axel and Foley go out to the grave, only to find it empty. Later, Warden kills Foley in his house: his body, along with Jessie's, is found in Warden's empty grave. The next night, Sarah and Megan are attacked by Warden in the grocery store—Megan is killed and has her heart torn out when she tries to escape through a window. Tom picks Sarah up from the hospital and drives her to the abandoned shack in the woods where Axel and Megan had their trysts. On the way, Axel calls her and tells her that Tom has been in and out of mental institutions for the past decade. Confused, Sarah tries to get control of the car but crashes instead, knocking Tom out. She makes her way to the shack where she discovers hundreds of empty, heart-shaped candy boxes right before she is attacked by Warden. Fleeing into the mine, Sarah is chased by Warden but is found first by Axel, then by Tom. As each man hurls accusations at the other, Sarah is caught in the middle, until Tom reveals something about Megan's murder that he could not have known unless he was present. Tom beats up Axel and claims to see Warden approaching, but Sarah sees nothing. Tom runs off to do battle with Warden while Axel joins Sarah and the two watch as Tom fights an imaginary foe. Finally Tom's schizophrenia is settled—he puts on the miner's gas mask and becomes Warden. After seriously wounding Axel, Warden disappears while Sarah tries to rescue her husband, only to reappear in the mineshaft, methodically smashing the lights. Taking her husband's gun, Sarah waits until Warden is right on top of them and fires at some nearby butane tanks—causing a fireball and a cave-in that consumes Warden.

'During the writing phase with Todd and the studio, I talked a lot about making *Scream*, what the preview process was like, what we learned from it,' Lussier told CHUD.com. 'The thing that Kevin [Williamson] and Wes [Craven] did so skilfully is that even though there is a lot of self-reference, the film works first and foremost as a mystery, which is one of those elements of great slasher movies of the '80s...We wanted to use that and capitalise on that and play the element of the love triangle–those kinds of classic story telling devices which always work. There's a reason why Agatha Christie sold so many damn books over the years. Once we grounded ourselves in that, everything else flowed from it–the nature of the kills, how the mystery of the killer and all those elements worked.'

EXT. COUNTRY ROAD—INT. TOM'S CAR—NIGHT

Sarah sits in the passenger seat. Tom drives.

SARAH
I can't get her face out of my head. Her eyes. Those words written in blood.

Tom seems jittery. He reaches for some pills. But the bottle's empty. Sarah notices.

> SARAH

What are those, Tom?

> TOM

They, uh...they help me, sort of focus. Bugs me that I need them. That some little pill has that much power over...

> SARAH

Half the town's on Prozac.

> TOM

Yeah, well, these little jewels beat up Prozac and take his lunch money.

> SARAH

Jesus, Tom. With what we all went through? What we're going through? At least you're doing something, right?

> TOM

What about you? How did you deal with your demons?

> SARAH

Twelve years of therapy.

> TOM

Twelve, but it was only ten years—

SARAH

—I'm paid up through 2010.

She forces a smile, struggling for some memory of normalcy.

TOM

And Axel? How did he—

SARAH

—You know Axel. Bottle it up and move on.

TOM

You know what happens to a bottle under pressure don't you?

SARAH

Axel? I don't think so. He's a rock. Sometimes wish he wasn't. And he has his vents. Nightmares mostly. Horrible things.

Sarah shudders, remembering some of them.

—Unfilmed exchange, from the original script

Before shooting began, several major changes were made to the script:

- The part of Jessie was cut. She was supposed to be the one who brokered the deal to sell the mine. She tries to attract Tom but is murdered by the miner.
- Sheriff Burke was supposed to die in his first encounter with Harry Warden in the mine. His death was moved to later in the film, though the nature of his demise (having his jaw ripped off by a pickaxe) remained the same. The role was significantly beefed up with the casting of genre favourite (and Pittsburgh resident) Tom Atkins (*The Fog, Halloween III, Night of the Creeps, et al*).
- It was originally intended that Ben Foley would try to convince Tom to sell the mine to a Detroit conglomerate with Tom refusing. This was reversed so that Tom instigates the sale over Foley's objections but ultimately changes his mind.
- A scene was cut involving Sarah's young son Noah who encounters the miner at their house, but the killer disappears before Sarah can confront him.
- The original ending had Tom being murdered by someone in miner's garb. This was changed to Tom murdering his would-be rescuer, switching uniforms and leaving the mine unnoticed.

Filming began in various Pennsylvania locations on May 12, 2008, on a $15 million budget and continued for two months. 'It was actually pretty brutal for all involved,' Lussier confessed to Bloody Disgusting. 'One location was voted by the entire crew as the hardest location they've ever shot.' Nevertheless, the director and his crew were energised by the opportunities that shooting in 3D afforded them: 'You have a whole dimension at your disposal that you don't in a 2D film. And you very quickly realise that the language of 3D affords the audience an opportunity to be completely immersed within the film, within the story, the thrills, etc. We very quickly realised we had the opportunity to turn this slasher remake into a theatrical event that goes beyond expectations.'

'It was important to build the film to 3D crescendos. You don't want everything out in your face like *Dr Tongue's 3D House of Pancakes*...you can't tell a story that way. What you want is to create a visual environment that lends itself to 3D space. 3D loves claustrophobic depth, a contradiction perhaps, but true nonetheless. That's why shooting underground in a real coal mine was the perfect setting for a 3D film. Once we discovered that we very quickly chose other locations that used that to our advantage. There's a huge sequence in a grocery store where we used the long, tunnel-like aisles to similar effect.'

Like its predecessor, this *Valentine* was going to pull no punches when it came to graphic violence: 'Gary Tunnicliffe, our special effects makeup guy...wrote this thing called 'A Document of Death', which outlined a million ways to kill somebody with a pick axe,' Lussier told *Cinefantastique*. However, the director was determined that *his* Harry Warden was not going to have his kills neutered by the MPAA, and decided on a strategy of deliberate overkill: 'We showed [the MPAA] a more extreme version the first time out...We had enhanced a few of the kills even further, so when they came back and said, "We have some problems here, here, and here," we said, "Oh, let us address that." Very quickly we sent them back the version of the movie we had been working on and really wanted. They said, "Oh yeah, this is fine."'

Another part of Lussier's ruse was to include a sequence that featured writer Farmer playing a truck driver who has sex with Irene (Betsy Rue) in a motel. After she discovers he has been video-recording their tryst, she angrily chases and confronts him in the parking lot, only to see him killed by Harry Warden, who then comes after her. To the delight of the male audience, Rue never puts on her clothes, leaving her full-frontal assets on display the entire time in eye-popping 3D. Amazingly enough, the director told CHUD, this whole adolescent fantasy had originally gone on even *longer*: 'We shot the sex scene deliberately long, and once we cut that out they let us get away with everything else. One of the things about Betsy in that sequence is that you start out very cognisant that she's naked, but by the end because you're so keyed into her terror you've forgotten that she's naked. It speaks to the power of her performance.'

Prior to release, the original opening scene, which sees teens Jason (Michael McKee) and Michael (Liam Rhodes) exploring the mine and relating its sordid history was dropped in favour of encapsulating the tragic events into a prologue of 3-Dimensional newspaper headlines, stills and voiceovers. Lussier explained the change: 'What the prologue was supposed to do was take all those '80s slasher movies, and even the original film to some degree, encapsulated in thirteen minutes. We could make that so much fun and chaotic that it would give us the right to make the rest of the movie with them grown up as adults in a mature environment.'

In the interest of tightening up the film's narrative, several other scenes ended up on the cutting room floor:

- Tom's late father Eli Hanniger (Tim Hartman) is featured in an early bar scene with Ben Foley (Kevin Tighe), discussing his son's negligence when Tom (Jensen Ackles) and Sarah (Jaime King) walk in.
- After returning to town, Tom goes to the mine and hears voices that make him reach for his pills.
- A nosy shopper (Ruth Flaherty) interrupts Tom and Sarah's reunion at her family's market.
- After dropping Sarah off at the market, Axel (Kerr Smith) exchanges a furtive glance with Megan (Megan Boone).
- Deputy Martin (Edi Gathegi) tells Axel that he is going to be a suspect in Megan's death because of their affair.

Released on January 16, 2009 (for some reason, Lionsgate decided to forego the scheduled Valentine's Day opening) to an opening weekend take of $21.2 million, *My Bloody Valentine 3D*'s US gross of $51.5 million was matched almost dollar-for-dollar overseas, where the film pulled in $49.1 million. The high profitability was further sweetened by some grudgingly positive reviews from *The Boston Globe* ('Lussier stages his movie not so much around nail-biting moments as novel ways to fling entrails at his viewers. But if you take pleasure in such mindless gore, there must be worse ways to spend 100 minutes'), the *Chicago Tribune* ('The technology is clearly the main draw and *Valentine* benefits from the novelty value of seeing an extra layer of visual depth added to a story that's basic slasher trash'), the *New York Times* ('A strange synergy of old and new, *My Bloody Valentine 3D* blends cutting-edge technology and old-school prosthetics to produce something both familiar and alien: gore you can believe in') and *Variety* ('An unabashedly retro work, revelling in the clichés and conventions of the slasher horror pics that proliferated in the early 1980s').

One person who was not impressed, however, was Dunning, who was still pining for his lost *Miner* script, telling The Terror Trap, 'The damn thing that bothered me about the remake is that everyone is running around being killed with an axe. The same axe. It gets boring. Absolutely boring. If you look at the original, we didn't use the pickaxe for everything. The rest were all tools of the mining trade. Nail guns. Cross saws. All kinds of different weapons were utilised...it certainly would have satisfied me more to see [my own] sequel because I wouldn't have gotten so bored.' Dunning did, though, have the satisfaction of seeing all the excised gore footage finally restored to the original *Valentine* when it was released in a Special Edition DVD by Lionsgate to coincide with the release of *Valentine 3D*. Not long after, he suffered a debilitating illness and died in September 2011 at the age of 84.

While there was talk of a sequel to *Valentine 3D*, it came to naught. Lussier and Farmer instead moved on to another 3D opus, the Nicolas Cage vehicle *Drive Angry* (2011) and at time of writing are attached to the fledgling *Halloween 3D* project after having exited Dimension's proposed *Hellraiser* reboot.

EPILOGUE

BACK AND FORTH TO THE FUTURE

As of 2012, there are some definite signs that the remake cycle is ending. Of the three horror makeovers released in 2011— *Don't Be Afraid of the Dark* (based on the 1973 TV movie), *Fright Night* (based on Tom Holland's 1985 homage to Hammer Films) and *The Thing* (technically a prequel to John Carpenter's version but it plays like a straight remake)—were all box-office failures. This comes after several other failed remakes, including that of *The Wicker Man* (2006), *The Hitcher* (2007), *Sorority Row* and *The Stepfather* (both 2009). Some remakes have actually eschewed the theatrical route altogether and gone straight to DVD, including *April Fool's Day, It's Alive* (both 2008), *Night of the Demons* (2009) and *I Spit on Your Grave* (2010).

The forecast for future remakes is no rosier. Besides Tim Burton and Johnny Depp's big-budget remake of the 1960s' horror soap opera *Dark Shadows,* the only project of any significance is the Bruce Campbell/Sam Raimi-produced reboot of the cult 1983 film that launched their careers, *The Evil Dead.* Even Platinum Dunes has announced that it has finished remaking the seminal horror titles of the '70s and '80s.

While 20th Century Fox took advantage of the ominous calendar date of June 6, 2006 (6-6-06) to release an updated version of 1976's *The Omen* (though still using essentially the same David Seltzer script), no one has yet had the courage to remake *The Exorcist,* seen by many as the *Gone with the Wind* of the genre. The influence of William Peter Blatty's tale of possession can still be seen, however, some 40 years on in such films as *The Exorcism of Emily Rose* (2005), *The Last Exorcism* (2010), *The Rite* (2011) and *The Devil Inside* (2012).

It is in these variations on a demonic theme that perhaps we have our answer as to whether or not the next decade will contain the same number of remakes as the previous one. A film need not necessarily be literally remade in order for its influence to be felt. After all, are not the *Twilight* books and films simply *Dark Shadows* translated for a new generation? Substitute Bella Swann, Edward Cullen and Jacob Black for Maggie Evans, Barnabas Collins and Quentin Collins and you get the idea. Given the *Twilight* phenomenon, it is not hard to see why Burton and Depp chose *Dark Shadows* to follow in the wake of their decidedly esoteric remakes of *Charlie and the Chocolate Factory* (2005), *Sweeney Todd* (2007) and *Alice in Wonderland* (2010).

In the final analysis, everyone asks the same question: are the remakes as good as the originals? From a technical standpoint, most of them are actually better: higher production values, state-of-the-art visual and make-up effects, more professional performances, slicker camerawork and editing. However, because most remakes are now studio films, they lack the independent spirit of their predecessors. They are, in fact, too polished, too professional, too predictable. None of the remakes have the gritty nihilism of the original *Night of the Living Dead*. Or the charnel-house atmosphere of *Texas Chain Saw Massacre*. Or the genuinely frightening shocks of *Halloween*. Or the bloody social satire of *Dawn of the Dead*.

In other words, none of the remakes are groundbreaking. None will create a new sub-genre or influence other films for decades. None seems to herald the arrival of a major new talent on the scene. They have mainly served as a means to an end for commercial directors to get a shot at the big time. To be sure, some of the remakes— *The Amityville Horror, Dawn of the Dead, Friday the 13th, The Hills Have Eyes, My Bloody Valentine 3D, Texas Chainsaw Massacre, When a Stranger Calls*—are undeniably entertaining and do not do any disservice to their predecessors. But this is hardly a compelling argument in their favour. Genres thrive only when ideas are renewed—not when they are recycled; when an Alexandre Aja makes a *Haute Tension* or an Eli Roth makes a *Hostel*—not when they remake someone else's film, no matter what kind of 'spin' they might put on it.

In the end, of course, remakes are made because studio executives like to minimise their risk with 'brand name' value. Hence the number of sequels, TV spin-offs and comic book adaptations—each with a supposed 'built-in' audience. So we, as the audience, will continue to get *X-Men* sequels and prequels, two-part *Harry Potter* and *Twilight* episodes and big screen versions of *The A Team* and *21 Jump Street*. And many, many more remakes. Our consolation in this age of Blu-ray, Netflix and YouTube is that we can always indulge our nostalgia with the real thing.

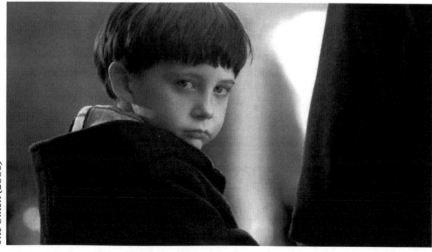

The Omen (2006)

FILMOGRAPHY

THE AMITYVILLE HORROR (1979)

Cast

James Brolin	George Lutz
Margot Kidder	Kathy Lutz
Rod Steiger	Father Delaney
Don Stroud	Father Bolen
Murray Hamilton	Father Ryan
John Larch	Father Nuncio
Natasha Ryan	Amy
K C Martel	Greg
Meeno Peluce	Matt
Michael Sacks	Jeff

Credits

Directed by Stuart Rosenberg
Written by Sandor Stern/Alison Cross
Based on the book by Jay Anson
Produced by Elliot Geisinger/Ronald Saland
Executive Producer Samuel Z Arkoff
Music by Lalo Schifrin
Cinematographer Fred J Koenekamp
Edited by Robert Brown Jr
Art Director Kim Swados
Visual Effects Supervisor William Cruse

Production Companies American International
Pictures/Cinema 77/Professional Films
Distributors American International Pictures (US)/
ITC Film Distributors (UK)
Produced October 1978/Released July 1979 (US)/
January 1980 (UK)
117 mins

THE AMITYVILLE HORROR (2005)

Cast

Ryan Reynolds	George Lutz
Melissa George	Kathy Lutz
Jesse James	Billy Lutz
Jimmy Bennett	Michael Lutz
Chloë Grace Moretz	Chelsea Lutz
Rachel Nichols	Lisa
Philip Baker Hall	Father Callaway
Isabel Conner	Jodie DeFeo
Brendan Donaldson	Ronald DeFeo
Annabel Armour	Realtor
Rick Komenich	Chief of Police

Credits

Directed by Andrew Douglas
Written by Scott Kosar/Sheldon Turner
Based on the book by Jay Anson
Produced by
    Michael Bay/Andrew Form/Brad Fuller
Executive Producers David Crockett/
    Randall Emmett/Ted Field/George Furla/
    Paul Mason/ Steven Whitney
Associate Producers
    Matthew Cohan/Stefan Sonnenfeld
Music by Steve Jablonsky
Cinematographer Peter Lyons Collister
Edited by Roger Barton/Christian Wagner
Production Designer Jennifer Williams
Art Director Marco Rubeo
Special Make-up Effects by
    Howard Berger/Greg Nicotero
Visual Effects Supervisor Sean Andrew Faden
Second Unit Director Mark Palansky

Production Companies Dimension Films/
Metro-Goldwyn-Mayer/Platinum Dunes/
Radar Pictures
Distributors Metro-Goldwyn-Mayer (US)/
20th Century Fox (UK)
Produced August 2004/Released April 2005
(US & UK)
90 mins

BLACK CHRISTMAS (1974)

Cast

Olivia Hussey	Jess
Keir Dullea	Peter
Margot Kidder	Barb
John Saxon	Lieutenant Fuller
Marian Waldman	Mrs Mac
Andrea Martin	Phyl
James Edmond	Mr Harrison
Douglas McGrath	Sergeant Nash
Art Hindle	Chris
Lynne Griffin	Clare

Credits

Directed/Written/Produced by Bob Clark
Written by Timothy Bond/Roy Moore
Produced by Gerry Arbeid
Executive Producer Findlay Quinn
Associate Producer Richard Schouten
Music by Carl Zittrer
Cinematographer Reginald H. Morris
Edited by Stan Cole
Art Director Karen Bromley

Production Companies August Films/Canadian
  Film Development Corporation/Famous
  Players/ Film Funding/Vision IV
Distributors Ambassador Films (Canada)/
  Warner Bros. (US)/EMI Films (UK)
Produced March 1974/Released November 1974
  (Canada)/May 1975 (US)/October 1975 (UK) 98 mins

BLACK CHRISTMAS (2006)

Cast

Katie Cassidy	Kelli Presley
Michelle Trachtenberg	Melissa
Kristen Cloke	Leigh Colvin
Mary Elizabeth Winstead	Heather Fitzgerald
Lacey Chabert	Dana
Andrea Martin	Barbara MacHenry
Crystal Lowe	Lauren Hannon
Oliver Hudson	Kyle Autry
Karin Konoval	Billy's Mother
Dean Friss	Agnes (16/22 yrs)

Credits

Directed/Written/Produced by Glen Morgan
Produced by Marty Adelstein/Ogden Gavanski/
  Steven Hoban/Kent Kubena/Satsuki Mitchell/
  Dawn Parouse/Victor Solnicki/Mike Upton/
  James Wong
Executive Producers Marc Butan/Bob Clark/
  Mark Cuban/Scott Nemes/Noah Segal/
  Todd Wagner
Music by Shirley Walker
Cinematographer Robert McLachlan
Edited by Chris Willingham
Production Designer Mark Freeborn
Art Director Tony Wohlgemuth
Special Make-up Effects by Toby Lindala
Visual Effects Supervisor James Tichenor

Production Companies 2929 Productions/
  Adelstein-Parouse Productions/Copperheart
  Entertainment/Corus/Dimension Films/Hard
  Eight Pictures/Hoban-Segal Productions/
  Movie Central Network/Province of British
  Columbia Production Services Tax Credit/
  Victor Solnicki Productions
Distributors Metro-Goldwyn-Mayer (US)/
  Pathe Distribution (UK)
Produced January 2006/Released December 2006
  (US & UK)
90 mins (rated)/95 mins (unrated)

THE CRAZIES (1973)

Cast

Lane Carroll	Judy
W G MacMillan	David
Harold Wayne Jones	Clank
Lloyd Hollar	Colonel Peckem
Lynn Lowry	Kathy
Richard Liberty	Artie
Richard France	Dr Watts
Harry Spillman	Major Ryder
Will Disney	Dr Brookmyre
Edith Bell	Lab Technician

Credits

Directed/Written/Edited by George A Romero
Story by Paul McCollough

Produced by A C Croft
Executive Producer Lee Hessel
Associate Producer Margaret Walsh
Music by Bruce Roberts
Cinematographer William Hinzman

Production Company Pittsburgh Films
Distributor Cambist Films (US)/Bloom Theatres (UK)
Produced March 1972/Released March 1973 (US)/
   February 1978 (UK)
103 mins

THE CRAZIES (2010)
Cast

Timothy Olyphant	David Dutten
Radha Mitchell	Judy Dutten
Joe Anderson	Russell Clank
Danielle Panabaker	Becca Darling
Christie Lynn Smith	Deardra Farnum
Brett Rickaby	Bill Farnum
Preston Bailey	Nicholas
John Aylward	Mayor Hobbs
Joe Reegan	Pvt Billy Babcock
Glenn Morshower	Intelligence Officer

Credits
Directed by Breck Eisner
Written by Scott Kosar/Ray Wright
Produced by
   Michael Aguilar/Rob Cowan/Dean Georgaris
Executive Producers
   Jonathan King/George A Romero/Jeff Skoll
Associate Producers
   Brian Frankish/Alexander W Kogan Jr
Music by Mark Isham
Cinematographer Maxime Alexandre
Edited by Billy Fox
Production Designer Andrew Menzies
Art Director Greg Berry
Special Make-up Effects by Robert Hall
Visual Effects Supervisor Ron Thornton
Second Unit Director E J Foerster

Production Companies Imagenation Abu
   Dhabi/Overture Films/Participant Media
Distributors Overture Films (US)/

Momentum Theatrical (UK)
Produced March 2009/Released February 2010
   (US & UK)
101 mins

DAWN OF THE DEAD (1978)
Cast

Sarah Polley	Ana
Ving Rhames	Kenneth
Jake Weber	Michael
Mekhi Phifer	Andre
Ty Burrell	Steve
Michael Kelly	CJ
Kevin Zegers	Terry
Michael Barry	Bart
Lindy Booth	Nicole
Jayne Eastwood	Norma

Credits
Directed by Zack Snyder
Written by
   James Gunn/Michael Tolkin/Scott Frank
Produced by Marc Abraham/Michael Messina/
   Eric Newman/Richard P Rubinstein
Executive Producers Armyan Bernstein/
   Thomas A. Bliss/Dennis E Jones
Music by Tyler Bates
Cinematographer Matthew F Leonetti
Edited by Niven Howie
Production Designer Andrew Neskoromny
Art Director Arvinder Grewal
Special Make-up Effects by
   David LeRoy Anderson
Visual Effects Supervisors Dennis Berardi/
   Aaron Weintraub
Second Unit Director Clay Staub

Production Companies Metropolitan
   Filmexport/New Amsterdam Entertainment/
   Strike Entertainment/Toho-Towa
Distributors Universal Pictures (US)/
   Entertainment Film Distributors (UK)
Produced June 2003/Released March 2004
   (US & UK)
101 mins (rated)/110 mins (unrated)

DAY OF THE DEAD

(1985) Cast

Lori Cardille	Sarah
Terry Alexander	John
Joe Pilato	Captain Rhodes
Jarlath Conroy	William McDermott
Antonè DiLeo	Pvt Miguel Salazar
Richard Liberty	Dr Matthew Logan
Howard Sherman	Bub
G. Howard Klar	Pvt Steel
Ralph Marrero	Pvt Rickles
John Amplas	Dr Ted Fisher
Philip G Kellams	Miller

Credits

Directed/Written by George A Romero
Produced by David Ball/Richard P Rubinstein
Executive Producer Salah M Hassanein
Associate Producer Ed Lammi
Music by John Harrison
Cinematographer Michael Gornick
Edited by Pasquale Buba
Production Designer Cletus Anderson
Art Director Bruce Miller
Special Make-up Effects by Tom Savini

Production Company The Laurel Group
Distributors United Film Distribution (US)/
  Media Releasing (UK)
Produced October 1984/Released July 1985 (US)/
  September 1986 (UK)
102 mins (US)/100 mins (UK)

DAY OF THE DEAD

(2008) Cast

Mena Suvari	Cpl Sarah Cross
Nick Cannon	PFC Salazar
Michael Welch	Trevor Cross
AnnaLynne McCord	Nina
Stark Sands	PFC Bud Crain
Matt Rippy	Dr Logan
Pat Kilbane	Dr Engle
Taylor Hoover	Judy
Christa Campbell	Mrs Leitner
Ian McNiece	Paul (DJ)
Ving Rhames	Captain Rhodes

Credits

Directed by Steve Miner
Written by Jeffrey Reddick
Produced by Boaz Davidson/James Dudelson/
  Randall Emmett/George Furla
Executive Producers Danny Dimbort/Robert
  Dudelson/Avi Lerner/Paul Mason/Jordan
  Rush/Trevor Short/David Varod
Music by Tyler Bates
Cinematographer Patrick Cady
Edited by Nathan Easterling
Production Designer Carlos Da Silva
Art Director Sonya Savova
Special Make-up Effects
  by Dean Jones/Starr Jones
Visual Effects Designer Nikolay Gachev
Second Unit Director Steve Griffin

Production Companies Emmett-Furla Films/
  Millennium Films/Taurus Entertainment
Distributor First Look Studios (US)/
  Optimum Releasing (UK)
Produced July 2006/Released April 2008 (US)/
  September 2008 (UK)
86 mins

THE FOG (1980)

Cast

Adrienne Barbeau	Stevie Wayne
Jamie Lee Curtis	Elizabeth Solley
Janet Leigh	Kathy Williams
John Houseman	Mr Machen
Tom Atkins	Nick Castle
James Canning	Dick Baxter
Charles Cyphers	Dan O'Bannon
Nancy Loomis	Sandy Fadel
Ty Mitchell	Andy Wayne
Hal Holbrook	Father Malone
Regina Waldon	Mrs Kobritz

Credits

Directed/Written/Music by John Carpenter
Written/Produced by Debra Hill
Executive Producer Charles B Bloch
Associate Producers
  Barry Bernardi/Pegi Brotman

Music by Dan Wyman
Cinematographer Dean Cundey
Edited by
  Charles Bornstein/Tommy Lee Wallace
Production Designer Tommy Lee Wallace
Art Director Craig Stearns
Special Make-up Effects by Rob Bottin

Production Companies Avco Embassy Pictures/
  Entertainment Discoveries Inc
Distributors Avco Embassy Pictures (US)/
  Rank Film Distributors (UK)
Produced April 1979/Released February 1980 (US)/
  November 1980 (UK)
89 mins

THE FOG *(2005)*
Cast

Tom Welling	Nick Castle
Maggie Grace	Elizabeth Williams
Selma Blair	Stevie Wayne
DeRay Davis	Spooner
Kenneth Welsh	Tom Malone
Adrian Hough	Father Malone
Sara Botsford	Kathy Williams
Cole Heppell	Andy Wayne
Mary Black	Aunt Connie
Jonathon Young	Dan (weatherman)

Credits
Directed by Rupert Wainwright
Written by Cooper Layne
Produced by
  John Carpenter/David Foster/Debra Hill
Executive Producers
  Derek Dauchy/Todd Garner/Dan Kolsrud
Associate Producers
  Randi Chernov/Shane Riches
Music by Graeme Revell
Cinematographer Nathan Hope
Edited by Dennis Virkler
Production Designers
  Michael Diner/Graeme Murray
Art Directors Michael Diner/Catherine Schroer
Special Make-up Effects by Toby Lindala
Visual Effects Supervisor Chris Watts

Second Unit Director David Barrett

Production Companies David Foster
  Productions/Debra Hill Productions/
  Revolution Studios
Distributor Columbia Pictures (US & UK)
Produced March 2005/Released October 2005 (US)/
  January 2006 (UK)
100 mins (rated)/103 mins (unrated)

FRIDAY THE 13TH
(1980) **Cast**

Betsy Palmer	Pamela Voorhees
Adrienne King	Alice Hardy
Jeannine Taylor	Marcie Cunningham
Robbi Morgan	Annie
Kevin Bacon	Jack Burrel
Harry Crosby	Bill
Laurie Bartram	Brenda
Mark Nelson	Ned Rubinstein
Peter Brouwer	Steve Christy
Rex Everhart	Enos

Credits
Directed/Produced by Sean S Cunningham
Written by Victor Miller/Ron Kurz
Executive Producer Alvin Geiler
Associate Producer Steve Miner
Music by Harry Manfredini
Cinematographer Barry Abrams
Edited by Bill Freda
Art Director Virginia Field
Special Make-up Effects by Tom Savini

Production Companies Georgetown
  Productions/Sean S Cunningham Films
Distributors Paramount Pictures (US)/
  Warner Bros (UK)
Produced September 1979/Released May 1980 (US)/
  June 1980 (UK)
95 mins

FRIDAY THE 13TH
(2009) **Cast**

Jared Padalecki	Clay Miller
Danielle Panabaker	Jenna

Amanda Righetti	Whitney Miller	Nancy Stephens	Marion Chambers
Travis Van Winkle	Trent DeMarco	Nick Castle	The Shape
Aaron Yoo	Chewie	**Credits**	
Derek Mears	Jason Voorhees	Directed/Written/Music by John Carpenter	
Jonathan Sadowski	Wade	Written/Produced by Debra Hill	
Julianna Guill	Bree	Executive Producers	
Ben Feldman	Richie	Moustapha Akkad/Irwin Yablans	
Arlen Escarpeta	Lawrence	Associate Producer Kool Lusby	

Credits

Directed by Marcus Nispel

Written by

  Mark Wheaton/Damian Shannon/Mark Swift

Produced by Michael Bay/Sean S Cunningham/

  Andrew Form/Brad Fuller/Alma Kuttruff

Executive Producers

  Walter Hamada/Guy Stodel/Brian Witten

Music by Steve Jablonsky

Cinematographer Daniel Pearl

Edited by Ken Blackwell/Glen Scantlebury

Production Designer Jeremy Conway

Art Director John Frick

Special Make-up Effects by Scott Stoddard

Visual Effects Supervisors

  Mitchell S Drain/Nathan McGuiness

Second Unit Director Mark Palansky

Production Companies Crystal Lake Entertainment/

  New Line Cinema/

  Paramount Pictures/Platinum Dunes

Distributors New Line Cinema (US)/

  Paramount Pictures (UK)

Produced April 2008/Released February 2009

  (US & UK)

97 mins (rated)/106 mins (unrated)

Cinematographer Dean Cundey

Edited by

  Charles Bornstein/Tommy Lee Wallace

Production Designer Tommy Lee Wallace

Production Company

  Falcon International Productions

Distributors Compass International Pictures

  (US)/Miracle Films (UK)

Produced April 1978/Released October 1978 (US)/

  January 1979 (UK) 91 mins

HALLOWEEN (1978)
Cast

Malcolm McDowell	Dr Samuel Loomis
Scout Taylor-Compton	Laurie Strode
Tyler Mane	Michael Myers
Daeg Faerch	Michael Myers (10)
Sheri Moon Zombie	Deborah Myers
William Forsythe	Ronnie White
Danielle Harris	Annie Brackett
Kristina Klebe	Lynda
Skyler Gisondo	Tommy Doyle
Danny Trejo	Ismael Cruz

Credits

Directed/Written/Produced by Rob Zombie

Produced by Malek Akkad/Andy Gould

Executive Producers Matthew Stein/Bob

Weinstein/Harvey Weinstein

Associate Producer Patrick Esposito

Music by Tyler Bates

Cinematographer Phil Parmet

Edited by Glenn Garland

Production Designer Anthony Tremblay

Art Director Timothy Kirkpatrick

Special Make-up Effects by Wayne Toth

Second Unit Director Rawn Hutchinson

HALLOWEEN (2005)
Cast

Donald Pleasence	Dr Sam Loomis
Jamie Lee Curtis	Laurie Strode
Nancy Loomis	Annie Brackett
P J Soles	Lynda van der Klok
Charles Cyphers	Sheriff Leigh Brackett
Kyle Richards	Lindsey Wallace
Brian Andrews	Tommy Doyle
John Michael Graham	Bob Simms

Production Companies Dimension Films/
Spectacle Entertainment Group/Trancas
International Films/The Weinstein Company
Distributors Metro-Goldwyn-Mayer (US)/
Paramount Pictures (UK)
Produced February 2007/Released August 2007 (US)/
September 2007 (UK)
110 mins (rated)/121 mins (unrated)

HALLOWEEN II *(1982)*

Cast

Jamie Lee Curtis	Laurie Strode
Donald Pleasence	Dr Sam Loomis
Charles Cyphers	Sheriff Leigh Brackett
Jeffrey Kramer	Dr Graham
Lance Guest	Jimmy
Pamela Susan Shoop	Karen
Hunter von Leer	Deputy Gary Hunt
Dick Warlock	The Shape
Leo Rossi	Budd
Gloria Gifford	Mrs Alves

Credits

Directed by Rick Rosenthal/John Carpenter
Written/Produced by
John Carpenter/Debra Hill
Executive Producers
Moustapha Akkad/Joseph Wolf/Irwin Yablans
Associate Producer Barry Bernardi
Music by John Carpenter/Alan Howarth
Cinematographer Dean Cundey
Edited by Mark Goldblatt/Skip Schoolnik
Production Designer J. Michael Riva

Production Companies Compass International
Pictures/Dino De Laurentiis Corporation
Distributors
Universal Pictures (US)/EMI Films (UK)
Produced April 1981/Released October 1981 (US)/
March 1982 (UK)
92 mins

HALLOWEEN II *(2009)*

Cast

Malcolm McDowell	Dr Samuel Loomis
Scout Taylor-Compton	Laurie Strode
Tyler Mane	Michael Myers
Sheri Moon Zombie	Deborah Myers
Brad Dourif	Sheriff Lee Brackett
Danielle Harris	Annie Brackett
Brea Grant	Mya Rockwell
Howard Hesseman	Uncle Meat
Angela Trimbur	Harley David
Mary Birdsong	Nancy McDonald

Credits

Directed/Written/Produced by Rob Zombie
Produced by
Malek Akkad/Mike Elliott/Andy Gould
Executive Producers Andy La Marca/Matthew
Stein/Bob Weinstein/Harvey Weinstein
Music by Tyler Bates
Cinematographer Brandon Trost
Edited by Glenn Garland
Production Designer Garreth Stover
Art Director Timothy Kirkpatrick
Special Make-up Effects by Wayne Toth
Visual Effects Supervisor Mark Dornfeld

Production Companies Dimension Films/
Spectacle Entertainment Group/Trancas
International Films/The Weinstein Company
Distributors Dimension Films (US)/
Entertainment Film Distributors (UK)
Produced February 2009/Released August 2009 (US)/
September 2009 (UK)
105 mins (rated)/119 mins (unrated)

THE HILLS HAVE EYES *(1977)*

Cast

Susan Lanier	Brenda Carter
Robert Houston	Bobby Carter
Martin Speer	Doug Wood
Dee Wallace	Lynne Wood
Russ Grieve	Big Bob Carter
John Steadman	Fred
James Whitworth	Jupiter
Virginia Vincent	Ethel Carter
Lance Gordon	Mars
Michael Berryman	Pluto

Credits
Directed/Written/Edited by Wes Craven
Produced by Peter Locke
Music by Don Peake
Cinematographer Eric Saarinen
Art Director Robert Burns

Production Company The Blood Relations Co
Distributors Vanguard Films (US)/New Realm
  Entertainment (UK)
Produced October 1976 /Released June 1977 (US)/
  February 1979 (UK)
89 mins

THE HILLS HAVE EYES (2006)
Cast

Aaron Stanford	Doug Bukowski
Kathleen Quinlan	Ethel Carter
Vinessa Shaw	Lynn Carter
Emilie de Ravin	Brenda Carter
Dan Byrd	Bobby Carter
Tom Bower	Gas Station Attendant
Billy Drago	Papa Jupiter
Robert Joy	Lizard
Ted Levine	Big Bob Carter
Desmond Askew	Big Brain

Credits
Directed/Written by Alexandre Aja
Written by/Art Director/Second Unit Director
  Grégory Levasseur
Produced by Wes Craven/Samy Layani/Peter
  Locke/Marianne Maddalena
Executive Producer Frank Hildebrand
Associate Producer Cody Zwieg
Music by tomandandy
Cinematographer Maxime Alexandre
Edited by Baxter
Production Designer Joseph C Nemec III
Art Director Tamara Marini
Special Make-up Effects by
  Howard Berger/Greg Nicotero
Visual Effects Supervisor Jamison Scott Goei

Production Companies Craven-Maddalena

Films/Dune Entertainment/Major Studio Partners
Distributors Fox Searchlight Pictures (US)/
  20th Century Fox (UK)
Produced June 2005/Released March 2006
  (US & UK)
107 mins (rated)/109 mins (unrated)

THE HILLS HAVE EYES PART II (1985)
Cast

Tamara Stafford	Cass
Kevin Spirtas (as Kevin Blair)	Roy
John Bloom	The Reaper
Colleen Riley	Jane
Michael Berryman	Pluto
Penny Johnson	Sue
Janus Blythe	Rachel/Ruby
John Laughlin	Hulk
Willard Pugh	Foster
Peter Frechette	Harry

Credits
Directed/Written by Wes Craven
Produced by Barry Cahn/Peter Locke
Executive Producer Adrienne Fancey
Associate Producer Jonathan Debin
Music by Harry Manfredini
Cinematographer David Lewis
Edited by Richard Bracken
Production Designer Dominick Bruno

Production Companies New Realm
  Entertainment/Video Tape Centre
Distributors Thorn EMI Video (UK)/
  Castle Hill Productions (US)
Produced September 1983/Released January 1985
  (UK)/August 1985 (US)
86 mins

THE HILLS HAVE EYES 2 (2007)
Cast

Michael McMillian	Napoleon
Jessica Stroup	Amber
Jacob Vargas	Crank
Flex Alexander	Sarge

Lee Thompson Young   Delmar
Daniella Alonso   Missy
Eric Edelstein   Spitter
Reshad Strik   Mickey
Ben Crowley   Stump
Michael Bailey Smith   Papa Hades

Credits

Directed by Martin Weisz
Written/Produced by
    Wes Craven/Jonathan Craven
Produced by Tina Anderson/Samy Layani/
    Peter Locke/Marianne Maddalena/Cody Zwieg
Executive Producer Jonathan Debin
Music by Trevor Morris
Cinematographer Sam McCurdy
Edited by Sue Blainey/Kirk M Morri
Production Designer Keith Wilson
Art Director Alistair Kay
Special Make-up Effects by
    Howard Berger/Greg Nicotero
Visual Effects Supervisor Jamison Scott Goei

Production Companies Craven-Maddalena
    Films/Dune Entertainment
Distributors Fox Atomic (US)/20th Century Fox (UK)
Produced September 2006/Released March 2007
    (US & UK)
89 mins (rated)/90 mins (unrated)

THE LAST HOUSE ON THE LEFT (1972)

Cast

Sandra Peabody (as Sandra Cassell)
           Mari Collinwood
Lucy Grantham   Phylis Stone
David Hess   Krug Stillo
Fred Lincoln   Fred 'Weasel' Padowski
Jeramie Rain   Sadie
Marc Sheffler   Junior Stillo
Richard Towers (as Gaylord St. James)
           Dr John Collinwood
Eleanor Shaw (as Cynthia Carr)
           Estelle Collinwood
Marshall Anker   Sheriff Frank Boone
Martin Kove   Deputy Harry Snark

Credits

Directed/Written/Edited by Wes Craven
Produced by Sean S Cunningham
Associate Producer Katherine D'Amato
Music by Steve Chapin/David Hess
Cinematographer Victor Hurwitz

Production Companies Esquire Theatres/
    Lobster Enterprises/Sean S Cunningham Films Ltd
Distributors Hallmark Releasing/American
    International Pictures (US)/Replay/VPD Video (UK)
Produced October 1971/Released July 1972
    (as Krug & Company and Sex Crime of the Century)/
    August 1972 (as The Last House on the Left) (US)/
    June 1982 (UK)
85 mins (US)/80 mins (UK)

THE LAST HOUSE ON THE LEFT (2009)

Cast

Tony Goldwyn   John Collingwood
Monica Potter   Emma Collingwood
Garret Dillahunt   Krug
Aaron Paul   Francis
Spencer Treat Clark   Justin
Riki Lindhome   Sadie
Martha MacIsaac   Paige
Sara Paxton   Mari Collingwood
Michael Bowen   Morton
Josh Cox   Giles

Credits

Directed by Dennis Iliadis
Written by
    Mark Haslett/Adam Alleca/Carl Ellsworth
Produced by Jonathan Craven/Wes Craven/
    Sean S Cunningham/Marianne Maddalena/
    Cody Zwieg
Executive Producer Ray Haboush
Associate Producers Vlokkie Gordon/
    Bryan Thomas/David Wicht
Music by John Murphy
Cinematographer Sharone Meir
Edited by Peter McNulty
Production Designer Johnny Breedt
Art Directors

Shira Hockman/Cecelia van Straaten
Special Make up Effects by
  Howard Berger/Greg Nicotero
Visual Effects Supervisor Jamison Scott Goei

Production Companies Film Afrika Worldwide/
  Midnight Entertainment/Relativity Media/
  Scion Films
Distributors Rogue Pictures (US)/
  Universal Pictures (UK)
Produced March 2008/Released March 2009 (US)/
  June 2009 (UK)
110 mins (rated)/114 mins (unrated)

MY BLOODY VALENTINE *(1981)*
Cast

Paul Kelman	Jessie Hanniger
Lori Hallier	Sarah
Neil Affleck	Axel Palmer
Keith Knight	Hollis
Alf Humphreys	Howard Landers
Cynthia Dale	Patty
Helene Udy	Sylvia
Rob Stein	John
Tom Kovacs	Mike Stavinski
Terry Waterland	Harriet

Credits
Directed by George Mihalka
Written by John Beaird
Story by Stephen Miller
Produced by
  John Dunning/André Link/Stephen Miller
Executive Producer Lawrence Nesis
Music by Paul Zaza
Cinematographer Rodney Gibbons
Edited by Gerald Vansier/Rit Wallis
Art Director Penny Hadfield
Special Make-up Effects by Thomas R Burman
Second Unit Director Ray Sager

Production Companies Canadian Film
  Development Corporation/Famous Players/
  The Secret Film Co
Distributor Paramount Pictures (US & UK)

Produced September 1980/Released February 1981
  (US)/May 1981 (UK) 90 mins

MY BLOODY VALENTINE 3D *(2009)*
Cast

Jensen Ackles	Tom Hanniger
Jaime King	Sarah Palmer
Kerr Smith	Axel Palmer
Betsy Rue	Irene
Edi Gathegi	Deputy Martin
Tom Atkins	Sheriff Jim Burke
Kevin Tighe	Ben Foley
Megan Boone	Megan
Karen Baum	Deputy Ferris
Joy de la Paz	Rosa

Credits
Directed/Edited by Patrick Lussier
Written by Zane Smith/Todd Farmer
Produced by
  Second Unit Director Jack L Murray
Executive Producers John Dunning/
  André Link/Michael Paseornek/John Sacchi
Associate Producer Hernany Perla
Music by Michael Wandmacher
Cinematographer Brian Pearson
Edited by Cynthia Ludwig
Production Designer Zack Grobler
Art Director Andrew Murdock
Special Make-up Effects by Gary J Tunnicliffe
Visual Effects Supervisors
  Mike Uguccioni/Marc Varisco
Second Unit Director Melissa R Stubbs

Production Company/
  Distributor Lionsgate Films (US & UK)
Produced May 2008/Released January 2009
  (US & UK)
101 mins

A NIGHTMARE ON ELM STREET
(1984) **Cast**

John Saxon	Lt Donald Thompson
Ronee Blakley	Marge Thompson

Heather Langenkamp	Nancy Thompson
Amanda Wyss	Christina Gray
Jsu Garcia (as Nick Corri)	Rod Lane
Johnny Depp	Glen Lantz
Charles Fleischer	Dr King
Joseph Whipp	Sgt Parker
Robert Englund	Fred Krueger
Lin Shaye	Teacher

Credits
Directed/Written by Wes Craven
Produced by Sara Risher/Robert Shaye
Executive Producers
  Stanley Dudelson/Joseph Wolf
Associate Producer John Burrows
Music by Charles Bernstein
Cinematographer Jacques Haitkin
Edited by Rick Shaine
Production Designer Greg Fonseca
Special Make-up Effects by David Miller

Production Companies Media Home Entertainment/
  New Line Cinema/Smart Egg Pictures
Distributors
  New Line Cinema (US)/Palace Pictures (UK)
Produced June 1984/Released November 1984 (US)/
  September 1985 (UK)
91 mins

A NIGHTMARE ON ELM STREET

(2010) Cast

Jackie Earle Haley	Freddy Krueger
Kyle Gallner	Quentin Smith
Rooney Mara	Nancy Holbrook
Katie Cassidy	Kris Fowles
Thomas Dekker	Jesse Braun
Kellan Lutz	Dean Russell
Clancy Brown	Alan Smith
Connie Britton	Dr Gwen Holbrook
Lia Mortensen	Nora Fowles
Julianna Damm	Little Kris

Credits
Directed by Samuel Bayer
Written by Wesley Strick/Eric Heisserer
Produced by Michael Bay/Andrew Form/

Brad Fuller/John Rickard
Executive Producers Richard Brener/
  Mike Drake/Walter Hamada/Michael Lynne/
  Dave Neustadter/Robert Shaye
Associate Producer Erik Holmberg
Music by Steve Jablonsky
Cinematographer Jeff Cutter
Edited by Glen Scantlebury
Production Designer Patrick Lumb
Art Director Craig Jackson
Special Make up Effects by Andrew Clement
Visual Effects Supervisor Marc Kolbe
Second Unit Director Robert Legato

Production Companies New Line Cinema/
  Platinum Dunes
Distributors New Line Cinema (US)/
  Warner Bros (UK)
Produced May 2009/Released April 2010 (US)/
  May 2010 (UK)
95 mins

NIGHT OF THE LIVING DEAD (1968)
Cast

Duane Jones	Ben
Judith O'Dea	Barbra
Karl Hardman	Harry Cooper
Marilyn Eastman	Helen Cooper
Keith Wayne	Tom
Judith Ridley	Judy
Kyra Schon	Karen Cooper
Charles Craig	Newscaster
Russell Streiner	Johnny
George Kosana	Sheriff McClelland

Credits
Directed/Written/Edited by/Cinematographer
  George A Romero
Written by John A Russo
Produced by Karl Hardman/Russell Streiner

Production Company Image Ten
Distributors Continental/Walter Reade (US)/
  Monarch Film Corporation Ltd (UK)
Produced July 1967/Released October 1968 (US)/

November 1969 (UK)

96 mins (US)/95 mins (UK)

NIGHT OF THE LIVING DE3D *(2006)*

Cast

Brianna Brown	Barb
Joshua DesRoches	Ben
Sid Haig	Gerald Tovar, Jr
Greg Travis	Henry Cooper
Johanna Black	Hellie Cooper
Adam Chambers	Owen
Ken Ward	Johnny
Alynia Phillips	Karen Cooper
Max Williams	Tom
Cristin Michele	Judy

Credits

Directed/Produced by Jeff Broadstreet

Written/Edited by/Second Unit Director
  Robert Valding

Executive Producer Ingo Jucht

Music by Jason Brandt

Cinematographer Andrew Parke

Production Designer Chris Davis

Art Director Josh Ritcher

Special Make-up Effects by
  Dean Jones/Starr Jones

Visual Effects Supervisor Adam Lima

Production Companies
  The Horrorworks/Lux Digital Pictures GmbH
Distributor Midnight Movies (US)/
  Stax Entertainment (UK)
Produced June 2005/Released September 2006 (US)/
  March 2010 (UK)
80 mins

PROM NIGHT *(1980)*

Cast

Leslie Nielsen	Mr Hammond
Jamie Lee Curtis	Kim
Casey Stevens	Nick
Anne-Marie Martin (as Eddie Benton)	
	Wendy
Antoinette Bower	Mrs Hammond

Michael Tough	Alex
Robert Silverman	Sykes
Pita Oliver	Vicki
David Mucci	Lou
Jeff Wincott	Drew

Credits

Directed by Paul Lynch

Written by William Gray

Story by Robert Guza Jr

Produced by Peter Simpson

Associate Producer Richard Simpson

Music by Paul Zaza/Carl Zittrer

Cinematographer Robert New

Edited by Brian Ravok

Art Director Reuben Freed

Special Make-up Effects by Warren Keillor

Second Unit Directors Dan Nyberg/Steve Wright

Production Companies Quadrant Trust
  Company/Simcom Productions
Distributors Avco Embassy Pictures (US)/
  Barber International (UK)
Produced August 1979/Released July 1980 (US)/
  February 1981 (UK)
89 mins

PROM NIGHT *(2008)*

Cast

Brittany Snow	Donna Keppel
Scott Porter	Bobby
Jessica Stroup	Claire
Dana Davis	Lisa Hines
Collins Pennie	Ronnie Heflin
Kelly Blatz	Michael
James Ransone	Detective Nash
Brianne Davis	Crissy Lynn
Kellan Lutz	Rick Leland
Mary Mara	Ms Waters

Credits

Directed by Nelson McCormick

Written by/Executive Producer J S Cardone

Produced by Toby Jaffe/Neal H Moritz

Executive Producers Chris J Ball/Marc Forby/
  Glenn S Gainor/Bruce Mellon/William Tyrer

Music by Paul Haslinger

Cinematographer Checco Varese
Edited by Jason Ballantine
Production Designer Jon Gary Steele
Special Make-up Effects by Robert Hall
Visual Effects Supervisor Rocco Passionino
Second Unit Director Lance Gilbert

Production Companies Alliance Films/
Newmarket Films/Original Film Distributors/
Screen Gems (US)/Columbia Pictures (UK)
Produced March 2007/Released April 2008 (US)/
June 2008 (UK)
88 mins (rated)/89 mins (unrated)

THE TEXAS CHAIN SAW MASSACRE

(1974) Cast

Marilyn Burns	Sally Hardesty
Allen Danziger	Jerry
Paul A Partain	Franklin Hardesty
William Vail	Kirk
Teri McMinn	Pam
Edwin Neal	Hitchhiker
Jim Siedow	Old Man
Gunnar Hansen	Leatherface
John Dugan	Grandfather
Robert Courtin	Window Washer
William Creamer	Bearded Man

Credits

Directed/Written/Produced/Music by Tobe Hooper
Written by/Associate Producer Kim Henkel
Executive Producer Jay Parsley
Associate Producer Richard Saenz
Music by Wayne Bell
Cinematographer Daniel Pearl
Edited by Larry Carroll/Sallye Richardson
Art Director Robert A Burns

Production Companies MAB Inc/PITS Investors/
Vortex
Distributors Bryanston Film Distributors (US)/
Hemdale Film Distributors (UK)
Produced July 1973/Released October 1974 (US)/
November 1976 (UK)
83 mins

THE TEXAS CHAINSAW MASSACRE (2003)

Cast

Jessica Biel	Erin
Jonathan Tucker	Morgan
Erica Leerhsen	Pepper
Mike Vogel	Andy
Eric Balfour	Kemper
Andrew Bryniarski	Leatherface
R. Lee Ermey	Sheriff Hoyt
David Dorfman	Jedidiah
Lauren German	Teenage Girl
Terrence Evans	Old Monty

Credits

Directed by Marcus Nispel
Written by Scott Kosar/Eric Bernt
Produced by Michael Bay/Joe Dishner/
Mike Fleiss/Kim Henkel/Tobe Hooper
Executive Producers Jeffrey Allard/Ted Field/
Andrew Form/Brad Fuller/Guy Stodel
Associate Producers
Matthew Cohan/Pat Sandston
Music by Steve Jablonsky
Cinematographer Daniel Pearl
Edited by Glen Scantlebury
Production Designer Greg Blair
Art Director Scott Gallagher
Special Make up Effects by
Howard Berger/Greg Nicotero
Visual Effects Supervisor Jason Schugardt

Production Companies Focus Features/New
Line Cinema/Next Entertainment/Platinum Dunes/
Radar Pictures
Distributors New Line Cinema (US)/
Entertainment Film Distributors (UK)
Produced July 2002/Released October 2003 (US & UK)
98 mins

WHEN A STRANGER CALLS

(1979) Cast

Charles Durning	John Clifford
Carol Kane	Jill Johnson

Colleen Dewhurst	Tracy
Tony Beckley	Curt Duncan
Rachel Roberts	Dr Monk
Ron O'Neal	Lt Charlie Garber
Rutanya Alda	Mrs Mandrakis
Carmen Argenziano	Dr Mandrakis
Kirsten Larkin	Nancy
William Boyett	Sergeant Sacker

Credits
Directed/Written by Fred Walton
Written/Produced by Steve Feke
Produced by Doug Chapin
Executive Producers Barry Krost/Melvin Simon
Associate Producer Larry Kostroff
Music by Dana Kaproff
Cinematographer Don Peterman
Edited by Sam Vitale
Production Designer Elayne Barbara Ceder

Production Companies Melvin Simon Productions/
The Movie Company
Distributors Columbia Pictures (US)/
United Artists (UK)
Produced October 1978/Released September 1979 (US)/
November 1980 (UK)
97 mins

WHEN A STRANGER CALLS

(2006) Cast

Camilla Belle	Jill Johnson
Tommy Flanagan	Stranger
Katie Cassidy	Tiffany
Tessa Thompson	Scarlet
Brian Geraghty	Bobby
Clark Gregg	Ben Johnson
Derek de Lint	Dr Mandrakis
Kate Jennings Grant	Kelly Mandrakis
David Denman	Officer Burroughs
Arthur Young	Will Mandrakis

Credits
Directed by Simon West
Written by Jake Wade Wall
Produced by
John Davis/Wyck Godfrey/Ken Lemberger

Executive Producer Paddy Cullen
Music by Jim Dooley
Cinematographer Peter Menzies Jr
Edited by Jeff Betancourt
Production Designer Jon Gary Steele
Art Director Gerald Sullivan
Visual Effects Supervisor Mitchell S Drain

Production Company Davis Entertainment
Distributors Screen Gems (US)/
Columbia Pictures (UK)
Produced July 2005/Released February 2006 (US)/
May 2006 (UK)
87 mins

ZOMBI/DAWN OF THE DEAD (1978)

Cast

David Emge	Stephen
Ken Foree	Peter
Scott H Reiniger	Roger
Gaylen Ross	Francine
David Crawford	Dr James Foster
David Early	Sidney Berman
Richard France	Dr Millard Rausch
Howard Smith	TV Commentator
Daniel Dietrich	Givens
Fred Baker	Police Commander

Credits
Directed/Written/Edited by George A Romero
Produced by Richard P Rubinstein
Executive Producers Claudio Argento/Billy
Baxter/Alfredo Cuomo/Herbert R. Steinmann
Associate Producer Donna Siegel
Music by Dario Argento/Goblin
Cinematographer Michael Gornick
Special Make-up Effects by Tom Savini

Production Companies
The Laurel Group/Seda Spettacoli/Titanus
Distributors Titanus (Zombi; Italy)/United Film
Distribution (Dawn of the Dead; US)/Target
International (Zombies: Dawn of the Dead; UK)
Produced November 1977/Released September 1978
(Zombi)/April 1979 (Dawn of the Dead)/July 1980

(Zombies: Dawn of the Dead)
118 mins (Zombi)/126 mins (Dawn of the
Dead)/125 mins (Zombies: Dawn of the Dead)

BIBLIOGRAPHY

Anson, Jay *The Amityville Horror* Pocket Books,
New York, 2005

Barbeau, Adrienne *There Are Worse Things
I Could Do* Da Capo Press, New York, 2006

Bracke, Peter M *Crystal Lake Memories:
The Complete History of Friday the 13th* Titan Books,
London, 2006

Etchison, Dennis *The Fog* Bantam Books, New
York, 1980

Ferring, David *The Hills Have Eyes Part II*
Granada, London, 1984

Gagne, Paul R *The Zombies That Ate Pittsburgh: The
Films of George A Romero* Dodd, Mead & Company,
New York, 1987

Grove, David *Making Friday the 13th: The Legend
of Camp Blood* FAB Press, Godalming, 2005

Jaworzyn, Stefan *The Texas Chainsaw Massacre
Companion* Titan Books, London, 2003

Martin, Jack *Halloween II* Zebra Books, New York,
1981

Russo, John *The Complete Night of the Living Dead
Filmbook* Harmony Books, New York, 1985

Russo, John *Night of the Living Dead* Pocket Books,
New York, 1981

Richards, Curtis *Halloween* Bantam Books, New
York, 1981

Romero, George A and Susanna Sparrow
Dawn of the Dead St. Martin's Press, New York, 1978

Szulkin, David A *Wes Craven's Last House on the
Left: The Making of a Cult Classic* FAB Press,
Guildford, 2000

www.hemlockbooks.co.uk

Hemlock Books is an independent publisher specialising in genre-related film titles, with particular emphasis on horror, mystery and the macabre.